D1268082

Banking in the Early Stages of Industrialization

A COMPARATIVE STUDY

Banking in the Early Stages of Industrialization

A STUDY IN COMPARATIVE ECONOMIC HISTORY

BY
RONDO CAMERON
University of Wisconsin

WITH THE COLLABORATION OF

OLGA CRISP
University of London

HUGH T. PATRICK
Yale University

AND
RICHARD TILLY
University of Michigan

New York
OXFORD UNIVERSITY PRESS
London 1967 Toronto

Library of Congress Catalogue Card Number: 67–10342
Printed in the United States of America

Dedicated with affection to

Claydean
Horace
Matsuno
Elisabeth

. . . it is always of the utmost importance for us to be thoroughly masters of the economic history of the time, the country or the industry, sometimes even of the individual firm in question, before we draw any inference at all from the behavior of time series. . . . General history . . . economic history, and more particularly industrial history are not only indispensable but really the most important contributors to the understanding of our problem. All other materials and methods, statistical and theoretical, are only subservient to them and worse than useless without them.

JOSEPH A. SCHUMPETER
Business Cycles, I, 13.

Since social phenomena . . . depend upon historic continuity, there can be no adequate knowledge of them without some reference to the past. It is, however, hasty and false to conclude that the full nature of social phenomena is to be found entirely in their history.

MORRIS R. COHEN
Reason and Nature (rev. ed.), p. 344.

The essential function of credit . . . consists in enabling the entrepreneur to withdraw the producers' goods which he needs from their previous employments, by exercising a demand for them, and thereby to force the economic system into new channels.

JOSEPH A. SCHUMPETER
The Theory of Economic Development, p. 106.

PREFACE

The primary purpose of this volume is to shed light on a pressing practical problem—namely, financing economic development. Thus, although the substance of the book is historical, our approach is analytical rather than narrative. For that reason we have not made a fetish of seeking out new primary sources, but have turned to them only when we found the existing secondary literature inadequate for our purposes. Readers acquainted with the economic history of the countries in question will therefore find much familiar factual information; but they will also discover significant new data not previously published, especially on Germany and Russia and, to a lesser degree, on France, Belgium, and Scotland. Similarly, the chapter on Japan presents much valuable information not normally available to Western scholars. The financial and industrial history of England, on the other hand, has been studied so extensively that it would be difficult to justify a fresh search for new and unutilized primary sources for a volume of this nature. In any event, we trust that whatever value the book possesses will be found principally in the novelty of our conceptual framework rather than in hitherto unknown factual information. As it is, we have been forced in the interests of readability to compress and omit much supporting evidence.

Modest though its pretensions are, this book would not have been possible without the generous financial assistance of the Rockefeller Foundation and the University of Wisconsin. The University of Glasgow extended its hospitality to me as a visiting research professor under a United States Government (Fulbright) award during the academic year 1962–63, and Professor Tilly spent the years 1961–63 in Germany with the assistance of the Social Science Research Council. Needless to emphasize, none of these institutions is responsible for the views expressed in this book.

Preliminary drafts of the substantive chapters served as background papers for a conference held at the Villa Serbelloni, Bellagio, Italy, August 16–22, 1964. Without implicating them in any way in our conclusions, we wish to express our appreciation for stimulating criticism and apt suggestions to the conference participants: Martin Bronfenbrenner, A. K. Cairncross, Wolfram Fischer, Raymond Goldsmith, David Granick, Karl-Gustaf Hildebrand, Richard W. Hooley, David Joslin, Maurice Lévy-Leboyer, Peter

Mathias, and Robert Triffin. Mr. and Mrs. John Marshall and the capable staff of the Villa Serbelloni made the conference as pleasant as it was intellectually rewarding.

Many other individuals and institutions have contributed directly and indirectly to the completion of this study. I should like to thank particularly Professors S. G. Checkland and Donald Robertson for a number of kindnesses before, during, and after my tenure in the University of Glasgow; Professors Kristof Glamann, Oscar Bjürling, Karl-Gustaf Hildebrand, A. J. Youngson, F. J. Fisher, Charles Wilson, W. H. B. Court, M. M. Postan, François Crouzet, Claude Fohlen, Herbert Kisch, Robert Fogel, and Drs. R. M. Hartwell and H. J. Dyos for permitting me to expose my ideas to their classes and seminars; Professors Lance Davis and J. R. T. Hughes, entrepreneurs of the annual Cliometrics conferences at Purdue University; Professors Roy Campbell, Robert V. Eagly, Fritz Redlich, and Mr. Maxwell Gaskin for critical readings of portions of the manuscript; Mrs. Brenda Gaskin, Mark Ehrenberg, and Clair Morris for research assistance; Don Stewart for computational assistance; Professor R. L. Bennett and my students and colleagues at the University of Wisconsin for suggestions, criticisms, and encouragement; and Professor T. C. Barker for kindnesses not elsewhere specified. Mrs. Mayvis Schneider, Miss Regina Ribeiro, and Mrs. Giovanna Holbrook provided efficient, cheerful secretarial and research assistance. Other acknowledgments appear at appropriate places in the footnotes. I have undoubtedly but unintentionally slighted others, especially those who rendered assistance to my collaborators. We all feel a special debt to our families for their deprivations.

Santiago de Chile RONDO CAMERON
February 1966

CONTENTS

TABLES

CHARTS

Banking in the Early Stages of Industrialization

A COMPARATIVE STUDY

I
INTRODUCTION

by Rondo Cameron and Hugh T. Patrick

A proliferation of the number and variety of financial institutions and a substantial rise in the ratio of money and other financial assets relative to total output and tangible wealth are apparently universal characteristics of the process of economic development in market-oriented economies.[1] This is an empirical generalization to which the historical record admits no exceptions to date. The causal nexus of this relationship is by no means clear, however. Does it run from financial institutions to industrialization or, on the contrary, does the process of industrialization throw up a wake of financial institutions, like a steamship cruising in calm waters?

The majority of economists who have dealt with this question tend to assume that financial institutions will grow more or less spontaneously as the need for their services arises—a case of demand creating its own supply. This view is associated with the notion that financial service (as opposed to real capital) is a passive, permissive, or facilitating agent, rather than a factor of production. Such an attitude disposes of a complex matter far too summarily. In the first place, there are a number of historical instances in which financial institutions constituted leading sectors in development; these institutions were "growth-inducing" through direct industrial promotion and finance. Secondly, even in the more common instances where financial institutions appear merely to respond to effective demand, the interactions of demand and supply in a dynamic situation are subtle and complex. The financial structure is shaped by a number of economic and noneconomic factors, and that structure affects the character and effectiveness of the system's functions. The efficiency with which any given financial system performs its functions depends not only on the strength of

[1] Cf. Goldsmith, "Financial Structure and Economic Growth in Advanced Countries," in Abramovitz (ed.), *Capital Formation and Economic Growth.*

the demand for its services, but on a host of legal, institutional, administrative, and even geographical factors as well.

From a broad spectrum of possible forms of interaction between the financial sector and the other sectors of the economy that require its services, one may isolate three type-cases: (1) the case in which inadequate finance restricts or hinders industrial and commercial development; (2) the case in which the financial system is purely permissive and accommodates all "credit-worthy" borrowers; and finally (3) the case in which financial institutions either actively promote new investment opportunities or encourage applicants for finance to come forward, provide them with advice and extra services, etc. In short, the structure of the financial system and the way in which it performs its functions will affect, for better or worse, the progress of industrialization.

A simple analogy may serve to emphasize the point. A machine cannot operate satisfactorily without lubricants. Different types of machines may require different amounts and types of lubricants, but for every type of machine there is an optimum amount and optimum quality or grade of lubricant. Too much or too little will cause the machine to malfunction, or at least reduce its efficiency. Similarly, if the wrong kind of lubricant is used the machine will not function properly. Metaphorically, finance is the lubricant of the process of economic growth, and the banking system is the chief dispenser of finance.

Or take a more realistic analogy. Transport facilities are generally regarded as essential for economic growth. A relatively widespread transportation network may exist in advance of the inception of industrialization (some facilities, however rudimentary, must exist for it to begin). More frequently, the transportation network and manufacturing industry develop together in response to the complex interactions of supply and demand. From the standpoint of growth, the question of which is the leading or lagging sector is less important than the character and efficiency of the transportation system, given the technological possibilities. The same is true of the financial system: it may be simultaneously growth-induced and growth-inducing, but what really matter are the character of its services and the efficiency with which it provides them.

For any given economy one can conceive that there exists an optimum financial structure (in its size relative to the whole economy, number and distribution of decision units and outlets, etc.) and an optimum pattern of institutional behavior (in the kinds of credits granted, kinds of credit instruments used, etc.). It would greatly facilitate empirical research as well as policy-making if banking theorists could specify a general set of criteria of optimality. Unfortunately they have not yet done so; quite possibly they cannot do so, since it is probable that economies in different stages of development—or differing in other respects—will impose different requirements on their banking systems, and hence will have different criteria of optimality. In any case our purpose is the more modest one of delineating and analyzing both the common features of and disparate responses to the problems of financing early manufacturing industries in a number of important historical instances. Hopefully this demonstration will contribute to the formulation of a general theory of financial institutions. At a minimum it will provide development economists, planners, and policy makers who are wrestling with the theoretical and practical problems of an industrial "take-off" with empirical grist for their respective mills.

THE HISTORICAL APPROACH

The historical approach employed in this book rests on several fundamental assumptions. The first and most important is that historical experience is relevant to the problems of the contemporary world. Recorded history is to the human race what memory is to the individual: it is the "collective memory" of society. This does not necessarily imply that the "lessons of history" can be applied directly to the solution of contemporary problems, much less that "history repeats itself." Neither do an individual's experiences repeat themselves in precisely the same manner—for that matter, no two apples fall to the ground in precisely the same manner—but the former fact does not lessen the importance of memory in the learning process of the individual any more than the latter invalidates the law of gravitation. Sir Arthur Lewis has written, "Every economist goes through a phase where he is dissatisfied with the deductive basis of economic theory, and feels sure that a much better insight into economic processes could be obtained by studying the facts of history. The instinct is sound, yet the enthusiasms of this phase seldom survive any serious attempt to get to grips with the facts of history." [2] The instinct, as Sir Arthur says, is sound; but historical experience is imperfectly known, and its discovery or recovery is a laborious, time-consuming, and frequently dusty undertaking, guaranteed to quell the enthusiasm of theorists and policy makers desirous of quick solutions. Moreover, "the facts" do not "speak for themselves," but yield satisfactory answers only in response to meaningful questions. If the questions are improperly phrased, or not put at all, then the "lessons of history" are likely to be garbled at best. Finally, although history cannot answer all the questions one would wish it to, it does not follow that it cannot answer some.

[2] Lewis, *Theory of Economic Growth,* 15.

It is a commonplace that each generation rewrites or restudies history in the light of its own problems and preoccupations. That is merely another way of saying that each generation wishes to ask of history a new set of questions. A major problem of the contemporary world, and a corresponding preoccupation of economists and economic policy makers, is the urgent necessity of achieving more rapid economic growth for the two-thirds of the world that still lives perilously close to the margin of subsistence. The historical approach is of special value in the study of this problem, for the historical experience of the nations that are already industrialized can be studied by the investigator as a completed process, and thus he has some of the advantages of hindsight. The method of comparative history, moreover, is particularly valuable in that the comparison of a number of cases not only reveals the variety of combinations by which development can be achieved, but also offers the possibility of observational controls, the closest approach to laboratory techniques available in most of the social sciences.

It is of the utmost importance, of course, that the cases chosen for comparison be really comparable in some meaningful sense. For that reason we have chosen chronological limits for the studies in this volume to correspond with comparable stages of development rather than using the same chronological period for all cases. This reveals our assumption that nations in similar stages of development face similar problems, and that the institutions and practices devised to cope with the problems of economies that are in earlier or later stages are not necessarily appropriate for economies in the early stages of industrialization.[3] Although this is an assumption, there is available a considerable body of historical evidence to substantiate it. A part of the evidence is negative in character, and suggests the dangers of indiscriminate institutional borrowing without making an adequate historical investigation of the borrowed institutions.[4]

The nations selected for inclusion in this comparative study have in common an experience of sustained, more-or-less successful industrialization. With one exception all shared the cultural inheritance of Western civilization. (By reason of its exceptional position the case of Japan is of unusual importance, and justifies the extra space devoted to it.) While having these features in common, the countries selected represent a suffi-

[3] Our use of the word "stages" is entirely innocuous in the sense of phase or period, and it has no connection with any "stage scheme" of history, early or recent. See Rostow (ed.), *Economics of the Take-off into Sustained Growth,* and Rosovsky, "Take-off into Sustained Controversy."

[4] The central banks foisted on the nations of Latin America by the "Kemmerer missions" in the 1920's are cases in point. The Kemmerer model was of doubtful utility in the nations that inspired it, and it was almost totally irrelevant if not downright harmful in the Latin American context. See also Chapter VIII for an interesting contrast.

cient variety in the nature and timing of their respective processes of industrialization, and particularly in the character of their financial systems, to enable us to draw meaningful conclusions respecting both their similarities and their differences.

But why should nations—political entities—be selected as the units for a study in economic history? It is generally appreciated that industrialization is a regional, not a national, phenomenon. In Great Britain, for example, industrialization tended to concentrate in Lancashire, the West Midlands, the Lowlands of Scotland, and South Wales. On the Continent the major industrial belt extended across northern France, eastern Belgium, and western Germany. Apart from the fact that statistics and many other types of evidence can usually be obtained only in national terms (which also requires that most other aggregative studies in economic history use nations as units), there is one overriding reason why this study should employ them. Although the growth of industry may be determined in part by other factors, less amenable to legislation and national policy, the financial system is shaped in large part by legislation, which, in most instances, extends to an entire nation. The major exception to this rule, the separate banking legislation for Scotland, together with the unique character of the Scottish banking system, justifies the treatment of Scotland as a separate case. A similar procedure might have been resorted to in the case of Germany, except for the minor importance of and paucity of information about many of the smaller German states. In fact, the chapter on Germany deals mainly with Prussia, with data from the other states brought in to illustrate exceptions to the general trend or to illuminate other significant features.

Unfortunately, a lack of resources and personnel has prevented us from extending the comparison in other promising directions. The major omission from our list of important industrial nations—the United States—can be justified only by reason of the enormous variety and complexity of the American financial system, which merits a separate comparative study of its own components. We had intended to include the Scandinavian countries, but they had to be dropped for lack of personnel. Even more serious is the omission of countries—with otherwise comparable conditions—that failed to achieve significant industrialization, such as the Austro-Hungarian Empire and the countries of Mediterranean Europe. To some extent this shortcoming may be offset by close attention to the history of France and Germany before 1850 and Russia before 1890; but it is a shortcoming nevertheless.

Another limitation on the conclusions to be derived from these studies is inherent in the method we have used. A knowledge of history, although useful in understanding social processes in general, cannot be used for purposes of prediction except in a most cautious and qualified sense. In the final analysis one discovers the limitations on the uses of history from history itself. But the theorist or policy maker who dismisses historical experience as irrelevant to the problems of the present with some such phrase as "everything is different now" is himself indulging in a historical generalization of very doubtful validity. In the words of Santayana, those who are ignorant of history are doomed to repeat it.

PRELIMINARY DEFINITIONS

Economic growth is defined here as a sustained increase in output per person; economic development is defined as economic growth accompanied by substantial structural change in the economy. Specifically, economic development involves an increase in the size of the secondary sector of the economy and a corresponding decrease in the relative importance of the primary sector. By "early stages of industrialization" we mean that transitional period in which manufacturing industries, normally the largest component of the secondary sector, adopt new, more capital-intensive techniques of production and grow rapidly relative to agriculture.

In what follows the term "financial sector" will frequently appear, along with its synonym, the "financial system." Technically the set of financial institutions is a subsector of the tertiary, or service-producing, sector of the economy. We use the shorter term merely for convenience. Within the financial sector the banking system is the most important component, and it is the one with which we are especially concerned, although we hope not to lose sight of its connections with other elements of the larger financial system. We are even more particularly concerned with the commercial banking system, though not to the exclusion of other banking and bank-like institutions. In some countries, as will be seen, the distinction between commercial banks and other types of financial institutions is not—or was not—so clear as in Anglo-Saxon countries.

THEORETICAL CONSIDERATIONS

Granted the interdependence of financial development and industrial development, what is the nature of the operational linkage? How do commercial banks and other financial institutions contribute to the formation of real capital in industry, if indeed they do? How does the industrial demand for bank-financed capital create its own supply, if that is the nexus? What is the role of the increase in the stock of money and other financial assets? How does the increase come about? In spite of a vast literature on the role of banks and other financial institutions in the economic system, and in spite of the recent deluge of scholarly publications, some theoretical, some empirical or descriptive, on various aspects of the problem of capital formation in underdeveloped economies, such questions have rarely been asked. Indeed, one influential school of banking theory has long denied that commercial banks can contribute in any significant manner to the formation of fixed capital, and hence to industrialization. Economic theory in general has had little to say on the matter. Schumpeter, who was the first modern economist to relate the banking system explicitly to economic development in a functional sense, and whose insights and intuitions must still command the admiration of all who work the field, made credit creation by banks one of the pillars of his theoretical schema, but he simply assumed the existence of commercial banks with the ability to create purchasing power, without inquiring more closely into the relationship.[5] More recently Gurley and Shaw have had a great deal to say about the proliferation of financial intermediaries and their importance for monetary policy in highly developed economies, but even in their work, stimulating and perceptive though it is, the financial institutions themselves are considered to be mere automatons, appearing to supply the demand for financial assets mechanically.[6]

It is our purpose in the historical chapters that follow to seek answers to the questions raised above. Obviously, however, the historical search should be guided by theoretical notions. In the absence of a full-blown theory of financial institutions we may begin by distinguishing analytically the functions that financial institutions may or should perform.

In the first place, financial institutions serve as intermediaries between savers and investors; in the contemporary world this function is the essential element in the definition of financial institutions. They serve as reservoirs for the accumulated liquid savings of the community, and they direct or allocate those savings, as well as their own "created" means of payment, among alternative investment opportunities. Each of these aspects will be the subject of further comment.

Secondly, financial institutions may supply part or all of the circulating media or means of payment. This function is intimately related to the allocative function, but it raises certain other questions as well. How did it happen that privately owned profit-making organizations got into the business of supplying the community with its means of payment, a function formerly monopolized and still legally reserved to the sovereign authority? What is

[5] Schumpeter, *Economic Development,* 60, 70 *et passim;* Schumpeter, *Business Cycles,* I, 109ff, 292ff.

[6] Gurley and Shaw, *Money in a Theory of Finance;* see also their earlier articles.

the relationship, if any, between this development and the process of industrialization?

Finally, although this function is not inherent in the definition of financial institutions, they may supply initiative and enterprise, as well as finance, for the creation, transformation, and expansion of industrial and other ventures. Schumpeter, among others, considered this function as antithetical to the very nature of commercial banking in a capitalist system,[7] but, as we shall see, such instances have been by no means uncommon in historical experience. It is a subject deserving of careful re-examination in terms of its consequences for the development of industry.

These are basic considerations pertaining to the financial system at any stage of development. For preindustrial economies and those in the early stages of industrialization certain additional features should be taken into account. For example, in such economies the financial system is likely to be rudimentary at best. Individuals may be unaccustomed to holding financial assets and unwilling to make use of financial intermediaries. Under such conditions, financial innovation—in the broadest sense, the introduction and utilization of new financial techniques and institutions—may assume an importance commensurate with technical innovation in industry. Obstacles to financial innovation, whether legal, social, or other, may hinder the growth of financial institutions and thus retard the progress of industrialization. On the other hand, the creation of a viable network of financial institutions appropriate to the circumstances of the economy in question, whether by deliberate public policy or in response to market demand, can materially facilitate and hasten industrial and commercial development.[8]

In an exchange economy individual savers are not necessarily the most efficient investors, since saving depends primarily upon income, whereas efficient investment depends upon entrepreneurial talents, knowledge, and willingness to take risks. As a result, in the absence of financial intermediaries marginal rates of return on real resources are not equated for different uses or among different users. If savers were willing to make their resources directly available to entrepreneurs the occasion for financial intermediation would not arise. Apart from the costs of information and communication, however, the characteristics of the securities issued by entre-

[7] Schumpeter, *Business Cycles,* I, 118, 251; see also Cameron, "The Banker as Entrepreneur."

[8] This assumes that financial institutions are in fact more efficient in the allocation of investable funds than individual savers are. The assumption is based on the following hypothesis and its empirical refutation: if banks in general were *less* efficient investors than individual savers (in general), one would expect that nations with high ratios of bank assets to national income would have lower rates of growth than nations with low ratios. Such is not the case. Q.E.D.

preneurs (equities, bonds, mortgages, bills of exchange, etc.) do not necessarily conform to the preferences of savers in terms of liquidity, security, divisibility, and other inducements to hold assets. Consequently, the function of financial intermediaries is to gain control of the surplus funds (representing claims to real resources) of savers and make them available to entrepreneurs. In the simple theory of financial intermediation they accomplish this by the payment of interest to savers for deposits of loanable funds, which they then lend at higher rates to entrepreneurs.[9] Financial institutions may use means other than payment of interest to acquire control of surplus funds, however. They may provide security, convenience in making payments and collections, and other services. They may combine such services with the payment of interest to offer a variety of financial assets of differing degrees of security, liquidity, yield, etc., such as demand deposits, time deposits, bonds, and insurance policies, to appeal to savers of diverse preferences and circumstances. In this fashion they may increase the absolute quantity of savings as well as modifying the allocation of investable funds.

Financial intermediation also provides a variety of incentives to investors. It is easily seen that reduction in the real or psychological costs of borrowing will encourage entrepreneurs to make larger investments. Financial intermediation does not necessarily imply that "the" interest rate will decline over time, however, since in a growing economy investment demand may become increasingly strong. Improvement of financial markets should nevertheless produce a narrowing of the dispersion of interest rates among different types of users, among geographical regions, and over periods of seasonal fluctuation. The development of a wide array of primary securities provides a more finely delineated spectrum of asset alternatives with greater possibilities of substitution by asset holders. This, in turn, permits borrowers who had been starved for funds under imperfect market conditions, but who would be willing to pay relatively high interest rates, to obtain access to capital.

For many entrepreneurs the increased availability of funds as a result of financial intermediation may be considerably more significant than a simple reduction in costs. Lenders typically use credit-rationing criteria in addition to interest-rate criteria in the allocation of funds. This is particularly important in underdeveloped countries, where most markets are much less perfect than in developed countries. The availability of funds from financial institutions enables the entrepreneur to assume a greater debt position than he otherwise could and, consequently, to undertake larger investments.[10] Ac-

[9] Cf. Hicks, *Capital and Growth,* 290.

[10] Cf. Patrick, "Financial Development and Economic Growth."

cess to funds on reasonable terms probably has favorable expectational or psychological effects on entrepreneurs. Closely related is the fact that the monetization of subsistence sectors resulting from increased financial intermediation encourages the shift to commercial production, and, because of specialization, increased work efforts, emphasis on high-yield products, and enhanced responsiveness to changes in relative prices of different products, there are attendant increases in output.

Another important possibility for growth opened by the introduction of appropriate financial institutions is that of a more efficient allocation of the initial stock of tangible wealth (capital in the broad sense) with which countries begin the process of industrialization. Typically, in preindustrial countries, a considerable proportion of tangible wealth is held in unproductive forms, such as excessive inventories and hoards of precious metals. In part this results from the technological characteristics of preindustrial countries, such as the slow cycle of production and the reliance on commodity money; in part it results from the lack of investment opportunities, or ignorance of their existence, and the absence of suitable financial assets. With the creation of financial intermediaries, and the initiation of industrial development, new investment opportunities arise. It also becomes possible for savers to hold their wealth in more convenient forms, including paper money, thus releasing real resources for productive purposes, either by means of foreign trade or through satisfying needs of workers engaged in producing capital goods. The additions to productive capital by this means were substantial in the cases of Scotland and Japan. Moreover, although the gain in productive capacity by the reallocation of the existing (preindustrial) stock of capital has something of a once-and-for-all character about it, even if the actual process is spread over a period of years or decades, a similar gain is obtained through financial intermediation as traditional or declining industries disinvest and their capital is reallocated to growing industries.

The ability of banks to create means of payment gives them the power to transfer resources directly from less productive to more productive uses. (Whether they actually use the power in that way depends, of course, on the structure of the system and the behavior of the bankers). Although Schumpeter probably exaggerated this feature of commercial banking in order to strengthen the theoretical novelty of his system, there is no doubt of its general importance. As he pointed out, the immediate effect of money creation by banks (assuming that it is lent to producers rather than to consumers or the government) is to give entrepreneurs increased command over real resources.[11] In the long run the productive activity of entre-

[11] Schumpeter, *Economic Development,* chap. III, esp. pp. 106–10; Schumpeter, *Business Cycles,* I, 113–20.

preneurs generates new streams of goods and services to offset the inflationary tendencies of the new money. (The offsetting influence need not balance exactly, of course. In Schumpeter's view it was precisely because increases in production did not match increases in money at every point in time that cyclical fluctuations took place.) Insofar as anyone loses in the process (cyclical fluctuations, crises, panics, etc., apart), it is those entrepreneurs who do not or can not gain access to funds to enable them to keep up the pace.[12]

Other points to be considered are the relationship of fixed to working capital needs in industry and the role of financial institutions in financing both forms of capital. Characteristically, commercial banks grant short-term credit for working capital. Partly for this reason many authorities have asserted that banking has made a negligible contribution to the formation of industrial capital. Apart from overlooking the many instances in which banks departed from the rule of short-term credit, this view fails to take into account the way in which entrepreneurs use short-term credit to free their own resources for fixed investment. In industries with high rates of profit and reinvestment—and these rates are typical of new firms in periods of rapid industrialization—the contribution made in this fashion could be considerable. A hypothetical example will illustrate the point. Let us imagine a firm with total assets of 100,000 currency units, of which one half was invested in fixed capital and the other half in working capital with an average turnover of three months. (It is now widely recognized that during the classic Industrial Revolution working capital normally constituted one-half or more, frequently much more, of the total capital of industrial enterprises.) If annual sales amounted to 200,000 units (equivalent to the annual turnover of working capital—a conservative hypothesis) and profits exclusive of the wages of management to 5 per cent of sales (also conservative), the annual profit would come to 10,000 units, or 10 per cent of total assets. Assuming that all profits are reinvested, the growth rate of the firm would also be 10 per cent per annum if it were completely self-financing, but double that, or 20 per cent, if it resorted to bank credit to satisfy its need for working capital. Such an example, far from being extreme, was in

[12] The statement in the text above bears a relationship to the so-called "real bills doctrine," generally regarded as fallacious, so its exact import may as well be clarified now. The only difficulty with the doctrine as a guide to bank policy is that one cannot tell with certainty, *in advance,* whether loans will be used for "genuinely productive purposes" or not—or even what purposes will be productive. There is also the matter of timing: planting a tree farm is a genuinely productive purpose, but a bank loan permitting a farmer to do so may have to be repaid before the timber is ready to harvest. What *is* valid about the real bills doctrine is that it describes a general tendency of bank loans to entrepreneurs to be "self-liquidating"—sooner or later.

fact typical of many enterprises in the eighteenth and nineteenth centuries, as the historical chapters will show.[13]

Finally, as A. O. Hirschman has emphasized,[14] one of the most crucial shortages in underdeveloped countries is the shortage of capable entrepreneurship. It should not occasion surprise, therefore, to discover that in successful cases of rapid industrialization truly creative entrepreneurs were to be found in such straegic sectors as the banking system, and that they used the leverage thus acquired for the promotion and finance of industrial undertakings. Financial innovation, after all, is not so very different from technical innovation. The former is frequently necessary for realization of the latter, and an individual experienced in one is likely to be in a good position to bring about the other. Such combinations may also allow the co-ordination of production and financial planning in several related industries, thus achieving a pooling of risks and economies of scale in finance as well as in manufacture.

Generally speaking, the advantages of industrialization stem from the higher productivity of human labor resulting from the application of machinery and mechanical power, together with organizational and marketing innovations necessary for their application. Capital in general did not have a higher rate of return in the eighteenth or nineteenth century than it does in the twentieth; indeed, the average rate of return on capital was probably substantially lower than it is in our own day. But capital in particular applications did have a much higher rate of return than the average. Typically, the highest profits resulted from the introduction of technical and organizational innovations that economized labor, or capital, or both. The firms that successfully introduced such innovations thus acquired the resources for rapid growth, whereas those that failed, or contented themselves with existing techniques, either disappeared or plodded along at the old rates of output.

But do banks finance innovations? There is a widespread impression—fostered, it must be said, by the conservative attitudes of many bankers in modern, developed countries—that banks lend only to already established, successful firms. Adrien Mazerat, the director-general of the French Crédit Lyonnais, put it more bluntly than most: "When a client insists energetically on obtaining some facility, it is because he needs it, and that is a reason for refusing it." [15] By and large, the impression is correct. For any given bank the majority of its borrowers must be both established and profitable,

[13] The argument of this paragraph, and of much of the following chapter, was anticipated elsewhere while this book was being prepared for publication. See Pollard, "Fixed Capital."

[14] Hirschman, *Strategy of Economic Development*, 26–8 *et passim*.

[15] Quoted in Bouvier, *Le Crédit Lyonnais de 1863 à 1882*, 886.

otherwise both the bank and its customers would soon go out of business. While the impression is correct in a general sense, the inference it suggests —that banks do not finance innovation—is wrong, or at least grossly oversimplified. Occasionally—some notable examples will be cited in the chapters that follow—banks have consciously and deliberately financed technical innovations of promise from a very early stage. More often, however, bank finance of industrial innovation is either unconscious or at least incidental on the part of the banker. Bankers' criteria for granting loans are numerous, and vary from time to time, country to country, and even bank to bank, but two are likely to be prominent in all times and places: (1) a reasonable prospect that the loan will be repaid when due, which may take the form of a pledge of marketable collateral, or may take less tangible forms, such as a demonstrated high rate of profit or trust and confidence in the borrower based on long personal acquaintance or, possibly, ties of kinship; and (2) a reasonable expectation that the loan will be part of and will contribute to a continuing profitable relation between the banker and the customer, which again may be based on previous experience, or on evidence of whatever nature that the proceeds of the loan will be used profitably and that the customer will again call on the banker for his assistance.

The consequence of successful innovation is increased productivity, hence profitability and growth. Under normal circumstances bankers will prefer to lend to profitable, growing firms and industries rather than to stagnant or declining ones. Thus, while it is rare for banks to finance directly a period of experimentation with a completely novel production technique by a new, inexperienced businessman or inventor—external finance for such experiments normally comes from those who can participate fully in the rewards if it is successful—it is quite common for bankers to finance the expansion of firms that have already introduced successful innovations, and also to finance the adoption of the innovation by imitators. Moreover, although the stereotype of the inventive genius tinkering in his basement or garret is congenial to the Anglo-Saxon mentality, it is probable that, historically as well as currently, the majority of technical innovations have been introduced by, if not generated within, established business enterprises. In such cases it is a simple matter for the entrepreneur to gain bank finance without the banker knowing or necessarily caring whether or not he is financing innovation.

Although this book deals with role of banking in the process of industrialization, it would be both impractical and unrealistic to attempt to isolate the relationship between the banking system and manufacturing industry as narrowly defined. Apart from the inherent difficulties in segregating bank loans by category of borrower in the historical records, such an approach would overlook the indirect contributions of the banking system to industrialization. For example, bank credit granted to the importers of industrial raw materials enabled the importers to extend credit in turn to the manufacturers. Bank financing of improvements in transportation lowered the costs of raw materials and fuel to manufacturers and of final products to purchasers, thus facilitating the extension of markets and bringing about economies of scale. Even mortgage loans to improving landlords and farmers contributed indirectly to industrialization by increasing productivity in agriculture and releasing labor for other uses. In short, wherever bank credit permitted a more efficient allocation of resources and increased productivity, it also promoted the progress of industrialization.

II
ENGLAND
1750 – 1844

by Rondo Cameron

England merits pride of place in this study not only because it was the land of the classic "Industrial Revolution," but because of the world-wide influence of its financial institutions and financial policies. In the course of their development the English financial, monetary, and banking systems were subjected to more public scrutiny and discussion than those of any other country. England's financial history has been investigated and analyzed in more detail and with greater thoroughness than any other. A large part of all monetary and banking theory, modern as well as classical, derives from the public discussion of English conditions and the disputes concerning English policy. Bankers, economists, and statesmen throughout the world have turned to England for the models of their banks, banking theories, and national policies. Whether or not English institutions and policies were the best that could have been designed given the times, and, much less, whether or not they were suitable models for other nations, are entirely separate questions. But that they have been used as such is a fact. It is entirely appropriate, therefore, that a study prompted by the needs of countries currently undergoing or hoping to achieve rapid industrialization should begin with England.

The period treated needs little justification. Although some of England's characteristic financial institutions antedated 1750 by more than half a century, 1750 marks the effective beginning of "country banking," the most important feature of the English banking system from the point of view of this study. At the other end 1844 is a clear watershed in English financial history. The private country banks were already in decline, their place being taken by the new joint-stock banks and branches. The banking legislation of that year radically altered the entire banking system, from the Bank of England outward. In any case, English industry had already successfully achieved its "take-off."

THE SETTING

It is tempting to read into English history a teleology whereby the ever-rising middle classes shaped their institutions, consciously or otherwise, in order to produce both broad political liberty and a free, capitalistic economy. The temptation must be resisted. Nevertheless, it cannot be denied that the precocious if precarious achievement of constitutional government in the seventeenth century favored the accumulation of capital in all sectors of the economy. Moreover, the fact that English financial and commercial policies after 1689 were controlled by men who were versed in the language and techniques of capitalistic enterprise, and who were not averse to increasing their own wealth by means of commerce or financial speculation, is not foreign to the subsequent industrial history of the country.

By the end of the seventeenth century England had established itself as a commercial nation of the first rank. From the beginning to the middle of the eighteenth century the total volume of English foreign trade (imports, exports, and re-exports) roughly doubled. By the mid-1780's it stood almost 50 per cent higher than in 1750, and in the next 15 years it doubled once more. In the mid-1840's it was more than three times as high as at the beginning of the nineteenth century.[1] This rapid growth was intimately related both to the development of the financial system and to the progress of industrialization.

The Pace of Industrial Change

In estimating the national income of England and Wales for the year 1688, Phyllis Deane, using Gregory King's calculations, reached a figure for "total national income" of £48 million.[2] In this total the income from agriculture, forestry, and fishing figured for 40 per cent, that of mining, manufacturing, and building for 21 per cent, and that of trade and transport for 12 per cent. Her estimate for the year 1801 relates to Great Britain, and shows a total national income in current prices of £232 million. (The inclusion of Scotland affects the absolute figure, of course, but as the industrial structure of Scotland in 1801 was not significantly different from that of England and Wales the percentage differences may be regarded as negligible.) At that time, according to Miss Deane's calculations, the share of the primary sector in the national income had fallen to 32.5 per cent, but the share of mining, manufacturing, and building had risen to only

[1] Mitchell and Deane, *British Historical Statistics*, 279–83.

[2] Deane and Cole, *British Economic Growth, 1688–1959*, 156.

23.6 per cent; the largest relative increase took place in trade and transport, which accounted for 17.5 per cent of the national income. In 1841 the percentages were 22.1, 34.4, and 18.4, respectively.[3]

These calculations reveal a number of interesting features about the evolving structure of the English economy. First, as early as the end of the seventeenth century it was substantially more "advanced" than the majority of underdeveloped countries in the twentieth century. The share of agriculture in the national income was only about half that found in many underdeveloped nations today, whereas the share of secondary and tertiary activities was proportionately higher. Secondly, the figures for 1801 show a surprisingly modest gain in secondary activities for a nation in the midst of an industrial revolution; on the other hand, they reflect the enormous growth of commerce and the corresponding increase in both inland transport and foreign shipping. At the beginning of the nineteenth century Blake's "dark, satanic mills" were still quite exceptional on the placid English landscape. The full thrust of the Industrial Revolution came in the next four decades. By 1841, as the figures show, the industrial structure had already taken on a substantially modern cast.

This interpretation is re-enforced by a study of growth rates of national income, which we also owe to Miss Deane and her collaborators.[4] These show a very slow rate of growth in the first half of the eighteenth century, scarcely averaging more than 0.5 per cent per annum. The curve rises somewhat after 1750, to about 1.5 per cent, but is then cut down during the years of the American Revolution. Finally it picks up again about 1785 and rises steeply thereafter into the nineteenth century, reaching an average over-all rate of some 3 per cent per annum in the 1830's.

Capital Accumulation and Investment

Over-all statistics relating to capital formation in England during the period of the Industrial Revolution are as yet unavailable. From two recent preliminary but careful surveys of the general question,[5] however, certain salient points can be affirmed.

1. In all probability capital formation as a proportion of national income was much lower than we have become accustomed to in more recent times. Phyllis Deane concludes that at no time during the eighteenth century did it rise above 7 or 8 per cent, reaching those figures, if at all, only in the last decade or so; for most of the century it did not rise above 5 per cent.

[3] Ibid. 161, 166.

[4] Ibid. See esp. chaps. II and IX.

[5] Deane, "Capital Formation in Britain before the Railway Age"; Crouzet, "Formation du capital en Grande-Bretagne."

Not until the railway boom of the 1840's did it reach the magic figure of 10 per cent.

2. Even at these relatively low levels, the largest part of new capital formation did not take the form of industrial investment as such; agriculture, transportation, residential construction, and urban embellishment in general each probably absorbed as much or more new capital as mining and manufacturing together.[6]

3. The rate of capital formation in mining and manufacturing varied enormously from industry to industry and from firm to firm. Some firms and industries grew rapidly, others slowly or not at all.

4. By far the largest part of industrial capital formation resulted from reinvested profits.

Acceptance of these tentative generalizations might seem to lead to three related conclusions: (1) formation of industrial capital was not a major problem during the Industrial Revolution; (2) insofar as it was a problem, it largely solved itself; (3) in any case, it had little to do with banking. None of these conclusions is valid, however, for reasons that will become evident in the remainder of this chapter. Several of these reasons are closely connected with the monetary situation of the time.

The State of Currency and the Supply of Money

Throughout the era of the Industrial Revolution monetary problems were a continual source of trouble for the nation. Although the country was nominally on a bimetallic standard in the eighteenth century, it had in fact gone over to a gold standard as a result of undervaluation of silver at the Mint. Prior to the minting of the first guineas, in the reign of Charles II, the amount of gold coinage in England had been negligible. During the eighteenth century, however, the total amount of gold coined at the Mint was in excess of £85 million. Silver, on the other hand, virtually disappeared from circulation. From 1662 to 1700 the annual average of silver coins turned out by the Mint was £288,000. Between 1701 and 1750 the average fell to slightly more than £15,000, and in 1751–1800 it fell to scarcely £3,000. The Mint made no silver coins at all in 24 of the last 50 years of the century, and in nine others it made no more than £100.[7] Most of the full-bodied silver coins that were issued were immediately melted down for export; those that remained in circulation were so badly worn and clipped that they constituted no more than tokens. The consequence,

[6] See also Pollard, "Fixed Capital," the theme of which is quite similar to that of this chapter.

[7] Craig, *The Mint,* Appendix I.

apart from the shift to the gold standard, was a drastic shortage of small change, since gold coins were generally too large to be used for the payment of wages or in retail trade. The Mint issued small quantities of copper coins in the first half of the century, but even those were discontinued in 1754. Thereafter the public had to supply its own need for small change. This it did with the assistance of foreign coins, counterfeit coins, and privately issued token money. The issuers of tokens were most often industrialists (especially in the metallurgical industries) who used the tokens for wage payments; some, building upon this experience, became full-fledged bankers as well as industrialists. A less happy solution to the problem of the shortage of wage money was the "truck" system, or payment in kind.[8]

Eighteenth-century England had means of payment in addition to its monetary gold and subsidiary coinage. Banknotes and deposits subject to withdrawal or transfer by means of checks (though checks were still in an experimental stage), had been in use since the middle of the seventeenth century. Contemporaries regarded them as mere substitutes for genuine money (i.e. gold), but in fact they performed virtually all of the functions included in the definition of money by modern monetary theorists. Their incidence in use was not spread evenly throughout the country, however. They were creations of London, and London employed them most extensively. With the growth of country banking after 1750 banknotes gradually became more common in the outlying areas, but demand deposits and the checking habit did not become important until well into the nineteenth century. This did not mean that merchants and industrialists outside of London relied exclusively on coin, or on coin supplemented by the issue of country banks. They had yet a third substitute for metallic money, the "inland bill," or bill of exchange.

The bill of exchange was far more ancient than either the banknote or the demand deposit; it had been developed in the Middle Ages. At first the bill was used as a device for avoiding the cost and risks of shipping coin or bullion over great distances, then as a credit instrument which circumvented the Church's prohibition of usury. When it first came to be used as a means of current payment is a moot question that may never be answered, but that it was so used in eighteenth-century England is beyond doubt. In some areas—Lancashire is the outstanding example—bills of exchange were so widespread that they drove out even banknotes.

[8] See Hilton, *The Truck System.* Payment in kind might be either direct or indirect, as by compulsory purchases from a company store. The use of private tokens, which Hilton also mentions, was not, properly speaking, a part of the truck system if the tokens were generally accepted by local merchants and redeemable in lawful money.

THE FINANCIAL STRUCTURE AND ITS EVOLUTION

Three distinct classes of institutions constituted the banking system of England in the second half of the eighteenth century. In a class by itself, with a legal monopoly of joint-stock banking, stood the Bank of England, founded in 1694. Slightly older (collectively) were the London private bankers, numbering some 50 or so.[9] The "country banks"—private banks outside London—made up the third class; there were only a handful in 1750, but their number grew rapidly in the next half-century and more rapidly still in the quarter-century following, reaching a peak of almost 800 in 1810 and peaking again in the boom year 1825. In the second quarter of the nineteenth century a fourth class joined those already existing. In 1826 Parliament passed legislation altering the terms of the Bank of England's monopoly and allowing the formation of other joint-stock banks. Their growth was rapid; with their branches, they already outnumbered the private banks before the legislation of 1844 radically changed England's financial system.

The Bank of England

The Bank of England deserves priority of consideration only by virtue of its political influence and legal status. Its creation resulted from the coupling of the government's urgent need for money with the bank promoters' desire for the profits of both speculation and monopoly. In this it set a pattern for the formation of national banks (later called central banks) in other countries, but its own contributions to industrial finance were negligible, if not negative. Nevertheless, by the middle of the eighteenth century it had achieved an impregnable position in the nation's financial structure. Its power and influence stemmed from its connection with public finance; its role in private finance was slight, and incidental to the former.

For the decade 1778–87 the Bank's holding of public securities averaged more than 70 per cent of its total portfolio. In 1795 its advances to the government amounted to 77 per cent of the total.[10] The majority of these

[9] Joslin, "London Private Bankers, 1720–1785," 173, gives the following figures, but emphasizes that they are probably understatements: 1754, 29; 1776, 51; 1786, 52. Clapham, *Bank of England,* I, 158, says "approximately fifty" for the 1770's. The number grew from 20 or 30 in 1750 to "nearly seventy" in 1800.

[10] Computed from semiannual figures supplied by the Bank in the inquiry of 1832; *PP, Report from the Commission of Secrecy on the Bank of England Charter,* Appendix 5, 13ff. See also Gayer, Rostow, and Schwartz, *British Economy, 1790–1850,* II, 893, for the comparable figures for the first half of the nineteenth century.

advances were made by discounting Exchequer bills issued for supplies and requisitions. The Bank also discounted other government bills—Navy, Victualing, and so on—and made advances against future receipts from land and excise taxes. In addition to its connection with short-term government finance, the Bank had the responsibility for managing the long-term, or funded, government debt, of which it owned directly a sizable fraction. It paid interest on the debt on behalf of the government, handled transfers of title, and was always consulted in connection with new issues. Even some of its private business was indirectly related to government finance, inasmuch as it advanced money on securities of the public debt to enable purchasers to make payments on subscriptions to new issues. Most government departments and many tax receivers also kept deposits, or "drawing accounts," with the Bank.

The Bank's private business was of two principal types. First, it accepted deposits from and maintained drawing accounts for wealthy individuals and business firms (and, in the case of a few large corporations, such as the East India and South Sea companies, permitted overdrafts on these accounts up to stipulated amounts). Secondly, it discounted bills of exchange and promissory notes (principally the former) for London merchants. The Bank's regulations for admission to discount were rather strict, however, and the number of discount accounts were correspondingly limited. Maintenance of a deposit account did not automatically entitle one to the privilege of discount. Eligibility to discount either notes or bills depended, first, on being a resident of London and "engaged in trade"; more than that, one had to be approved by a committee of directors with whom personal consideration might carry considerable weight. For the period 1800–1815 (the earliest for which figures are available), the number of private individuals entitled to discount varied between 1,200 and 1,400 only.[11] It is unlikely that the number was greater in the eighteenth century; among other reasons, bankers were not admitted to discount until 1797. Direct advances by the Bank to its customers (other than by discount) were rare, and usually for the purpose of meeting subscriptions on new public loans.

In spite of the subsidiary importance of its private business, the Bank did occupy a key position in the English economy—or, at least, in the economy of metropolitan London. That it did so resulted from two facts: it was the holder of the nation's reserves of metallic money, and its banknotes were used as a means of payment for virtually all large transactions in the City of London.

Under early legislation the Bank did not possess a monopoly of note

[11] Clapham, *Bank of England,* I, 205.

issue, but only of joint-stock banking. Nevertheless, its superior legal position and its connection with government finance gave it a great advantage over its would-be competitors, and by the second half of the eighteenth century the London private bankers had virtually ceased to issue. The Bank had already achieved in fact what the legislation of 1826 conferred on it in law: a monopoly of note issue in the immediate environs of London. Once in circulation, whether by means of government or private advances, the notes generally remained out for a considerable period. In addition to being used in ordinary commercial transactions, they were used in payment of customs and excise taxes, for subscriptions to government loans, and, after the establishment of the London Clearing House in 1773, to settle balances between bankers. Although both the Bank and the private bankers accepted deposits from their customers, checks were rarely used except to withdraw notes or specie for actual payments. However important the Bank's notes were for the mercantile and financial transactions of the metropolis, nonetheless they rarely circulated beyond the immediate environs of London.

As holder of the nation's gold reserve the Bank had much more than local significance. This function, however, was unofficial and largely unacknowledged. In the latter half of the eighteenth century the Bank was far from being a "banker's bank"; not only did it exclude private banks from discounting until 1797, but very few even maintained deposit accounts with it. Nevertheless, the Bank had already begun to assume, albeit unwillingly and almost unconsciously, some of the characteristics of a "central" bank. In the mid-1770's its holdings of bullion (mostly gold) averaged almost £5 million at a time when the total monetary gold stock of the country did not exceed £20 million.[12] Although its metallic reserve fluctuated over a wide range, from a low of £367,000 in 1763 to a high of £8,646,000 in 1789, the Bank's importance received its decisive test in 1797. When, under the pressure of an internal drain of specie and the threat of a French invasion, the Bank suspended cash payments with government authorization, the English country banks and the banks of Scotland likewise spontaneously ceased to redeem their notes in gold, though they had no formal authorization to do so until much later.

The London Private Bankers

London private bankers can trace their professional origins back at least as far as the middle of the seventeenth century. Before the end of the century they already possessed, if only in rudimentary form, the three major

[12] See below, p. 42.

modern credit instruments: bills of exchange, deposits subject to check (or draft), and banknotes. By the middle of the eighteenth century the London bankers were clearly becoming members of a specialized profession. The unfair competition of the Bank of England forced them to give up their note issue, but this merely encouraged them to develop their two remaining facilities still more.

Between 1750 and 1844 the most important business of the bankers in the City was that of serving as London agents for their country correspondents. Even before 1750 they had begun, to some extent, to tie together the isolated country districts into something resembling a nationwide financial system centered on London. With the growth of commerce and industry and the increasing commercialization of agriculture, accompanied and fostered by the rise of the country banks, the London bankers became the indispensable linchpins in the system, connecting the country banks not only with the London money market but also with one another. Alternately holding surplus funds and discounting bills for country correspondents, they linked the wealthy agricultural counties of East Anglia and the Southwest with the capital-hungry counties of the Industrial Revolution, to the benefit of all.[13]

The Country Banks

The statistics on the growth of country banking provide powerful circumstantial evidence bearing on the relationship between banking and industrialization.[14] In 1750 not more than a dozen firms in the whole of England and Wales, outside London, specialized in banking. Their growth there-

[13] Dr. Peter Mathias and Prof. David Joslin have emphasized that the integration of the credit structure brought about by the London and country banks together was not merely geographical, but social and industrial as well. That is, financial integration tapped sources of capital which, in its absence, would have remained unutilized or would have been utilized less efficiently as a result of barriers erected by distinctions between social classes and differences in industrial structure. In their view there was no shortage of capital in the aggregate in the eighteenth century, but shortages only in particular applications. The development of the banking system made the financial market less imperfect.

[14] The statistics, unfortunately, are not exact. The earliest annual series begins with the year 1800, and the first official figures with the year 1809; even those are subject to error. For earlier years there are only isolated estimates. A difficulty with individual cases is in deciding when a draper, ironmaster, or whatever, who carried on some banking functions incidental to his original business, shed that business and specialized in banking—if he ever did. For a comprehensive discussion of the reliability of the statistics, see Pressnell, *Country Banking,* chap. 2. The general trend, in any case, is clear enough.

after was rapid, if uneven: in the early 1780's there were more than 100; by 1800 there were more than 300. The curve rose rapidly until 1810, stabilized for a few years, dropped off slightly after 1815, and rose again to a new peak in 1825. After the crisis of 1825 the number of private country banks began to decline, but the spectacular growth of joint-stock banks in the provinces, authorized by legislation in 1826, more than made up the difference. (See Chart II.1.) The number of licenses to issue banknotes (which covered some, but not all, branch offices; nonissuing banks did not require a license) reached a maximum of 783 in 1810. The Post Office directories of country correspondents of London bankers give an initial peak of 660 in 1813, and a new, higher one of 684 in 1825. Between 1836 and 1844 the total number of country banks and branches, both private and joint-stock, exceeded 1,000.

The origins of country banking were diverse. Among the early bankers were men who had formerly been engaged—and frequently still were—in wholesale or retail trade, in manufacturing of both the domestic and factory types, in mining, and in tax collecting. The early lists also included attorneys and an occasional landed proprietor. The economic forces that called the country banks into existence as a specialized profession were equally diverse, but they may be grouped under three easily identifiable headings. The demand for remittance facilities, especially on London, was perhaps the most important. This was obviously the case with tax receivers, and scarcely less so in the case of most merchants who became bankers. Secondly, the increasing demand for the services of financial intermediaries led many money scriveners (brokers) to take up banking as a full-time occupation. Closely related was the need, in agricultural areas in particular, for safe repositories for idle funds. Finally, but by no means of minor significance, the deficiencies of the coinage and the need for a local circulating medium, especially for the payment of wages in industrial districts, led to the use of token coins and paper currency, which soon took on the characteristics of banknotes. From that it was a short step to full-fledged banking. In this way many industrialists entered the ranks of the bankers; occasionally shopkeepers and even publicans made use of the same route.

The average size of the country banks was not impressive; they were restricted by law to partnerships of not more than six persons. No less an authority than Pressnell appears to accept, *faute de mieux,* contemporary estimates of £10,000 as the "average" or "typical" capitalization of country banks. This figure seems to refer to the last decade of the eighteenth century or the first decade of the nineteenth. The average size was probably smaller in earlier years, almost certainly larger in later. In any event, the restriction on the size of the banks, together with the relative lack of

CHART II.1

COUNTRY BANKS (INCLUDING BRANCHES) IN ENGLAND AND WALES, 1800–1844

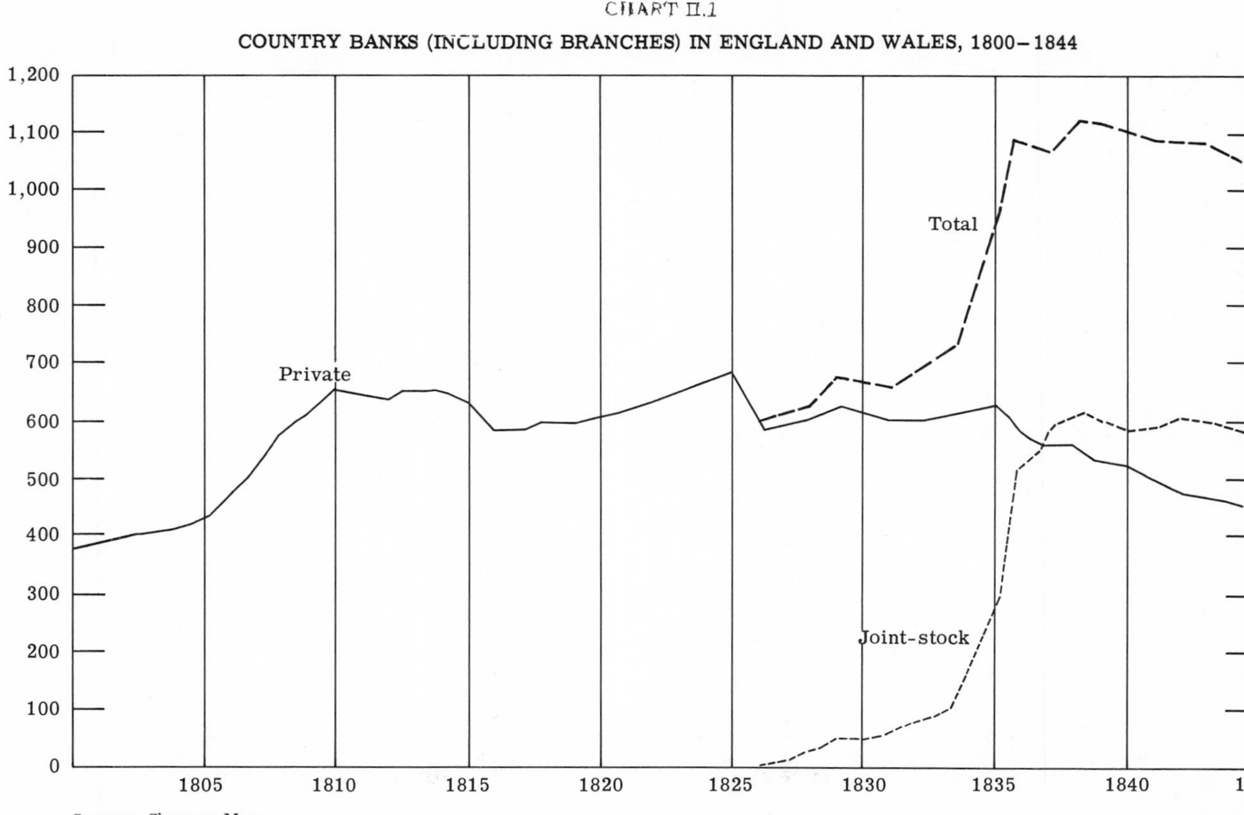

Source: Shannon Mss.

experience of bank managers and their sometimes unorthodox practices, weakened the ability of the banks to withstand the frequent financial crises of the era and gave them a possibly exaggerated reputation for instability. Yet another consequence of limited size was the predominance of unit banking. Though branches were not unknown, they were relatively rare. Finally, the low capital requirements and the absence of any legal impediment facilitated entry into banking; these circumstances, together with the rapidly increasing demand for banking services, account for the rapid growth in the number of country banks.

The geographical distribution of country banks is of some interest in considering their relationship to industrialization. At the beginning of the nineteenth century every county in England, except tiny Rutland, already had at least one bank. The West Midland region was best served, insofar as the density of bank offices is a measure of service; it had approximately one office for each 12,000 inhabitants—a greater banking density than London, which had one bank for each 17,000. For England and Wales as a whole the figure was approximately 21,000 if London is included, and slightly higher if London banks and population are excluded. (Size of banks, or banking capital per inhabitant, is a quite different matter, of course, as is geographical concentration.) At the opposite extreme, the area with the lowest density of bank offices in 1800 was the industrial northwest (Lancashire and Cheshire); although Lancashire had at least 14 banking establishments in 1800, the ratio of banks to population was only one to 48,000, less than half the national average. This low density would seem to belie any close correlation between banking and industrialization. In the case of Lancashire, special circumstances account for its wide departure from the national average. Prior to the development of the deposit business on a large scale in the 1830's, the principal source of profit for most country banks had been note issue. Lancastrians had had several unhappy experiences with bank failures, however, notably in the crisis of 1788, and these produced a lasting effect. The result was that Lancashire was the only county that had no significant local note circulation of its own. Most Lancashire banks were not banks of issue; instead, Lancashire merchants and manufacturers relied on bills of exchange drawn on one another for most local transactions. The metallic circulation was supplemented by Bank of England notes—the only case of any significance in which these notes circulated outside London before the banking reform of 1826. Moreover, mere number is by no means the only criterion of the adequacy of banking facilities. Whereas many note-issuing banks in agricultural districts were flimsy affairs at best, such substantial concerns as Leyland, Bullins & Co. of Liverpool, and Jones, Lloyd & Co. of Manchester, could rival the larger London banks in importance. In 1815, for example,

Leyland, Bullins had total assets of more than £1 million sterling, and in 1836 almost £3 million.[15]

By the beginning of the 1840's bank offices were not only more numerous, but they were also far more equally distributed throughout the country. Insofar as it is possible or meaningful to generalize about the small deviations from the national average, it appears that the density of bank offices relative to population was greatest in those regions in which the geographical density of the population was smallest—that is, in primarily rural regions such as the Southwest, the North, and Wales, where small local banks of issue continued to supply the largest part of the circulating media. (See Chart II.2.) By the 1840's the majority of banks in the more populous urban areas were no longer the private banks of old, but branches of joint-stock banks of regional or even national significance.

The Rise of Joint-stock Banking

The private country bankers had long been objects of suspicion and complaint. Their extreme critics held them uniquely responsible for the periodic financial crises that shook the country, and they made occasional demands for their complete suppression. Better informed persons realized that the country could not do without a banking system, and that what was needed was the strengthening of that system, not its abolition. Such sentiments grew stronger in the years after 1815, which were characterized by both falling prices and increasing demands for banking services. In 1822 Thomas Joplin discovered the "flaw" in the Bank of England's charter—that joint-stock banks as such were not illegal so long as they did not issue notes—but he was unable to secure financial support for his projected bank in Newcastle because of the prevailing opinion that the Bank's monopoly was impregnable.[16] In the same year the Cabinet toyed with the idea of explicitly authorizing joint-stock banks beyond a 65-mile radius from London—the germ of the Act of 1826—but was deflected by other considerations, notably the opposition of the Bank of England and especially the private bankers.

The severe crisis of 1825–26, in which 60 country banks failed, made demands for reform irresistible. The government moved promptly on several fronts, but the most important result was the Act of 1826 (7 Geo. IV, c. 46), which specifically authorized joint-stock banks beyond the 65-mile radius. The country bankers, still recovering from the crisis, were unable to protest effectively, and the opposition of the Bank of England was muted

[15] Pressnell, *Country Banking,* 177, 517.

[16] Thomas, *Joint Stock Banking,* 74–7. In 1824 Joplin proposed a similar but larger bank for London.

CHART II.2

BANKS PER 10,000 INHABITANTS, BY REGION, ENGLAND AND WALES, 1801 and 1841

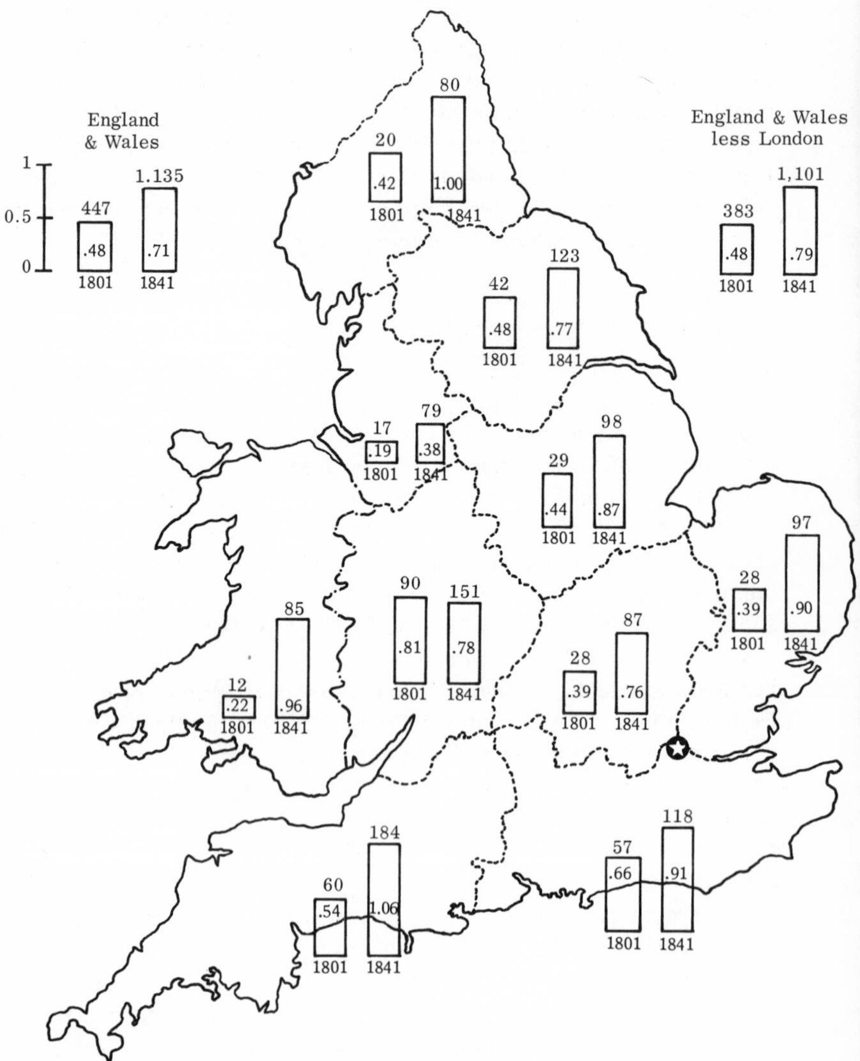

Number above column represents bank offices.

by the government's implied threat to oppose renewal of its charter in 1833.

The Act of 1826 was a piece of near-emergency legislation, and it contained several flaws and ambiguities; yet its main intent was clear. Nevertheless, the response to it was sluggish at first. In the first year of the new law only three joint-stock banks entered business (one of them was a converted private bank), and only three more were established in the next. By the end of 1830, almost four years after the law took effect, only 14 banks had been established under it. Various reasons for this slow response have been advanced, but the most likely explanation, apart from the novelty of the idea, was the depressed state of business in the wake of the crisis. In any case, by 1833 there were approximately 30 joint-stock banks in operation, which, with branches, added more than 100 bank offices to the lists of country banks. In that same year the law renewing the charter of the Bank of England clarified the Act of 1826 by explicitly allowing joint-stock banks in London if they did not issue banknotes. Growth was extremely rapid for the next few years. By 1844 approximately 150 had been established, more than half in the three years 1834–36. Including branches, the total number of joint-stock bank offices amounted to approximately 600 in the early 1840's.

Although the provincial joint-stock banks were allowed to issue notes if they did not have an issuing office within a 65-mile radius of London, by no means all of them took advantage of the opportunity. Almost 90 per cent of those established before 1837 did so, but only seven of the 37 created between 1837 and 1844 did. Among the reasons for not issuing notes was the attitude of the Bank of England. The Bank granted special facilities to those banks that handled its notes instead of their own and, on the other hand, refused to rediscount bills for joint-stock banks of issue. During the crisis of 1836 the latter policy was especially effective in persuading some banks to give up the issues they already had and in discouraging new ones from beginning. Perhaps the most important reason for the relative unimportance of the issue function, however, was that joint-stock banks in the provinces, like London private banks in the previous century, had discovered that it had become possible to carry on a profitable business by means of deposits alone.

Savings Banks

Savings banks, the main original purpose of which was to alleviate poverty by encouraging providence and thrift among the working classes, grew out of the charitable efforts of the late eighteenth century.[17] The "Society for

[17] On savings banks see Horne, *History of Savings Banks,* and Fishlow, "Trustee Savings Banks, 1817–1861."

Bettering the Condition of the Poor," founded in 1796, was representative of the movement. The Society was followed in the next decade by a number of "penny banks," "Sunday banks," "benefit banks," etc. For the most part these had little success, even in terms of their own limited objectives. The real origins of a successful savings-bank movement came from Scotland, with the formation of the Ruthwell savings bank in 1810 and the Edinburgh Bank for Savings in 1813. Within a few years more than a hundred such banks existed in Scotland. The movement developed more slowly in England for a variety of reasons (attributed by Scots to "deficiencies of national character"), of which the most important was probably the difficulty of finding suitable investment outlets for the resources of the savings banks. Parliament remedied this situation in 1817 by providing for trustee savings banks. The most important principles of the legislation were the requirements for honorary (unpaid) trustees and managers and the provision for investment of the resources of the savings banks with the National Debt Commissioners at a fixed rate of return that was higher, on the average, than the market rate. Both principles reflected the philanthropic nature of the savings-bank idea.

In 1817 fewer than 80 savings banks existed in England and Wales; in contrast, there were more than twice that number in Scotland. Within a year 150 new banks were created in England. By the 1840's, in the United Kingdom as a whole, there were more than 500 savings banks, almost a million depositors, and total deposits of almost £30 million. The evidence suggests, however, that the majority of the depositors were domestic servants and members of the lower middle class, such as shopkeepers, rather than the workers for whom the savings banks were originally intended. Moreover, whatever their influence in encouraging thrift, the savings banks could not contribute directly to the formation of industrial capital because of their connection with government finance.

Bill Brokers and the Discount Market

Another important group of financial intermediaries that developed in the course of the Industrial Revolution was the bill-broking fraternity. Precisely when the bill brokers became a distinct, specialized profession is not clear. King, the historian of the London discount market, thought they originated in the latter half of the eighteenth century and consolidated their position during the Napoleonic Wars.[18] Pressnell, on the other hand, found no trace of them before the final decade of the eighteenth century, and regarded their activities prior to about 1830 as limited and unimportant.[19] The dif-

[18] King, *History of the London Discount Market,* chap. I.

[19] Pressnell, *Country Banking,* 84–105.

ference is partly a matter of emphasis and interpretation. In any case, both authorities agree that the character of their functions changed importantly after the Napoleonic Wars and especially after the crisis of 1825. Prior to that time the brokers acted merely as agents for country banks, gathering up bills put out for discount by the banks in the capital-hungry industrial areas and sending them off to banks with surplus funds seeking investment. For this service they charged a small commission. During the periods of low interest rates, in 1817–18 and again in 1822–25, some country banks began to leave money at call with the bill brokers, who invested it directly by discounting suitable bills, thereby becoming principals in the transactions. In this case their earnings came from the difference between the interest rates that they paid for money left with them at call and the rate of discount they charged on bills. The panic of 1825 at first threatened the very existence of the bill brokers, but in the long run it turned them in the direction that led ultimately to the delicate, highly organized money market depicted in Bagehot's *Lombard Street*. After the crisis was over the London private bankers ceased paying interest on money deposited with them by country bankers, and gave up their reliance on rediscounting with the Bank of England in periods of stringency, relying instead on higher cash reserves of their own and larger deposits in the Bank of England. The country banks therefore cut their deposits with London bankers to a minimum and left the surplus with the bill brokers at low call money rates. The London private bankers also put out their own surplus funds with bill brokers, and even the joint-stock banks began to employ them. After 1830, when the Bank of England first admitted bill brokers to the privilege of rediscount, the classic system began to take shape, although it did not attain its perfection until the 1850's. The existence of a highly organized money market is symptomatic of a fully articulated capitalistic economy rather than one in the early stages of industrialization.

Other Financial Institutions

Several minor types of financial institutions either already existed or grew to prominence between the mid-eighteenth and mid-nineteenth centuries. Charitable foundations, some tracing their origins to the Middle Ages, frequently extended credit for a variety of purposes. So-called "loan charities," in fact, "were especially created to assist young men beginning their careers, and in innumerable cases they must have provided at least a part of the capital necessary to open a new business." [20] Those working class associations called "friendly societies," which provided financial help for

[20] James, "Charity Endowments as Sources of Local Credit," 159.

funeral expenses and other misfortunes, as well as fellowship, also had a long history. Yet another kind of self-help financial institution was the benefit building society. The earliest recorded institution of this type was founded in Birmingham in 1781, but they did not receive legal recognition until 1836.[21]

Two other important classes of financial intermediaries grew to maturity in England during the Industrial Revolution. Organized markets for dealings in negotiable securities, the London stock market in particular, originated in that pregnant era between 1689 and 1720, and by the early decades of the nineteenth century they had acquired a key position in the British financial structure, rivaling in importance that of the Bank of England. The insurance industry, with still earlier roots, also dates in its modern form from the end of the seventeenth and the beginning of the eighteenth century. By the 1840's, when more than 100 companies were listing stock with an aggregate value of more than £25 million, it had clearly become a major industry. Until the mid-nineteenth century, however, the stock market dealt chiefly in government securities. Insurance companies probably invested a portion of their assets in industrial investments, but little detailed information is available. In any case these two categories of financial institutions lie outside the immediate scope of this study.

The Size of the Banking Sector

In attempting to assess the importance of the banking system it would be helpful to have a quantitative estimate of the size of the banking sector relative to the whole economy. By applying Pressnell's figure of £10,000 as the "average" capitalization of country banks to the numbers of banks at various dates, we get what might be regarded as a maximum estimate for the earlier years and a minimum for the later. On this assumption it would appear that around 1775 not more than £1 million was involved; around 1800, about £3,700,000; and in 1825 not less than £6 million. That is for country banks only. The London banks were certainly substantially larger on the average. If Curries & Co. can be regarded as typical, the proprietary capital of London banks was between two and three times as large as that of the typical country bank in the 1770's. [22] On this basis it appears that the capital invested in banking, exclusive of the Bank of England, amounted in 1775 to about £2,500,000; in 1800, to £5,-

[21] Hobson, *A Hundred Years of the Halifax,* 1.

[22] Curries & Co. had a capital stock of £30,000 in the 1770's, reduced to £20,000, then raised again to £22,500 in the 1780's. I am obliged to the secretary of Glyn Mills and Company for providing me with a copy of the surviving balance sheets.

500,000; and in 1825 to £8,500,000.[23] When we include the "Rest," or surplus account, of the Bank of England,[24] the figures become (approximately) £3,500,000, £9,800,000, and £11,400,000.

After 1825 the average capitalization of both London and country banks increased substantially. Many of the smaller banks failed in the 1825 crisis; many of those that survived increased their capital, partly as a matter of public relations if not of security, but chiefly to meet the competition of the new joint-stock banks. The joint-stock banks typically began operations with capitals of £25,000, £50,000, even £100,000; the legislation of 1844 set £100,000 as the minimum, of which at least one-half had to be paid up. A conservative estimate indicates that capital invested in banking in England and Wales in 1844 was at least £30 million.[25]

It is a commonplace that commercial banks do not operate primarily on their own capitals. One of the distinctive features of banking as a business is that banks mobilize the temporarily idle funds of others and persuade the public to accept their own liabilities in the form of notes and deposits

[23] The calculations are as follows.

Year	*Country banks*			*London banks*			
	No.	Av. Cap.	Total	No.	Av. Cap.	Total	Grand Total
1775	100	£ 10,000	£ 1,000,000	50	£ 30,000	£ 1,500,000	£ 2,500,000
1800	370	10,000	3,700,000	60	30,000	1,800,000	5,500,000
1825	600	10,000	6,000,000	50	50,000	2,500,000	8,500,000

The figure of £ 30,000 for the average capital of London banks in 1800 is probably too low, and for 1825 it certainly is; I have, accordingly, raised it to £ 50,000 (which may still be too low) since the purpose of the calculations is to give merely a rough approximation. As noted above, the estimate of £ 10,000 for country banks in 1825 is also probably too low. The numbers of both London and country banks have been rounded.

[24] The Bank of England's entire nominal capital was permanently invested in government securities, and hence was not available for banking purposes.

[25] London joint-stock banks account for £ 250,000 and 52 reporting provincial joint-stock banks for £ 7,250,000, or an average of £ 140,000 each; 48 provincial joint-stock banks did not report. The nonreporting banks were probably smaller, on the average, than the reporting banks; assume an average of £ 100,000, or a total of £ 4,800,000. Assume a further £ 100,000 average capitalization for the 63 London private banks, and a £ 25,000 average for the 273 private country banks, for a grand total, exclusive of the Bank of England, of £ 27,375,000. The Bank of England's "Rest" in 1844 was £ 3,375,000.

Newmarch estimated total capital employed in banking (i.e. proprietors' equity, deposits, and circulation) at the end of 1849 as £ 190 million. Deducting £ 140 million for deposits and circulation (cf. Table II.2, p. 42) leaves £ 50 million, including the capital of the Bank of England. Allowing for that, we are left with the £ 36 million as the active capital invested in banking at the beginning of 1850. See Newmarch, "Magnitude and Fluctuations of Bills of Exchange."

in the settlement of debts. Thus the total of assets or liabilities of the banking sector is a more important measure of its importance in the national economy than is its equity capital. It will come as no surprise that the estimates of those quantities are no more reliable or precise than those for bank capitalization. We might begin by taking as a bench-mark figure Newmarch's estimate of £190 million for 1849–50.[26] Another method of proceeding is to anticipate the findings of Table II.2 with respect to note issues and deposits, addding them to the estimates given above for capitalization. Accordingly, we reach the following figures for total liabilities and net worth of the banking sector:

1775	£20,500,000	
1800	54,800,000	
1825	80,000,000	(interpolated)
1844	139,000,000	

These indicate an over-all rate of growth of 2.8 per cent per annum (continuous compounding) for the banking sector, compared with 1.6 per cent per annum for national income and 3.1 per cent for industrial production.[27]

The figures above, even if they are of the correct order of magnitude, still do not tell us the relative importance of banking in the economy. Ideally, we should like to know the ratio of the total assets (or liabilities) of the banking sector to the total national wealth. Rather than make arbitrary assumptions about capital/output ratios in the absence of reliable statistics, it seems preferable to relate bank assets to national income. The relevant data for selected dates are given in Table II.1.

Such estimates cannot, of course, be regarded as accurate for purposes of statistical manipulation. If used with the caution that their derivation indicates, however, they can serve a useful purpose in international and intertemporal comparisons.

[26] Ibid. Deducting the Bank of England's immobilized capital, the comparable figure is £ 176 million.

[27] The growth rates over shorter periods are as follows.

Period	Capital employed in banking	National income	Industrial production
1775–1800	3.9	1.5	3.5
1800–1825	1.5	1.2	2.6
1825–1844	2.9	2.1	3.4

The rates for national income are based on Table II.2; the index of industrial production is from Hoffmann, *British Industry, 1700–1950*. Continuous compounding yields slightly lower rates of growth than periodic compounding.

TABLE II.1

BANK ASSETS AND NATIONAL INCOME, ENGLAND, 1775–1844

Year	Bank Assets (£ million)	National Income (£ million)	Ratio (%)
1775	20.5	135.0	15.2
1800	54.8	196.7	27.9
1825	80.0	270.0	29.6
1844	139.0	403.8	34.4

Sources: Bank assets as estimated above; national income from Deane and Cole adjusted for England and Wales as in Table II.2, p. 42. Figures for 1825 are interpolated.

ASPECTS OF INDUSTRIAL FINANCE

English industrial enterprise developed in the shadow of the Bubble Act. That Act, passed in 1720 at the height of the South Sea Bubble mania, remained on the books for 105 years; the spirit that underlay it continued to influence English company law for almost half a century after its repeal.[28] On its face the purpose of the law was to prevent unincorporated enterprises from acting as if they possessed a corporate charter. At that time corporate charters could be obtained only by a grant from the Crown or by special Act of Parliament, and they were usually associated with an additional grant of special privilege, such as the monopoly of a particular branch of trade. After the collapse of the South Sea Bubble (to which the passage of the law itself contributed), both Parliament and the legal officers of the Crown became extremely reluctant to grant corporate charters. The process of incorporation thus became lengthy, expensive, difficult, and uncertain of outcome. Moreover, a tendency developed both in the procedure of incorporation and in interpretations of the courts for the articles of the charter to stress the limits of corporate action, to restrict the corporation to the express purposes of the charter. For all of these reasons businessmen rarely petitioned for corporate charters. There is little doubt, nevertheless, that the mere existence of the Act hindered the flow of capital into industry.[29] That circumstance served to increase the importance

[28] See Dubois, *The English Business Company after The Bubble Act;* Cooke, *Corporation, Trust, and Company;* Hunt, *Development of the Business Corporation.*

[29] Such, at least, was the opinion of Alfred Marshall and many other commentators. Cf. *Industry and Trade,* 312; also Scott, *Joint-Stock Companies,* I, 348. For a more recent view, based on extensive research, see John, *Industrial Development of South Wales, 1750–1850,* 53.

of short-term finance for working capital provided by banking and other sources of credit.

The Demand for Capital

Since the beginning of the English Industrial Revolution factories, steam engines, and blast furnaces have been the symbols of industrialism. Students of the phenomenon from Marx and Engels to Harrod and Domar have emphasized the importance of capital in the process of economic growth. Only recently, however, have we begun to get empirical studies that enable us to judge the quantitative importance of capital in its various forms. These indicate that capital investment was a much smaller proportion of total national income than had previously been supposed, that investment in manufacturing enterprises constituted but a small part of total investment, and that fixed capital accounted for but a small part—substantially less than half—of all capital invested in manufacturing.[30] Moreover, insofar as the newer forms of industry had a greater need for capital, both fixed and circulating, than the old, the transition was gradual, not sudden. The size of the average firm increased somewhat over time, and new firms entering most industries in the 1830's were probably larger than new firms entering the same industries in the 1780's; but for the most part growth was internal—within the firm—by means of reinvested profits. The proportion of fixed to working capital varied from industry to industry, and may have increased slightly over time. Rarely, however, did the "representative firm" in any industry invest as much as 50 per cent of its total assets in fixed capital. Of greater importance collectively were the liquid funds or access to credit needed for the purchase of raw materials, the payment of wages (and, in some cases, of rents and royalties), and the extension of credit to buyers. In this respect the difference between the new industrialism and the old was one of degree only, not one of kind.

Benjamin Gott, the owner of the first large integrated woolen mill, had total assets of almost £100,000 in 1801, but only £28,000 was tied up in fixed investment.[31] In Black Dyke Mills, the total assets of which rose from £11,399 in 1834 to £398,706 in 1867, the value of "buildings and machinery" rose from 20 per cent of total assets in 1834 to 41 per cent in 1837 (after the construction of a new factory), then fell continuously to less than 5 per cent in the 1860's.[32] In the first modern linen factory,

[30] See above, p. 17, n. 5.
[31] Crump, *Leeds Woollen Industry,* 257.
[32] Sigsworth, *Black Dyke Mills,* 228–9.

Marshalls of Leeds, the ratio of fixed to total assets was "always . . . well below the 50 per cent mark." [33]

The cotton industry, after the adoption of steam power and the machinery of its technological revolution, seems to have had slightly higher ratios of fixed to total capital than other textile industries. According to Pollard, "in the typical up-to-date mill in the period 1780–1830, fixed capital represented only just a little more than one-half of the capital invested." [34] It was not necessary for the entrepreneur to own all—or any—of his fixed capital, however. Renting space in mills, with power furnished by the mill owner, was a common practice in the Manchester industry.

One might expect to find the largest demands for capital, both fixed and total, in the mining and metallurgical industries, but this was not necessarily the case. Many coal mines were small-scale family affairs, operated on a part-time basis by the farmer on whose land the coal was found. Even in larger concerns the value of equipment represented but a small fraction of the total capital involved; the largest outlays were for wages and the royalties paid to the landowners as the coal was dug. In the brass and copper industry typically "only a sixth of a concern's capital was in the form of permanent capital." [35] In the iron industry it was possible for the three Walker brothers—a schoolmaster, a nailmaker, and a farmer—to set up a small foundry out of their meager savings and part-time labor. In 1746, after five years in the business, they took in a new partner and *raised* their capital to £600.[36] A number of other firms in the iron industry also began on a small scale, usually in the finishing trades, and expanded backward into the more capital-intensive branches of refining, blast-furnace production, and mining as their profits and need for raw materials grew. Thomas Attwood declared in 1812 that a complete new set of ironworks would cost at least £50,000; the capital of the Cyfartha works in that year was almost £165,000, but less than £70,000 was invested in plant and equipment.[37] By that time the age of the pioneers was already in the past, and the optimum scale of plant was considerably larger than it had been 50 or even 25 years before. In the eighteenth century the number of firms in the iron industry that undertook integrated operations from the beginning, such as Carron Company in Scotland, was extremely small.

Capital requirements in other leading industries exhibited similar patterns. The famous firm of Boulton and Watt, so intimately associated with

[33] Pollard, "Fixed Capital," 303; also Rimmer, *Marshalls of Leeds,* 43–4.

[34] "Fixed Capital," 302.

[35] John, *Industrial Development of South Wales, 1750–1850,* 49.

[36] Ashton, *Iron and Steel,* 46.

[37] Pollard, "Fixed Capital," 303.

the Industrial Revolution, began with the modest capital of £3,370. As late as 1822 its total assets amounted to only £35,000, and of that less than 10 per cent took the form of buildings and machinery. The Albion steam flour mill, "the most highly mechanized unit of its kind," had less capital sunk in plant and equipment than in inventories and other forms of working capital.[38]

The Supply of Capital and Entrepreneurship

Granted the limitation placed on company formation by the Bubble Act, the establishment of new enterprises does not appear to have been a major problem. The counterpart of the difficulty of securing incorporation was the ease with which single individuals or small partnerships might enter into business without licensing, registration, or other legal impediment. Usually all that was required was a willing entrepreneur, a small initial capital, and access to credit and markets. All were relatively easy to come by, especially in the textile trades.

The early industrialists in the cotton industry were of quite diverse social origin, but they came chiefly from the lower middle class of both town and country. Arkwright was a barber and wig maker, Owen the son of a small-town saddler and ironmonger. The Peels and Philipses came from yeoman stock, but many others were mere cottagers who combined hand spinning and weaving with a bit of subsistence farming. Several who subsequently became prominent figures in the Lancashire cotton industry were Scottish country boys, as were the partners in the famous firm of McConnel and Kennedy. Capital requirements being small, it was by no means unthinkable for a hand weaver or spinner to go into business for himself, put out rovings or yarn to his neighbors in the vicinity, and, at the opportune juncture, when the new machinery was coming into use, set up as a factory spinner.[39]

A similar situation existed in the woolen industry, which, however, was slower to adopt factory methods.

> £100–£150 would be more than ample. . . . The initial expenses were comparatively light, and it was generally easy for a man with a clean reputation to get credit to the extent of a week's supply of wool. Thus the apprentice . . . could look forward to the day when he would . . . be able to set up as his own master. He might borrow the money at once, or work as a journeyman until he had saved the requi-

[38] Ibid. 304–5.

[39] See the testimony of one who did so in Radcliffe, *Origin of the New System of Manufacture.*

site sum; then he acquired his house, ground, and looms and set to work as an independent manufacturer.[40]

At the very end of the eighteenth century and in the first half of the nineteenth, when the woolen and worsted industries began to adopt power machinery, the first factories were established by the sons and grandsons of some of the men who had made the transition from part-time spinner or weaver to master manufacturer.

Whatever the initial source of capital, once a new firm was established its growth took place predominantly by means of the reinvestment of profits. The usual practice among English industrialists, especially in the early days of the Industrial Revolution, was to allow themselves 5 per cent on their invested capital for their living expenses. Only the net income in excess of that amount was called profit, and it was usually reinvested in the business. Of course, there were instances when more than 5 per cent of net income was withdrawn, but there were also cases in which the 5 per cent proved more than ample for a gracious style of living. For example, the additions to capital of Black Dyke Mills regularly exceeded its accounting "profits" from 1842 to 1859, the difference coming from the interest which the owners allowed themselves but did not use for consumption.[41]

The rate of growth of capital in the firms is therefore a good general guide to the rate of profit, especially in the early years of a firm's history; as firms grew older the rate of growth tended to decline, either because of a declining rate of profit or because a larger percentage of profits was withdrawn from the business either for consumption or for investment elsewhere. Crouzet has assembled data on capital invested in a number of important firms, especially those in metallurgy and textiles. These show that a rate of growth of 15 per cent per annum was not at all unusual among the more progressive firms. In the 15 years from 1795 to 1810 the rate of growth of the young firm of McConnel and Kennedy, Manchester cotton spinners, averaged almost 30 per cent per annum.[42] (See Chart II.3.)

While these considerations may settle the question of the ultimate source of capital for English industrial expansion, they do not, in themselves, answer the equally interesting question of how the expansion was financed. Appearances to the contrary notwithstanding, the reinvestment of profits was by no means direct or automatic. The majority of the most rapidly growing enterprises made extensive use of credit, both bank and "trade." We have already noted Heaton's reference to the ease with which a manufacturer could get "a week's supply of wool." In Lancashire "credit was

[40] Heaton, *Yorkshire Woollen and Worsted Industries,* 294.

[41] Sigsworth, *Black Dyke Mills,* 226.

[42] Crouzet, "Formation du capital en Grande-Bretagne," Table B.

CHART II.3
GROWTH RATES OF ENGLISH MANUFACTURING ENTERPRISES

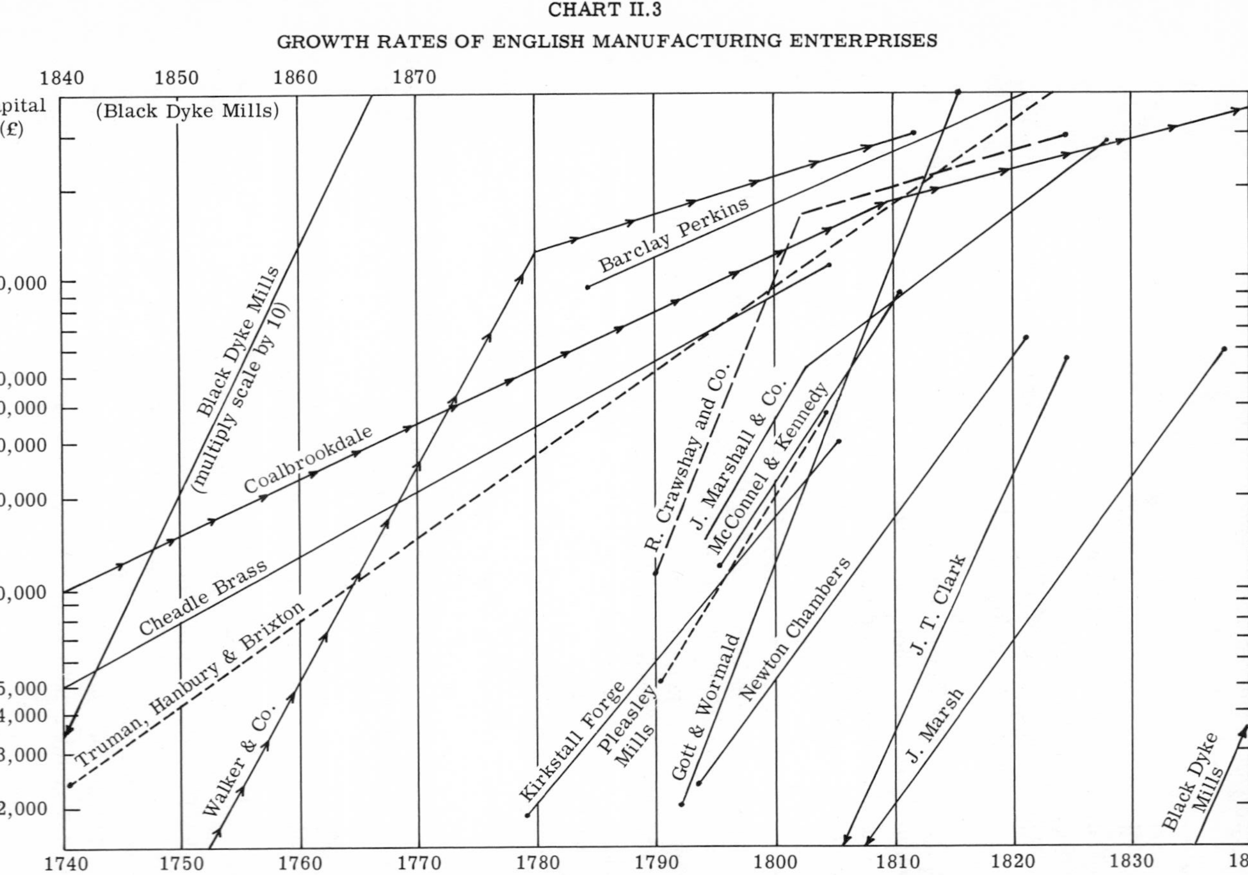

Source: Crouzet, "La Formation du capital en Grande Bretagne pendant la revolution industrielle."

almost as indispensable . . . as it is today. As Defoe remarked, every stage of manufacture and distribution, except the payment of the wages of the spinners and weavers, involved some amount of credit." [43] Again,

> . . . the merchant who imported cotton enabled the young manufacturer to set up for himself by giving him three months' credit, whilst the exporting merchant rendered similar assistance by paying for the manufacturer's output week by week. It was in this way, by a flow of capital inwards from commerce, that most of the early industrial enterprises of Lancashire got started and the immense expansion of the cotton industry was rendered possible.[44]

Such extensions of credit typically depended upon the banking system for discounting facilities. In the final analysis, therefore, we must consider the role of the credit system generally and banking in particular.[45]

THE ROLE OF THE BANKS

Given the inelastic supply of the precious metals, one of the most important functions of the banking system was that of providing an increased supply of the means of payment to meet the rapidly increasing demand for money associated with industrialization, higher incomes, and the "monetization" of the entire economy.

Attempts to estimate the quantity of money available during the Industrial Revolution, insofar as they aim at numerical accuracy, are bound to fail.[46] It is helpful, nevertheless, to make rough estimates in the hope of arriving at the correct order of magnitude. Table II.2 presents such estimates, and the sources and procedures used in deriving them, from which their limitations will be obvious. A few general comments are in order at this point, however.

[43] Wadsworth and Mann, *Cotton Trade and Industrial Lancashire,* 91–2. Even wages might involve credit under the "long pay" system; in a sense wages paid in tokens or scrip also involved credit.

[44] G. Unwin, Introduction to Daniels, *Early English Cotton Industry.*

[45] Crouzet concludes from his masterly survey of capital formation in the Industrial Revolution that the contribution of banking capital was "very weak." His data, however, relate principally to net worth or ownership equity, not to total liabilities. As noted above, the bulk of the evidence (not all of which can be presented here) testifies to the prominent role of credit in financing the Industrial Revolution.

[46] Pressnell, dealing with the note issues of the country banks, a far more limited problem, concluded after a careful and searching analysis of the underlying data that they were worse than useless, and issued a stern injunction to any who might be so rash as to attempt to use them (*Country Banking,* 189). The purpose of this section, however, is different from that envisaged by Pressnell in his valuable study.

TABLE II.2

STOCK OF MONEY, MEANS OF PAYMENT, NATIONAL INCOME, AND VELOCITY OF CIRCULATION IN ENGLAND AND WALES, SELECTED DATES, 1688–1913

	1688–89	1750	1775	1800–1801	1811	1821	1831	1844	1855	1865	1875	1885	1913
Components of Money Stock and Means of Payment (£ millions)													
Specie in circulation	10.	15.	16.	20.	15.	18.	30.	36.	50.	70.	105.	109.	145.
Banknotes	2.	5.	10.	25.	45.	32.	29.	28.5	26.7	27.	32.2	27.7	44.7
Deposits		[a]	[a]	5.[b]	15.[b]	25.[b]	40.	80.5	145.	270.	409.	458.	1,074.5
Total Money (M_1)	12.	20.	26.	50.	75.	75.	99.	145.	221.7	367.	546.2	594.7	1,264.2
Other	8.	20.	37.	115.[c]	140.[c]	76.	67.	75.	153.	–	32.4	–	–
Means of payment (M_2)	20.	40.	63.	165.	215.	151.	166.	220.	374.7		578.6		
Components of Money Stock (percentages)													
Specie	83.3	75.	61.5	40.	20.	24.0	30.3	25.	22.6	19.1	19.2	18.3	11.5
Banknotes	16.7	25.	38.5	50.	60.	42.7	29.3	20.	12.0	7.4	5.9	4.7	3.5
Deposits		[a]	[a]	10.[b]	20.[b]	33.3[b]	40.4	55.	65.4	73.5	74.9	77.0	85.0
Total (M_1)	100.0	100.	100.0	100.	100.	100.0	100.0	100.	100.0	100.0	100.0	100.0	100.0
Components of Means of Payment (percentages)													
Specie	50.	37.5	25.4	12.1	7.0	11.9	18.1	16.4	13.3		18.1		
Banknotes	10.	12.5	15.9	15.2	20.9	21.2	17.4	12.9	7.1		5.6		
Deposits		[a]	[a]	3.0	7.0	16.6	24.1	36.6	38.7		70.7		
Other	40.	50.	58.7	69.7	65.1	50.3	40.4	34.1	40.9		5.6		
Total (M_2)	100.	100.0	100.0	100.0	100.0	100.0	100.0	100.0	100.0		100.0		
National Income (£ millions) and Velocity of Circulation													
National Income	50.8	100.	135.	196.7	255.9	247.4	290.7	403.8	474.5	640.7	896.9	928.2	2,265.
V_1 (= Y/M_1)	4.2	5.0	5.2	3.9	3.4	3.3	2.9	2.8	2.1	1.7	1.6	1.6	1.8
V_2 (= Y/M_2)	2.5	2.5	2.1	1.2	1.2	1.6	1.75	1.8	1.3	–	1.5	–	–
Per Capita Income (£)	9.24	16.27	18.17	21.71	24.79	20.50	20.77	24.42	25.2	30.3	37.3	34.1	49.6

[a] Due to the dubious "moneyness" of deposits in the eighteenth century, they have been included in "Other means of payment" rather than in "Total money." The figures are for 1750, 5.0; for 1775, 7.0.

[b] For reasons analogous to that given in note a, only one-fourth of estimated deposits have been included in M_1 in 1800–1801, three-sevenths in 1811, and five-sevenths in 1821. The remainders have been included in "Other."

[c] The figures for "Other" (bills of exchange primarily) for 1800–1801 and 1811 are especially suspect; they are, however, in accord with contemporary estimates.

SOURCES AND PROCEDURES FOR TABLE II.2

1688–89. Horsefield, *British Monetary Experiments, 1650–1710,* Appendices 2-4, based on contemporary estimates. Horsefield, following Sir Isaac Newton, accepts estimates for specie in the 1690's substantially higher than that given here. My figure corresponds closely to those given by Davenant, King, and almost all other contemporary authorities. It is also more consistent with the figures for Mint output, which totaled £11.6 million, 1660–1689. "Other" consists of £6 million in government tallies and £2 million in inland bills. The national income figure is "national product at market prices," from Deane and Cole, *British Economic Growth, 1688–1959,* 2, based chiefly on contemporary estimates by Gregory King.

1750. Estimates of specie are based on the following facts and assumptions: the total silver coinage during the years 1696–99 (including the recoinage of 1696–97) was £6.7 million; silver coinage from 1700 to 1750 totaled less than £1 million, giving a maximum possible of £7.7 in silver in 1750. However, due to the undervaluation of silver most full-bodied coins were melted down for export; those that remained, amounting possibly to £2 million, were lightweight, in effect mere tokens. Gold coinage for 1701–50 amounted to £18.8 million, in addition to an estimated £6 million in circulation in 1700. Allowing for normal loss and export, and £2 million in the Bank of England's reserve, a figure of £15 million appears to be a reasonable approximation for total specie in circulation.

Banknote circulation of the Bank of England was £4.3 in 1750 (Mitchell and Deane, *British Historical Statistics*, 441). The estimate allows £700,000 for the circulation of London and country banks. Deposits of £5 million (£1.9 for the Bank of England, £3.1 for others—chiefly London private banks) are included with "other means of payment," the remainder of which consists of bills of exchange and is a guess pure and simple. The estimate for national income is an interpolation based on Deane and Cole, *British Economic Growth, 1688–1959,* p. 156.

1775. Specie: the recoinage of gold in 1774–78 "produced £18,221,000 of new gold money, of which about £16,500,000 came from deficient coins, the rest from gold supplied by the Bank in the ordinary way" (Clapham, *Bank of England,* I, 177). Silver in circulation approximated £800,000. A deduction of £3 million has been made for the normal gold holdings of the Bank in the 1770's, although because of the recoinage they were more than twice that in 1775.

Banknotes: The figure is hypothetical, derived by multiplying the demand notes of the Exchange Bank of Bristol outstanding on 17 June 1779 (£18,874, from Pressnell, *Country Banking,* 142) by 100, which is the estimated number of country bankers (no allowance is made for issues of the London private bankers, which may now be regarded as negligible), adding the result to the circulation figure of the Bank of England for 1775 (£8.76 million), and rounding downward.

Deposits: In the mid or late 1780's the combined deposits of four of the largest private banks in London amounted to about £1.5 million, but many banks of importance had less than £100,000 (Joslin, "London Private Bankers, 1720–1785," 346ff.). Curries, for example, ranged from a low of £76,000 in 1774 to a high of £130,000 in 1779, before going on to new highs in excess of

£300,000 at the end of 1789. The estimate of £7 million assumes average deposits of £100,000 in the (approximately) 50 London private banks, plus £2 million in drawing accounts in the Bank of England. No allowance is made for deposits in country banks.

Bills of exchange: £30 million, a guess.

National income: same procedure and source as for 1750.

1800–1801. Specie: Clapham, *Bank of England,* I, 171–2, citing contemporary estimates. A deduction of £5 million has been made for the gold reserve of the Bank of England.

Banknotes: composed of £15 million for the Bank of England and £10 million for the country banks, on the assumption that the former figure was "probably greater than the volume of private issues before 1797, and probably still in excess though to a slight degree only, during the Suspension" (Pressnell, *Country Banking*, 159).

Deposits: The estimate of £20 million for total deposits assumes average deposits of slightly less than £200,000 in the 70-odd London private banks, plus £7 to £8 million in the Bank of England. Still no allowance for country bank deposits, although a few, at least, of the country banks had begun to accept deposits. Only one-fourth of total deposits are included in M_1, the remainder in "other means of payment."

Bills of exchange: Vansittart estimated the average daily circulation of bills in 1793 at £200 million, and Benjamin Heywood, a Liverpool banker, accepted the figure, as does Pressnell, at least as a rough order of magnitude (*Country Banking*, 171). It seems utterly fantastic, however, that the daily circulation of bills should equal or surpass the annual national income. Even reducing Vansittart's figure by half appears to leave it too high, judging by better-authenticated estimates of bills of exchange for later dates.

National income: derived from Deane and Cole, *British Economic Growth, 1688–1959,* 166, on the assumption that per capita income was the same in Scotland as in England and Wales. This may impart a slight downward bias, but it can scarcely be a serious one inasmuch as Scots constituted only 15 per cent of the population of Great Britain.

1811. Specie: official statistics of specie exports and coinage indicate a net outflow of approximately £8 million, 1801–10, of which £3 million came from the gold reserve of the Bank of England.

Banknotes: Pressnell, *Country Banking*, 160: "during the most flourishing period of country banking, that of the Suspension of Cash Payments, the country bankers appear to have provided about as much of the ordinary currency of the country as did the Bank of England and the Mint." The Bank of England circulation in 1811 was £23.3 million. Later (p. 171) Pressnell writes of "the £40 and £50 millions of the combined note-issues of the Bank of England and the country banks" about 1812. Boase, *Banking in Dundee*, 272, gives a total of £44,825,000 for 1811, presumably using Sedgwick's estimates of country banks' issues.

Deposits: total of £35 million estimated on the assumptions that average deposits in the 70 London private banks amounted to £250,000, that country bank deposits averaged one-third of country note issues (Vincent Stuckey to Committee on Resumption of Cash Payments, 1819, 245), and Bank of England deposits of £11.3 million. Only three-sevenths are included under M_1, the remainder in "Other."

Bills of exchange: £120 million. W. Leatham, a contemporary banker (*Letters on the Currency*, 2nd ed., 1840), made an estimate of £119 million for 1815, based on stamp tax returns. By Leatham's own estimates the quantity of bills declined drastically thereafter until about 1830.

National income: same procedure and source as for 1800–1801.

1821. Specie: extrapolated backward from 1831 on the basis of international specie and bullion movements from Imlah, *Economic Elements in the Pax Britannica*, 70, and changes in the Bank of England's gold reserve.

Banknotes: Boase, *Banking in Dundee*, 318.

Deposits: In the absence of any firm estimates by contemporaries, I have assumed the same figure for 1821 as for 1811. This is at least consistent with scattered data from individual banks, which show little net change between the one year and the other. On the other hand, deposits in the Bank of England fell from £11.3 million in 1811 to £5.7 million in 1821. As a result of the increasing use of deposits for normal payments, five-sevenths have been included in M_1.

Bills of exchange: total bills created in 1821 amounted to £199.2 million, down from £477 million in 1815 and £264 million in 1818. Assuming an average usance of four months, the average daily circulation in 1821 would have been £66.4 million, the figure used here. If the average usance were three months, the daily circulation would have been £49.8 million.

National income: same source and procedure as for 1800–1801.

1831. Specie: Vincent Stuckey to Select Committee, 1836, IX, Q. 1401. This is supported by extrapolation backward from 1844 of gold and silver specie and bullion movements presented in Imlah, *Economic Elements in the Pax Britannica*, 71, and changes in the Bank of England's gold reserve.

Banknotes: estimate based on extrapolation of country bank circulation from official returns, 1833–37, and Bank of England circulation, 1830–35; Mitchell and Deane, *British Historical Statistics*, 450.

Deposits: Bank of England, £10 million (Mitchell and Deane, *British Historical Statistics*, 443); London private banks, £20 million, assuming average deposits of slightly less than £500,000 for the 40-plus private banks; and country banks, £10 million, in accordance with the evidence of contemporaries that by 1831 the deposits of country banks equaled or exceeded their note issues.

Other (bills of exchange): Newmarch, "Magnitude and Fluctuations of Bills of Exchange," 175. The estimate assumes that the ratio of bills in England and Wales to the total for Great Britain is the same as the average of the years 1832–35. Deposits in Trustee Savings Banks (not included in Table II.2) amounted to £14.6 million (Horne, *History of Savings Banks*, 386).

National income: same source and procedure as for 1800–1801.

1844. Specie: Tooke and Newmarch, *History of Prices*, VI, 701.

Banknotes: Mitchell and Deane, *British Historical Statistics*, 444, 450.

Deposits: Bank of England, £12.6 million (ibid., bankers' deposits excluded); London joint-stock banks, £7.9 million; London private banks, £27 million (Crick and Wadsworth, *A Hundred Years of Joint-Stock Banking*, 22); country banks, £33 million, based on contemporary estimates of £25-40 million cited by Pressnell, *Country Banking*, 162. If the 100 provincial joint-stock banks had average deposits of £200,000, and the 273 private country banks had average deposits of £50,000, the resulting total would be £33.5 million. Baxter, "On the Principles Which Regulate the Rate of Interest and on the Currency Laws," estimated deposits for 1844 at £70 million, on no very clear basis.

Other (bills of exchange): Newmarch, "Magnitude and Fluctuations of Bills of Exchange," 175. Deposits in Trustee Savings Banks (not included in Table II.2) were £29.5 million.

National income: interpolated from Deane and Cole, *British Economic Growth, 1688–1959*, 166, on the same assumptions as for 1800–1801.

1855–1885. Specie: 1855 and 1875, Hollingsbery, *Handbook on Gold and Silver*, 263-5; 1865, Walter Bagehot, in France, Conseil supérieur, *Enquête...*, I, 29; 1885, Triffin, *International Monetary Standard*, worksheets.

Banknotes: Mitchell and Deane, *British Historical Statistics*, 450-51.

Deposits: 1855 and 1865: Baxter, "On the Principles Which Regulate the Rate of Interest and on the Currency Laws," 278. Baxter's figures are very rough, and they refer to 1856 and 1866. Deductions have been made for deposits in Scottish and Irish banks from Dun, "The Banking Institutions, Bullion Reserves, and Non-Legal Tender Note Circulation of the United Kingdom Statistically Investigated," 74-5. 1875, Dun, 118. Dun's estimate refers to December 1874; deductions have been made for interbank deposits as indicated by Dun, ibid. 123; 1885, Crick and Wadsworth, *A Hundred Years of Joint-Stock Banking*, 34 (estimate refers to end of 1884).

Other: 1855, bills of exchange, average daily circulation from Tooke and Newmarch, *History of Prices*, VI, 588; a proportionate reduction has been made for Scotland. 1875, acceptances only (December 1874), from Dun, ibid. 118. Total bills discounted, £208.6 million.

National income: Mitchell and Deane, *British Historical Statistics*, 367, derived on the assumption that per capita income in England and Wales was 10 per cent higher than in the United Kingdom as a whole.

1913. (N.B. The 1913 estimates pertain to the United Kingdom as a whole.)

Specie: Triffin, *International Monetary Standard*, worksheets. Banknotes; Mitchell and Deane, *British Historical Statistics*, 451. Deposits; ibid. 447; National income; ibid. 368.

Whatever the deficiencies of the estimates, and however one chooses to define the money supply, Table II.2 shows clearly the declining relative importance of specie and the correspondingly increased importance of bank-created money. In large measure this was no doubt a natural development, as bank money proved its greater convenience for many purposes. At the same time one should recognize the importance of the deficiencies of the eighteenth-century coinage, and of the suspension of specie payments during the wars with France, in bringing the advantages of bank money forcibly to the attention of the public, and thus hastening its adoption. After the wars many bankers obtained quantities of gold coin in preparation for the resumption of specie payments, but they discovered to their amazement that there was little demand for it; the public generally preferred the banknotes to which they had become accustomed.[47]

Scarcely had the public become fully accustomed to the use of notes, however, than the authorities began to take steps to restrict their issue. The resumption of specie payments after the wars with France was, of course, to be expected; nevertheless many voices were raised in favor of maintaining the existing system, at least in modified form, without a return to a full gold standard at the prewar parity.[48] Even Ricardo proposed a bullion standard and a national note-issuing agency. The government, under the influence of naïve theories, persisted in policies that culminated in the Bank Act of 1844, the clear intent and effect of which was to make the quantity of paper money as rigid and inelastic as the quantity of specie. Had the entire money supply behaved in this fashion, it is not too extreme to suppose that the English economy would have entered a period of stagnation in the 1850's and 1860's instead of the renewal of expansion which actually occurred. A glance at Chart II.4, which attempts to depict the behavior of money, industrial production, and national income, is suggestive in this respect.[49]

[47] Feaveryear, *The Pound Sterling,* 126; cf. Pressnell, *Country Banking,* 447. The increase of specie in circulation between 1819 and 1823 and the corresponding decrease in Bank of England issues was due chiefly to the Bank's deliberate withdrawal of its small notes.

[48] See Viner, *International Trade,* 203–17.

[49] Chart II.4 is based largely on Table II.2; hence it suffers from the same deficiencies, in addition to special ones of its own. Hoffmann's index of industrial production has been justly criticized on both methodological and substantive grounds, and it can be regarded as only a rough indicator of the progress of British industrialization. A special difficulty in its use here is that the inclusion of Scotland in the index imparts a slight upward bias, inasmuch as the rate of growth of industrial output in Scotland was higher than in England during the period covered. Much the same is true of the series for national income; although the absolute figures have been reduced to apply to England and Wales only, by the use of the rather arbitrary assumption indicated in the Sources for Table II.2, the rate of growth is essentially that attributed to Great Britain as a whole. In view of the small size of the Scottish economy and its generally similar pattern of growth, however, these difficulties pale in comparison with other deficiencies of the chart.

The chart's most serious shortcoming, apart from the dubious value of the underlying estimates, is that it does not show (except for the series on note issues) either annual or smoothed cyclical variations. The estimates of both money and national income are for individual years, rather than quinquennial or decennial averages, which would be preferable; hence they are affected by random fluctuations. By a singular misfortune 1811, 1821, and 1831 were all years of depression or "slack trade," though not all to the same degree. Thus the correlations indicated between the stock of money, national income, and industrial production must be regarded with exceptional reserve.

CHART II.4

NATIONAL INCOME, MEANS OF PAYMENT, AND INDUSTRIAL PRODUCTION, ENGLAND, 1750–1844

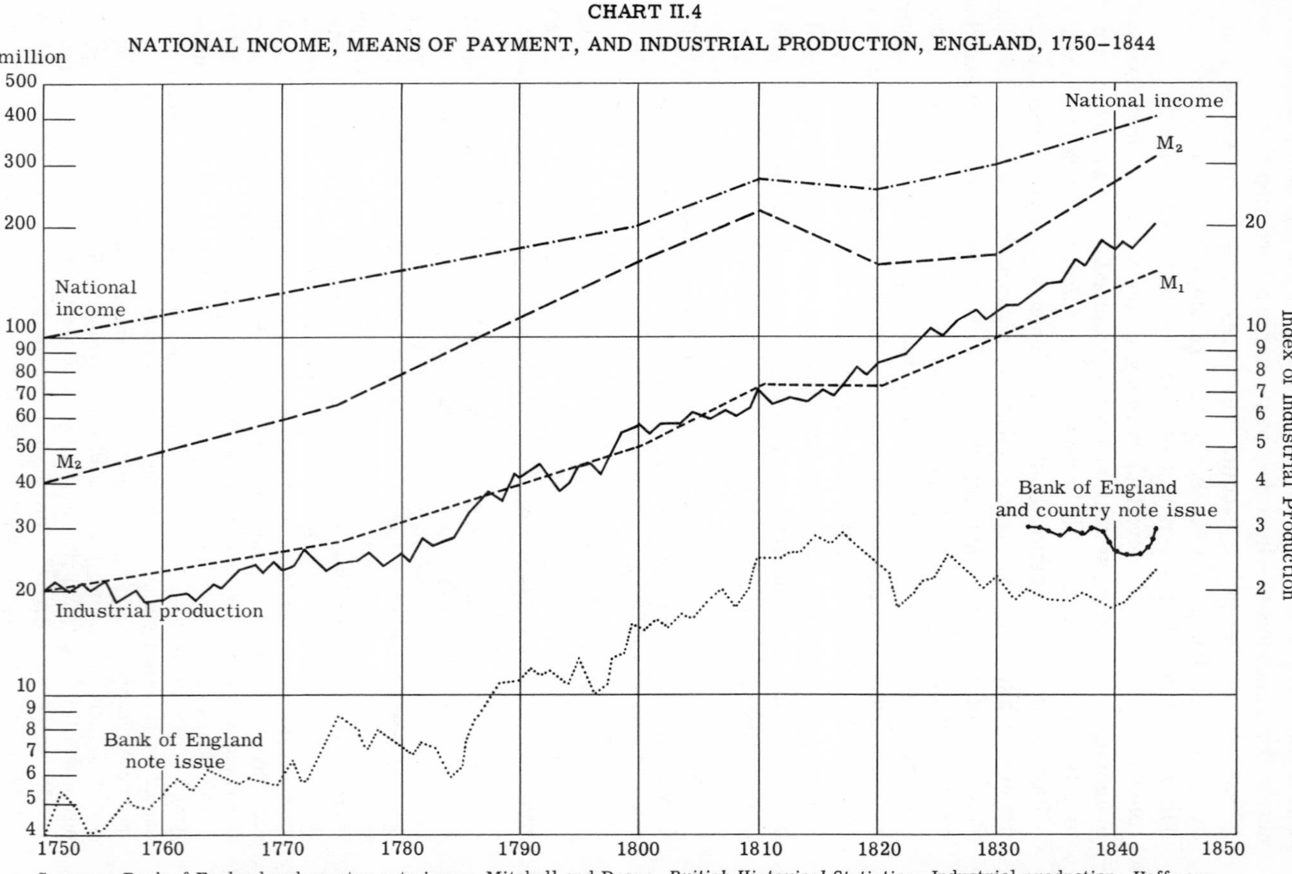

Sources: Bank of England and country note issue: Mitchell and Deane, *British Historical Statistics*. Industrial production: Hoffmann, *British Industry, 1700–1950*, Table 54, col. J. National income, Total money (M_1), and Means of payment (M_2): Table II.2, p. 42.

Fortunately for the country, bankers and businessmen could resort to demand deposits and bills of exchange in order to circumvent the effects of an inelastic currency. As early as 1750 bank deposits apparently constituted a significant if still minor element in the stock of money. The quantitative estimates must be interpreted with care, however, quite apart from doubts as to their reliability, for the statistical difficulties are compounded by confusion over the meaning of the term "deposits." There were various kinds of deposits, and practice varied from district to district and even from bank to bank; but it is probably safe to say that until well into the nineteenth century, except in London, "deposits" meant what we today would call time deposits, deposit accounts, or savings accounts, as opposed to demand deposits or current accounts. It is questionable whether, before the second quarter of the nineteenth century, even the whole of demand deposits or current accounts should be included among the means of payment. Debits to such accounts most often took the form of cash paid out over the counter; payments by book transfer were usually reserved for interbank payments making use of the banker's draft. In any case, the concept of the bank deposit was well established and the technique of payment by check existed even if it had not been widely used.[50] The restriction on note issues beginning in the 1820's served to stimulate a greater use of checks, even for relatively small payments. The new London joint-stock banks in the 1830's made a special point of encouraging them, and by 1844 deposits constituted the largest single element in the money supply. As early as 1840 an anonymous "Country Bank Manager" asserted that two-thirds of all payments were made by check, and a sample of payments into banks in 1865 showed that 97.3 per cent of such payments were in the form of checks. The continued rapid growth thereafter is evident from Table II.2.[51]

Businessmen resorted to the use of bills of exchange as currency long before they began using checks as substitutes for specie and banknotes. Precisely how long before is a difficult question, since the primary purpose of a bill was to extend credit rather than to serve as a medium of exchange, but they may have been used for the latter purpose as early as the seventeenth century. In the eighteenth century businessmen made scant distinction between a bill of exchange and a promissory note in ordinary practice,

[50] I am indebted to L. S. Pressnell for allowing me to consult an unpublished paper by him on the history of the check. See also his *Country Banking,* 167–72; Clapham, *Bank of England,* I, 221–3; Horsefield, "Duties of a Banker," 24–5.

[51] The growth of the checking habit might have been still greater but for a strict interpretation of the Truck Act of 1831, which severely hampered payment of wages by check. A special legislative provision removed the obstacle—in 1960! See Hilton, *The Truck System,* 149–53.

although the legal distinction was clear.[52] In 1775 Parliament passed "An Act to restrain negotiation of Promissory Notes and Inland Bills of Exchange under a limited sum within that part of Great Britain called England." The main effect of the Act was to prohibit the country banks from issuing notes of less than £1 (extended to £5 in 1777), but a phrase from the preamble of the Act is revealing: "Whereas various notes, bills of exchange, and drafts for money, for very small sums, have for some time past been circulated or negotiated in lieu of cash . . . and many of such bills and drafts being payable under certain terms and restrictions, which the poorer sort of manufacturers, artificers, labourers, and others cannot comply with, otherwise than by being subject to great extortion and abuse." [53]

That bills formed the most important part of the circulating medium of Lancashire in the heyday of its industrial revolution is generally appreciated by economic historians,[54] but they were also used in other times and places. A near-contemporary testified that "it is the recollection of many persons that all the woollen business of the West Riding was conducted by Bills of Exchange at two months' date, as low as £5, drawn without stamps, with gold for wages, without the intervention of bank notes previous to the last war." [55] Newmarch, the foremost authority on the subject, indicated that many bills circulated in parts of the country other than where they originated, since bankers and businessmen feared that bills circulated locally might divulge trade secrets. Although the use of bills as currency probably declined somewhat with the development of checking facilities in the 1830's and 1840's, they still constituted an important part of the total means of payment at least as late as the 1850's.[56] Newmarch marshaled convincing evidence to show that the volume of bills fluctuated directly with bank rate and thus, presumably, inversely with other media of exchange, indicating

[52] A letter from Thos. Evans & Sons, bankers at Derby, to Samuel Oldknow in 1786 indicates that bankers, at least, were becoming increasingly conscious of the distinction: "Bills at two months on a good House in London, either your own drawings or indorsements will suit us. We do not much like [promissory] notes, tho' we have the utmost confidence in the drawer, because if we happen to have any particular occasion for money, they are not readily discounted in London; & indeed our own opinion is against the custom of passing notes." Quoted by Unwin, *Samuel Oldknow,* 177.

[53] Quoted by Newmarch, "Magnitude and Fluctuations of Bills of Exchange," 153.

[54] See Ashton, "The Bill of Exchange and Private Banks in Lancashire, 1790–1830."

[55] Leatham, *Letters on the Currency* (1840), 38, quoted by Newmarch, "Magnitude and Fluctuations of Bills of Exchange," 154.

[56] Hughes, *Fluctuations in Trade, Industry and Finance,* 258; Tooke and Newmarch, *History of Prices,* VI, 587–8.

that businessmen resorted to them especially when other forms of credit were scarce and money "tight." [57]

It is therefore beyond doubt that bills of exchange played an important monetary role, but the precise degree of their "moneyness," much less the extent of their use, remains very much an open question. Even if we had good estimates of the total quantity of bills for the entire period of interest (such as Newmarch's for 1830–53), there would remain the vexing problems of the average usance and the proportion of bills that actually functioned as money. Many bills, perhaps most, performed no monetary functions at all, others did so only once or twice in the course of their existence.[58] Still others, however, especially the small bills characteristic of Lancashire, circulated from merchant to merchant with dozens, even scores, of endorsements. Nevertheless, it is clear from Table II.2 that the average velocity of bills was much lower than that of other components of the means of payment. Although in principle banks were not necessary for the drawing and circulation of bills, the willingness of banks to discount them is what gave them currency. In effect, the entrepreneurs of Lancashire constituted a kind of mutual credit bank whose obligations bore a collective guarantee; even there, large and powerful banks stood behind the community as primitive lenders of last resort.

The interpretation of the series of velocities in Table II.2 leads to some interesting speculation. The gradual decline in velocity is consistent with experience elsewhere [59] and makes us somewhat confident of the general validity of the estimates of the various types of money. The data, such as they are, support the hypothesis that the demand for money rises with income; but they also indicate that the changing composition of the money supply is correlated with both rising incomes and declining velocity. Ignoring bills of exchange, whose special features explain their lower velocity, it would appear that specie has a higher velocity than bank-created money, especially deposits. Are these apparent differences in velocity inherent characteristics of the various media (as with bills of exchange)? Or is the appearance simply due to the accidental fact that the various media assumed prominence at different stages of development? If the former, does a shift from high-velocity to low-velocity forms of money contribute to

[57] Tooke and Newmarch, *History of Prices,* Appendix XI.

[58] Newmarch, on the other hand, believed (and gave illustrative examples) that a typical bill always served a minimum of seven transactions, even without going into general circulation. Such a turnover does not, of course, correspond to an income velocity of circulation.

[59] Cf. Friedman and Schwartz, *Monetary History of the United States, 1867–1960,* esp. Chart 57 and Table A-5.

industrialization and the growth of income? Or, on the contrary, does the growth of income create a demand for money having a low velocity (i.e. is the income elasticity of demand for banknotes and deposits higher than for specie)? While theoretical reasoning would appear to support the latter view, the way in which the various forms of money assumed prominence supports the former. That, in turn, implies that the money-creating (or money-supplying) function of the banking system was an important stimulus to industrialization. While the data are too fragmentary and unreliable to support refined statistical analysis, the subject merits further study.

Short-term Credit

According to orthodox banking theory, the main function of commercial banks is to provide short-term credit, secured by goods in process or in transit, to merchants and manufacturers to serve as their working capital. In this view the ability of the banking system to contribute to fixed capital formation, and hence to industrialization, is strictly limited by the requirement that it maintain a high degree of liquidity. The marginal contribution that the banking system can make to industrialization results from its ability to help industrialists economize their own limited capital and from the more efficient allocation of resources due to its brokerage function, which reduces the rate of interest to borrowers and raises the rate of return to holders of idle funds.

While it is true that, during the Industrial Revolution, English bankers dealt primarily in short-term credit, the traditional view of their limited contributions to industrialization requires modification at several points. In the first place, the traditional view overlooks or underestimates the high ratio of working to fixed capital typical of most industrial firms, and thus underestimates the proportion of capital provided by bank credit. Given the high rate of profit that was characteristic of successful firms, and the regularity with which these profits were reinvested (usually but not always in fixed capital), it becomes evident that bank credit could be highly instrumental in promoting the growth of fixed capital even when banks did not lend directly at long term for purposes of fixed investment.

Thanks to the recent work of Pollard,[60] it is unnecessary to present in detail the evidence relating to industrialists' reliance on short-term bank finance for both fixed and working capital. A couple of illustrative examples may nevertheless be useful in visualizing the process.

The history of Black Dyke Mills, unusually well documented during the period of its early rapid growth, illumines what may have been a typical

[60] Pollard, "Fixed Capital," 304–5.

pattern for successful firms in textiles, and perhaps in other industries as well.[61] The firm originated in 1819, when John Foster, the son of a farmer and colliery owner, married at the age of 21 and soon thereafter began to put out yarn to local weavers in accordance with traditional practice. (It is not clear whether his initial capital came from his father, his own savings, or his bride's dowry; in any case it could not have been great.) Apparently Foster prospered, for when he adopted the factory system in 1834 his net worth amounted to £11,185 in total assets of £16,864, including a farm, a colliery, cottages for his workers, his own substantial home (£1,500), and a share in the Bradford Banking Company. This was only the beginning of his prosperity, however; after a few difficult but successful years the value of the firm soared rapidly to £1,463,155 in 1867, when Foster retired from active participation. No less significant than its rapid growth is the pattern of finance that emerges from the firm's records. It made extensive use of short-term credit, both trade and bank, in its struggling early years. By 1845 its production was great enough to allow it to bypass the wool factors and buy its raw material directly from the producers; this required cash payment, and the entry for trade creditors which had loomed large in the previous decade dwindled in importance thereafter. In spite of large profits and continuous reinvestment, however, the accounts show continued year-end deficits with the Bradford Banking Company until 1852. Then, with total assets of £275,000 and net profits of £40,000, the firm at last began to maintain a net credit position with the bank. Funds continued to accumulate thereafter to such an extent that they could not all be employed in the business, and, in addition to growing figures for "cash on hand" and "in bank," the accounts reveal investments in securities that eventually amounted to half the total assets.

Another example is that of William Balston, an orphan who served his apprenticeship in the paper industry under James Whatman and rose to become Whatman's foreman. Balston began his career as an independent entrepreneur (in partnership with two others, who knew nothing of paper-making) in 1794. His equity in the company amounted to £5,000, all borrowed from Whatman at 5 per cent interest on no security but a note of hand. Balston repaid his debt by 1798, and by 1805, when he withdrew from the firm to build his own mill, he was worth £15,000. Within seven years he sunk £47,000 in the new mill, £31,000 of it borrowed by means of mortgages, promissory notes, bank overdrafts, and finance bills. "From the start it was clear the every penny would be sunk in the initial outlay, and that there would be nothing left for working capital." [62] He purchased raw materials on three months' credit, quickly turned them into paper,

[61] See Sigsworth, *Black Dyke Mills.*

[62] Balston, *William Balston—Paper Maker,* 53–4.

sold the paper to London stationers, also on credit, and discounted the resulting bills either with his London bank or his local bank in Maidstone in order to obtain the funds with which to pay his suppliers and workers. There were financial difficulties, especially in periods of depression, but Balston survived, prospered, and served for many years as chairman of the Master Paper Makers Trade Association. The firm he founded still exists.

The very nature of bank operations is another point on which the traditional theory of commercial banking requires modification to fit the facts of English country banking during the Industrial Revolution. The typical country bank was not primarily a broker between lenders (depositors) and borrowers, but an "engine of credit," however puny, pumping out a stream of new money. This was most obviously the case with those industrialists who, like the Crowleys, issued their own currency, whether they engaged in full-fledged banking or not.[63] It is no less true of bankers without direct or indirect industrial interests of their own, both those who issued notes and those who, in the second quarter of the nineteenth century especially, used the more subtle means of deposit creation.

Long-term Credit

Yet another reason why orthodox banking theory is not an adequate guide to the role of banks in the English Industrial Revolution is the fact that most bankers either were not acquainted with the theory or chose not to follow its precepts if they were. This was conspicuously the case in long-term lending for industrial purposes. It is obviously impossible to specify what proportion of bank loans were made for periods of more than, say, one year, but it is no less certain that the proportion was far from insignificant. All authorities on English banking history have noted the existence of such loans; some deplore them, others merely report them, most try to minimize their importance, but none can ignore them.

In general, three types of long-term lending by banks can be distinguished. The easiest is the long-term loan pure and simple, secured by a mortgage, other securities, or a mere promissory note. In this category was the loan of £25,000 by Child & Company of London to the Duke of Bridgewater, that of £20,000 by Parr's Bank to the St. Helens Crown Glassworks, and that of £20,000 to £25,000 by Esdaile & Company

[63] Flinn, *Men of Iron,* passim. The list is surprisingly long, and includes the names of many industrialists of the first rank, among them John Wilkinson, Robert Peel, the Walkers of Rotherham, Samuel Oldknow, the Lloyds of Birmingham (who became more famous as bankers than as industrialists), the Darbies and Reynolds of Coalbrookdale, and many others.

(also London bankers) to the Llanelly Copper Company of South Wales.[64] Many other examples might be cited, but they still would not tell us the proportionate importance of long-term lending, either to the banks or to the industries they financed.

The second category consists of those loans which in form were short-term but by prior agreement of banker and borrower could be periodically renewed so long as the borrower needed the funds and the banker did not. Apparently this was the most common method of long-term lending. Horsefield cites the case of a loan for £1,000 "renewed on a fresh promissory note every three months for nine or ten years," and another which "ran for varying but always large sums, from 1780 to 1803." [65] Lloyds Bank counts "among its most prosperous and largest customers to this day . . . firms whose capital was at some stage provided substantially . . . by Lloyds. . . . The finance would begin as 'temporary finance,' but the bank's confidence in the customers would increase and in lean times dependence on bank finance would be allowed to grow far beyond the limits of working capital." Sayers adds that "the successes that have followed are among the most creditable in England's industrial history during the last hundred years." [66] Loans of this type, involving the use of so-called "finance" or "accommodation" bills, apparently financed the periodic booms in the Lancashire cotton industry.[67]

The third category of long-term loan was the involuntary type: a short-term loan that the borrower was unable to repay at the due date, and so had to be carried over. It is no more possible to estimate the quantitative importance of this type than of long-term lending in general; less so, in fact, in that such loans that were eventually repaid would be difficult to distinguish from those in the second category. In all probability, however, the majority were never repaid in full. No doubt all banks had their share of difficulty with this type of loan, but it is rather surprising to discover that the Bank of England "was sufficiently involved in the affairs of the Company of Copper Miners to appoint its own manager of the Cwmavon Works in 1849 when that Company found itself unable to repay the loans advanced by the Bank." [68] The Bank did not ordinarily make direct ad-

[64] Barker and Harris, *A Merseyside Town,* 481; Wadsworth and Mann, *Cotton Trade and Industrial Lancashire,* 222; John, *Industrial Development of South Wales, 1750–1850,* 43.

[65] Horsefield, "British Banking Practices, 1750–1850," 319.

[66] Sayers, *Lloyds Bank,* 95.

[67] Pressnell, *Country Banking,* 91; Mathews, *Trade-Cycle History,* 196–8.

[68] John, *Industrial Development of South Wales, 1750–1850,* 48; also Clapham, *Bank of England,* II, 206–7. The Bank advanced £150,000 to the company in 1847. Its governor, who later went bankrupt, was also a director of the Bank.

vances to industry at long term *or* short, but, though unusual, this was not an isolated case.[69]

Direct Participation in Industrial Ventures

It is frequently difficult to distinguish long-term loans by bankers from their direct participation in industrial enterprises. This is notably the case where a single firm or individual is identified with both banking and industry. As previously noted, such cases were by no means rare. In many of them the banking sideline originated as a result of experience with "shop notes," "current bills," and token money devised to overcome the shortage of coins for wage payments. It would quickly become apparent to the industrialist that a banking adjunct not only solved his payments problem but also enabled him to raise a substantial capital from the general public at a zero real rate of interest, regardless of accounting conventions. The history of Lloyds Bank offers an instructive example. The bank was founded in Birmingham in 1765 as Taylors and Lloyds, with an initial capital of £8,000. Throughout the first several decades of the bank's history one of the largest borrowers on open account was the iron business of S. N. & C. Lloyd, sons of the founder and also partners in the bank. In 1773, eight years after the bank was established, the more or less continuous deficit of the iron firm with the bank was temporarily reduced to £8,000 (i.e. the original capital of the bank) "by ploughing in the profits divided by the Bank." [70]

The Coalbrookdale Company, one of the oldest and most distinguished firms in the iron industry, had family ties with several banks. In the 1720's Thomas Goldney, a partner in the firm and its Bristol agent, acted in effect as its banker. From about 1780 Richard Reynolds, another partner, took over as the firm's principal banker. That relationship was continued by his son Joseph, who founded a bank in Wellington in 1805. Abraham Darby IV, manager of the Coalbrookdale works from 1827 to 1849, was also a partner in Darby & Co., bankers of Coalbrookdale, founded in 1810. Darby & Co. amalgamated with Reynolds' and other private bankers in the area to become the Shropshire Banking Company in 1836; Abraham Darby became a director in 1839 and chairman of the board in 1845. The Shropshire Banking Company eventually became a part of Lloyds Bank.[71]

As these examples show—along with those of the Crowleys, Wilkinsons, Walkers, and several others which might be cited from the South Wales

[69] For other examples see John, *Industrial Development of South Wales, 1750–1850,* 51, and Clapham, *Bank of England,* II, 108–9, 145–6.

[70] Sayers, *Lloyds Bank,* 10.

[71] Ibid. 334; Raistrick, *Dynasty of Ironfounders,* 8, 13.

iron industry—the intermixture of banking and industry was especially common in the iron trade. Significantly, Quakers were active in both, though not to the exclusion of other religious denominations. Brewing is another industry that reveals a similar pattern. In both London and the country it was exceptional for a brewery *not* to have a banker among its partners, or at least among the relatives of the partners.[72] In some cases bankers became partners in breweries after a long and satisfactory experience of both short- and long-term lending: the names Barclay, Bevan, Gurney, Hanbury, Brown, Hobhouse, and Hoare all testify to this movement. In other cases, especially in more or less isolated country districts, banking frequently developed as a sideline to brewing.

At the end of the eighteenth century William Gillett "combined banking activities with plush weaving" and did business with "Messrs. Cobb & Co. of Banbury, who were bankers as well as manufacturers of webs and horse-girths." [73] William's son Joseph married the daughter of Joseph Gibbins, "a banker at Birmingham and Swansea, and the family had interests in copper, glass, chemicals, and Birmingham small wares." [74] Joseph Gillett initiated his own long and successful career as a banker with his wife's dowry and funds borrowed from her family, but he ran into difficulties in the crisis of 1847–48 as a result of "injudicious support of other family concerns, including an inventor brother . . . an early example of the perils involved in financing inventors." [75] The bank survived, however—indeed, it was one of the last surviving private banks when purchased by Barclay's Bank in 1919—and in the early twentieth century it lent a young bicycle mechanic, W. R. Morris—subsequently Lord Nuffield—£4,000 on an unsecured note to launch Morris Motors.

Although the intermixture of banking and industry appear to have been most common in iron (or, perhaps, heavy metallurgy in general), textiles, and brewing, instances may be cited from mining, shoemaking, soap manufacture, sugar refining, and many others.[76] Such an association should not be surprising in view of the industrial origins of many country bankers, but it raises problems of interpretation for the economic historian. Schumpeter,

[72] See Mathias, *Brewing Industry,* 293–4, 325–30. On p. 329 Mathias gives a table of banker-brewers. It contains more than 50 names of families and partnerships (with nine other "possibles"), including all of the large London brewers as well as many provincial ones.

[73] Taylor, *Gilletts,* v, 1–2.

[74] Ibid. 4.

[75] Ibid. v. In 1840 the bank's largest debtor was the plush-manufacturing firm of J. E. & J. Gillett, whose debit balance amounted to £5,764.

[76] Pressnell, *Country Banking,* 14–36; also Ashton, *An Eighteenth-Century Industrialist,* 182–3, 186–7; Glover, "Thomas Cook and the American Blanket Trade"; Church, "Family Enterprise"; Bellamy, "Cotton Manufacture in Kingston upon Hull."

whose theory of economic development receives striking confirmation from so many aspects of English industrial and financial history, was categorical in his assertion that, for money creation by banks to contribute to sustained and genuine economic growth, the banker should be entirely independent of the business borrower.[77] It should now be evident that this was not the case with many English industrialists and bankers of the first rank. Schumpeter had in mind, of course, the possibility that in such situations the banker's cool judgment might be carried away or overridden by the entrepreneur's dynamic optimism. That this did happen on occasion is beyond question; some of the most spectacular failures in English business history resulted from overextension of credit by a single bank to a single firm. The consequences of such failures were aggravated by the general absence of limited liaibility for either banks or industrial firms, and by the interlocking network of banking throughout the island. But to recognize that failures occurred, whether or not the banker had a direct interest in the business to which he lent, is very different from maintaining that the country banking system was either uniquely or mainly responsible for the periodic crises that affected English industry during the Industrial Revolution. Many other factors were responsible for those crises, not least of which were the unenlightened and sometimes pigheaded policies of the monetary and fiscal authorities, including the Bank of England. In the final analysis the remarkable feature of the intermixture of banking and industry is not that so many banks came to grief as a result, but that so many vigorous and progressive industries developed from it.

CONCLUSION

The English banking system from 1750 to 1844 was far from ideal in its contributions to either stability or growth of the economy as a whole. Yet England did experience the first industrial revolution, and the available evidence indicates a positive and significant contribution thereto by the banking system. If this interpretation is correct, it puts the well-known English genius for "muddling through" in a somewhat different light. At almost every point at which banking and monetary policy might have been used constructively to promote economic growth, the authorities either made the wrong decision or took no action at all.[78] The monopoly of the Bank

[77] Schumpeter, *Business Cycles,* I, 118.

[78] This statement is not intended to imply moral censure, but to report a fact. Policy makers in the eighteenth century were not so "growth-minded" as those of the mid-twentieth, did not have the benefit of modern economic theory, etc. But the fact remains.

of England, the gross inefficiency of the Mint, the restrictions on small notes, the Resumption Act of 1819, the piecemeal and halfhearted reforms of 1826 and 1833, and, finally, the Act of 1844 itself, are all cases in point. Paradoxically, however, the very obstacles placed in the way of a rational banking and monetary system stimulated the private sector to introduce the financial innovations necessary for realization of the full benefits of the technical innovations in industry. (Fortunately for England, the law was sufficiently loose and its administration sufficiently lax that the obstacles to innovation were not insurmountable.) Among these financial innovations were the country banks themselves, the issues of token money and "shop notes," from which many of them grew, and the use of bills of exchange and checks as currency. Without these or similar devices it is scarcely conceivable that English industrial progress would have been either so rapid or so far-reaching. With them, innovating entrepreneurs gained control over real productive services in true Schumpeterian fashion. The financial system that developed to provide them, though not the best that could be imagined, did respond to the needs and demands of the times.

III
SCOTLAND
1750–1845

by Rondo Cameron

Scotland in 1750 was a poor country by almost any standards. The majority of its sparse population still engaged in near-subsistence agriculture, and in large areas the tribal system of social and economic organization remained intact. It had few industries worthy of the name. The most important commodity in its foreign commerce, imports as well as exports, was tobacco, from which the economy as a whole received little direct benefit. More significant generally was the trade in live cattle driven south to England.

Less than a century later Scotland stood with England in the forefront of the world's industrial nations. It had flourishing textile, metallurgical, and chemical industries and was the acknowledged leader in the strategic new technology of engineering. Its booming export surplus enabled Scottish investors to contribute to the development of new lands throughout the world. Scotland's transformation from backward household economy to leading industrial economy was even more spectacular than the contemporary industrial revolution in England.

THE SETTING

Perhaps the greatest of Scotland's many obstacles to growth was the land itself. A petition of 1720 put the matter fairly: "Scotland is a country the most barren of any Nation in these Parts of Europe, they have nothing of their own growth to export, except corn, coals, cattle and some wool; nor nothing to form any Manufactures but what they receive from their neighbors." [1] Approximately three-fourths of the land area consists of rocky hills

[1] *A Short View of some probable effects of laying a duty on Scotch linen imported,* quoted by Hamilton, *Economic History of Scotland,* xiii.

and mountains, entirely barren in many places and with thin, scattered soil in others. Nor is the climate favorable to agriculture. At the end of the eighteenth century less than 15 per cent of the Highlands was in cultivation; the proportion in the southern uplands was little higher, if at all. Great stretches of thousands of acres supported a few hundred sheep or cattle at best. The coastal plain of the east and north had more fertile land; normally it produced a surplus of oats and barley for consumption in the few urban areas, in the Highlands, and occasionally even for export. The best endowed area, however, was the narrow Lowland belt between the firths of Forth and Clyde. It contained some of the best agricultural land, as well as almost all of Scotland's coal, the country's only mineral resource of any significance.

The difficult, barren terrain also hindered transportation and communications. At the beginning of the eighteenth century wheeled vehicles were a rarity even in the vicinity of towns; they were virtually unknown in the hinterland. Scotland, unlike England, has few rivers that are navigable above the firths and sea lochs. Sailing ships and small coastal vessels served to connect the ports with one another and with the outside world, but most inland transportation was accomplished on foot or horseback until the nineteenth century. Canal building at the end of the eighteenth century provided improved transportation in the Lowlands, but, except for the Caledonian through the Great Glen, canals could not penetrate the Highlands. Much the same was true of railways, which in any case had little impact until after the middle of the nineteenth century.

The dominant political event affecting Scotland's potentialities for economic development was the Union of 1707, which made Scotland an integral part of the United Kingdom. The Treaty of Union abolished the Scottish Parliament, and in the next year the Scottish Privy Council was abolished. These acts left Scotland without a distinct administration until 1885. Although this situation was deplored by those who felt that a distinctly Scottish government might have taken more vigorous and effective action to promote economic welfare; it seems more likely that the absence of a central government for Scotland was a blessing in disguise. With respect to financial matters in particular, it prevented the banking system from being turned into an instrument of government finance and left it free to develop in accordance with the demands of the private economy.

Far more importantly, the Treaty of Union provided for the integration and assimilation of Scotland into the English system of taxation, currency, and markets—and the most significant of these was markets. Access to markets alone does not assure the industrial development of a nation; Ireland had access to the same markets but had a very different economic history. Scotland, however, had the ability to buy and sell freely in the markets of both England and the British colonies, and this constituted a sort of *sine qua non* for its rapid industrial development. The benefits of the enlarged market area did not emerge as quickly as the Scottish advocates of Union had hoped. Nevertheless, by 1750 the merchants of Glasgow had taken a leading position in the Virginia tobacco trade, and, after the American Revolution, they played an important role in the West Indian trade as well. England was probably even more significant as a market than the colonies, however. Unfortunately, statistics of trade between England and Scotland were not recorded after 1707, but it is clear that England was the principal destination for linen and cattle, the two most important exports of domestic production in the eighteenth century. According to Adam Smith, the growth of the cattle trade was the greatest "of all the commercial advantages which Scotland . . . derived from the union with England." [2] In the nineteenth century the complementarity of the two industrial economies, with the possibilities for specialization and economies of scale, constituted an even greater boon.

The Pattern of Industrial Change

Whereas England's staple industry in the eighteenth century had been the manufacture of woolens, that of Scotland was linen. The industry had been in a perilous state early in the century, but it secured official encouragement and subsidization from the Board of Trustees for Improveing Fisherys and Manufactures in Scotland. The Board's program achieved moderate success, and the amount of linen stamped for sale rose from 2 million yards in 1728 to 7.5 million in 1750. By 1821 the output exceeded 36 million yards.[3] Such progress was encouraging, but it scarcely constituted the basis for an industrial revolution. Indeed, the linen industry remained predominantly a handwork and cottage industry until the second quarter of the nineteenth century. Scotland also had a small woolen industry, but it mainly produced cheap, coarse wares, likewise on a handwork basis.

The cotton industry constituted the leading edge of the industrial revolution in Scotland as in England. It grew up in the first half of the eighteenth

[2] Smith, *Wealth of Nations,* I, 222. For the importance of the English market generally, see Campbell, "Anglo-Scottish Union of 1707," 468–77.

[3] Hamilton, *Economic History of Scotland,* Appendices IV and V. The figures do not include linen produced for home use, or linen yarn sold to England and Ireland, which at one time was estimated at one-fourth the value of the officially stamped linen.

century as an adjunct of the linen industry in the vicinity of Glasgow (Lanarkshire and Renfrewshire), where weavers used a weft of cotton on a linen warp for the fine and fancy cloths for which they were noted. As early as 1755, when the first import statistics were collected, Scotland imported directly more than 100,000 pounds of raw cotton, in addition to yarn purchased in England. The rapid growth of the industry dates from the introduction of mechanical spinning in 1778, however. By 1787 there were 19 spinning mills in Scotland, of which the most important was New Lanark, built in 1784–86 by David Dale in partnership with Richard Arkwright. The New Lanark mill alone employed more than 1,200 workers. This pace of growth continued during the next two or three decades. According to the returns of the factory inspectors in 1835, Scottish mills employed 32,580 workers, or 15 per cent of the total for the entire British industry, a slightly higher proportion than that of total population. Given Scotland's smaller base and later start, this indicates a more rapid growth of the industry in Scotland than in England. Moreover, the value of output of the Scottish industry was proportionately higher than that of England, owing to the quality of Scottish products. According to contemporary estimates, as early as 1812 Scotland accounted for 22 per cent or more of the total value of British cotton production.[4] The finishing trades, notably bleaching, dyeing, and printing, also grew rapidly, and through their demands for raw material they gave a powerful fillip to the growing chemical industry, to which Scottish scientists made so many notable contributions.

Coal mining had been an important industry in Scotland from the sixteenth century. In the first half of the seventeenth century the principal industrial use for coal was in the manufacture of salt, although it was also used in sugar refining and the manufacture of rope, cordage, hardware, soap, glass, porcelain, and earthenware, as well as for domestic heating. With the growth of these industries in the later eighteenth and nineteenth centuries the demand for coal naturally increased, but even greater demands arose from new industries, iron and engineering in particular.

Unlike England, Scotland produced only negligible quantities of iron before the second half of the eighteenth century. The birth of the modern iron industry in Scotland came with the founding of Carron Company in 1759. This enterprise, which was unusual in many respects, was conceived on a large scale and with progressive intentions from the beginning. In spite of many difficulties, both financial and technical, it soon won a reputation of renown; for many years it was the largest enterprise of its kind

[4] Deane and Cole, *British Economic Growth, 1688–1959,* 186; see also Daniels, *Early English Cotton Industry,* 180.

in Europe, and the largest of any kind in Scotland. By the end of the eighteenth century, however, it had a number of domestic competitors, and Scotland accounted for about one-eighth of the total British iron production. Growth of the industry was still more rapid in the first half of the nineteenth century; in 1854, at the time of the first official statistics, Scotland, with less than one-seventh of the population of Great Britain, produced more than one-fourth of its output of pig iron.

A large part of the output of the iron industry went to supply the associated engineering and shipbuilding industries. Although the engineering industry has many facets, it was long associated primarily with the steam engine. The modern steam engine was conceived at the University of Glasgow and gestated in the Carron ironworks; but the technological and industrial base of Scotland at that time was still too narrow to give it birth. Nevertheless, in later years Scotland reclaimed its heritage of engineering supremacy. The growth of sugar refining and cotton spinning in the west of Scotland created a demand for skilled mechanics and millwrights who soon proliferated in Glasgow. In 1812 the *Comet,* the first successful steam-propelled vessel in Europe, was launched on the Clyde. By mid-century Clydeside was far and away the world's leader in shipbuilding, heavy engineering, and associated branches of industry.

Capital Accumulation, Investment, and the Currency

At the time of the Union Scotland's population amounted to about one-fifth that of England and Wales, but its taxable capacity only amounted to about one-fortieth.[5] Undoubtedly the latter ratio reflects the prevalence of the subsistence features of the Scottish economy; it is far too low to serve as a true measure of the relative levels of wealth of the two countries. It is nevertheless a significant indicator of both past levels of performance and future prospects for growth. Yet Scotland's industrial growth in the century after 1750 was more rapid than that of England, supporting the view that capital accumulation is more often a result than a precondition of industrialization. Scotland did, however, accumulate sizable sums of capital in the eighteenth century. The most important channel through which capital was accumulated before the Industrial Revolution itself was the tobacco trade. Glasgow's "tobacco lords" were noted for their great wealth and ostentatious demeanor, but their most important common characteristic was their shrewd intelligence and general business ability. Most of them foresaw the American Revolution; on the eve of the war they laid in

[5] Smout, "Anglo-Scottish Union of 1707," 455.

huge stocks of tobacco, liquidated their American assets, and escaped with negligible losses. It used to be thought that the rise of the cotton industry was traceable directly to transfers of capital from the tobacco trade to manufacturing.[6] Recent research has failed to reveal many massive direct transfers of this nature; some of the tobacco merchants shifted to the West Indian sugar trade instead, and others invested in a variety of industrial and mercantile ventures or purchased landed estates.[7] A favorite investment of Glasgow traders, both before and after the American Revolution, was in banking. The most significant feature of the war as it affected the Scottish economy was that it released large quantities of capital from an employment that had few linkages either backward or forward, and made it available for domestic investment generally.

The history of Scottish currency bears out the picture of the general backwardness of the economy in the first half of the eighteenth century, and suggests how much of the subsequent investment was financed. The recoinage of 1707 produced £411,117, mostly silver, of which less than £240,000 was native coin, £40,000 English, and £132,000 foreign. In addition, contemporaries estimated up to £30,000 in gold that was not brought in for recoinage, about £60,000 in copper tokens, and as much in banknotes. In all, the Scottish money stock totaled about £500,000, or approximately 10 shillings per capita, compared with more than £2 per capita in England and Wales in 1688–89. In the second half of the century the stock of gold and silver in Scotland was even less, both total and per capita, than it had been at the beginning, in spite of the substantial growth of wealth. According to one estimate the supply of gold in Scotland in the 1790's amounted to no more than £50,000.[8] Most of that was held by the banks. We have it on the authority of Adam Smith that "silver very seldom appears except in the change of a twenty shillings banknote, and gold still seldomer,"[9] and Robert Owen testified that even gatekeepers on public turnpikes were entirely unacquainted with gold coins.[10] The largest part of the circulation consisted, in fact, of those 20 shilling notes, along with some of larger (and for a time, of smaller) denomination.

[6] Hamilton, *Industrial Revolution,* 120–21.

[7] Hamilton, *Economic History of Scotland,* 168; Campbell, "Anglo-Scottish Union of 1707," 472; Campbell, "Economic History of Scotland," 18; Campbell, *Scotland since 1707,* 46.

[8] Clapham, *Bank of England,* I, 168.

[9] Smith, *Wealth of Nations,* 281.

[10] Owen, *Life,* 52.

TABLE III.1

EVOLUTION OF THE SCOTTISH BANKING STRUCTURE, 1704–1865

	1704	1750	1760	1770	1780	1790	1800	1815	1825	1836	1845	1865
Banks of issue	1	5	5	12	12	17	18	30	31	29	19	12
Other banks	0	8	18	17	14	13	11	10	7	3	1	0
Branches	0	0	2	11	17	54	64	84	141	229	368	682
Total offices	1	13	25	40	43	84	93	124	179	261	388	694
Persons per office (1,000's)	1,000	100	52	34	32	18	17	16	13	10.6	7.2	4.6
					(£ 1,000's)							
Circulation	51	163	393	700	1,200	2,100	3,500	3,164	4,058	3,281	3,351	5,003
Deposits	0	140	290	600	1,000	2,000	7,000	15,000	21,000	25,000	33,192	57,180
Net worth	12	186	284	500	560	1,250	2,750	–	–	8,000	10,794	12,426
Total assets	63	600	1,224	3,665	3,760	5,350	13,250	24,000	31,000	40,000	60,000	77,222
Assets per person (£)	.06	.5	.9	2.7	2.7	3.6	8.3	12.4	14.1	16.0	21.9	24.2

Sources: See p. 67, n. 11.

THE FINANCIAL STRUCTURE AND ITS EVOLUTION

Table III.1 presents in bare outline the main quantitative indicators of the structure of Scottish banking over a period of more than a century and a half.[11] It shows the evolution of the system from a single privileged institution at the beginning of the eighteenth century to a dozen large, powerful, and competitive banks, each operating numerous branches on a national scale, in the second half of the nineteenth century. In the intervening years the system passed through several phases, each one of importance for the development of industry.

The Chartered Banks

The Bank of Scotland, authorized by act of the Scottish Parliament in 1695, represented the feeble hope that the bank might create the prosperity that was sadly lacking in the disordered state of the country. For almost half a century, however, it had to struggle desperately and by means of dubious expedients merely to survive. The Royal Bank of Scotland, instituted by royal charter in 1727, owed its existence to the political influence of the holders of the Equivalent debentures, government securities issued to com-

[11] Table III.1 was compiled from a wide variety of sources, primary and secondary, published and unpublished, of varying reliability, and it is sprinkled with estimates and interpolations. Behind each figure lies a separate table, and in some cases several tables, which makes detailed citations impracticable. Fortunately for the purpose of depicting over-all trends, the most reliable and comprehensive data pertain to the earliest years included as well as the latest (cols. 1, 2, 3, 11, and 12).

The most helpful and illuminating sources were records of the banks themselves, incomplete and frequently difficult to interpret though they are. For gentlemanly hospitality as well as generous permission to consult their records I am greatly indebted to the officers of the banks, and especially to their secretaries, Mr. John Rankin (Bank of Scotland), Mr. W. Lyall (Royal Bank of Scotland), and Mr. Robert Allan (National Commercial Bank of Scotland). Mrs. Brenda Gaskin performed the labor of extracting relevant data from the general ledgers of the Bank of Scotland with skill and intelligence.

The principal published works utilized were Kerr, *History of Banking in Scotland,* and that invaluable compilation of primary data and gossip, Boase, *Banking in Dundee.* The histories of the individual banks are truly remarkable for their almost total lack of any relevant information. A few scattered figures were obtained from Malcolm, *Bank of Scotland;* Malcolm, *British Linen Bank;* Munro, *Royal Bank of Scotland;* Rait, *Union Bank of Scotland;* Keith, *North of Scotland Bank Limited;* Reid, *Clydesdale Bank.* The circulation figures from 1815 onward are from Parliamentary Papers.

pensate claimants on the Crown at the time of the Union in 1707. Until the very eve of Scotland's industrial revolution these constituted the only banks of importance in the country. The British Linen Company, chartered in 1746 to assist the linen industry, did not turn exclusively to banking until the 1760's, but it constituted the third of the three great joint-stock banks enjoying limited liability.

The Growth of Competition

All three chartered banks were located in Edinburgh. Although they lent to individuals in other areas as well,[12] entrepreneurs in Glasgow, Aberdeen, Dundee, and several smaller cities felt that their interests were unduly neglected by the great Edinburgh institutions. In 1749 a partnership of Glasgow merchants established a company which they called the Ship Bank. They obtained a cash credit of £10,000 from the Bank of Scotland and indicated that they intended to circulate the bank's notes in Glasgow and the west. In earlier years the two Edinburgh banks had engaged in vigorous competition with one another. Not to be outdone by its rival, therefore, the Royal Bank made a similar grant for a similar purpose to another partnership, which called itself the Glasgow Arms Bank. Much to the chagrin of both Edinburgh banks, they soon discovered that the Glasgow men used the credits simply as a reserve for issuing their own notes. This development forced the Edinburgh banks to settle their mutual grievances and to make a secret agreement to put down "private Persons erecting themselves into Banking Companys without any Publick Authority, particularly the two Banking Companys lately set up at Glasgow." [13] After warnings to Glasgow to cease and desist, the Edinburgh banks withdrew their credits, but by that time the Glasgow institutions were already well under way. The Edinburgh banks then resorted to the classic tactic (which they had previously used against each other) of hiring an agent to round up as many notes as possible of the offending banks and present them in quantity for immediate payment. The Glasgow banks defended themselves with the equally classic device (also pioneered by their Edinburgh mentors) of paying in sixpences and making use of the optional clause, which the Bank of Scotland had first used against the Royal Bank in 1730. This clause, printed on the banknotes, gave the bank the option of paying the bearer specie on demand, or paying with interest at six months after sight. The citizens of Glasgow also came to the aid of their local banks, and "with great readiness and alacrity

[12] An early account book of the Royal Bank, from 1728–29, shows that several Glasgow merchants had cash credits with the bank.

[13] Bank of Scotland, *Minutes of the Court of Directors,* vol. 5, 2 January 1752.

paid in large sums of specie" to the Arms and Ship banks.[14] The representative of the Edinburgh banks then brought a legal suit against the Glasgow banks, but that, too, failed to stop them.

The successful defiance of Edinburgh by the Glasgow banks encouraged others. By the early 1760's there were a dozen or more similar banks issuing notes in all parts of Scotland. Legally they took the form of partnerships, in some cases with several scores of partners; functionally they scarcely differed from the old chartered banks except for their smaller size and the fact that the partners lacked limited liability. In addition many enterprising individuals—shopkeepers, publicans, and others—issued their own notes of hand during the "small note mania," when notes for as little as one shilling Scots (equal to one penny sterling) circulated freely. Moreover, most of the notes contained the optional clause, which made it virtually impossible to obtain specie for them. In this state of affairs the Edinburgh banks appealed to Parliament for a law to restrict the right of issue in Scotland to institutions chartered for that purpose—meaning themselves, of course.

A great many Scots had become aware of the inconvenience of the multitude of small, unknown, and inconvertible notes, but few were prepared to see note issue monopolized in Edinburgh. On 13 December 1763, the "Justices, Freeholders, and Commissioners of Supply" of Renfrewshire held a meeting, with Sir James Maxwell of Pollock (a stockholder in one of the Glasgow banks) in the chair, and resolved:

> That paper money, under proper regulations, is advantageous to the country, tending to promote agriculture, manufactures, and trade: That the limiting of the circulation of paper money to the Banks of Edinburgh would be highly prejudicial to the landed and commercial interests of this part of the United Kingdom, by creating a dangerous monopoly to these Banks, in a branch of business so very important: That several Banking Companies in Scotland appear to be established upon as firm and solid foundations as either of the banks in Edinburgh . . .[15]

The Renfrewshire delegates did concede, however, that the optional clause was harmful, and petitioned Parliament "to oblige all Banks or branches in Scotland to make ready and punctual payment, on demand, of the Notes issued by them, in good and lawful money of Great Britain." [16] The result

[14] *Scots Magazine,* May 1756, quoted in Rait, *Union Bank of Scotland,* 29.

[15] Quoted in Boase, *Banking in Dundee,* 45.

[16] Ibid. 46.

was a law, passed in 1765, that abolished the optional clause and prohibited notes for less than 20 shillings, but left the right of issue free.

In 1752, at the time of their agreement to fight the Glasgow banks, the Bank of Scotland and the Royal Bank instituted a regular meeting of committees of their directors to confer on matters of common interest and established a weekly note exchange with running credits for the balance due. In 1771, having failed in their attempt to suppress the new banks, they made the best of what was for them a bad situation and agreed to accept at their counters the notes of ten of the most solidly established banks in other parts of Scotland (including those erstwhile reprobates, the Glasgow Arms and Ship banks, as well as the British Linen Company), and to admit them to their note exchanges.

Under these conditions the banking system made rapid strides in both stability and efficiency. Freedom of issue insured healthy competition and adequate banking services wherever they were in demand. The regular note exchanges made the banks watchdogs of one another and prevented any bank from getting seriously out of line with the general development of the economy. The note exchanges were forerunners, in fact, of modern clearing houses. Scotland did not altogether avoid bank failures, but its record with respect to stability was much better than those of most countries in similar stages of development.

Other Private Banks

In addition to the issuing banks, which were frequently referred to as joint-stock banks even though they lacked corporate charters, a number of small partnerships carried on a banking business without issuing notes. The earliest originated as merchant firms in the 1730's and 1740's, adding dealings in bills of exchange to commodity trade; a few even accepted deposits to supplement their own trading capital. The most important ones were located in Edinburgh, where they had connections with the old chartered banks, their partners frequently serving as directors of the latter. There were never more than 15 or 20 of these firms in business at any one time; they did not constitute a major element in the banking system. They gradually declined after 1815, and had virtually disappeared by 1845.

The Rise of Branch Banking

The Bank of Scotland opened a few branches in 1696 and again in 1731, but on both occasions the ventures proved unsatisfactory and the branches were closed within a few years. Agents of the British Linen Company began circulating its notes in 1759, and possibly earlier; the company established its first formal branches, in Aberdeen and Dundee, in 1760, thus inaugurating the continuous history of branch banking in Scotland. By 1800 the company had 17 branches. The Bank of Scotland opened two branches in 1774 and three more in 1775. By 1800 it had 27 branches, but in the next 20 years it closed several, reducing the number of its branches to 13 in 1820. In 1783 the Royal Bank established a branch at Glasgow, with the enterprising merchant and manufacturer David Dale as agent. Within a few years the volume of business transacted in Glasgow exceeded that of the bank's main office in Edinburgh; in 1817 the discounts and advances in Glasgow totaled more than £1 million, as against less than £300,000 in Edinburgh,[17] and the Glasgow office was widely reputed to have the largest business of any bank in Great Britain outside London. In spite of this promising beginning, the Royal Bank established no more branches for half a century. A number of the smaller provincial banks did, however.

Typically a bank would have three or four branches, usually in near-by satellite communities, but many banks also maintained branches in Glasgow; in 1809, of 19 note-issuing banks in Glasgow, 16 were branches whose head offices were elsewhere. With more than 100 offices altogether, including branches and private banks, Scotland in that year had a substantially higher density of banking facilities than England.

The Beginnings of Consolidation

Branches not included, Scotland had 18 note-issuing institutions at the beginning of the nineteenth century: three in Edinburgh, two each in Glasgow, Aberdeen, Dundee, Stirling, and Paisley; and one each in Perth, Greenock, Falkirk, Ayr, and Leith. In addition at least 11 private (nonissuing) banks catered to the banking needs of the country. The period of Bank Restriction witnessed the proliferation of new banks in Scotland as in England; by 1810 there were more than 40 independent banks, a number which was maintained with negligible fluctuation for the next ten years. One reason for the rapid increase was dissatisfaction with the increasing conservatism of the old established banks. During the Napoleonic Wars the chartered banks invested heavily in government securities (see Chart III.3, p. 84), thus reducing their capacity to lend to local industry and commerce. The close affiliation of the chartered banks with Edinburgh private bankers also incurred criticism on the ground that the private bankers acted as retailers

[17] Royal Bank of Scotland, "State of Affairs of the Royal Bank . . . 1817."

of credit for the chartered banks, obtaining large cash credits on specially favored terms. The Commercial Bank of Scotland, founded in Edinburgh in 1810, took advantage of the current of opinion by advertising that it would prohibit private bankers from serving on its board of directors, and stressing its liberal lending policy. The National Bank of Scotland, founded in 1825 in Edinburgh also, took a similar line. Both banks acquired charters in 1831, and both engaged in a vigorous policy of branch expansion, forcing their older rivals to do likewise. The 1830's saw the formation of several new large joint-stock banks, in Glasgow especially. These banks projected themselves on a regional or national scale at once, frequently absorbing smaller banks as well as creating new branches. The ultimate effect of this amalgamation movement, together with the restrictive legislation of 1845, which extended to Scotland the main principles of the Bank Act of 1844 in England, was to reduce the number of Scottish banks to ten by 1880 and to five in the mid-twentieth century.

At the time the new Act took effect Scotland had 19 banks of issue and one lingering private bank. Edinburgh and Glasgow each had five large banks with nationwide branch networks. The somewhat smaller provincial banks also had sizable regional branch systems. Altogether Scotland had almost 400 bank offices, a ratio of one office for each 7,200 persons, almost double the "bank density" of England and Wales. This combination of a few substantial banks, each with a large number of branch offices, gave Scotland the strongest, most competitive, most efficient banking system of the times.

Savings Banks

Savings banks originated in Scotland. No doubt the already widespread familiarity of the public with banks of issue facilitated this innovation, but, on the other hand, the savings banks stimulated the willingness to save among those of the lowest income classes and led many directly to regular deposit banks. The movement began with the formation of the Ruthwell savings bank in 1810, followed by the Edinburgh Bank for Savings in 1813. By 1815 savings banks were well established, with a dozen or more in various parts of Scotland.

Unlike their imitators in England, the Scottish banks enjoyed no special government recognition until 1835, and they followed independent investment policies. In the early years they deposited their funds with regular banks at 5 per cent interest. When an individual's account reached £10, the minimum deposit in the joint-stock banks, it was transferred to a regular deposit account. The joint-stock banks dropped their fixed interest rate policy in the 1820's, and the rate fell as low as 2.5 per cent. The savings banks thereupon began to invest in government securities, in loans to municipalities, and even in loans on personal security. The Stonehaven Savings Bank, for example, lent £2,000 at 5 per cent to a local distillery.[18]

In 1835 the Scottish savings banks were given the option of joining the English system of Trustee Savings Banks. Most did, but some retained their old independence. In 1846 total deposits in Scottish savings banks amounted to £1,384,000,[19] an average of more than £15 per depositor, at a time when the per capita annual income did not exceed £25. Nor does that figure take into account the large number of persons who had graduated to regular deposit banking.

Monetary and Financial Aspects

The lower portion of Table III.1 shows the evolution of the banking system in monetary terms. It would appear that in the 95 years from 1750 to 1845 the total assets of the system grew almost exactly 100-fold, or at an annual rate of approximately 4.85 per cent. It would be interesting to know the real rate of growth, corrected for changes in the price level. Unfortunately there is no suitable price index covering the entire period, even for England or Great Britain, much less for Scotland. By decade intervals the undeflated growth rates show sizable fluctuations, corresponding to what appears to have been, from nonquantitative and some quantitative evidence, the rhythm of growth of the economy as a whole. The two decades from 1750 to 1770 show a large increase in bank assets, concomitant with strong upsurges in agricultural output, linen production, and foreign trade. In the decade of the American Revolution, a decade of stagnation in both production and trade, the rate of growth fell substantially, but it still appears at a respectable figure. Growth resumed in the 1780's, when the cotton industry began to adopt factory methods, and it continued at a high rate during the Napoleonic Wars. During the postwar decade the rate fell abruptly once more but still remained positive. Growth resumed after the crisis of 1825–26, and in the final decade the rate approached the century-long average. The average annual rates are given in column 1 of Table III.2.

In an attempt to reduce the growth rate of bank assets to real terms, several deflators, none really satisfactory, have been employed. In column 2 an unweighted index of grain prices at the Haddington fiars (the fiars

[18] Horne, *History of Savings Banks,* 54.

[19] Porter, "On the Accumulation of Capital by the Different Classes of Society," 194.

TABLE III.2

GROWTH RATE OF TOTAL BANK ASSETS
BY INDICATED INTERVALS, SCOTLAND, 1750–1845

(per cent per annum)

	Undeflated	Deflated		
1750–60	7.1	8.5	–	7.8
1760–70	11.0	6.7	–	10.8
1770–80	2.6	(–0.3)	–	(–0.7)
1780–90	3.8	1.5	–	2.3
1790–1800	9.1	(–0.8)	3.8	3.7
1800–1815	10.0	–	5.0	4.7
1815–25	2.2	–	4.0	–
1825–36	2.3	–	3.5	–
1836–45	4.5	–	6.8	–
1750–1800	8.8	3.1	–	4.6
1800–1845	3.4	–	4.7	–
1750–1845	4.85	–	–	–

prices were used to determine the cost of living for the purpose of setting ministers' salaries) shows the same general pattern of fluctuation as the raw data, but at a substantially lower level. The grain price index (see Chart III.9, p. 95) is, of course, open to the objection that it was unduly influenced by variations in harvest conditions. Moreover, if it is true that during the Industrial Revolution the price of manufactured goods fell relative to grain prices this would impart a downward bias to the index. Column 3 uses the Gayer-Rostow-Schwartz index of British domestic and imported commodities (1821–25 = 100). It is probably somewhat better for the purpose than the grain price index, but it is not obvious how applicable it is to Scotland. Column 4 is the Schumpeter-Gilboy index of English consumer goods prices (1701 = 100). Besides the fact that it includes no Scottish prices at all, it is also heavily weighted with grain prices. The general impression one gains is that the rate of growth of bank assets in real terms was somewhat lower than in money terms in the second half of the eighteenth century, but slightly higher in the first half of the nineteenth century. Over the period as a whole it was probably lower, too, but only to a slight degree. It seems clear in any case that, whether measured in real or money terms, the growth of bank assets was substantially more rapid than in England (see above, p. 34).

The same conclusion emerges even more positively from a comparison of bank assets per inhabitant. In money terms the two countries were on a par in the 1770's, with about £2.7 per person. By 1800 the ratio was more than 4 to 3 in favor of Scotland, and by 1844 about 5 to 2. This is strong circumstantial evidence of the superiority of the Scottish banking system over the English; it also gives a great deal of support to the thesis that the Scottish banking system played a major role in Scotland's more rapid industrialization.

BANK POLICIES AND PRACTICES

Precocious though it was, the Scottish banking system developed largely in response to the changing needs and circumstances of the Scottish economy. The chartered banks attempted to model themselves to some extent on the Bank of England, and they were influenced by Dutch practice as well. But Scotland's economic environment differed greatly from those of London and Holland, and Scottish bankers did not hesitate to depart from traditional ways when they did not suit the needs of the developing economy. The result was that a number of significant innovations in bank policy and practice were made which account for much of the system's unusual effectiveness in promoting and facilitating economic growth.

Lending Policy and Practice

Perhaps the most effective device employed by the Scottish banks, from the viewpoint of rapid economic development, was their method of granting loans. Contrary to the orthodoxy of other times and places, which held that banks should lend only on the security of goods in transit or in process, and for periods of not more than 90 days, the Scottish banks did not hesitate to lend for unspecified periods with no tangible securities at all. Bills of exchange, the staple assets of many contemporary banks in other countries, were the least important earning assets of the Scottish banks. Of greater importance were loans on personal or heritable bonds. These were long-term loans, usually made to substantial proprietors, secured either by pledges of real property (heritable bonds) or by the signature of the borrower and two or more co-obligants (personal bonds). The largest volume of lending, however, took place by means of loans on cash account, which were also called "cash credits." Under this system an enterprising merchant or manufacturer could obtain a "running cash" (credit) against his own signature, along with those of two or more of his friends as sureties. The agreement with the bank stipulated a maximum amount that the customer might borrow; he was then free to withdraw, in the form of the bank's own notes, any sums that in total did not exceed the agreed limit. He paid interest only on the amount actually borrowed, and repaid the principal at such times and in such amounts as his circumstances permitted. No fixed terms were set for the loans, but cash accounts were expected to have a fairly rapid turnover. An Englishman with more than 40 years' experience as a banker in Scotland estimated that the average turnover was four times a year.[20]

The cash credit system apparently was originated by the Royal Bank of Scotland soon after its own establishment. The bank had a large capital but few liquid resources, and it may have hit upon the system as a device to encourage the circulation of its notes. In any event the Bank of Scotland soon followed suit, and by the middle of the century when new banks came into existence it was a standard feature of Scottish banking. The surviving records of the Bank of Scotland show that, on 27 March 1750, it held cash accounts for 279 individuals and business firms with an aggregate debit balance of more than £75,000, or more than half of the bank's earnings assets.[21] The largest credit was to Thomas and Adam Fairholme, private merchant bankers who were also directors of the bank, for £3,000, but the largest debit balance, £1,405, was owed by Hugh and Robert Clerk, merchants, against a total credit of £2,000. The majority of debit balances ranged between £200 and £500, and were owed mainly by merchants and manufacturers of Edinburgh and the immediate vicinity, although a few were located in more distant places, including Glasgow.

An analysis of the credits granted by the Dundee Bank at the beginning of its operations will illustrate the way in which this device was used in a provincial center on the eve of the Industrial Revolution. (See Charts III.1 and III.2.) The bank was founded in 1763, at the height of the "small note mania," with a paid-in capital of £1,260. Its note circulation quickly rose to about £30,000 to £40,000, a level at which it stabilized until near the end of the century. The population of Dundee at the time was about 6,000. In its first four years the bank granted cash accounts to 162 individuals and firms for a total of £59,385; the average per account was thus £306. Just over half the credits went to men who styled themselves merchants. Landed proprietors, mainly the local gentry with a scattering of titled nobles, had 32 accounts, although this figure included the £500

[20] Boase, *Banking in Dundee,* 560.

[21] Bank of Scotland, *General Ledger,* vol. 11 (1747–50), fols. 425ff.

credit to George Dempster of Dunnichen, the bank's principal promoter, and similar credits to all of the other partners in the bank. Farmers and factors (estate managers) had seven accounts together, as did "writers" (attorneys), some of whom undoubtedly functioned as brokers and dealers. Six credits went to "manufacturers" (industry not specified), and one to a "founder." Five of the bank's debtors were men of the cloth, and five others doctors, druggists, or apothecaries. The list also included three shipmasters, two tailors, a glover, milliner, stationer, vintner, brewer, carpenter, and "Ann Robertson & Sisters" (for £300). In addition to credits granted to individuals they went also to the "Forfar Weaver Trade," the "Dundee Tailor Trade," the Dundee Whale Fishing Company, the burgh of Brechin, and the city of St. Andrews. The credits ranged from a minimum of £100 to a maximum of £500, with a single exception: John Young, merchant of Coupar-Angus, had a credit of £1,000. About 50 of the 162 credits went to persons residing elsewhere than Dundee (in addition to the farmers and proprietors); most lived in towns and villages near by, but several lived in Perth, Montrose, St. Andrews, and Arbroath, and one in Aberdeen. On 1 February 1767, 108 accounts showed debit balances totaling £25,177, or an average of £233 per account, from which Boase concluded that the beneficiaries of cash accounts utilized them to the extent of three-fourths of the total credit.[22]

In subsequent years the average value of the credits increased somewhat, and, with the growth of industry, more loans were made to industrialists, although it appears that the majority of credits continued to be granted to merchants for commercial purposes. In the immediate post-Napoleonic period (1815–1820) the Commercial Bank of Aberdeen opened cash credits for shipbuilders, cotton manufacturers, distillers, brewers, and a variety of other industrialists. The majority of the credits ranged from £1,000 to £2,000, but in 1820 the bank granted credits to two cotton manufacturers for £10,000 each.[23] Cash accounts remained an important lending device of the Scottish banks until at least the second quarter of the nineteenth century. In 1826 Thomas Kinnear, an Edinburgh private banker sent by the Scottish banks to argue against the prohibition of £1 notes, which was then under consideration in Parliament, estimated the number of cash accounts to be more than 10,000 and the total credit outstanding upon them to be £6,000,000. Meanwhile, however, a variety of other forms of lending had been developed to supplement the cash account.

[22] Boase, *Banking in Dundee,* 64ff.

[23] Minute book of the Commercial Bank of Aberdeen, now in the archives of the National Commercial Bank of Scotland.

CHART III.1

DUNDEE BANKING COMPANY, PRINCIPAL ASSETS, 1764–1864

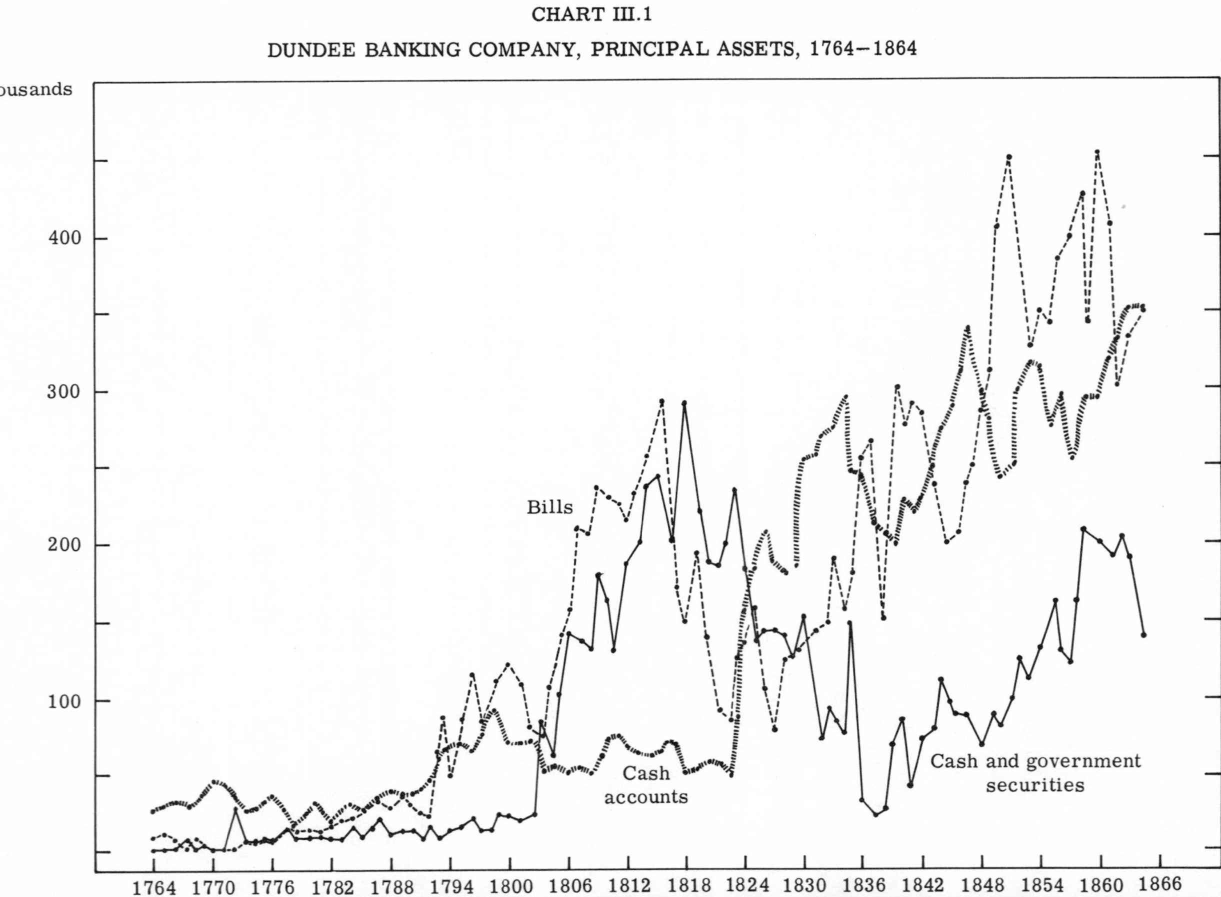

CHART III.2

DUNDEE BANKING COMPANY, PRINCIPAL LIABILITIES, 1764–1864

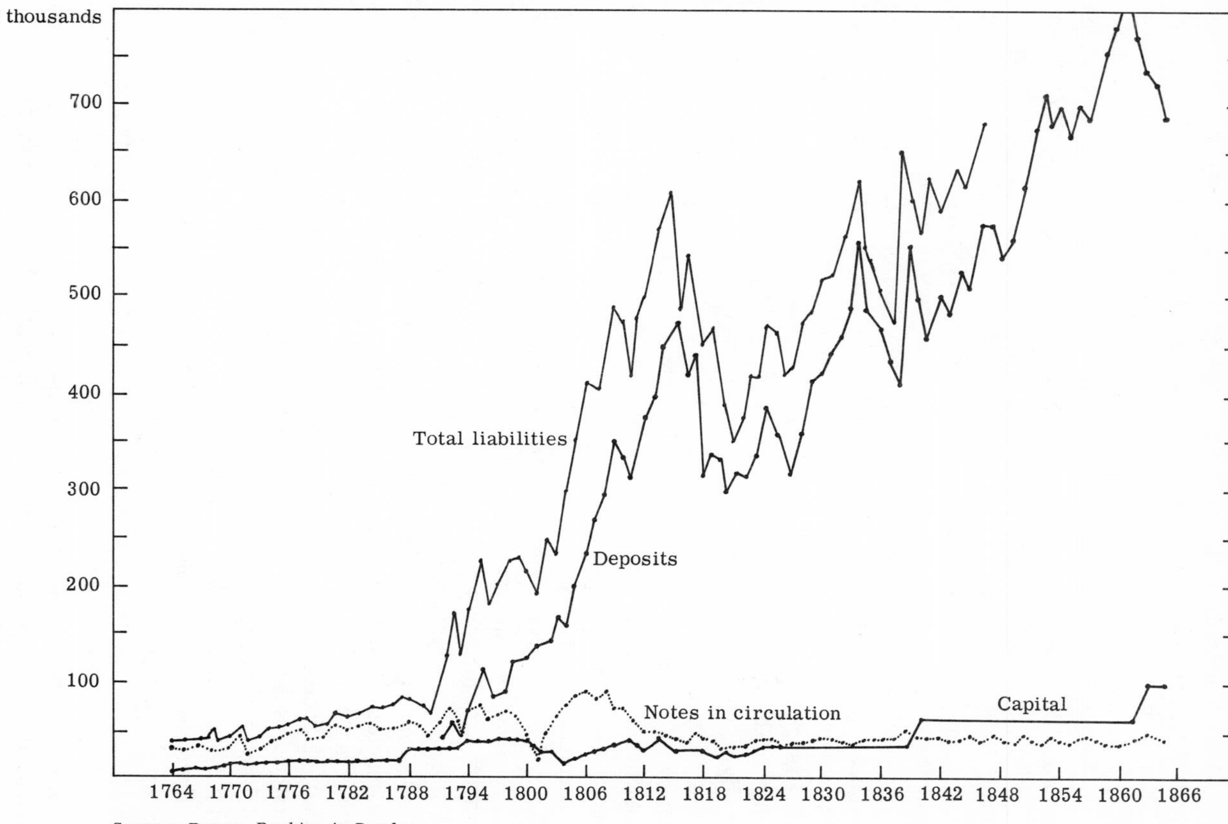

Source: Boase, *Banking in Dundee*.

Loans on personal and heritable bonds constituted an important part of Scottish bank lending in the middle of the eighteenth century, but declined in relative importance in subsequent decades (although the Dundee Bank did not begin to lend on "Heritable Subjects" until 1822). Heritable bonds differed from personal bonds chiefly in the kind of security offered; the latter differed from loans on cash account principally in the uses to which the proceeds were put. The records of the Bank of Scotland for 1750 show £57,000 due on these accounts. The 14 loans on heritable bond ranged in size from £500 to 5,000, with interest charged at a flat rate of 5 per cent. At that time most of the loans were of several years' standing, and on some the interest payments also were several years in arrears. Surprisingly, no interest was charged on arrears of interest; on one account a payment had been made in 1750 of the interest due for 1747 at the standard rate of 5 per cent, and credited in full for that year. The 84 loans on personal bond ranged in size from £100 to £2,500, with the great majority in the range £200 to £500. Like the loans on heritable bond, these were mostly of some years' standing, earned interest (frequently in arrears) of 5 per cent, and were generally repaid in irregular installments. Most of the borrowers in both categories were substantial proprietors, sometimes noblemen. Most likely they used the proceeds of the loans to improve their estates, to purchase the securities of local bridge and turnpike trusts, perhaps to educate a son or make a trip to London or the Continent. The personal tie between banker and borrower is evident not only in the nature of the security required for loans on personal bonds, but also in the lax provision for the payment of interest.

Bills of exchange, a minor element in Scottish bank portfolios in the 1750's, increased gradually in importance until, in the second quarter of the nineteenth century, they became the principal means by which the banks provided funds for commerce and industry. On 27 March 1750, the Bank of Scotland held only £11,150 in bills, or less than 5 per cent of total assets at that date. By 1800 the bill account had increased to £418,242, or 15 per cent of total assets, and in 1844 discounts and commissions on bills yielded more than 25 per cent of gross profits. The Scottish bankers distinguished among bills according to the centers on which they were drawn. Thus "bills of exchange" meant bills payable in London or other cities outside Scotland, "inland bills" referred to bills on other cities or towns in Scotland, and "bills discounted" meant simply local bills. For small local banks such as the Dundee Bank the two latter categories were much the most important; the great Edinburgh banks dealt more extensively in bills on London, but even they did most of their business in Scottish bills. In the nineteenth century "bills receivable" appear for relatively large amounts in the accounts of the Bank of Scotland and the Royal Bank. These appear to represent direct lending by the banker to his customer, with the individual bill or promissory note replacing the open credit on cash account. Another new asset account that crops up with increasing frequency in the nineteenth century is the overdraft. There is very little difference in principle between the overdraft and the cash credit; most likely the increasing prominence of the former was linked to the spreading use of checks in place of banknotes for commercial transactions.

Investments

In the early years the earning assets of the banks consisted almost exclusively of loans and discounts in Scotland. A small amount of government securities first appeared in the accounts of the Bank of Scotland in 1766, but they did not become a permanent feature until the American Revolution. Such investments, including Bank of England and East India stock, shot up dramatically after 1792, quickly overshadowing ordinary lending. Mr. F. S. Taylor, secretary of the Institute of Bankers in Scotland, has kindly brought to my attention this letter, written in 1800 by the treasurer of the Bank of Scotland to the bank's agents (branch managers), cautioning them against lending for speculative purposes.

> Sirs,
>
> At the commencement of the present War, the Directors, by circular letters, to which I refer to you, cautioned you and the other Agents of the Bank, against all Transactions, by which the Bank's funds might be misemployed and wasted, in accommodating persons who speculated with their money, or with their credit, in the Stocks or otherwise, instead of being employed, as the Directors always wish them to be, in supporting the fair and industrious Merchant, Manufacturer, and Farmer. The Agents then, and indeed during the continuance of the War, have (with very few exceptions) seconded the intention of the Directors, and the Country and the Bank have both reaped the benefit of it.
>
> As however the necessity of that prudent caution is again become as strong as ever, not only upon account of the continuation of the War, and the consequent increase of public burdens, but also upon account of the present high price of the Necessaries of Life, and the prospect of a large expense for Corn to be imported before next Crop; the Directors find that they have too good reason to renew the former caution to the Bank's Agents. And therefore I have by their orders to recommend and to request, that without respect to the persons of men who

may apply to you for Loans of the Bank's money, you will use your most impartial judgement in discriminating between Speculators, and fair Borrowers, for the usual purposes of manufacture, etc. Particularly, that you will discount no bills to Dealers in Corn, excepting the Importers of it; Nor to Landholders, Farmers, Merchants, and others, whom you may suspect of borrowing money for the purpose of enabling them to keep back their Corn or Meal from the Market; Nor to persons who have not Residence or property within the District of your Branch, because we see persons going from Branch to Branch, for discounting Bills, in order to borrow as much money as they can, at the manifest hazard of the Agents, who cannot possibly know how deeply such persons are engaged in the whole; That when applications are made to you for large sums, for any purpose, whatever, you will desire them to be made first to the Board of Directors; That you will not discount bills however good, for the purpose of Retiring Bills due or nearly due; not when the proceeds of them are to be used for taking Bills from you on London; In a word that you will avoid not only all Transactions in Discounting and in Drawing Bills, that are pernicious, but also that are unprofitable to the Bank, or dangerous to yourselves. But on the other hand you will continue to give every Encouragement and Aid, consistent with the Bank's Interest and your own Security; which the fair Dealer, especially the old steady friends of the Bank may require.

(Signed) James Fraser,
Treasurer.
Bank of Scotland.

The bank may very well have wished to prevent others from using its funds for speculation, but it is clear from the bank's own records, presented in graphic form in Charts III.3 and III.4, that it invested heavily in government securities at the expense of ordinary loans and discounts.

As previously noted, this policy, which was apparently also followed by the other Edinburgh banks, drew criticism on the grounds that it deprived Scottish industry of capital and was not unconnected with the vigorous new competition the old banks had to face in the first quarter of the nineteenth century. Lord Cockburn, one of the founders of the Commercial Bank of Scotland, declared that "No men were more devoid of spirit, and even of the proper spirit of their trade, than our old Edinburgh bankers. Respectable men they were, but without talent, general knowledge, or any liberal objects, they were the conspicuous sycophants of existing power." [24] The

[24] Cockburn, *Memorials of His Own Times,* 238–9.

Commercial Bank was generally regarded as a "Whig bank," but in its prospectus it promised to lend on good security without regard to party. Whether it lived up to that promise we have no way of knowing, but it clearly abided by its promise to lend liberally to Scottish industry and commerce, and prospered thereby.

The smaller provincial banks, to judge by the records of the Dundee Bank and a few other fragmentary accounts, invested a much smaller proportion of their assets through London. Even that was largely for the purpose of maintaining liquid earning assets in London in place of idle balances with other banks or cash in their own vaults. In its summary accounts the Dundee Bank iumped "cash and government securities" under one heading.

The Growth of Deposits

The Scottish banks apparently accepted deposits from the beginning of their existence, but they made no serious attempt to attract deposits from the general public until near the end of the eighteenth century. The earliest deposits in the Bank of Scotland were made in exchange for "treasurer's bonds." (The treasurer was the bank's chief executive officer.) These deposits were few in number but for large amounts (£1,000 to £5,000), and they were generally owned by stockholders of the bank, sometimes as partial security for cash credits. They received interest, usually at 4 per cent but occasionally at 5, and were clearly expected to remain in the bank for long periods.

In 1762, in the early stages of competition connected with the "small note mania," the Bank of Scotland advertised that it would pay 5 per cent for money left "for 6 months certain," and 4 per cent on demand deposits. Apparently it was unable to employ the funds profitably, however; it ceased accepting deposits at 5 per cent within six months, and the following year advised all depositors to withdraw their funds. This experiment was repeated at intervals during the next several years. Not until 1787 did the bank regularly accept deposits, but from then until 1824 it paid a steady 3 per cent on demand deposits. Unfortunately the bank's surviving accounts do not show the full effect of this decision, for its general ledgers treated the branches as though they were separate banks. Thus Chart III.4 shows deposits at the main office only.

The Royal Bank apparently began to accept deposits at the same time as the Bank of Scotland. The British Linen Company did not do so until forced by competition about 1800. In Glasgow, on the other hand, where deposits with merchants and manufacturers for use in their business had preceded banking proper, the banks made a big business of deposits. The

CHART III.3

BANK OF SCOTLAND, PRINCIPAL ASSETS,* 1750–1850

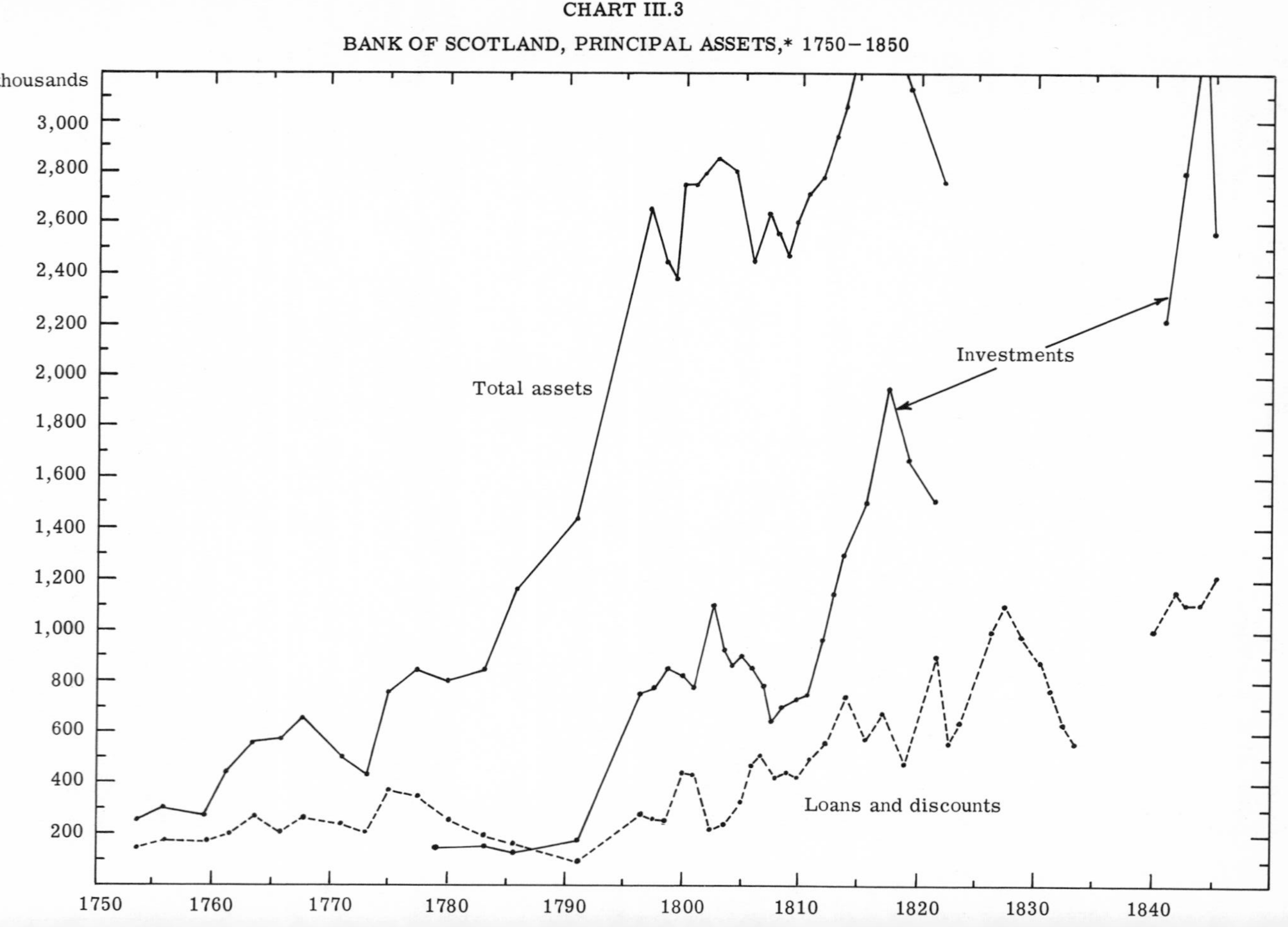

CHART III.4

BANK OF SCOTLAND, PRINCIPAL LIABILITIES,* 1750–1850

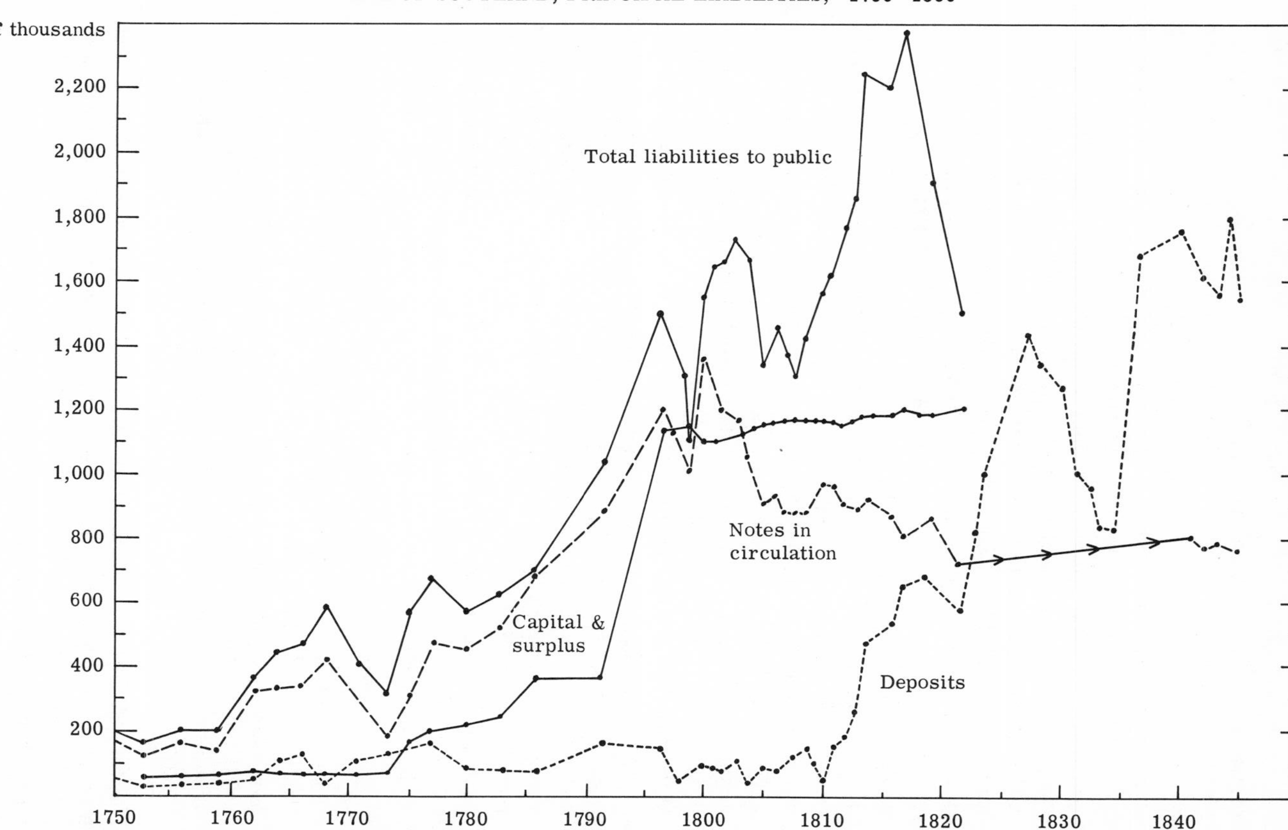

*Figures misleading; see pp. 82–89.

smaller provincial banks also began to accept deposits, and by 1800 aggregate deposits were double the amount of notes in circulation. Their progress was steady and rapid thereafter.

The character of the deposits contains some ambiguities. It is not clear when they first became transferable by check, nor when banks first began to "create" deposits. As noted, the earliest deposits took the form of "treasurer's bonds" or interest-bearing non-negotiable promissory notes of the banks. In 1810 the Bank of Scotland introduced the "deposit receipt," also non-negotiable, which paid 4 per cent if held for at least six months. Meanwhile the bank continued to pay 3 per cent on demand deposits or "accounts-current." The effects of the new deposit receipts are evident in Chart III.4, even though that chart does refer only to the head office. Other banks soon followed suit. About the same time, or possibly earlier, the banks began to accept deposits for sums as small as £10, which, together with the attractive rate of interest, was a great stimulus to savers of modest means. Of course £10 still represented a sizable capital for the typical laborer or artisan, but the new savings banks gave even them the chance of accumulating a small "*rentier* capital."

The banks followed a policy of stable interest rates on deposits until the sharp decline in bond yields after the Napoleonic Wars. In 1817 they reduced the rates on deposit receipts as well as on current accounts to 3 per cent. During the disturbed 1820's deposit interest fluctuated between 2 and 3 per cent (with a brief interval at 4 per cent during the crisis of 1825–26), but in 1829 it settled down again at 2 per cent, where it remained until it was raised to 3 per cent again in 1836. For the next ten years it fluctuated gently between 2 and 3.5 per cent.

The banks also attempted to follow a policy of stable interest rates in their lending activities. In 1836 the manager of the British Linen Company wrote to the chairman of the Parliamentary committee on banks of issue:

> The Bank fixed their deposit Interest on its present general rate with some local exceptions about six years ago, previous to which time it was higher and varied with the . . . rate of discount. The Bank's rate on Discount on Bills and charge on Advances had been steady for a number of years at 4 per cent on all current transactions without distinction.[25]

The earliest direct reference to the use of checks in Scotland that I have seen refers to the year of 1801. At that time an agent of the Dundee Bank

[25] Quoted in Malcolm, *British Linen Bank,* 115.

went to Montrose twice weekly with a valise full of banknotes "to discount Bills and pay cheques on Cash Accounts." [26] In this case, it appears, the checks were used merely to withdraw banknotes from the bank with which the customer had established credit. The notes themselves, not the checks, still served as the means of payment. But that was in the provinces. Practice may have been different in Edinburgh and Glasgow. In 1826 Thomas Kinnear testified before the committee on small notes that "the exchange of notes and cheques between the Edinburgh Banks is settled by a bill on London . . ." [27] This clearly implies that checks were then being used as means of payment. A modern authority indicates that customers' "draughts" were in use as early as 1729 to withdraw sums from cash accounts; however, "the printed cheque as it is known today came into use in Scotland shortly before the end of the eighteenth century, but it probably was not common until the 1820's or 1830's." [28] The first clearing house in Scotland specifically for checks did not come into being until 1856, in Glasgow. The note exchanges, as Kinnear indicated, probably served the purpose earlier.

It is unlikely that "deposit creation" originated before the use of checks. So long as banknotes were the principal means of exchange the cash credit served precisely the same function as deposit creation. The rapid growth of deposits after 1800 was due not only to the voluntary savings of individuals, but also to the practice of granting current account overdrafts. Significantly, it was at just this time that banknote issues, which had shown a steady increase over the previous 100 years, began to level off.

Cash Reserves

However "conservative" the Edinburgh bankers may have been in other respects, their conservatism did not extend to their reserve policies. The same was true in at least equal measure of bankers elsewhere in Scotland. "Cash" reserves were typically low, probably 10 per cent or less on the average for the entire century. Actually, no firm generalization can be made on the subject, for the bank records rarely distinguished between specie and the bank's own notes held in its cash box. In the few instances where the records do show that distinction it is unusual for specie reserves to exceed 5 per cent of total liabilities to the public; more often they are less than 1 per cent. The reserve policy of the Dundee Banking Company,

[26] Boase, *Banking in Dundee,* 217.

[27] Ibid. 343.

[28] Leslie, *Note Exchange and Clearing House System,* 44.

depicted at ten-year intervals in Chart III.5, appears to be on the "conservative" side in comparison with the general practice.

The surviving accounts of the Bank of Scotland are the most comprehensive and continuous of any Scottish bank, past or present. The earliest date for which a separate accounting of specie holdings is given refers to the year 1842. At that time the specie in the bank's possession, both in the head office and branches, amounted to £65,568, compared with total (nominal) assets of £5,610,000. The ratio of specie to liabilities to the public was less than 2 per cent, although the nominal "cash" ratio (specie plus the bank's own notes) was about 8 per cent. (We should make a partial exception to the statement that no reference to specie appears before 1842: the bank temporarily suspended payments twice, early in its career, and on both occasions published its accounts to show its solvency. In 1704 it held £1,600 in old Scottish merks against debts to the public of £50,487; in 1728 it had an actual cash reserve of £585 against liabilities of £72,455.) [29]

The earliest extant balance sheet of the Royal Bank refers to the year 1817 (See Charts III.6 and III.7.) It shows a cash reserve of £353,000 against liabilities to the public of £2,897,000, indicating a cash ratio of 12 per cent. Actually, as indicated in a footnote to the balance sheet, the bank held only £22,200 in specie, or less than 1 per cent of its liabilities. No other balance sheet until after 1845 yields comparable information.

In 1752 the Glasgow Ship Bank held £600 in silver against notes in circulation of £41,000, a ratio of less than 1.5 per cent; its total liabilities to the public amounted to more than £95,000, bringing the ratio to less than 0.7 per cent. In 1761 its cash/notes ratio was 1.8 per cent, and its cash to total liabilities ratio again was less than 1 per cent.[30] A final example: in 1800 the Dundee Commercial Bank had a capital of £2,500, liabilities to the public of £97,850, and "cash on hand and at call" of £23,424. Almost £20,000 of the latter item consisted of balances in London, Edinburgh and Glasgow; the "on hand" part, consisting of "Notes & Specie" (not separately designated), came to £3,744.[31]

The banks' casual reserve policies appear to have been linked to their even more casual accounting techniques, though it would be difficult to determine which was cause and which effect. The Bank of Scotland did not prepare annual balance sheets until 1797. Before that time it merely balanced individual accounts in the general ledger at irregular intervals, usu-

[29] Rait, *Union Bank of Scotland,* 5, 11–12.

[30] Ibid. 36–7.

[31] Boase, *Banking in Dundee,* 215.

CHART III.5

CASH RATIOS OF THE DUNDEE BANK, 1764–1864

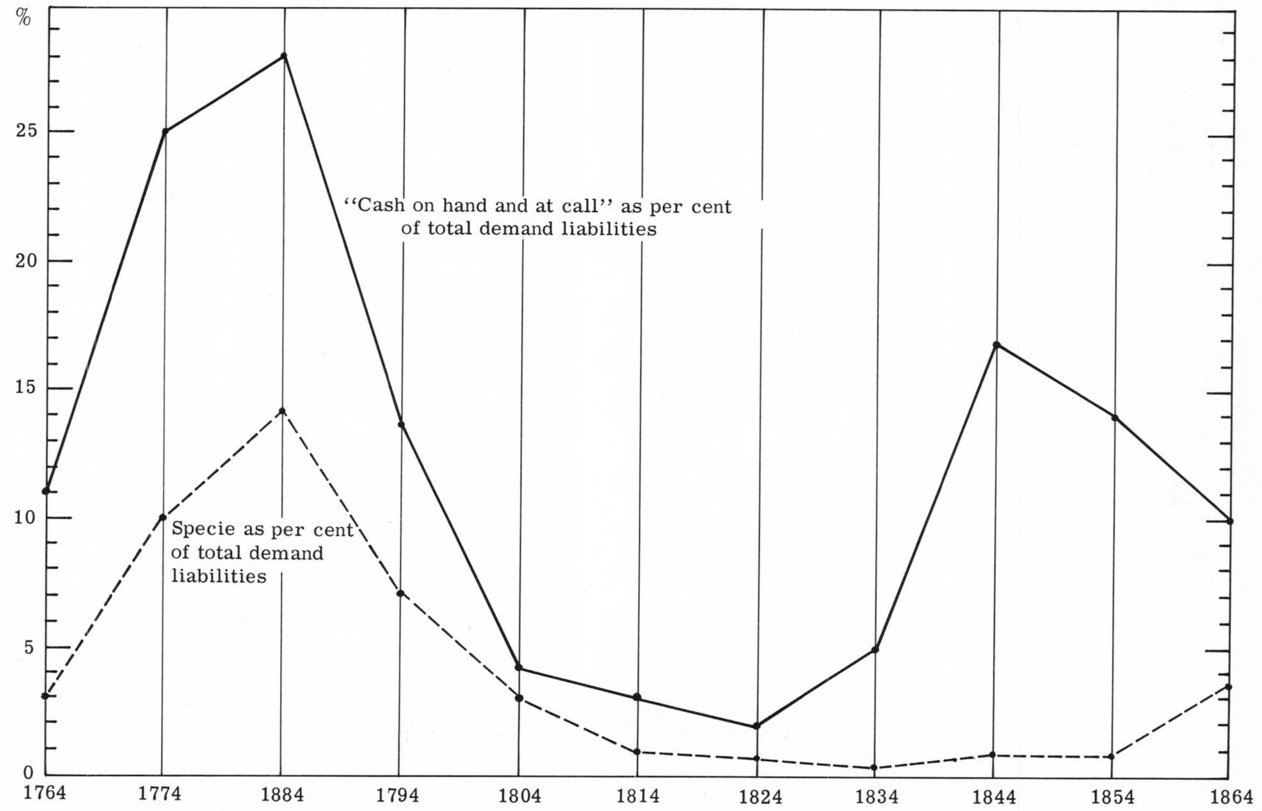

Source: Boase, *Banking in Dundee*.

CHART III.6

ROYAL BANK OF SCOTLAND, PRINCIPAL ASSETS,* 1817–1845

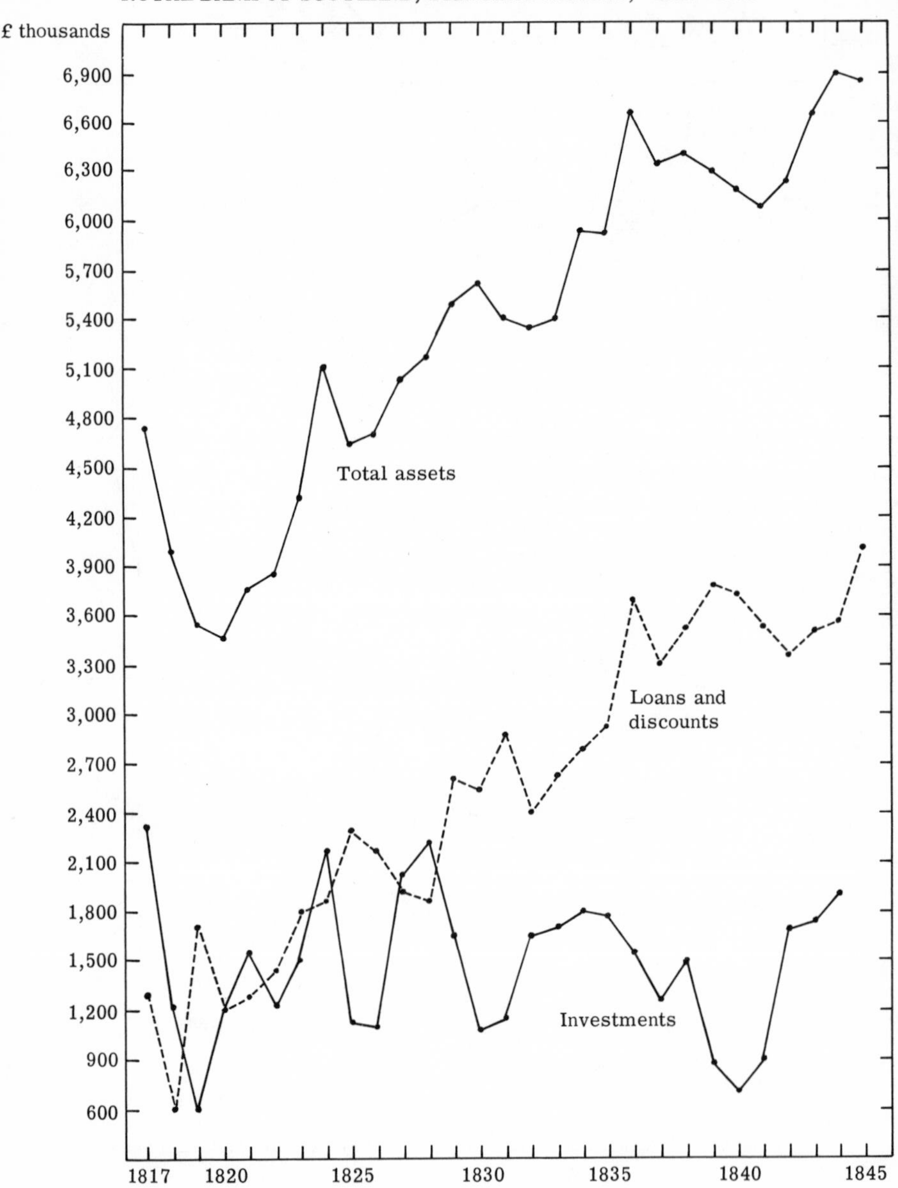

*Total assets inflated; see pp. 80-89.

CHART III.7

ROYAL BANK OF SCOTLAND, PRINCIPAL LIABILITIES,* 1817–1845

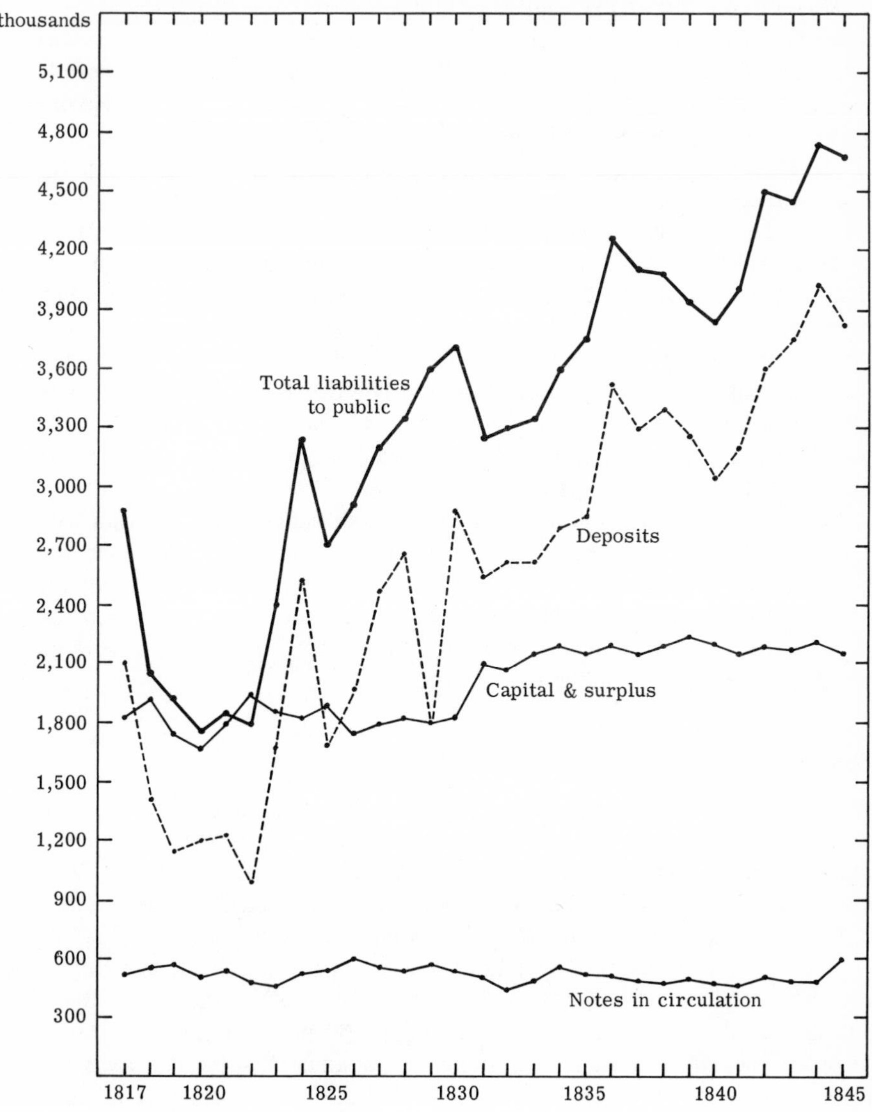

*Figures misleading; see p. 88-89.

ally every three years, from which it has been possible to prepare summary balance sheets. Those are not entirely accurate, however, due to the bank's practice of counting its own unissued notes and repurchased stock as both assets and liabilities. Even after 1797 accounting practice was by no means consistent; there is a long gap from 1823 to 1842 for which it is impossible to determine total assets (even in accordance with the bank's own reckoning) and several other major items.

The Royal Bank and apparently most other banks followed similar practices, which encompassed not merely accounting techniques and reserve policies. The "remarks" that accompany the Royal Bank's "State of Affairs of the Royal Bank on 29th Sept. 1817—with Remarks" give every indication that that was the first occasion on which the bank's own directors had been treated to such an intimate view of its situation. Banks in the Dundee district may have been exceptions to the general rule, but it is more likely that the admirable sets of accounts of the Dundee Banking Company and some other banks in the district have been preserved for posterity in the valedictory of the bank's last general manager because of Mr. Boase's own indefatigable energy and curiosity.

More fundamentally, the fact that the Scottish banks could function with such slender real reserves was due to widespread public acceptance of their notes, along with fractional coinage, as the most desirable if not the only legal form of money. Given this public attitude, it was quite reasonable for the banker to regard his own unissued notes as a reserve with which to meet sudden public demands for cash.

Bank Profits

Insofar as the rate of profit in a competitive industry under dynamic conditions is a measure of that industry's contribution to growth, the Scottish banks deserve a high rating, for banking was a profitable business in Scotland. Again, the Dundee Banking Company is our model; possibly it is a typical example. Founded in 1763 with an initial paid-in capital of £1,260, it amalgamated with the Royal Bank exactly a century later, exchanging the shares of its £100,000 capital at parity for those of the Royal Bank, whose own shares commanded a premium of 60 per cent. In the hundred years of the Dundee Bank's existence its annual gross profits averaged more than 25 per cent of its paid-up capital. Deducting expense of management and losses through bad debts, its "real total profit" averaged 11.7 per cent, from which dividends averaging 10 per cent were paid and the surplus, amounting to £57,171, or more than half its eventual capital, was plowed back.

Scattered figures for other banks suggest that 9 or 10 per cent may have been the average earning for the period as a whole, although wide variations existed, of course, both from year to year and among the banks. The general trend of profits seems to have been downward throughout the period and on until the 1860's, but this trend reversed itself in the 1870's and 1880's. In the 1830's and 1840's the typical dividend was between 6 and 8 per cent. The manager of the British Linen Company wrote in 1836 that his bank had paid a dividend of 8 per cent "for a considerable number of years." It continued to do so for a considerable number thereafter. The North of Scotland Bank, established in Aberdeen in 1838, had net profits of 8.8 per cent for its first eight years, but in the same period the newly established Clydesdale Bank in Glasgow averaged only 5.9 per cent.

Almost all Scottish banks followed a policy of building up reserves. The earlier partnerships, in fact, such as the Glasgow Arms and Ship banks, followed the traditional mercantile policy of paying "interest" of 5 per cent and returning the excess, if any, to capital. Most of the increases in capital of the large joint-stock banks in the nineteenth century resulted from conversions of surplus earnings.

Table III.3 shows the average rate of return of the Dundee Banking Company and the Bank of Scotland over an entire century. These are the only banks for which such continuous reçords exist. The comparison gives rise to some significant if tentative inferences. The smaller provincial bank had a higher over-all average than the Bank of Scotland, but much wider fluc-

TABLE III.3

AVERAGE RATES OF PROFIT IN SCOTTISH BANKS

(annual averages by decades, per cent)

	Dundee Bank	Bank of Scotland
1764–73	12.6	11.0
1774–83	19.1	6.8
1784–93	8.2	8.05
1794–1803	1.6	3.7
1804–13	23.0	7.1
1814–23	0.65	10.85
1824–33	10.1	8.5
1834–43	8.3	6.7
1844–53	10.05	6.8
1854–63	16.5	8.2
Over-all average	11.0	8.05

tuations about the mean. This was especially true during the difficult wartime and immediate postwar years. Whereas the Bank of Scotland invested heavily in government securities and similar investments through the London market, the Dundee Bank continued to devote the greater part of its resources to discounts and advances for local entrepreneurs. The Royal Bank and the British Linen Company resembled the Bank of Scotland in this respect, whereas the Commercial and most Glasgow and provincial banks resembled the Dundee Bank. Apparently the sure way to survival in the banking world of Scotland was to take the low road of relatively riskless invesments. Of those who took the high road, many did not survive, but those who did not only earned higher profits (this was true of at least the Commercial and the National, as well as the Dundee); they also had the satisfaction of contributing to the development of the national economy.

Chart III.8 has a dual purpose. On the one hand, it exhibits the annual variations of the rate of net profit of the Dundee Bank. On the other, it shows gross profit as a percentage of total assets, which is intended as a rough measure of the real cost of capital to the Scottish economy. Their divergence is not evidence of monopolistic profits or usurious lending practices. On the contrary, it is itself a measure of the contribution of the bank to capital formation and economic growth. In the absence of banks, as in much of Germany until after 1850, or with a bank monopoly or quasi-monopoly, as in France between 1800 and the 1850's, the cost was surely higher.

CONCLUSION

It is most unfortunate that there are no separate statistics of national income for Scotland for this period. It would not be unreasonable to infer, however, that in 1750 the per capita income of Scotland was no more than half that of England, but that by 1845 it very nearly equaled England's. A contemporary Scottish estimate for 1750 set a figure of £5,360,000 for total national income, giving a per capita figure of little more than £4, less than one-third of English per capita income of £16/5/2 as determined by Miss Deane. In the mid-twentieth century, on the other hand, per capita income in Scotland stood at about 92 per cent of England's. But Scotland in the mid-nineteenth century, nearing the peak of its greatest relative prosperity, was surely better off compared to England than is the depressed Scotland of the mid-twentieth century. Whether or not Scotland ever caught up with England in per capita income and industrial production, it is clear that its rate of progress between the mid-eighteenth

COMPARATIVE RATES OF RETURN, DUNDEE BANKING COMPANY, 1764–1845

CHART III.9

GRAIN PRICES IN SCOTLAND AND ENGLAND

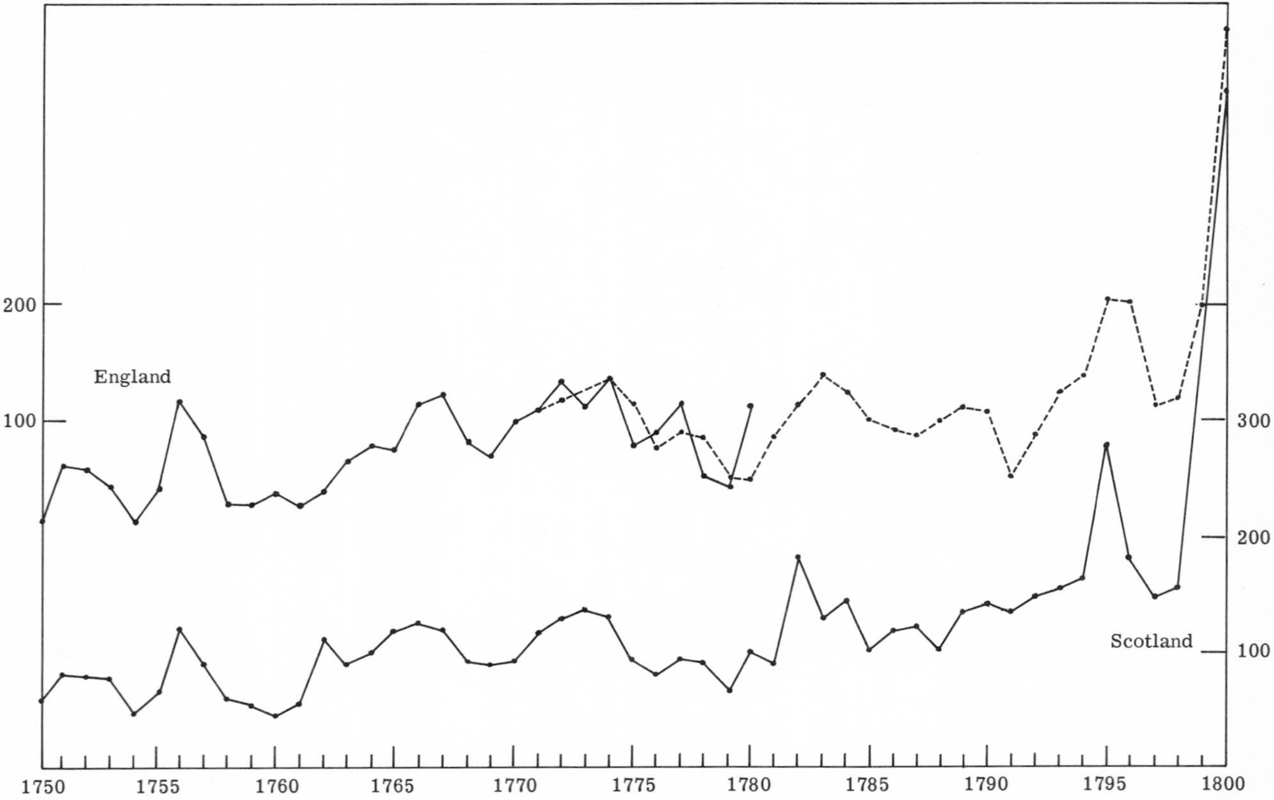

Base: 1771–79 = 100.

and mid-nineteenth centuries was far more rapid. The comparison with France is even more telling in Scotland's favor. Given its many disadvantages and few positive advantages for growth compared with its neighbors, the superiority of its banking system stands out as one of the major determining factors. Indeed, there is only one other that can rank with it: Scotland's educational system. (It is not without significance that Scotland's relative decline in the twentieth century has been accompanied by an increasing assimilation of Scottish educational and banking policies and practices into those of England. In banking, the process began in 1845.)

The superiority of the Scottish system consisted in (1) the freedom of issue, which facilitated the establishment of new banks, increased competition, and immediately provided the banks with the means to engage in productive credit creation; (2) the early establishment of branch banking, which further stimulated competition and assured the nation of an adequate supply of banking facilities, small enough in the individual unit to cater to the needs of small entrepreneurs but large enough in the aggregate to ensure stability and safety; (3) the tradition of small notes, which, as Adam Smith correctly pointed out, saved the nation thousands of pounds annually in the unnecessary expense of maintaining a large stock of sterile metal;[32] and (4) the resulting popularization of the banking habit, which led to the early development and widespread use of bank deposits as both outlets for saving and means of payment.

Given both freedom and competition, the banks developed a number of important financial innovations. High on the list of these is the cash credit system, the Schumpeterian "engine of credit" in almost pure form. David Dale, founder of the New Lanark Mills, and Royal Bank agent in Glasgow, received a cash credit of £1,000 from the Royal Bank in the same month that he secured the land on which the mills were built.[33] The bank also loaned to the Forth and Clyde Navigation Company, builder of the Forth and Clyde Canal; to Carron Company; to the Estate of Harris for the development of the kelp industry; and to thousands of enterprises of lesser note. Bankers also engaged directly in industry: the Dunlops of Glasgow, former "tobacco lords" and one of the notable families of that thriving, bustling city, participated in banking, coalmining, ironworking, textiles, and eventually rubber. On the other hand, as Thomas Kinnear pointed out, the willingness of bankers to grant cash credits to manufacturers on liberal terms "took away the temptation to issue their own notes,

[32] Smith, *Wealth of Nations,* 276–82.

[33] Royal Bank of Scotland, *Minutes,* vol. 13, p. 369, 19 May 1784.

as in England, where often a good manufacturer became a bad banker, and brought misery on his district." [34]

Among the other innovations and notable practices of the Scottish banks were the acceptance of small sums on deposit, the payment of interest on deposits, and the differentiation of deposit liabilities to accommodate the needs of a variety of depositors. These practices both stimulated the supply of savings and made it more mobile. On the other side, by providing for a variety of ways of borrowing in addition to cash credits (bills receivable, personal and heritable bonds, etc.) the banks enabled men of "good character and ability" but small means to go into business for themselves. In the words of a contemporary, "the general prosperity of the country and the facilities of procuring money on credit has promoted an uncommon spirit of enterprise of late and multiplied and extended manufactures of all kinds." [35]

While it might be thought that the multiplicity of note-issuing agencies and the use of small notes, which forced gold out of the country, would lead to inflation, monetary derangement, and instability, there is no evidence that this was the case. Chart III.9 compares grain prices in Scotland and England from 1750 to 1800, when the inflationary pressures, if such there were, should have been felt. Although the indexes are not the best imaginable, they are the only ones available. In any case, if strong inflationary pressures were at work, the prices of grain, the raw material for the staff of life, would surely show it—as indeed they do after the suspension of specie payments by the Bank of England in 1797. Such monetary derangement as occurred, apart from the brief and inconsequential "small note mania," was, in fact, introduced from England or from abroad. The same is broadly true for instability in general. Although Scotland had some bank failures, only that of the Ayr Bank (Douglas, Heron & Co.) of 1772 was of magnitude in its effects, and even that was partly introduced from abroad. By and large, the Scottish system rode through the numerous crises of the era with far less turbulence than did the English and some other, less developed systems.

The modern financial economist or historian can scarcely improve upon the judgment of one of Scotland's earliest and ablest bank historians:

> The comparative immunity from legislative interference which characterized banking in Scotland until the year 1844 has been an unmistakable blessing to the country, and has saved the banks from those vexatious and unnecessary distinctions and restrictions which have

[34] Quoted in Boase, *Banking in Dundee,* 342.

[35] *Considerations of the Present Scarcity and High Price of Coals in Scotland* (1793), quoted in Hamilton, *Economic History of Scotland,* 205n.

hampered and distorted English banking. In Scotland, banking was permitted to develop as the country advanced in wealth and in intelligence. Nay, it was even enabled to lead the nation on the path of prosperity, and to evolve, from practical experience, a natural and healthy system of banking, which would have been impossible under close state control similar to that followed in other countries.[36]

[36] Kerr, *History of Banking in Scotland,* 69–70.

IV
FRANCE
1800–1870

by Rondo Cameron

At the beginning of the nineteenth century France was the wealthiest nation in Europe. Its population was three times that of England, which was probably the only country with substantially higher levels of per capita income and wealth. During the next two generations France gained relative to England in per capita terms, but its lead in total wealth and income steadily dwindled, and ultimately, in the 1860's, it disappeared [1] (see Table IV.1). In the same decade the population of the states that were to become the German Empire in 1871 surpassed the population of France. The German states also took the lead in coal and iron production, although German income per capita probably continued to lag. Meanwhile, however, several smaller nations gained relative to France in per capita income.

The causes of the comparatively poor performance of the French economy in the industrial era, and in the nineteenth century in particular, have been debated extensively. Many contributory factors have been adduced, but as yet the debates have produced no clear consensus. In part the problem is illusory: when all growth rates are reduced to per capita terms much of the disparity between France and its neighbors disappears. Nevertheless a residue remains. A satisfactory explanation of this could have an important bearing on the understanding of the determinants of economic

[1] According to recent calculations by Jean Marczewski, the total "physical product" (i.e. excluding services) of Great Britain (England, Wales, and Scotland) did not exceed that of France until the 1880's or even 1890; much depends, however, on the method of weighting selected and on various other adjustments to the raw data. See Marczewski, *Histoire quantitative,* Part Two, chap. IV, esp. Tables 12–15. On a per capita basis, according to Marczewski, the British physical product fluctuated irregularly at levels 5 to 40 per cent above the French between 1815 and 1900. (Ibid. Table 30.)

TABLE IV.1

NATIONAL AND PER CAPITA INCOME, FRANCE AND GREAT BRITAIN, SELECTED YEARS, 1801–72

	National Income (£ million)		Per Capita Income (£)	
Year	France (NNP)	Great Britain (GNI)	France	Great Britain
1801	288	232	10.5	21.7
1847	544		14.5	
1851		523		25.0
		United Kingdom (NNI)		United Kingdom
1859	776	656	21.3	22.9
1872	888	1,072	24.6	33.6

Sources: Mitchell and Deane, *British Historical Statistics*, 366–7; Perroux, in Kuznets (ed.), *Income and Wealth*. The conversion of the French figures has been made at 25 francs/£, which probably undervalues the figures for 1801. The comparison, while very rough, is probably valid for depicting relative standing and general trends.

growth in general. In previous discussions elsewhere financial factors have received only secondary consideration when they have been considered at all. Even my own earlier contributions, though concerned in part with the development of financial institutions, did not deal systematically with their role in the process of industrialization.[2] It now appears that this neglect may have been a serious oversight. One need not, of course, go to the opposite extreme and classify financial institutions as a "major determinant" of either growth or stagnation. It is sufficient to accept the tautological assertion that, given a different financial structure and different monetary and banking policies, growth might have been either more or less rapid.

THE FINANCIAL STRUCTURE AND ITS EVOLUTION

France entered the nineteenth century with virtually a clean slate as far as financial institutions were concerned. The French had bitter recollections of John Law's ill-fated "system," the unfortunate Caisse d'Escompte, and, more recently, the disastrous episode of the *assignats*. Nevertheless, the new regime that issued from the *coup d'état* of *dix-huit*

[2] See, for example, Cameron, *France and Europe*, esp. chaps. VI and VII.

brumaire had a free choice of financial institutions. Unfortunately for France, the regime's choice—and the effects of that choice, which were re-enforced in subsequent legislation—contributed little to economic development and may have been a positive hindrance.

Origins and Early Years of the Bank of France

After the *coup d'état* Bonaparte needed a ready source of credit to finance the consolidation of his power within France and the extension of his conquests beyond its borders. Following the demonetization of the *assignats* in 1796 and the return to a metallic currency, several small note-issuing banks had sprung up in Paris and the provinces under the regime of common law. None of them was adequate for Bonaparte's purposes, but he quickly reached agreement with the directors of one, the Caisse des Comptes Courants, to enlarge it and transform it into the Bank of France. The Bank was capitalized at 30 million francs but had difficulty in placing its shares in spite of the personal example of the First Consul and his decree requiring government agents to purchase shares and to deposit their surplus funds in the Bank; almost two years elapsed before the entire capital was paid in. Meanwhile, however, the Bank opened its doors for business on 20 February 1800, in the offices of the former Caisse des Comptes Courants.

The Bank's principal functions consisted of discounting bills of exchange and making advances to the government. It also accepted deposits on current account, but inasmuch as it had no facilities for payment by check and did not permit overdrafts, these did not amount to much except for the government's deposits. Although it enjoyed government favor, it did not at first have a monopoly of issue; the other banks continued to discount bills and issued notes in competition with it, and at least one new bank arose after it. In 1803, however, the government granted the Bank a monopoly of issue, raised its capital to 45 million francs, and introduced a number of other changes in its organization. Some of its smaller erstwhile competitors amalgamated with it; others ceased to exist.

The government made heavy demands on the Bank in return for its favor. In December 1805, at the time of the battle of Austerlitz, short-term government obligations accounted for 80 million in a total of 97 million francs of securities in the Bank's portfolio; for the year as a whole advances to the government amounted to 228 million, against private discounts of 260 million. As early as September the Bank's specie reserve had fallen to little more than 1 million francs, whereas its liabilities to the public amounted to almost 100 million. In the face of this strong pressure the Bank restricted its private discounts still more and resorted to a partial suspension of specie payments. Napoleon blamed the Bank for the resulting crisis and reorganized it once more. Up to that time active management had been in the hands of a committee of directors. Napoleon replaced these with a governor and two deputy governors named by the government. The *conseil d'administration* (board of directors, composed of twelve *régents* and three *censeurs*) became a purely advisory body; in addition, Napoleon required that three of the regents be named from among the receivers-general of taxes. The Bank had become, in effect, an agency of the state.

The last years of the Empire again strained the Bank's resources, even though its capital had been raised to 90 million francs. In 1812 its advances to the government totaled 273 million francs, against 231 million in private discounts; in 1813 the figures were 341 million and 430 million, respectively, and in 1814 they were 269 million (mostly in the first four months) and 96 million.[3] In April 1814 the Bank went into virtual liquidation. Its portfolio of discounted bills held less than 2 million francs; it reduced its note circulation to 10 million by the simple expedient of refusing new discounts, and watched its deposits drop to little more than 1 million.

With the abdication of Napoleon, Jacques Laffitte, a private banker and regent of the Bank, became provisional governor. Laffitte attempted a wholesale reorganization of the Bank, but he was only partially successful. He reduced the capital to 67,900,000 francs and gave up the Bank's pretensions to a monopoly of issue for the whole of France (his fellow regents, however, could not be persuaded to give up their monopoly of Paris). Laffitte wanted to convert the Bank into a "simple commercial bank"; above all, he wanted to free it from government control. Baron Louis, the new finance minister, at first expressed approval, but, reflecting that the Bank might be as useful to the Restoration government as it had been to Napoleon, he subsequently reneged on his promises. Jaucourt wrote to Talleyrand:

> Forgetting all his past principles, so often and so long professed in so many gatherings of bankers, forgetting all that he had promised Laffitte, the conduct of the latter, the friendship which united them, he [Baron Louis] changed his mind and, pressed to declare his intention, told the representatives of the Bank, "You want to be independent, but you will not; you will have a governor, I will name him, and he will not be the one who currently occupies the post." [4]

[3] Banque de France, *Statistique annuelle.*

[4] Jaucourt (deputy minister of foreign affairs) to Talleyrand, Paris, 30 September 1814. Archives des Affaires Etrangères (Paris), *Mémoires et documents,* vol. 681, fol. 18 (copy in Archives de la Banque de France).

Provincial Banks and the Drive for Monopoly

Napoleon, against the wishes of the regents, had forced the Bank to establish branches at Lyon, Rouen, and Lille. It closed down these branches as quickly as possible after the fall of the Empire, and it did not object when the government chartered local banks of issue in Rouen (1817), Nantes (1818), and Bordeaux (1818). In function these banks resembled the Paris institution, although they operated on a far more restricted scale. Their notes had currency only in the *départements* in which they were located, and they could discount only those bills of exchange that were payable locally or in Paris. The government refused their request for mutual acceptance of one another's notes and drafts and in other ways circumscribed their freedom of action.[5]

Between 1835 and 1838 six new banks were chartered in such important cities as Lyon, Marseilles, and Toulouse. The Bank of France had earlier opposed branch banks on the grounds that they would be unprofitable and difficult to manage, but the government-appointed officials of the Bank overcame the elective regents' objections to the extension of the Bank's field of operations. One of the deputy governors made this statement.

> Since 1817, in very different circumstances from today, when the [old] branches of the Bank were closed at the request of the board, one has seen and one sees every day the principal commercial cities of France create similar establishments on their own initiative. Soon there will be nothing left of the monopoly of the Bank, the exercise of which could be profitable to the *départements* as to the Bank itself, and which would establish a more uniform and centralized circulation than that of isolated banks. . . . If the Bank does not wish to be completely disinherited in the *départements,* it must hasten to take steps to occupy the cities of the second order, in default of those of the first, in order to merit its title of *Bank of France,* and to preserve, in view of the approaching renewal of its charter, a facility which might otherwise be compromised.[6]

The Bank thereupon undertook to establish branches in a number of provincial cities, and at the same time the government refused to charter any new banks in the *départements.* Between 1836 and 1848 the Bank set up branches in 13 provincial centers. During the political and economic crisis of 1848, when all banks suspended specie payments, the Bank, with gov-

[5] Lévy-Leboyer, *Banques européennes,* 495–6.

[6] Banque de France, *Procès-verbaux du Conseil général,* vol. 20, fol. 220, 25 February 1836.

ernment authorization, forcibly absorbed the departmental banks. Thenceforth its monopoly of issue extended to the whole of France.

Other Financial Institutions before 1848

The Bank of France discounted bills of exchange payable only in Paris and, after 1836, in cities where it had branches. Moreover, the terms the Bank set for discount were so restrictive that they prevented many legitimate bills from being presented to it. The numerous voids thus created were filled, however imperfectly, by myriads of private bankers and discount merchants in both Paris and the provinces. It was they who, with their networks of correspondents, facilitated the movement of goods throughout the country and, by means of local discounts, provided working capital for domestic commerce and industry. They worked primarily with their own capital, and frequently engaged in commodity trade or served as commission merchants as well as dealing in bills of exchange. Some of the larger and best established houses, in Paris especially, also accepted deposits on which they paid interest; but insofar as they did so it was at long term only, from relatives or friends, for use in their own businesses. The absence of checking facilities limited their powers of credit creation to acceptances, and those had a very limited circulation.

A few of the private bankers in Paris could trace their origins to the old regime. Others grew out of the lucrative business of military contracting during the wars. Still others were foreigners, mainly Protestants from Switzerland and Jews from the Rhineland, who moved to Paris during the Empire or soon after. Some came from provincial centers. The wealthiest and most successful of this group became known collectively under the Restoration as *la haute banque parisienne*. They financed the bulk of international trade, frequently with the assistance of relatives in other countries. Even more significantly, they pioneered the techniques of investment banking. The first important moves in this direction came when they competed with Hope & Co. of Amsterdam and Barings of London for the privilege of underwriting the liberation loans of 1817–18. Rothschild soon acquired a virtual monopoly of the underwriting business, but prudence dictated that he occasionally share its profits with his fellow bankers. During the canal-building era of the 1820's and 1830's these same bankers took the lead in promoting canal companies and underwriting their issues of securities, an apprenticeship for similar work with railways in subsequent decades.

Another field for promotion pioneered in France by the *haute banque* was insurance. Insurance attracted them not only as a profitable field for the investment of their own capital and for underwriting profits, but also as a means of gaining control over additional funds. Laffitte and Benjamin Delessert took the lead in 1816 by founding a joint-stock insurance company with a royal charter, the Compagnie Royale d'Assurances Maritimes. Others followed quickly. By 1848 30 joint-stock insurance companies with a combined nominal capital of 175 million francs had their shares listed on the Paris Bourse. There were also many smaller companies, both in Paris and the provinces. The members of the *haute banque* kept a firm hand on the leading companies by means of interlocking directorates.

Delessert also took the lead in creating the first savings bank (*caisse d'épargne*), mainly from philanthropic motives. This was in 1818. By 1845 there were more than 350 of these institutions throughout France holding deposits amounting to nearly 400 million francs. The average balance per account came to 575 francs, indicating that the savings banks scarcely reached the day laborers and other low-income groups for whom they were designed. Like their English models, their assets were invested exclusively in government-guaranteed securities.

The Paris Bourse, or stock exchange, dated from the old regime. It had been suppressed during the Revolution, but was re-established under the Directory and reorganized by Napoleon. In 1815 it listed only French government securities, but soon thereafter the obligations of foreign powers and the shares and bonds of the canals and insurance companies were added. By 1848 railway securities and a few industrial stocks had made their appearance, greatly facilitating the work of the underwriting bankers.

Between 1800 and 1848 hopeful promoters made literally hundreds of applications to the government for charters for joint-stock banks. Many of the projects were hopelessly utopian or bizarre, but some were solidly conceived or had real merit as experimental ventures. Most involved note issue, but not all did. Nevertheless, except for the few departmental banks of issue, the government—with the wholehearted approval of the Bank of France—rejected all of them. Such formidable opposition resulted in the abandonment of most of the projects, but a few hardy entrepreneurs, such as Jacques Laffitte, who had been alienated from both the Bank and the government, persevered.

In 1837 Laffitte established the Caisse Générale du Commerce et de l'Industrie, using the *commandite* form of enterprise, which did not require government authorization. (He had intended to use "Banque" in the title, in place of "Caisse," but was dissuaded by the threat of sanctions from the Bank of France.) Effectively capitalized at 15 million francs (later raised to 20 million), Laffitte's Caisse Générale granted both short-term commercial credit and long-term industrial credit, as well as engaging in promotional activities. Discounts of commercial paper rose steadily from 276 million francs in 1838 to more than 400 milllion in 1846–47. The most notable innovation of the Caisse Générale was the issue of *billets à ordre,* negotiable interest-bearing notes payable at 5 to 30 days from sight, given in exchange for deposits. Although Laffitte was prevented from issuing notes payable to bearer on demand, with this device he was able to secure the control of resources several times as large as his own capital, and thus he also added an element to the monetary circulation.

Following Laffitte's establishment of the Caisse Générale several other similar institutions arose in both Paris and the provinces. In 1847 the five *caisses* in Paris had a combined capital of 57 million francs and discounted commercial paper for more than 1.65 billion francs. At least 20 *caisses,* with a combined capital of more than 70 million francs, were created in the provinces in the decade following 1838.[7] These new institutions played a significant role in the industrial boom of the 1840's, but the limitations of their structure, together with the hostility of the Bank of France, destined them to ultimate failure. Almost all perished in the financial crisis that accompanied the Revolution of 1848.

The Rise of Joint-stock Banks

Prior to 1848 the financial structure evolved slowly, almost imperceptibly. Apart from the *caisses* there were no important innovations in institutions, although the development of investment banking qualifies as a major innovation in techniques. The Revolution of 1848 opened the way for a series of major innovations in both institutions and techniques. In one way or another, all were associated with the creation of new joint-stock banks.

To meet the financial crisis the Provisional Government decreed the establishment of *comptoirs d'escompte* in all principal cities, to serve as intermediaries between merchants and industrialists and the Bank of France. Funds were provided or guaranteed in equal amounts by the state, the city administrations, and the patrons of the *comptoirs,* either by subscription or by deductions from the face value of bills offered for discount. Although the *comptoirs* were intended as temporary expedients, several eventually received more permanent status. That in Paris became a privately owned *société anonyme* in 1854, capitalized at 20 million francs. The *comptoir* at Lille eventually became the Crédit du Nord, a large regional bank. Both it and the Comptoir d'Escompte de Paris granted long-term as well as short-term credit and provided a variety of other financial services.

After the *coup d'état* of 1851 resolved the political uncertainties that had hampered full business recovery since 1848, the French economy entered the decade of its most rapid growth of the entire century. The gov-

[7] Gille, *Banque et crédit,* 121, 122, 124, 143; Lévy-Leboyer, *Banques européennes,* 504.

ernment of Napoleon III, wishing to encourage prosperity, facilitated the creation of several new financial institutions.

The Crédit Foncier de France, the earliest and one of the most important of these, was a centralized, nationwide mortgage bank. Capitalized at 30 million francs (one-half paid in) and with a government subsidy of 10 million, it obtained the bulk of its funds by issuing long-term bonds which soon became favorites with French investors. It played a large role in financing the reconstruction of Paris and other French cities, and financed many public works as well. To handle rural credit needs it created the Crédit Agricole and the Comptoir de l'Agriculture as subsidiaries. New loans granted annually rose from 25 million francs in the 1850's to 350 million in 1866.

The characteristic financial institution of the Second Empire, the Société Générale de Crédit Mobilier, also came into existence in 1852 as a part of the government's attempt to provide a counterweight to the influence of the Bank of France and the financiers of the *haute banque,* most of whom were hostile or at best lukewarm to the new regime. Capitalized at 60 million francs, the company could accept deposits on current accounts to twice that figure. Its statutes also conferred the right to issue both short-term obligations, similar to Laffitte's *billets à ordre,* and long-term bonds; it made scant use of either for a variety of reasons, including political considerations and the opposition of other financiers and the Bank of France.[8] The Crédit Mobilier was a *banque d'affaires,* the forerunner of the great "mixed banks" that became characteristic of Continental Europe in the latter part of the nineteenth century. It specialized in company promotion and provided general financial services for the enterprises it patronized. It was especially active in railways and other public works, and engaged extensively in foreign as well as French promotion and investment. In 1867, after it became involved in unsuccessful real-estate speculation, its enemies in the Bank of France took advantage of its embarrassment to force it into liquidation.

Requests for charters for banks, credit companies, and financial institutions of all types poured into government offices in the 1850's, but the Conseil d'Etat, the deciding authority in such matters, flatly rejected the great majority. As a result the entrepreneurs, as they had in the 1830's and 1840's, again resorted to the *commandite* form of organization, in even greater numbers than before. Numerous small *caisses d'escomptes,* brokerage houses, loan companies, and investment trusts sprang up in all parts of the country. Individually they were mostly trifling affairs; collectively, they added considerably to the nation's ability to mobilize capital.

[8] See Cameron, *France and Europe,* 137–46.

After the depression of 1857 revealed the undesirability of excessive reliance on the *commandite* form of organization for large-scale industry and commerce, the Conseil d'Etat liberalized its procedures for granting corporate charters. This liberalization eventually resulted in laws providing for free incorporation, passed in 1863 and 1867. In 1859 the government chartered the Crédit Industriel et Commercial. The founders represented themselves as wishing to create a large deposit bank and "naturalize" the English system of payment by check. In fact, in its early years the operations of the Crédit Industriel resembled in large measure those of the Crédit Mobilier. In 1863 it set up a subsidiary with a similar aim, the Société de Dépots et de Comptes Courants, and in the following year it assisted in the formation of similar banks in Lyon, Marseilles, and Lille. Deposit banking and the use of checks developed slowly, however.

The most important of the many new banks and credit companies that came into existence in the 1860's were the Crédit Lyonnais and the Société Générale pour Favoriser le Développement du Commerce et de l'Industrie en France. Both were primarily deposit and discount banks, although in their early years both also engaged in mixed banking. In the 1870's, both, along with the Comptoir d'Escompte, engaged in a vigorous campaign of expansion, covering France with competing networks of branches. This development was just barely visible prior to 1870, however.

In 1857, when the Bank of France had 37 branches in operation, the law renewing its privilege required it to establish at least one branch in every *département* if the government so requested. In 1870 the Bank had 60 branches in operation, leaving more than 25 *départements* without its services. The large deposit banks had only a few branches each. Nevertheless, by 1870 the basic pattern of the modern French banking structure had been fixed. It included the Bank of France in the center, the sole source of paper currency and supreme regulator of the system; a relatively small number of large joint-stock deposit banks—four or five—operating on a national scale; a much larger number of small local and regional banks in the provinces; a few *banques d'affaires;* and a number of specialized institutions for foreign commerce, mortgage credit, etc., some of which, like the Crédit Foncier, had quasi-official status. The old private bankers, though they were still in business, operated primarily as investment trusts; they transferred banking operations proper to the joint-stock banks that they controlled.

Some Quantitative Measures and Comparisons

Quantitative data on the French banking system in the nineteenth century are even more elusive and less reliable than those on England and Scotland in the eighteenth century. Gille, the foremost authority on French banking in the first half of the nineteenth century, makes no over-all estimates even of the number of banks. The major difficulty in that respect lies with the private bankers, especially in the provinces. Not only is there no list to which one can turn, but it is not even clear when, and to what extent, those individuals and partnerships who are known to have discounted bills and performed similar functions actually engaged in banking. Many did so only sporadically; almost all combined their banking functions with other occupations, and their operations were notoriously unstable. Even estimates of the number of joint-stock banks (including *sociétés en commandite par actions*) are subject to a large element of guesswork.

Granted the uncertainties regarding the number of banks, estimates of capital involved are almost wholly a matter of guesswork. The only element one can look upon with some certainty as to its validity is banknote circulation—one of the few obvious virtues of having a monopolistic note-issuing agency. Figures for equity capital can be derived only by adding to the few known figures (for the Bank of France and the larger joint-stock banks) the estimated average capitalization for the estimated number of banks—that, in turn, is derived from the haphazard but probably not representative sample of scattered data in surviving business records. Figures for deposits are obtained in the same fashion and suffer from an additional handicap when regarded as monetary liabilities, for not only were the majority of deposits not subject to check, most were not even payable on demand.

Subject to the reservations and qualifications indicated above, Table IV.2 attempts to give quantitative expression to the main components of the banking system. No sources are cited, for the simple reason that for more than half the "total resources," and for a still larger proportion of the number of banks, there are no sources properly speaking, only guesses. In spite of its fictional character, however, the table does yield some interesting insights. Even if the results are incorrect by a factor of 2 (and that is probably the appropriate confidence interval, with equal probability that the true figures are over- or understated) the inferences to be drawn would not be radically different. Comparison with English and Scottish data reveals that the complaints of French businessmen were justified: bank facilities were too few, and bank resources pitifully inadequate. At the end of its "take-off" period the French economy had approximately the same bank density as Scotland had had in the middle of the eighteenth century. France had fewer bank assets per inhabitant in the mid-nineteenth century than England or Scotland had had in 1770, and in 1870 had not reached the position that they had held before the beginning of the nineteenth century.

TABLE IV.2

EVOLUTION OF THE FRENCH BANKING STRUCTURE, 1800–1870

	1800	1810	1820	1830	1840	1850	1860	1870
				Number of Banks				
Joint-stock banks:[a]								
Paris	3	1	1	1	6	4	10	17
Provinces	1	0	3	3	15	20	98	132
Branches	0	3	0	0	3	25	48	100
Private banks:								
Paris	10	15	25	30	30	25	25	20
Provinces	50	60	100	150	250	200	200	200
Total offices	64	79	129	184	304	274	371	469
Persons per office (1,000's)	430	370	234	176	112	130	98	82
			Bank Resources (millions of current francs)					
Circulation	55	101	162	236	278	486	750	1,544
Deposits	20	60	120	160	300	400	600	1,200
Capital	27	110	132	178	370	350	900	1,000
Total resources	102	271	414	576	948	1,236	2,250	3,744
Assets per person (francs)	4	9	14	18	28	35	62	101

[a]Includes banks *en commandite* if shares were transferable.

These estimates, dubious though they are, seem to indicate an intimate correlation between the tardy development of the banking structure and the equally slow progress of industrialization in France. They do not, however, indicate whether the nature of the causal relation lay with an inadequate demand for banking services or with artificial restrictions in the supply. Proper consideration of the former possibility requires a discussion of the problems of industrial finance.

ASPECTS OF INDUSTRIAL FINANCE

The *Code de Commerce* of 1807 set forth the legal forms of business organization. Apart from individual enterprise, which remained free for most occupations, it provided for three types of associations: (1) *sociétés en nom collectif,* simple partnerships in which all partners were equally liable for the debts of the firms; (2) *sociétés en commandite,* limited partnerships in which the "active" partner or partners assumed unlimited liability, whereas the silent, "sleeping," or limited partners risked only the amounts they subscribed; and (3) *sociétés anonymes,* true joint-stock companies with limited liability for all shareholders. In addition, the *commandite* form had two subdivisions, the *commandite simple,* requiring re-organization or dissolution if any of the partners died or withdrew, and the *commandite par actions,* with transferable shares for the limited partners.

Until the passage of free incorporation laws in 1863 and 1867 each *société anonyme* required explicit and individual authorization by the Conseil d'Etat, frequently with special privileges, obligations, or restrictions attached. Generally speaking the Conseil d'Etat granted charters sparingly, and usually restricted them to industries vested with a public interest, although, as previously indicated, it was loath to grant them to banks because of the influence of the Bank of France. Insurance companies, in contrast, were required to assume the *anonyme* form. From 1819 to 1867 inclusive only 599 companies received charters. One-fourth were in transportation—canals, railways, shipping and transport, and bridge companies—and more than one-fifth were in insurance. Mining was the only industry not obviously in the public utility field to secure a sizable number, although some charters were granted in heavy metallurgy, textiles, sugar refining, glass, and paper.

The majority of industrial enterprises whose capital requirements surpassed the limits of simple partnerships therefore had to make use of the *commandite* form, which did not require special authorization but merely registration with a notary. After a court decision in 1832 gave legal approval to the practice of making shares "to bearer," the *commandite par actions au porteur,* whose shares could be listed on the Bourse, became the most common form of organization in many branches of industry. From 1826 to the end of 1837 only 157 *anonymes* obtained authorization, but more than 1,100 *commandites,* with a combined nominal capital four times as large as that of the *anonymes,* registered with the Tribunal de Commerce of the Seine (Paris) alone. In the first seven months of 1838, at the height of the boom, 301 *commandites,* with aggregate capital of 800 million francs, registered in Paris, although many disappeared in the financial crisis that followed. In the two decades from 1840 to 1860 *commandites par actions* were formed at an average rate of more than 200 per year, as against only 14 per year for *anonymes.* In addition, many small firms—more than all *commandites* and *anonymes* together—in light industries as well as the service trades continued to use the simple partnership or individual proprietorship.

Within this legal framework the French laid the foundations of modern industry. There is little if any reliable evidence of a marked "shortage" of either entrepreneurial talent or risk capital. The figures just cited are indicative of a heightened awareness of the possibilities of new enterprise and a desire to capitalize on them. The sharp rise in the price of government securities after the re-establishment of peace (the 5 per cent *rente* rose above par—100—early in 1824, having dropped to 55 as recently as 1817) proves that capital was available, and the willingness of investors to purchase foreign securities, even those of the revolutionary Spanish, Portuguese, Greek, and Haitian regimes, argues against the existence of a generalized high risk-aversion factor. The greater part of investable funds, however, went into domestic commerce, industry, and public works.

Between 1820 and 1860—that is, before the full development of the modern banking system—French industry underwent a profound structural transformation and a substantial if not spectacular expansion. Coal production, which averaged less than 1 million tons from 1816 to 1820, exceeded 8 million tons in 1860. Imports of coal rose even more rapidly, in spite of high tariffs, which points up the strong demand by growing industries. The iron industry, which was fired entirely by charcoal before 1820, quickly adopted the puddling process in refining, and completed the transition to coke smelting in the 1850's. Output of pig iron quintupled during the period. Until after 1850 France had more steam engines than all other Continental countries combined, and became a major producer of both steam engines and other industrial machinery. Most of the new machines went to the domestic textile industries, woolens and cotton in particular, which were the largest users of steam engines and other mechanical equipment as well as the most important industries. Consumption of raw cotton, which rose from 12 million to 60 million kilograms between 1815 and 1845, expanded still more rapidly in the 1850's. The chemical, glass, porcelain, and paper industries, among others, grew rapidly and benefited from constant technical improvements. A number of new industries either originated or were quickly naturalized in France in this period, including gas lighting, matches, photography, electroplating and galvanization, and the manufacture of vulcanized rubber.

The capital for this transformation came in part from established firms, in textiles especially, and in part from private bankers, notably in mining and heavy metallurgy. In both cases the expansion was carried forward by the reinvestment of profits. Among the outstanding characteristics of the banker-entrepreneurs of the period were their versatility and the variety of their interests. Benjamin Delessert, before promoting insurance companies and savings banks, founded a cotton spinnery (1801), built the first refinery for sugar beets, and played a leading role in the Société d'Encouragement pour l'Industrie Nationale. Jacques Laffitte, in addition to his banking and political interests, had investments in newspapers and printing establishments, a gas company, a cotton mill, a chemical factory, a glass-works, and several coal mines and ironworks. Casimir Perier, before succeeding Laffitte as second prime minister under the July Monarchy, reorganized the Anzin coalmining company, the greatest in France, and had an interest with his brother in the foundry and machine shops of Chaillot, where, before the Revolution, the first Continental steam engines had been built. André Koechlin, head of Dollfus-Mieg et Cie., the first French cotton mill to use a steam engine (in 1812), founded the machine shops that produced the first French locomotives; he also had extensive industrial interests in Germany as well as in France. François Seillière, from a Vosges textile family, financed the Schneider brothers in the famous ironworks and machine shops of Le Creusot and also had investments in German mining and metallurgical establishments; as one of the leading personalities in the Crédit Mobilier he played a major role in railway finance both in France and abroad.

With this record in view one might well ask in what respect the French banking system was inadequate. The main problem was the shortage of working capital for industry, which limited the rate of expansion of output and kept firms under constant financial pressure. The larger scale of enterprise in the nineteenth century required larger initial outlays of capital than in eighteenth-century Britain, and, until the development of a broad market for industrial securities, immobilized the promotional capital in fixed plant and equipment. The initial capital of the Société des Houilleres et Fonderies de l'Aveyron in 1826, 1.8 million francs (equal to £72,000 at the rate of exchange then current), may be compared with the initial capital of Carron Company in 1759, £12,000, or with the £50,000 estimated as the cost of a complete new ironworks in England in 1812.[9] To be sure, within a decade the capital of Carron Company had increased fivefold and the company was still in financial straits; but the same was true of Aveyron ten years after its establishment, in spite of the support of five prominent Paris bankers. Nor was Aveyron an isolated or extreme example

Faced with such difficulties, French entrepreneurs sought to overcome them in two different ways. One was to broaden the market for industrial securities, and in this they eventually succeeded. The experience of the *haute banque* in underwriting government loans and promoting insurance and canal companies in the 1820's stood them in good stead. With the advent of the railways in the 1830's a broader market became an absolute necessity. For major undertakings, such as the Chemin de fer du Nord or

[9] See above, p. 37.

the Paris-Lyon, a large consortium of bankers was necessary merely to underwrite the initial issue of securities for distribution to the public, even with a Rothschild in their midst. Without a Rothschild, only a large joint-stock bank could do the job. In fact, the immediate occasion for the founding of the Crédit Mobilier was the withdrawal of the Rothschilds from the syndicate formed to build the Chemin de fer du Midi.[10] The spectacular early success of the Crédit Mobilier, and the impetus it gave to the establishment of similar institutions both in France and abroad, derived in large measure from its ability to interest numerous investors of moderate means both in its own securities and in those of the enterprises it patronized.

The other means of dealing with the shortage of working capital, repeatedly attempted by Laffitte from 1814 until his death in 1844, was to reorganize the commercial banking system. Laffitte failed in this, as did numerous other reformers after him. This failure, which affected even large enterprises like Laffitte's and Aveyron, was especially serious for the numerous small industrialists who could not interest the great bankers in their enterprises or, if they could, feared loss of control and independence. Lack of easy access to short-term credit for working capital condemned them to remain small, and eventually bred the psychological outlook associated with petty capitalism. Thus resulted the schizophrenic development of French industry and commerce, traces of which can still be seen today: on the one hand a highly capitalized, technically efficient and progressive sector, on the other a sector composed of small firms, undercapitalized, traditional but tenacious.

MONETARY AND CREDIT POLICY

The principal reasons for the scarcity of short-term credit for working capital lay with the monetary and credit policies pursued by the government and the Bank of France. The primary determinants of these policies were, in order, the needs and convenience of the Treasury, the attitudes of the *hautes fonctionnaires* named to the posts of governor and deputy governor of the Bank, and the pecuniary interests of the Bank's stockholders.

The Stock of Money and Its Composition

Table IV.3 presents estimates of the stock of money by principal categories at various dates. The tenuous nature of the estimates scarcely needs em-

[10] Cameron, *France and Europe,* 136–7. The promoters of the Crédit Mobilier intended it as a "railway bank" and proposed to call it the "Banque de Travaux Publics."

TABLE IV.3

STOCK OF MONEY, NATIONAL INCOME, AND VELOCITY OF CIRCULATION, FRANCE, 1789–1910

	1789	1803	1845	1870	1885	1900	1910
Components of the Stock of Money (billions of francs)							
Gold		.65	.5	5.0	4.6		
Silver		1.20	3.0	2.0	2.8		
Total specie		1.85	3.5	7.0	7.4	6.7	8.4
Less reserves		a	.3	1.1	1.9	.5	.7
Specie in circulation	2.2	1.80	3.2	5.9	5.5	6.2	7.7
Banknotes	.1	.10	.3	1.5	3.1	4.2	5.3
Deposits	a	a	.4	1.2	2.0	5.0	10.4
Total money	2.3	1.90	3.9	8.6	10.6	15.4	23.4
Components of the Stock of Money (percentages)							
Specie in circulation	96.	95.	82.	68.	52.	40.	33.
Banknotes	4.	5.	8.	18.	29.	27.	23.
Deposits			10.	14.	19.	33.	44.
National Income (billions) and Velocity of Circulation							
Net national product	6.1	7.2	12.5	24.0	26.5	32.0	38.2
V(= NNP/M)	2.7	3.8	3.2	2.8	2.5	2.1	1.6

[a]Less than 50 million.

Sources: Net national product: Perroux, in Kuznets (ed.), *Income and Wealth*, Series V (interpolated where necessary).
Banknotes: Banque de France, *Statistique annuelle*, except as otherwise indicated.
Deposits: my estimates, except as otherwise indicated.
Specie: 1789, Palmade, *Capitalistes et capitalisme français*, 35n, citing various authorities. (Banknotes of the Caisse d'Escompte from Courtois, *Histoire des banques*, 328).

1803 and 1845, Bigo, *Banques françaises*, 39–41, citing contemporary authorities.

1870, Victor Bonnet, cited by Hollingsbery, *Handbook of Gold and Silver*, 205.

1885, Foville, *Economiste français*, 19 September 1891.

1900 and 1910, all figures on money stock from *Annuaire statistique de la France, edition retrospectif* (1961), 326 (original estimates by I.N.S.E.E.).

phasis. The series on deposits is, of course, open to the same objections as in Table IV.2. The estimates of specie in circulation, on the other hand, are probably better than for most other countries, including Britain. In the latter part of the nineteenth century the Ministry of Finance conducted a series of experiments, sampling the stocks of coin in public offices and the larger banks to determine their age and rate of survival. From the data obtained it is possible to estimate the total quantity of specie with a fair degree of accuracy.[11] The series on banknotes in circulation is about as reliable as such can be.

The outstanding features of Table IV.3 are the unusual predominance of specie and the slow development of deposits. With the experience of John Law and the *assignats* behind them, the French monetary authorities made it a cardinal point of policy to maintain a specie standard. Twice during the nineteenth century, in 1848 and in 1870, the Bank of France had to suspend specie payments, but on both occasions it resumed them before the date specified by law. Nominally France maintained a bimetallic standard throughout the century. In fact, silver constituted the greater part of the coinage before 1850, gold did thereafter. In the 1840's Léon Faucher estimated that France possessed one-third of all money metals in Europe; other estimates ranged even higher. From 1848 to 1867, following the gold discoveries in California and Australia, France alone coined 40 per cent of total world production of gold. It is easy to understand, therefore, why Frenchmen gained a reputation for hoarding. Every peasant, it was said, had his *bas de laine* stuffed with silver *écus,* gold *Napoléons,* and their equivalents. The figures on velocity, however, show that, on the average, Frenchmen held a lower proportion of their income in the form of money than did Englishmen. This is what one would expect in view of the higher per capita incomes of Englishmen and the elasticity of demand for money with respect to income. Moreover, whatever the propensity to save or the state of liquidity preference, the precise form in which cash balances are held depends upon the costs of the various alternatives. The main reason why gold and silver figured so prominently in the stock of money in France was that there was a limited supply of, and a high cost of holding, other monetary assets.

Until 1847 the smallest denomination of note issued by the Bank of France was 500 francs—a sum larger than the annual per capita income in France. In 1847, under pressure from the government after numerous complaints by the Paris Chamber of Commerce and other business groups, the Bank began to issue notes for 200 francs, and during the suspension of specie payments in 1848 it issued still smaller notes, also at government insistence; but, characteristically, it began to retire the small notes even before the resumption of payments. As a result its notes circulated (except during the suspension) only among wealthy financiers and wholesale merchants. Even in Paris the majority of inhabitants had never seen a banknote,

[11] See *Bulletin de statistique et législation financière,* XXX (1891), 121ff; *Economiste français,* 19 September 1891; Dolléans, *Questions monétaires contemporaines,* 48ff.

much less owned one; in most *départements* banknotes were completely unknown.

The Bank had stated its position on small notes as early as 1803.

> The appetite for gain must not lead a great establishment to issue notes for petty sums which have no other purpose than to attain the hands of the people, to descend to daily transactions and drive out silver. . . . [They would] fall into the hands of a great number of individuals who would soon form crowds at the door of any bank and spread alarm among all holders of notes. . . . It is by dividing notes into small fractions that they can be used for discounts in retail trade, where it is dangerous to introduce facilities that would produce an accumulation of merchandise out of proportion to local consumption.[12]

After the crisis of 1848 the government insisted that the Bank continue to issue notes of 100 francs and in 1865 pressured it to issue notes of 50 francs as well. During the second suspension of specie payments, 1870–75, the Bank again issued notes of 25, 20, and 5 francs, but again withdrew them before the full resumption of cash payments. By this time the increase in the number of the Bank's branches and the *cours forcé* had accustomed the population to the Bank's notes, and they figured more prominently in the money supply. But the Bank by preference continued to issue large notes whenever possible; the aggregate value of its 1,000 franc notes surpassed all other denominations and usually amounted to half or more of total issues.

At no time in the nineteenth century, except during periods of suspension, did banknotes equal the quantity of specie in circulation, not because the public would not accept them—the contrary was the case [13]—but because the Bank chose not to issue them in appropriate denominations.

There are a number of reasons for the slow growth of deposits. Perhaps the most important was the refusal of the government to charter joint-stock banks before 1848. The Bank of France paid no interest on its *comptes courants,* private bankers could not accept demand deposits because of the nature of their assets, and the *caisses* were forbidden by law to redeem their *billets à intérêt* on demand. The statutes regulating the Crédit Mobilier forbade it to accept deposits for more than twice its paid-in capital, and similar restrictions applied to other chartered banks. Another important obstacle to the growth of deposits was the fact that checks were not recog-

[12] Quoted in Ramon, *Banque de France,* 45–6.

[13] In 1865 a petition of textile merchants and manufacturers, protesting the restrictive credit policies of the Bank of France, stated that they would view "without fear" legal tender status for the Bank's notes, which they felt should be issued in small denominations so as to replace specie in ordinary transactions. See France, Conseil supérieur, *Enquête . . .*, I, 61–140.

nized by law until 1865. Moreover, the law that gave them legal definition was hedged with qualifications to prevent them from being used as "instruments of credit" instead of simple means of payment: post-dating and overdrafts were specifically forbidden. In 1871 a tax of 10 centimes was imposed on each check, and it was soon raised to 20 centimes on checks payable in cities other than the one in which they were drawn. In 1872 the principal Paris banks created a *chambre de compensation,* or clearing house, but after ten years its clearings amounted to but a tiny fraction—less than 5 per cent—of similar operations in London and New York. As late as 1900 clearings in Paris totaled less than 17 billion francs, compared with more than 200 billion (equivalent) in London and 446 billion in New York.[14]

Table IV.3 contains no estimates for bills of exchange. The omission is regrettable, for bills certainly circulated as money, but there are few data on their quantitative importance. It was said that an annual commerce of 200 million livres was carried on in Marseilles before the Revolution with only 700,000 to 800,000 livres in specie,[15] and pre-Revolutionary Lyon was famous for its *Quatre Payements,* quarterly settling days on which all bills were cleared, thus obviating the use of much specie. In 1836 the regents of the Bank of France, discussing an application for a new bank of issue in Lille, admitted the importance of bills of exchange as a means of payment: "The discount of bills on Paris is a necessity for Lille, for such bills form, as in other commercial centers, the principal element in the circulation. They are a sort of money with which the greater part of merchandise is paid for." [16] Estimates of the annual drawings of bills of exchange in the 1830's and 1840's range from 11 billion to 22 billion francs.[17] Professor Lévy-Leboyer has suggested annual drawings of 20 billion francs for the years around 1840; if the average usance of these bills were 90 days, the average daily circulation of bills of exchange would have exceeded all other means of payment by more than 25 per cent.

Such attempts to economize on specie availed little in the absence of more adequate banking facilities. Fewer than 10 percent of the estimated number of bills were discounted or rediscounted by banks of issue. The Bank of France itself was the greatest "hoarder" of metal. As Chart IV.1 indicates, the Bank's specie reserves rarely fell below 80 per cent of its note liabilities, even in periods of crisis; it was not unknown for its reserves

[14] Courtois, *Histoire des banques,* 364; Dolléans, *Questions monétaires contemporaines,* 108; Vigne, *La Banque à Lyon,* 242–3.

[15] Palmade, *Capitalistes et capitalisme français,* 35.

[16] Banque de France, "Déliberations du Conseil général," vol. 20, fol. 210, 25 February 1836.

[17] Lévy-Leboyer, *Banques européennes,* 501.

CHART IV.1

BANK OF FRANCE, PRINCIPAL ACCOUNTS, ANNUAL AVERAGES, 1800–1880

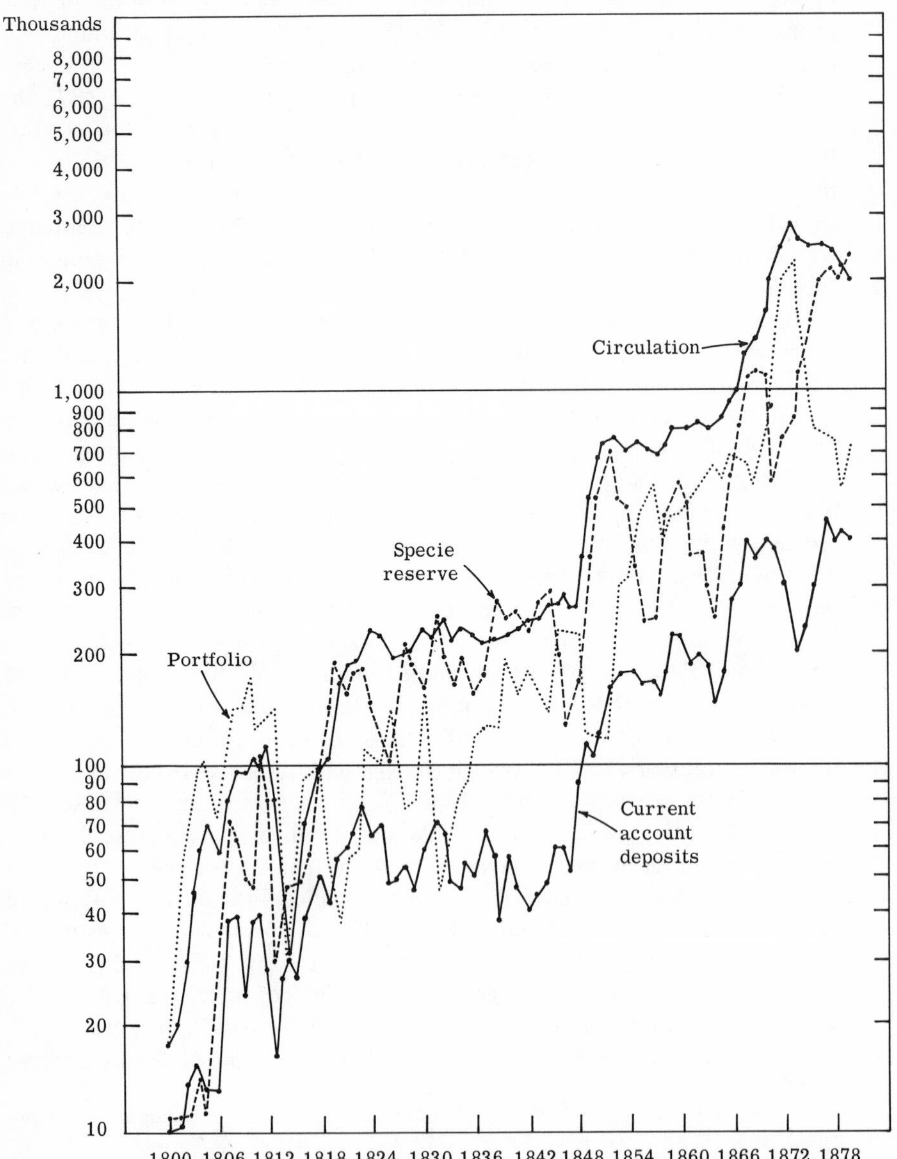

to exceed its issues. Such policies, though "sound" and "prudent" for the Bank, were expensive for the country at large.

The Conditions of Credit

The immediate cause of the scarcity of short-term credit is to be found in the conditions under which such credits were granted. The Bank of France, the only institution with the power to create generally acceptable means of payment, did so sparingly and on terms which effectively proscribed the use of short-term credit for development purposes. (See Chart IV.2.) For the first three decades of the Bank's existence the only channel of any significance by which its notes could get into circulation, apart from advances to the government, was by commercial discount. (The Bank also made advances against deposits of gold and silver bullion, but these were of little quantitative importance and in any case did not create additional means of payment.) The conditions for admission to discount were severe. Before being approved a merchant or banker usually had first to open a current account with the Bank, then undergo a careful screening of his character and financial resources by a committee of Bank directors. The potential client also had to reside in Paris, although exceptions were occasionally made for important receivers-general of taxes in the provinces.[18] Most important of all were the fixed rules for the eligibility of paper for discount: every bill presented had to carry the signature of three merchants or bankers "of notable solvency," have a term of 90 days at most (and less in time of stringency), and be payable in Paris. Even then there was no guarantee that it would be accepted. In effect, this limited the Bank's function to rediscount for the relatively small group of merchants and bankers who formed its select clientele. The benefit of its moderate rate of discount—4 per cent for most of the first half of the century—thus went to them, and not to the original borrowers, who paid the intermediaries from 4.5 to 8 per cent, according to their financial standing and bargaining power. Small merchants, manufacturers, and artisans were effectively prohibited, as the founders of the Bank had intended: until 1848 the average value of bills discounted never fell below 1,000 francs, and that at a time when per capita annual income was between 200 and 300 francs.

On numerous occasions attempts were made, both from within and without the Bank, to modify and relax this rigid regime of credit. In 1814, at the time Laffitte tried to free the Bank from government control, a modest proposal was made in the *Conseil général* to allow the substitution of Bank shares or government securities for the third signature. Among the

[18] Gille, *Banque et crédit,* 86.

CHART IV.2

BANK OF FRANCE, DISCOUNTS AND ADVANCES, ANNUAL TOTALS, 1800–1880

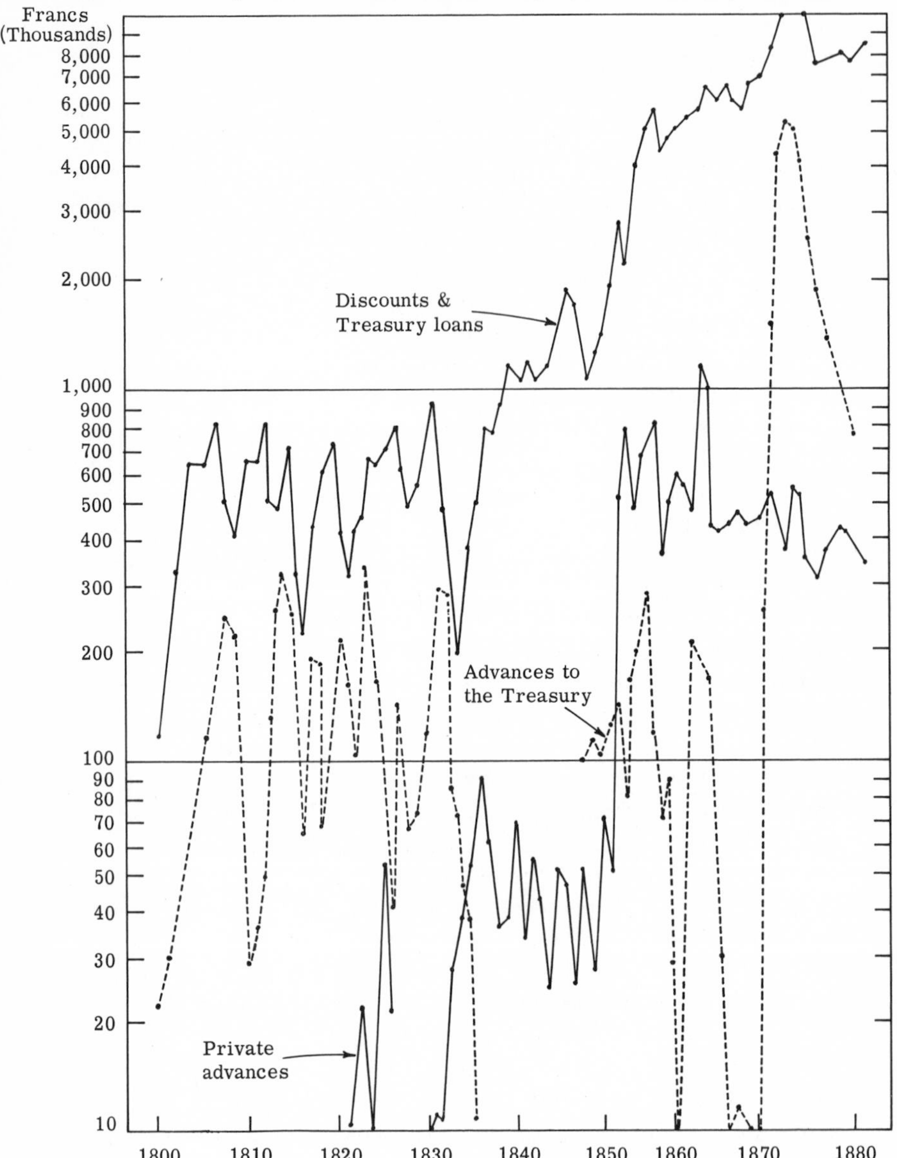

arguments in favor was that "manufacturers and wholesale merchants who sell on credit can obtain only bills with two signatures." [19] To this it was objected that there would be problems of "unknown" or "little known" merchants bringing bills for discount, creating additional risk and bother. Although the *Conseil* adopted the proposal in principle, the failure of the Bank to get its charter revised postponed implementation until 1833, when government-guaranteed securities were accepted in lieu of the third signature. The following year a new law authorized the Bank to make direct advances upon deposit of *rentes*—in part a measure to improve their marketability—but at the same time the Bank and the government together successfully opposed an amendment which would have authorized the Bank to create a special *comptoir* for retail merchants which would discount two-signature paper for terms up to six months at a fixed rate of interest of 5 per cent.

The charter renewal of 1840 was the occasion of numerous petitions to amend the conditions on which the Bank granted credit, but the Bank and the government again resisted all "radical" innovations. Adolphe Thiers, then prime minister, personally led the defense of the Bank's position: "It is an excellent thing to require industry to undertake only short-term engagements, because in obliging it to renew its engagements more frequently you habituate it not to trust too much to its future and you insure that there will be more payments, more liquidations, more movement, a greater circulation of capital." [20] As a member of the opposition pointed out, the logical conclusion of the argument was that no credit at all should be granted. The *rapporteur* for the committee of the Chamber of Deputies which reported in favor of charter renewal came very close to this position: "Your Committee approve the limits within which the action of the Bank has been circumscribed; they cannot give their assent to any of the projects contained in the petition which the Chamber has received, and which would make of the Bank of France a merchant *or a banker*." [21]

Complaints against the Bank's policy continued to be made throughout the century, but such improvements in its services as were made usually resulted from competition or for the convenience of the government. Prior to 1837 the Bank discounted bills only three days each week, and did not credit the borrower with the sum discounted until the following day. Laffitte's Caisse Générale discounted daily and paid the value of the discount immediately; within a few weeks of its establishment the Bank of

[19] Banque de France, "Déliberations du Conseil général," 11 July 1814.

[20] Ramon, *Banque de France,* 190; the Bank presented Thiers a special gold medal in appreciation of his services.

[21] English translation in British State Papers, *Report of Select Committee on Banks of Issue,* 1840, Appendix 36, p. 361. Italics mine.

France did likewise. In 1852, in order to facilitate the government's encouragement of railway construction and the rebuilding of Paris, the Bank began to make advances on railway securities and bonds of the City of Paris, and in 1854 it opened a "depository for securities" for the collection of interest and dividends in order to compete with the Crédit Mobilier and the *commandite* banks specializing in stock market speculation. By 1870 the competition of the new joint-stock banks forced it to accept deposits of a variety of negotiable securities in lieu of the third signature, and it ceased to be exclusively a bank of rediscount. The Bank held aloof from the *chambre de compensation* at first, but in the first year of its institution the Bank's deposits on current account fell drastically—by almost 100 million francs—while those of the clearing banks rose accordingly; the Bank joined the *chambre* shortly after the beginning of its second year.

However onerous the terms of borrowing from the Bank of France were, directly or indirectly, the great majority of French entrepreneurs had no access to its funds at all until well into the second half of the nineteenth century. In the 1840's, when the cost of credit in Paris varied from 3 to 8 per cent, depending upon the status of the borrower, it ranged from 6 to 18 and even 30 per cent in cities without banks of issue.[22] It was conditions such as these that were responsible for the strong movement for departmental banks of issue in the late 1830's and early 1840's. The Bank's reaction has already been noted, but it should be pointed out that its opposition to new banks concerned not only objection to the number of competitors but also to the forms of competition.

The Suppression of Competition

The decision to establish branches and to oppose the formation of new departmental banks of issue was not unanimous within the Conseil. Benjamin Delessert, for example, alleged that branch managers would be "tempted to extend credit imprudently"—especially to their friends—in the expectation that the head office would bail them out if necessary.[23] He opposed the establishment of branches but was perfectly willing to see the establishment of independent departmental banks, using local capital. The majority of the regents, however, fell in with the government-appointed governor and deputy governors. They sought not only to protect their monopoly, but also to impose their orthodoxy on the provinces by preventing such "dangerous innovations" as the payment of interest on

[22] Gille, *Banque et crédit,* 147.

[23] Banque de France, *Procès-verbaux du Conseil général,* vol. 20, fol. 235, 17 March 1836.

deposits.[24] Above all, they feared a departure from that fundamental canon of "sound banking," the restriction of lending to short-term self-liquidating commercial purposes.

> By a rule of prudence which experience has not yet falsified, banks of discount (except those of the United States) have generally adopted as a base of their operations the number of three endorsements and the term of three months. [The projected bank in Lille] would reduce the number of endorsements and extend the term. . . . It is all the more necessary to prevent *loans on a single signature with pledges of securities;* otherwise the bank could become a lender [*maison de prêts*] on industrial shares, merchandise, mortgages . . . [etc.]. One cannot be too severe in preventing such an indeterminate extension [of credit] on such a dangerous base.[25]

The Bank of France was consulted regularly by the government whenever applications for new banks came in, and it succeeded in killing projected banks in Chartres, Foix, Amiens, Nimes, Avignon, Bourges, Nevers, Limoges, Angouleme, and Dijon, and imposed delays and modifications in the terms of charters granted to banks in Lille, Toulouse, and other cities. The regents forced the proposed bank at Lille to change its name from "Banque du Nord" to "Banque de Lille," and exhibited a paternalistic attitude in turning down its request to discount bills on Bordeaux, Lyon, and other cities with banks of issue: "We propose *to authorize* the projected bank to take bills on Lille, Paris, Tourcoing and Roubaix." [26] In almost every case the Bank objected to any variation from the form of its own statutes in proposals for new banks. One of the heresies of the proposed bank in Dijon, which resulted in its outright rejection, was its intention to create branches within a range of 150 kilometers of Dijon.[27] The Bank also vetoed a proposed second bank in Rouen, although the project had the support of the Chamber of Commerce of that city.[28]

When the Bank's own charter came up for renewal in 1840 the departmental banks tried to take advantage of the occasion to secure modifications in the conditions of their own operations. Acting in concert, they petitioned the Chambers for permission to discount bills drawn on any city in which an authorized bank existed, to accept one another's notes and to form a nation-wide note exchange, to substitute deposits of their own shares for the third signature on bills of exchange, to pay interest on deposits, to

[24] Ibid. vol. 21, fols. 57–9, 30 March 1837, with reference to the proposed bank at Dijon.

[25] Ibid. vol. 20, fol. 211, 25 February 1836. Italics in the original.

[26] Ibid. fol. 212. Italics mine.

[27] Ibid. vol. 21, fols. 57–9, 30 March 1837.

[28] Ibid. vol. 20, fols. 313–19, 14 and 21 July 1836.

liberalize the use of current accounts, and to issue notes for as little as 100 francs. The Bank and the government stood together, however, and the law renewing the Bank's charter was adopted with only minor modification. Not only were the proposals of the departmental banks rejected, but the law specified that in the future new charters *or renewals* for departmental banks would require a special law, whereas the Bank might establish additional branches merely on the authority of a royal ordinance. The stage was thus set for the final take-over in 1848.

The Revolution of 1848 and its sequel, although it resulted in an absolute monopoly of note issue for the Bank, temporarily weakened its ties with the government and opened the way for additional competition in other spheres. The Provisional Government, when it created the *comptoirs d'escompte,* did not consult the Conseil d'Etat, long the bastion of the Bank's defenses within the government. The new powers that issued from the *coup d'état* of 1851 declared an uneasy truce with the Bank of France and the old-line private bankers so closely allied with the Orleanists. Persigny, hatchet-man for Louis Napoleon, personally railroaded the charter of the Crédit Mobilier through the Conseil d'Etat. In subsequent years, however, after the new regime had proved its staying power, a rapprochement was effected between it and the powers of the old. In 1857 the Bank obtained a renewal of its privilege for 40 years, on condition that it double its capital, make additional advances to the state and provide additional support for public credit, and ameliorate in various minor ways the conditions on which it granted credit.

The last serious attack on the monopoly of the Bank grew out of the annexation of Savoy after the Italian War of 1859. The Bank of Savoy, although but a small local bank of issue, possessed a perpetual charter of considerable latitude, including the rights to establish branches and to issue notes for as little as 20 francs on securities of its own choosing. The treaty of annexation provided that it "would continue to enjoy in Savoy the rights and privileges which have been accorded it." Its directors hoped to sell out to the Bank of France, but the Bank regarded the price they set as excessive, and it decided to let the upstart wither on the vine. Émile and Isaac Péreire, the powers in the Crédit Mobilier, who had engaged in running battles with the Bank of France over a period of 30 years, attempted at this point to use the Bank of Savoy to break the Bank's monopoly. Technically, the Bank possessed a monopoly of note issue only in Paris and those cities in which it maintained branches; thus a rival bank might legally set up in Versailles or St. Denis—provided it obtained the authorization of the government. But the government in this case decided against the Péreires, in favor of the Bank. In retaliation the Péreires instigated a public inquiry into "the principles and the general facts which regulate the monetary and fiduciary circulation,"[29] but the outcome was a foregone conclusion. Once again the government confirmed the monopoly of the Bank. As late as the charter renewal of 1897 the advocates of freedom and competition in banking still hoped for a reversal, but the practical consequences of the issue had long since been overshadowed by other developments.

CONCLUSION

France at the end of the eighteenth century already possessed the technical capacity for an industrial revolution. The legal and political reforms of the Revolutionary era endowed it with most of the institutional prerequisites. Demographic factors, which eventually played a major role in retarding French economic growth, did not seriously affect it before 1850. France did, in fact, lay the foundations for subsequent industrialization in the first half of the nineteenth century. Its progress, however, might have been more rapid. That it was not must be attributed in large measure to its banking system, characterized by an inadequate number and distribution of bank offices, an insufficient variety of specialized financial institutions, artificial and unnecessary restrictions on the total volume of credit, and an inelastic and unnecessarily expensive stock of money. The root cause of these deficiencies lay in the monopolistic position of the Bank of France and in the restricted vision and inflexible attitudes of the men who controlled its destinies.

After 1849 the inflow of gold and the resulting world-wide inflation compensated in some degree for the inelastic currency and the restrictions on note issue. The new political regime of the Second Empire temporarily broke the Bank's stranglehold on the country's financial system, and introduced a number of financial innovations. It would be foolish, of course, to attribute the prosperity of the Second Empire and the rapidity of the industrial transformation that it witnessed solely to financial reforms. Moreover, in spite of the reforms many deficiencies in the financial structure remained. Nevertheless, the correlation between the rate of growth and changes in the financial structure before and after 1848 is striking, and cannot be laid to mere chance.

In 1865 Walter Bagehot, called upon to testify as a disinterested expert in the French monetary investigation of that year, asserted that the English country banks had performed a valuable service, in spite of their deficiencies, in habituating the population to credit instruments, thus permitting

[29] France, Conseil supérieur, *Enquête*. . . .

development of deposit banking, concentration of savings, and reduced dependence on metallic currency. For Britain in the 1860's he regarded it as a matter of indifference whether there was a single bank of issue or a multiplicity, inasmuch as the country banks had already popularized the banking habit. But, he added, "where one wishes to develop an economic system based on bank currency, it is preferable to have a multiplicity of instruments, that is to say, of banks of issue." [30] As early as 1833 Émile Péreire regarded Britain's financial system, and the extensive use it made of paper currency and bank deposits in particular, as "the secret of the industrial and political power of Great Britain." [31]

In the 1830's and 1840's, when French industry was straining for its "take off," the country supported the charge of a stock of sterile metals almost five times as large as that of contemporary Britain. Had France managed with the same proportion of gold and silver in its money supply as England and invested the surplus (by means of imports) in real resources yielding a return of only 5 per cent per annum, the annual addition to real income would have been on the order of 1 to 1½ per cent—an increase in the annual growth rate of between 50 and 100 per cent! That is one measure of the cost to France of its financial system.

[30] Ibid. I, 35.

[31] I. and E. Péreire, *Œuvres,* I, 365.

V
BELGIUM
1800–1875

by Rondo Cameron

Belgium, although a small country, is of unusual interest for this study. At the beginning of the nineteenth century the Belgian Netherlands were, like the rest of Continental Europe, primarily agrarian. They had a long urban-industrial tradition going back to the Middle Ages, but almost 300 years of oppressive, unenlightened rule by Spain and Austria had stifled that tradition and had produced economic stagnation. Then, in 1795, through the French Revolutionary Wars, the area fell under French control. The spillover of the French Revolution inaugurated a new era economically as well as politically by rekindling the spirit of enterprise and opening the country to the invigorating winds of change. Until after 1830, however, when the Belgians achieved national independence, the economic changes were less dramatic than the political gyrations that affected the area. Subsequently the economy entered a period of explosive growth accompanied by the development of a unique set of banking institutions. By 1870 Belgium was the most highly industrialized nation on the Continent, with more than 40 per cent of its labor force engaged in mining, manufacturing, and construction.[1] It also had one of the most highly developed banking systems.

THE SETTING

Among Belgium's advantages for industrialization were its location in the "cockpit of Europe," its several navigable rivers, and its plentiful mineral resources, especially coal. The political changes of the first third of the

[1] Calculated from data of the general census of 1866, reported in *Annuaire statistique de la Belgique,* 1880, 57. In 1846 the proportion of the total population (not of the labor force) dependent upon those industries had been approximately 30 per cent (ibid. 1870, 39); in 1800 the proportion had been less than 15 per cent.

century, although producing some dislocations, also helped to set the stage for rapid industrialization. Incorporated with France from 1795 to 1814, the country experienced in full measure the purgative effects of the revolutionary reforms, as well as the benefit of the large French market. The industrial and commercial development that began in that period continued in the next, when the Belgian provinces were placed under the rule of the Dutch king, William I, an enthusiastic if somewhat paternalistic advocate of material progress. Although economic issues played a minor role in triggering the Belgian revolution of 1830, the successful outcome of that revolution produced several important economic consequences, not least of which was the developmental psychology of the leaders of the new government, which soon infected the country at large.

One reason for the relatively slow development of industry before 1830 was the difficulty of securing suitable forms of business organization. The coal industry, for example, was organized on the basis of *sociétés civiles,* holdovers from the *ancien régime,* in which miners, coal merchants, and others interested in the mines shared in both the direction and the profits. Ownership could not be easily transferred, and great difficulties attended the raising of new capital for expansion and technical innovation. The Dutch government authorized but 23 *sociétés anonymes* in the southern provinces, of which 13 were insurance companies. Only six were industrial concerns, and some of those failed before or during the Belgian revolution.

Another obstacle hindering the growth of industry was the rudimentary state of the financial system. In the sixteenth century Antwerp had been the leading financial market in Europe, but the intervening centuries had taken their toll on the market as on all other aspects of economic life. The bourses of Antwerp and Brussels were reorganized under Napoleon, but until the 1830's the market was narrow and circumscribed, dealing principally in domestic and foreign government securities. Yields were relatively low, but that reflected the weak demand rather than a plentiful supply of capital. Belgian capitalists invested between 100 and 200 million francs in foreign securities before 1830, in addition to approximately 200 million francs in domestic government debt, but they would not trust their funds to their own entrepreneurs. William I, personally and through government agencies, invested approximately 10 million francs in Belgian industry between 1815 and 1830 by means of both loans and participations,[2] but was unable to inspire his moneyed subjects to emulate him. Whatever surplus funds they did not use to purchase government securities, or land,

[2] Westebbe, "State Entrepreneurship," 207–8 *et seq.* John Cockerill, the famous "iron king of Liège," obtained 4 million of it, but loans also went to 94 other industrialists, usually in sums ranging from 20,000 to 100,000 francs. See also Hodges, *Iron King,* 108ff.

they preferred to invest in mortgages, generally for short terms at high interest rates. Owing to the absence of suitable financial intermediaries, most small-scale industries either relied on trade credit or were entirely self-financing.

During the Napoleonic period the Belgians used the French coinage, principally silver. Under the Dutch the florin was the nominal money of account, but it was undervalued in terms of the franc. As a result French francs continued to be the usual medium of exchange in the Belgian provinces, though they were supplemented by old and worn Dutch and Austrian coins. No paper money was issued in the Belgian provinces until 1823, and the maximum circulation attained between 1825 and 1828 was but 9 million francs; by the end of 1830 only 2 million remained in circulation. After independence the Belgians continued to rely on French, Dutch, and Austrian coins until the latter two were demonetized in 1844. Belgium adopted the franc as its standard money, and both French and Belgian coins were accepted as legal tender. As industrialization got under way in earnest, however, the use of banknotes and deposits was of increasing importance.

THE FINANCIAL STRUCTURE AND ITS EVOLUTION

Under the French and Dutch regimes the banking system was rudimentary at best. The earliest list of private bankers dates from 1833, and it mentions 84 bankers for the country as a whole. The number was probably less in earlier years. As with private bankers elsewhere, they combined banking with brokerage and mercantile operations, and were known indifferently as "bankers" and "merchants." They operated primarily with their own resources, occasionally accepting long-term deposits or sleeping partners. Their principal activity as bankers consisted of making interlocal payments (especially with Holland, which had a different currency system) and collecting on bills of exchange. Demand deposits and normal discounting were virtually unknown except in Antwerp.[3] The beginning of the modern financial system of Belgium dates from the founding of the first joint-stock bank in 1822, also under the Dutch, although it had little effect on the economy until after the Belgian revolution.

The Société Générale

The world's first joint-stock investment bank, which antedated the French Crédit Mobilier by 30 years, was the Algemeene Nederlandsche Maatschappij ter begunstiging van de Volks-slijt, more commonly known as the

[3] Chlepner, *Banque en Belgique,* 30–33.

Société Générale de Belgique.[4] It was chartered by William I on 23 December 1822. The stated purpose of the bank was to "contribute to the progress, development, and prosperity of agriculture, manufactures, and commerce" of the Belgian provinces.[5] According to its statutes it could issue banknotes payable in specie on demand, discount bills of exchange and other commercial paper, accept deposits and make payments to order against them, and make advances on public and private securities, bullion, merchandise, and real property. The bank could also issue its own interest-bearing bonds at short or long date, and administer for its own account (including sale or alienation) certain royal domains granted to it in return for annuities to the king's civil list and bureau of amortization.

In spite of the apparent need for a bank, and its own ample attributions, the public response to the new institution was something less than overwhelming. Its authorized capital was 30 million florins (approximately 63 million francs) in 60,000 shares of 500 florins each, plus the royal domains, which were arbitrarily valued at 20 million florins. An institution of that size in a country as small as Belgium was little short of phenomenal. In a subscription campaign that remained open for six months the general public took fewer than 6,000 shares, notwithstanding the king's personal guarantee of a 5 per cent annual dividend. The king himself was obliged to subscribe for 25,800 shares to enable the bank to begin operations. It did so in 1823, with assets consisting of 12,144,000 florins in government securities (accepted at market price in payment for the shares, principally from the king) and 3,649,000 florins in specie. (Converted to francs, the initial capital amounted to 33.2 million.) In addition the bank had its real estate, which eventually proved to be worth substantially more than 20 million florins.[6]

Until after 1830 the results of the bank's operations were no more successful than the subscription for its shares, scarcely responding to its large size and impressive theoretical functions. The first governor of the bank, appointed by the king, was a Dutch politician without experience in finance. The bank did not attempt to liquidate the royal domains, which would probably have been impossible to accomplish within a short period in any case. It served as fiscal agent of the Dutch government (the current account of the Treasury was more than twice as large as all other liabilities together, reaching a maximum of 37 million francs in 1825), and engaged in a strictly limited fashion in commercial discounts and advances and in dealings in government securities. Its private deposits were negligible. Its specie reserve was normally twice as large as its note circulation and private de-

[4] *Statuten van de Naamlooze Maatschappij, AGR, SG* I.

[5] Ibid. 19–20.

[6] Chlepner, *Banque en Belgique,* 124.

posits combined; thus the net effect of the bank's operations before 1830 may have been deflationary. Nevertheless its operations were sufficiently profitable that it did not have to have recourse to the king's guarantee.

The bank's nearest approach to investment banking before 1830 came in 1828–29, when it attempted, unsucessfully, to operate a slate quarry and a lead mine. It also made advances to canal and coal companies, which, during the commercial crisis that accompanied the revolution, it was obliged to convert into equities. Indirectly this fortuitious event set the stage for its further development. During the revolution the bank had to suspend specie payments, and it was saved from bankruptcy only by the consideration of the Provisional Government.[7] The Dutch governor of the bank fled during the revolution, and the Provisional Government appointed in his place Ferdinand Méeus, a 32-year-old private banker in Brussels without previous connections with the Société Générale. After the depression had run its course and the bank had resumed its normal activities, it set about liquidating the properties it had unintentionally acquired during the revolution. Early in 1835 it obtained permission from the government to reorganize the two coal companies as *sociétés anonymes,* and floated their shares on the market with the assistance of James de Rothschild of Paris.[8] Instead of severing all connections with the new enterprises it maintained representation on their boards of directors, served as their fiscal agent, and in general directed their affairs. This procedure became the standard pattern in its subsequent industrial promotions, which followed rapidly.[9]

Developments from 1835 to 1850

In March 1835, the government authorized the creation of a new joint-stock bank, the Banque de Belgique. Capitalized at 20 million francs, the new bank was headed by Charles de Brouckère, a prominent political figure, but it drew much of its financial support from France. The statutes of the Banque de Belgique were modeled on those of the Société Générale, including the right of issue, and it lost no time in imitating its predecessor in matters of industrial promotion. Indeed, for almost four years the two banks engaged in a frantic promotional duel which resulted in the creation of 55 new joint-stock companies with an aggregate capitalization of more than 150 million francs.

In spite of a large inflow of French capital, the market was not broad enough to absorb all the new security issues resulting from the promotional

[7] Ibid. 57–8.
[8] Cameron, *France and Europe,* 121–2; Lévy-Leboyer, *Banques européennes,* 603–5.
[9] See below, p. 144.

boom, and the two banks were forced to retain a substantial share in their own portfolios. Meanwhile the banks continued to engage in ordinary commercial banking on a modest scale. The Société Générale, owing to its larger size and more numerous branches, had a substantially larger note circulation than the Banque de Belgique; at the beginning of December 1838, the former had 14 million francs in notes outstanding against the latter's 4 million. Because of the industrial boom that was stimulated by the banks and the construction of the state railway network, the international depression of 1837–38 was slow in reaching Belgium, but in the fall and winter of 1838 the threat of war between Belgium and the Netherlands caused a liquidity panic. The two banks had earlier practiced note exchanges, but when the Banque de Belgique was unable to redeem all its notes held by the Société Générale, the latter sought to rid itself of a pesky competitor by forcing the Banque de Belgique to suspend payments. In the ensuing crisis the Société Générale very nearly had to stop payments as well, but timely aid from the Paris Rothschild bailed it out. To prevent a deepening of the crisis the government loaned the Banque de Belgique 4 million francs to resume payments; the bank was subsequently reorganized with the infusion of 10 million francs of new capital.[10]

Meanwhile several lesser financial institutions had been added to the evolving structure. In 1835 the government authorized the Banque Liègeoise with a nominal capital of 4 million francs, but only 700,000 was paid in immediately. It had the privilege of note issue, but was forbidden to discount bills of exchange, with the result that its circulation of notes was negligible. It obtained most of its resources by means of bond issues, and lent on mortgages, other securities, and on current account. It had a slow but steady growth, relatively untroubled by financial crises.[11]

Two joint-stock banks were established in Antwerp during the period, but both were short-lived. The Banque Commerciale d'Anvers, created in 1837, had a nominal capital of 25 million francs, of which only one-fifth was paid in. It failed in the crisis of 1848. The Banque de l'Industrie, dating from 1838, was capitalized at 10 million francs (one-half paid in) for the purpose of encouraging exports. It failed in 1846.

The Banque de Flandre, established at Ghent in 1841, with an authorized capital of 10 million francs, was intended as a bank of issue for the western provinces. Its main business was commercial discounting, but, owing to the depression of the Flemish textile industry in the 1840's, its

[10] The basic documentation on this episode is to be found in the archives of the Société Générale, dossiers 170 and 171, deposited in the Archives Générales du Royaume (Belgium). See also Chlepner, *Banque en Belgique,* 155–72, and Cameron, *France and Europe,* 124.

[11] Chlepner, *Marché financier,* 22; Chlepner, *Banque en Belgique,* 67.

activity was not great until after 1850. It had some British capital, but became almost a subsidiary of the Société Générale, which rediscounted its paper.

Three mortgage banks were established in 1834–35. The Banque Foncière, a creation of the Société Générale, failed in 1843. The rival Caisse Hypothécaire, under the auspices of the Banque de Belgique, had greater success. In 1866 it became the Crédit Foncier de Belgique. A smaller institution, the Caisse des Propriétaires, also under the tutelage of the Banque de Belgique in its early days, far outlived its mentor.

The vigorous promotional activity of the two large banks, together with the limited financial market and the reluctance of Belgian investors to purchase industrial securities, stimulated the banks to a notable financial innovation—joint-stock investment trusts or holding companies. In 1835 the Société Générale created the Société de Commerce de Bruxelles, capitalized at 10 million francs, and the Société Nationale pour Entreprises Industrielles et Commerciales, capitalized at 15 million. The following year it established the Société des Capitalistes Réunis dans un But de Mutualité Industrielle, with an authorized capital of 50 million francs, of which 12 million was raised at once. The main purpose of all these institutions was to purchase and hold the shares of the industrial concerns founded by the Société Générale. The Société des Actions Réunies, with a capital of 12 million francs, and the Société d'Industrie Luxembourgeoise, with 5 million francs, both founded in 1837 by the Banque de Belgique, had a similar purpose.

After the crisis of 1838 the pace of promotion fell off considerably. In fact, the two banks required most of the next decade to liquidate the securities that had immobilized their assets in the preceding four years. Moreover, the 1840's were characterized by agricultural crises and stagnation in the linen industry, capped by another international industrial depression beginning in 1847. The news of the Paris revolution of February 1848 set off runs on all banks in Belgium. The Banque Commerciale d'Anvers failed, but the government, to prevent a greater crisis, allowed the Société Générale and the Banque de Belgique to suspend specie payments, and gave their notes legal tender status. Immediately before the crisis their combined note issues amounted to 21 million francs. The government set the maximum limit on their legal tender issues at 66 million francs, but in fact the issues did not exceed 42 million during suspension. Moreover, the notes did not depreciate relative to silver. Both banks made loans to the Banque de Flandre and the Banque Liègeoise to tide them over the crisis, as well as to industry and commerce generally. By June 1848 the crisis in Belgium had passed. The wise actions of the Belgian government and banks on this occasion had few counterparts elsewhere in Europe.

Developments from 1850 to 1875

The prompt and liberal actions of the government and banks eased the financial crisis, but the ultimate result of that crisis was a substantial reform of the banking system. The principal element in the reform was a new institution, the Banque Nationale de Belgique, which opened for business on 2 January 1851. Although it was intended as a central bank of issue, it did not have a complete monopoly of issue at first. The Société Générale, the Banque de Belgique, and the Banque de Flandre all gave up their note issues, but the Banque Liègeoise and possibly one or two other small banks did not. In any case, their issues were negligible in quantity and of purely local circulation. In effect, the Banque Nationale became the sole bank of issue. The bank also served as fiscal agent for the government, and was clearly intended to be a "bankers' bank," a lender of last resort.

The Banque Nationale, capitalized at 25 million francs, had the legal status of a *société anonyme* with private ownership. The government, however, appointed both the governor of the bank, who served as chief executive officer, and also a special commissioner to oversee the bank's operations and to report to the minister of finance. The bank was allowed a large measure of autonomy, but in the last analysis it was dependent upon the will of the government.[12] To compensate the Société Générale and the Banque de Belgique for the loss of their issue rights, the government allowed them to subscribe jointly for the entire capital of the new bank, from which operation they reaped considerable benefit, as the market for its shares proved brisk and bouyant.

Six new joint-stock banks were created between 1850 and the end of 1870, at Seraing (1857), Antwerp (1865), Charleroi (1866), Dinant (1869), Antwerp (1870, formerly a branch of the Société Générale), and Liège (1870). They were all relatively small, with a combined capital of only about 15 million francs, but they spread banking facilities more broadly through the nation. In the promotional boom preceding the crash of 1873 ten more new joint-stock banks were formed, of which five were former branches of the Société Générale. The most important of the new banks were the Banque de Bruxelles, with a paid-in capital of 21.8 million francs; the Banque Centrale Anversoise, with 30 million; and the Banque Belge du Commerce et de l'Industrie, with 21.1 million. The passage of a free incorporation law in 1873 resulted in the creation of five more banks in 1874–75 in spite of the depression; two were formerly branches of the Société Générale. In addition, 16 new banks created in the period 1850–75,

[12] Kauch, *Banque Nationale,* 45–52.

with an aggregate capital of 39.5 million francs in 1875, took the form of *sociétés en commandite.*[13]

Other Financial Intermediaries

Several Belgian cities established communal savings banks on the model of those in France and Britain as early as the 1820's. In 1831 the Société Générale established its own *caisse d'épargne*—actually only a special window for time deposits. Unlike the communal banks, the Société Générale used the deposited funds in its general operations instead of investing them in government securities. Several other banks, and one large industrial concern, the Société de la Vieille Montagne, also instituted savings banks. The mining districts had their *caisses de prevoyance,* and in the 1860's a number of *banques populaires* appeared. In 1865 the government set up its own savings bank with numerous branches throughout the country. In 1876 the savings banks counted more than 160,000 depositors with total deposits of more than 90 million francs.[14]

A more unusual type of institution than the savings banks were the mutual credit societies. The first of these, the Union de Crédit de Bruxelles, grew out of the crisis of 1848. In some respects it resembled the *comptoirs d'escompte* of France, except that it had no official representation or standing. The members were mostly retail tradesmen and artisans or small manufacturers. Each member received a credit equal to his subscription to capital (minimum share 500 francs), paying 5 per cent in cash to provide the society with working capital and giving his note for the balance. Following the success of the innovation in Brussels, similar societies were founded in Ghent and Liège in 1856, Antwerp in 1864, Mons in 1868, Charleroi in 1871, and Verviers in 1873. At the end of 1867 the four societies then in existence had almost 5,000 members and a combined capital of almost 60 million francs. During that year they discounted 330,572 bills totaling 160 million francs. They also accepted deposits on current account for 12 million francs.[15]

Quantitative Aspects of the Financial Structure

Table V.1 presents a summary quantitative view of the evolution of the Belgian banking structure. Unfortunately, many of the figures are estimates, and for other desiderata there is not even sufficient information on which

[13] Chlepner, *Marché financier,* 62–3.

[14] *Economiste français,* 2 November 1878; *Annuaire statistique de la Belgique,* 1880, 185–96.

[15] *Economiste français,* 2 November 1878.

TABLE V.1

EVOLUTION OF THE BELGIAN BANKING STRUCTURE, 1825–75

	1825	1830	1835	1845	1850	1860	1870	1875
Number of Banks								
Joint-stock banks[a]	1	1	3	6	4	6	21	47
Branches	1	5	7	b	b	b	b	b
Private banks (est.)	60	80	b	b	b	b	b	b
Total bank offices	62	86	b	b	b	b	b	b
Persons per office (1,000's)	61	46	b	b	b	b	b	b
Resources of Joint-stock Banks Only (millions of francs)								
Capital and reserves	34.	31.5	51.	146.	100.	277.8		362.
Banknotes in circulation	9.	2.1	17.	30.	45.	120.9		350.
Demand deposits[c]	37.	28.	8.8	40.	20.	110.1		492.
Other liabilities to public	1.	1.9	25.9	115.	60.	75.1		119.
Total resources	81.	63.5	102.7	331.	225.	584.		1,323.
Resources per inhabitant (francs)	21.	16.	25.	78.	51.	115.		249.

[a]Does not include mortgage banks, savings banks, mutual credit societies, etc.

[b]Not available.

[c]Including governmental deposits.

Sources: Chlepner, *Banque en Belgique*; Chlepner, *Marché financier*; Frère, *Sociétés anonymes*; Heuschling, *Resumé de la statistique générale*; Malou, *Société génerále*; Schoubroeck, *Evolution des banques belges*.

to base estimates. The figures for bank resources for columns 1, 2, 3, and 8 are, however, quite firm. Private bankers flourished during the second and third quarters of the century, but there are no good estimates of their number, much less of their resources.

The figures for total bank resources clearly show an accelerating trend. For the period 1825–50 the average annual growth rate of total resources was 4.1 per cent; for the period 1850–75 it was 7.1 per cent. For the period 1825–75 as a whole it was 5.6 per cent.

THE ROLE OF THE BANKS

Money Supply and the Means of Payment

Banknotes were not widely used in Belgium before 1850. This was due in part to public mistrust (the Belgians had also experienced the *assignats* during the French Revolution) and in part to the fact that before 1851 the banks of issue concentrated on industrial promotion and investment, with a corresponding neglect of short-term commercial credit. It was also due to the intense rivalry between the Société Générale and the Banque de Belgique; after the crisis of 1838 they refused to accept one another's notes, thus impairing the circulation of both. Prior to 1848 banknote circulation per capita in Belgium was less than 5 francs, compared with a relatively stable figure of about 7 francs in France. In Scotland, to go to the opposite extreme, even before 1800 note circulation had exceeded £1 per capita, roughly the equivalent of about 25 francs. After the creation of the Banque Nationale de Belgique the use of banknotes expanded appreciably; we should note here that, unlike the Bank of France, the Banque Nationale issued notes for 20 and 50 francs, as well as for larger denominations. Both Belgium and France by 1870 had approximately the same per capita circulation, about 40 francs, but in Belgium by 1875 small notes accounted

TABLE V.2

RATE OF EXPANSION OF BANKNOTE CIRCULATION IN FRANCE AND BELGIUM

(per cent per annum)

	Belgium	France
1825–75	7.4	4.8
1850–70	7.5	5.8

for approximately 15 per cent of the total circulation. Thus the rate of growth of note circulation was somewhat higher in Belgium than in France, as indicated in Table V.2.

The Société Générale held government deposits before 1830, but private deposits, although they existed, were quantitatively negligible. After 1831 the bank effectively used time deposits to increase the resources at its command. At first it paid 4 per cent interest and required only eight days' notice for withdrawal, but in 1843 it reduced the interest rate on new deposits to 3 per cent and increased the required notice to 60 days. Until then, time deposits had risen steadily, surpassing both note circulation and current account deposits, which paid no interest. The maximum sum on time deposit in 1842 was 61.6 million francs; it declined gradually thereafter to a low of 12.2 million in 1870, then rose again slightly.[16]

[16] Schoubroeck, *Evolution des banques belges,* Table II.

The Société Générale also maintained demand deposits (*comptes courants,* later sometimes called *comptes chèques*). In addition to government deposits (before 1850), these consisted principally of the idle funds of the companies it patronized and for which it served as fiscal agent. The maximum before 1850 (not including government deposits, which fluctuated widely) was 26.7 million francs in 1838. From 1851 to 1872 the average balance of current accounts was only 12 million francs, but this rose rapidly after 1866, when the bank began to pay interest on funds deposited on current account by private individuals. In 1865 current account deposits totaled only 6.3 million francs, virtually all of which belonged to companies in which the bank was interested; by 1872 the figure was 28 million francs, of which 12.4 million belonged to individuals.[17]

The Banque de Belgique instituted a *caisse d'épargne* to accept time deposits as soon as it began business. Deposits in it reached a maximum of about 1 million francs in 1838, but after the bank suspended payments the deposits fell off drastically for several years. By 1843 time deposits were back up to 1.9 million francs; then the bank announced that in the future it would repay depositors either in specie or in government securities valued at market price, and deposits immediately declined again. After 1848 the Banque de Belgique discontinued its *caisse d'épargne* but continued to accept time deposits on which it paid interest of 3 per cent. In addition it paid interest of 2 per cent on demand deposits. For the period 1851–72 the year-end average balance of demand deposits was 11.5 million francs.[18] The bank also made a determined effort to develop payment by check by granting overdraft credit to businessmen and firms. The importance of this element of the means of payment was superior to that of the bank's demand deposits; it averaged 13 million francs from 1851 to 1872.

The Banque Nationale held the government deposits from its creation in 1851. These averaged 50 million francs for the period 1851–72. The bank also accepted private deposits, but it did not pay interest. As a result private deposits were of minor importance until 1864, when the bank began to allow and accept payment by check. Thereafter private deposits rose rapidly to 60.9 million in 1872. The smaller banks also accepted deposits; in 1875 the total liabilities to the public of 39 of these banks (not including the three large banks discussed above, nor mortgage banks, mutual credit societies, savings banks, etc.) amounted to 297 million francs.[19] By contrast, the three large banks in 1872 had aggregate liabilities to the public

[17] Ibid.

[18] Ibid. Table V.

[19] Chlepner, *Marché financier,* 62–3.

of 214 million francs not including the note circulation of the Banque Nationale, 512 million including it.[20] These figures, fragmentary though they are, indicate the increasing importance of the banking system in providing the nation's means of payment.

Short-term Credit

Prior to 1850 the Société Générale and the Banque de Belgique neglected short-term commerical credit except for the enterprises they patronized directly. Discounts of either bank rarely rose above 10 million francs, and the accounts labeled *portefeuille-escompte* or *effets escomptés* usually included bills turned over to them for collection and foreign bills; the latter served the bank as secondary reserves. One reason for the shortage of commercial credit was the fact that both banks centralized their operations in Brussels. The Société Générale had five branches in other major cities in the 1830's, and the Banque de Belgique had two, but these appear not to have been very active, and did not reach the population of smaller communities at all. The credit needs of the large industrial enterprises founded and patronized by the two banks was handled by means of current account advances. Since many of the transactions of such companies as coal mines, foundries, and machine works were with one another, payments were made by means of book transfers in the banks.

The Banque Liègeoise was forbidden by its statutes to discount bills of exchange. It made direct loans on mortgages, merchandise, and perhaps open account, but its operations were of strictly minor importance before 1850. The banks in Antwerp may have been somewhat more active in discounting. The Banque de Flandre between 1842 and 1850 averaged discounts of about 10 million francs per year, half of which it normally rediscounted with the Société Générale. Elsewhere in the country commercial credit was in the hands of private bankers, who typically charged as much as 8 per cent for discounts. The deficiency of short-term commercial credit before 1850 was definitely a weakness of the Belgian banking system; it handicapped small entrepreneurs in particular. That deficiency, together with the two large banks' policy of favoring large integrated industrial concerns, helps to explain the concentrated, oligopolistic nature of Belgian industry.

After 1850, with the founding of the Banque Nationale and the proliferation of small local banks and mutual credit societies, the conditions of commercial credit were substantially improved. The Banque Nationale dealt exclusively (in principle, at least) in short-term commercial credit, prin-

[20] Schoubroeck, *Evolution des banques belges,* Table VIII.

cipally by means of discount and rediscount. Its year-end portfolio amounted to 124 million francs, on the average, from 1851 to 1872; it reached 263 million in 1872.[21] For more than a decade after the crisis of 1848, the Banque de Belgique also devoted its activities primarily to short-term credit; then it veered back toward industrial promotion and finance in the 1860's. In 1861 80 per cent of its earning assets, amounting to more than 30 million francs, were in the form of short-term credits. For the period 1851–72 as a whole, 57 per cent of the total credit it granted took that form.[22] The Société Générale, in contrast, continued to specialize in long-term credit and industrial participations. Typically its short-term credits accounted for only 25 to 30 per cent of its earning assets, although because of its larger size the total short-term credit granted was greater than that of the Banque de Belgique. The Société Générale's year-end annual average of short-term credits, 1851–72, was 36.8 million francs, of which 13.8 million took the form of discounts, 4.9 million advances on merchandise and securities, and 18.1 million current account advances.[23] The relatively large size of the last item probably indicates that the Société Générale gave even its short-term credit primarily to the firms in which it took direct participations. The aggregate short-term credit granted by the three major banks (advances to the government excluded) rose from 86 million francs in 1851 to 340 million in 1872, for an average annual growth rate of almost 7 per cent. Figures for the smaller banks are not available, but given the growth in their number and in their total assets, and the fact that most of them engaged primarily in short-term credit, it seems likely that total short-term credit increased even more rapidly than 7 per cent.

Long-term Credit

Long-term lending for fixed industrial investment was one of the distinguishing features of the Belgian banking system. Nevertheless there is some difficulty in determining its precise quantitative importance because of the ambiguity of the term. On the one hand, current account advances and other forms of short-term borrowing might in fact be used to finance fixed investment, and might remain on the books of the bank for several years. The evidence suggests that this was of considerable importance in the 1830's and 1840's in particular. For example, between 1835 and 1838 John Cockerill borrowed more than 2 million francs from the Banque de Belgique on mortgages and short-term notes. The loans were still outstanding when Cockerill died in 1840. In 1842 the bank and other creditors of the firm

[21] Ibid. Table I.
[22] Ibid. Table VI and p. 112.
[23] Ibid. Table III.

(including the Belgian government) created the Société Anonyme des Etablissements John Cockerill, but not until 1846 were the loans repaid.[24] On the other hand, much industrial investment was financed by bank purchase of shares of industrial firms; technically, therefore, the banks were not lenders, but owners. Here we will focus our discussion on the role of the Société Générale and the Banque de Belgique, since these were by far the largest banks, the ones which specialized in industrial finance, and the ones on which documentation is most nearly adequate.

Both the Société Générale and the Banque de Belgique loaned on mortgages, made long-term loans on promissory notes and other securities, and purchased bonds and shares of industrial enterprises (including railways and utilities). The Société Générale began operations in 1822 with considerable real estate and a large quantity of government securities which it had accepted in payment of shares. Before 1830 it was preoccupied with its real estate, which it did not sell; on the contrary, it purchased more.[25] During the first decade of its activity its holdings of government securities accounted for between 20 and 25 per cent of its total assets. Its first tentative steps toward investment banking came in 1828 or 1829, when it made advances to canals and coal mines.[26] After the Belgian revolution loans became a normal part of its business. The account "shares and bonds" first appeared in its balance sheet in 1835; it grew steadily thereafter until the crisis of 1848. In 1847 its holdings of shares and bonds amounted to almost 70 million francs and constituted more than 30 per cent of total assets. In addition, it is likely that the account for "loans and carry-overs," which amounted to 61 million francs in 1847 and had been as high as 73 million, represented long-term loans primarily, since it was listed separately from bills discounted and debit current accounts.[27] The accounts for "shares and bonds" and "loans and carry-overs" between them constituted more than 50 per cent of total assets for most of the 1840's. The third large item was current accounts in debit, which may also have concealed a certain amount of (perhaps unintentional) long-term lending.

The accounts of the Banque de Belgique reveal similar proportions. Until 1839 the two largest accounts on the asset side of the ledger were "advances and carry-overs on shares and bonds," which indicates that the bank was financing the purchasers of the shares in its companies, and "current accounts of companies." The latter continued to be important in the

[24] Hodges, *Iron King,* 329.

[25] Chlepner, *Banque en Belgique,* 52.

[26] Ibid. 55–6. At the urging of William I the bank also loaned John Cockerill 500,000 florins to establish a cotton mill. The loan was secured by a mortgage on Cockerill's half interest in the Seraing ironworks. Hodges, *Iron King,* 113–14.

[27] Chlepner, *Banque en Belgique,* 76–7.

1840's, but the account "shares and bonds (property of the bank)" replaced the former as one of the two largest accounts.[28]

The Société Générale was relieved of its note-issuing responsibility after 1850, and thereafter it was able to devote itself more single-mindedly to industrial finance. It did this primarily by direct participation, however, rather than by lending. Its holdings of industrial shares and bonds—predominantly the former—averaged 60 to 70 per cent of total assets. As previously noted, it is probable that most of its short-term operations financed the working capital needs of the firms it patronized.

The Banque de Belgique, which also lost its issue function in the financial reorganization of 1848–50, followed a different, somewhat wavering course. It emerged from the reorganization with almost 30 per cent of its assets in relatively immobilized form: it had almost 6 million francs of badly depreciated industrial securities and more than 4 million in mortgage credits. It undertook no new industrial promotions or long-term loans for several years, but devoted itself to supplying short-term credit while it attempted to liquidate its portfolio of long-term investments. In the late 1850's it did another about-face and began to invest heavily, especially in foreign and domestic railways. In 1863 40 per cent of its assets consisted of investments in industrial securities and mortgages—well over half in railway bonds. The sharp depreciation of Italian and Spanish railway bonds in the 1860's caused it to reverse its tactics once again, not without severe losses, but it then became involved in a series of complicated and questionable promotions in Belgium which absorbed its resources and set the stage for the eventual embezzlements by one of its high officials.[29]

Several of the banks founded in the promotional boom of the early 1870's, notably the Banque de Travaux Publics, the Banque de Bruxelles, and the Banque Belge du Commerce et de l'Industrie, also devoted themselves to industrial finance. On the other hand, with the continued growth of large-scale industry, *autofinancement* became more prominent; hence the relatively greater reliance on short-term or "commercial" credit for working capital, usually by means of current account advances.

Entrepreneurial Activity of the Banks and Direct Participation in Industry

Industrial promotion and finance was the outstanding characteristic of the Belgian banking system. The Société Générale pioneered this type of activity in the 1830's. All other Belgian banks, with the obvious exception of the Banque Nationale, engaged in it to some extent. As practiced by the Société Générale, and, for a time, by the Banque de Belgique, the banks

[28] Ibid. 78–9.

[29] Chlepner, *Marché financier,* 67–8.

did not respond passively to demands for credit, but actively sought new firms, underwrote their stock issues, financed potential stockholders, held stock in their own names, placed their officers on the boards of directors of the companies they promoted, and ministered to the companies' needs for both working capital and new capital for expansion. In effect, the industrial concerns in which they participated were merely operating subsidiaries of the banks. The Société Générale boasted in 1860 that, of the total joint-stock capital of 1 billion francs in Belgium, 200 million represented the capital of firms under its aegis.[30]

In Belgium's first industrial boom, from 1835 to 1838, the Société Générale, with the assistance of James de Rothschild of Paris, promoted, organized, and financed 31 new *sociétés anonymes* with an aggregate capital of more than 100 million francs.[31] The firms included Belgium's first joint-stock coal mining companies, several integrated ironworks, sugar refineries, glassworks, a textile factory, a machinery and engineering works, and the Antwerp Steamship Company. Several of those firms, especially in the metallurgical industries, are among the leading firms in Belgium today.

The Banque de Belgique, although much smaller, was no less active in the boom than its elder rival. It created 24 *sociétés anonymes,* with an aggregate capital of 54 million francs. They also included coal mines, metallurgical establishments, textile mills, sugar refineries, and a machinery and engineering company. Each bank had a virtually self-contained industrial empire. As with the Société Générale, several of the companies founded by the Banque de Belgique are still among the leaders in their industries. One of them, the Société de la Vieille Montagne, is one of the world's largest producers of nonferrous metals. It was established in 1837 on the foundations of a small single proprietorship for the production of zinc, which was at that time a new metal for industrial purposes. The main reasons for converting the company to joint-stock form were to relieve the founder, then 83 years old, of the responsibilities of management, and to obtain capital for expansion. The enterprise was capitalized at 5 million francs in 5,000 shares of 1,000 francs each, of which the founder and his heirs received 4,200 for their *apports.* The Banque de Belgique took the remaining 800 shares for a cash subscription of 800,000 francs, and in addition advanced the company 3.5 million francs in anticipation of a new stock issue for the construction of a large new foundry. The stock issue did not

[30] Schoubroeck, *Evolution des banques belges,* 99.

[31] Briavoinne, *Industrie en Belgique,* II, 233–4; Frère, *Sociétés anonymes,* chap. I, *passim;* Chlepner, *Banque en Belgique,* 74, 85ff; Lévy-Leboyer, *Banques européennes,* 604–16; Cameron, *France and Europe,* 121–3, 346–7. The archives of the Société Générale, although not complete, contain much valuable detailed information on this period.

take place, owing to the crisis of 1838–40, but the new plant was so successful that the company was able to repay the loan from retained earnings. Dividends rose steadily from 5 per cent in 1837 to 48 per cent in 1846, dropped precipitately to 4 per cent in 1848, and averaged nearly 20 per cent for the remainder of the century. In addition, reinvested profits soon dwarfed the nominal value of the initial capital. Three of the first six directors of the company were drawn from the board of the Banque de Belgique. Charles de Brouckère, chairman of the board of the bank, served as chief executive officer of the company from 1841 to 1846, when he resigned as the result of a policy dispute with the French directors. By that time a majority of the shares were held in France, and French bankers replaced the Banque de Belgique as the company's principal financiers. For a time in the 1850's the company had close relations with the French Crédit Mobilier.[32]

The extremely ambitious scale on which the banks operated in their early years, together with the narrow market for industrial securities and their own inexperience in both industrial promotion and ordinary banking procedures, resulted in immobilization of their assets. This proved to be acutely embarrassing during the political and economic crises of 1838 and 1848. Given the chance to disengage by means of emergency loans (in 1838) and suspension of convertibility (in 1848), however, both banks continued to contribute to the development of industry. The solutions arrived at on those two occasions were much less costly and destabilizing for the nation than enforced liquidations would have been. The creation of a central bank of issue, relieving the other banks of their currency-supply function, freed them to continue their work.

After 1850 the Société Générale devoted itself almost exclusively to industrial promotion and finance, chiefly by stock participations. Its holdings of industrial securities averaged 77.5 million francs, 1851–72, and did not fall below 80 million after 1864. In contrast to the earlier period, when its attention was directed primarily toward mining and metallurgical enterprises, after 1850 it specialized in railway promotion and construction, both domestic and foreign. In this way it could assure the mining and metallurgical enterprises which it had created earlier of a market for their products. One result of this policy was that Belgian industry was less susceptible to the periodic depressions that afflicted the international economy in the second half of the nineteenth century. The industrial distribution of the security holdings of the Société Générale is given in Table V.3.

The Banque de Belgique, though much less important both relatively and absolutely than the Société Générale, nevertheless made a substantial con-

[32] For a more detailed account see Cameron, *France and Europe,* 353–64, which is based on the company's archives.

TABLE V.3

SOCIÉTÉ GÉNÉRALE, PORTFOLIO OF INDUSTRIAL SECURITIES, ANNUAL AVERAGE, 1851–72

Industry Group	Million Francs	Per Cent	Per Cent of Total Assets
Transport and construction	31.6	40.8	
Coal mining	24.5	31.6	
Metallurgy	10.1	13.0	
Miscellaneous	11.3	14.6	
Total	77.5	100.00	64.4

Source: Schoubroeck, *Evolution des banques belges*, Table IV.

tribution. The industrial distribution of its security holdings is presented in Table. V.4.

Something of the contribution of the banks to Belgian industry may be judged from the fact that the industries in which they were most deeply involved were also among the most important industries in the Belgian economy, quantitatively, and the ones which exhibited the highest rates of growth. Whether the high growth rates were attributable directly to the services of the banks, or whether the banks selected the industries with the highest potential growth rates, does not affect the conclusion as to the efficacy of their assistance. Table V.5 presents data on the output and growth rates of several of the more important industries. Unfortunately, output data for the textile industries are not available; they were among the most

TABLE V.4

BANQUE DE BELGIQUE, PORTFOLIO OF INDUSTRIAL SECURITIES, ANNUAL AVERAGE, 1851–72

Industry Group	Million Francs	Per Cent	Per Cent of Total Assets
Metallurgy	3.7	32.0	
Transport	3.5	30.0	
Textiles	2.1	18.0	
Coal mining	.8	7.0	
Miscellaneous	1.5	13.0	
Total	11.6	100.00	28.5

Source: Schoubroeck, *Evolution des banques belges*, Table VII.

TABLE V.5

OUTPUT AND GROWTH RATES FOR SELECTED INDUSTRIES, BELGIUM, 1830–75

Industry (units)	Output 1830	Output 1850	Output 1875	Growth Rate (% per annum) 1830–50	Growth Rate (% per annum) 1850–75	Growth Rate (% per annum) 1830–75
Coal (million tons)	2.0	5.8	15.0	5.3	3.8	4.5
Pig iron (1,000 tons)	n.a.	145.	565.0[a]	–	6.8	–
Steel (1,000 tons)	n.a.	3.2[b]	47.2	–	17.9	–
Zinc (1,000 tons)	2.0[c]	22.0	73.0	20.0	4.8	9.7
Lead (1,000 tons)	n.a.	1.3	10.0[d]	–	10.2	–
Copper (1,000 tons)	–	0.9	2.6	–	4.2	–
Glass (mill. frs.)	n.a.	8.3	43.5	–	6.6	–
Steam engines[e] (1,000 h.p.)	11.3	54.3	510.0	7.9	9.0	8.5
Railways[f] (km.)	0.0	898.0	3508.0	–	5.4	–

[a]1870. [b]1860. [c]1838. [d]1870. [e]Installed h.p. [f]Trackage in place; does not include foreign railways built by Belgian firms.

Source: *Annuaire statistique de la Belgique*.

important export industries, but probably had a lower rate of growth than the industries listed.

SUMMARY AND CONCLUSIONS

The Belgian banking system contained several unique features, and Belgian bankers were responsible for a number of highly significant financial innovations. The Société Générale de Belgique was the first joint-stock bank created especially for the purpose of promoting the development of industry. At first the novelty of the institution and the inexperience of its officers rendered it relatively ineffective. The realization of its promise was in part fortuitous: the Belgian revolution inspired a favorable developmental psychology among the country's middle-class revolutionaries; the man who was appointed governor of the bank in 1830 was exceptionally able and imaginative; the inspiration for the bank's first promotional activity came from meditation on the problem of how to dispose of properties acquired by default. Success was immediate, but it required a number of years, including two severe crises and a complete reorganization of the financial system, to perfect the operating procedures of promotional banking.

The rapid success of the Société Générale, as well as the political opposition that it inspired, led to the creation of the Banque de Belgique, which modeled its activities on those of the Société Générale. Although much smaller, the Banque de Belgique in its early years made a significant contribution to the industrialization of Belgium, in spite of notable errors of judgment. Subsequently the bank wavered between ordinary commercial banking and promotional banking before eventually falling prey to dishonest officers. Nevertheless, both banks were able to supply the entrepreneurial leadership as well as finance which otherwise might not have been forthcoming, at least not in sufficient quantity for the rapid, broad-scale development that did in fact take place.

The Belgian system, successful though it was in contributing to rapid industrialization, was vulnerable to criticism on several grounds. The combination of note issue with promotional operations proved to be unfortunate. The Scottish banks had been able to make effective use of their note issues in part because the population became habituated to them at an early date and preferred banknotes to specie, but mainly because the banks did not participate directly in industrial enterprises. The mixture of issue and promotional functions is unlikely to be workable for extended periods, especially when it is necessary for the banks themselves to hold industrial shares in their own portfolios until they can be taken off the market. On the other hand, the use of deposits is quite compatible with promotional activities under certain conditions. One key to successful mixed banking is bank control of its own liabilities, either by means of contractual deposits or through control of the companies that make the deposits.

Although the banks' note issues before 1850 were large enough to be an embarrassment to them during liquidity crises, they were not large enough to benefit the economy as much they should have in normal times. The neglect of short-term commercial credit before 1851 hampered the development of small enterprises in particular. Moreover, the small circulation of notes caused the country to bear the cost of an unnecessarily large stock of specie, as in France.

The "bicephalic" nature of the system before 1850 generated unnecessary instability—especially with one head so much larger than the other. The system became "tricephalic" in 1851. That was an improvement, but other alternatives would have been still better. More banks of more or less equal size, with the same total resources as the existing system, would probably have produced greater stability without appreciably lowering the rate of growth. Alternatively, a single large promotional bank with several smaller note-issuing banks to provide short-term credit under competitive conditions could have produced both a high growth rate and stability. The very existence of the Société Générale and the Banque de Belgique discouraged potential bank entrepreneurs until the government stepped in to remove the banks' rights of issue.

Finally, along with its other lessons, the Belgian experience would seem to indicate that different institutional arrangements can produce equally favorable results—and perhaps that different circumstances even require different institutions. Of the four countries surveyed thus far, the Scottish and the Belgian banking systems show the greatest dissimilarities; yet they were also the ones that contributed most forcefully and positively to industrialization and economic development in their respective countries.

VI
GERMANY
1815–1870

by Richard Tilly

During the first half of the nineteenth century the industrial development of the German states lagged behind that of Britain, France, and Belgium by a considerable margin. This relative backwardness has led some scholars to discuss Germany's economic expansion at the end of the nineteenth century as an example of the "advantages of backwardness" for rapid industrialization.[1] Whatever the merits of this view, there are a number of plausible reasons for Germany's backwardness earlier in the century. Political fragmentation was clearly one important element. In 1815 "Germany" consisted of 38 sovereign states, some of them large and relatively powerful, like Prussia or Bavaria, but most of them small and insignificant. This fragmentation hindered the development of a unified German market, forced the maintenance of a number of unnecessary and unproductive government establishments, and reduced political bargaining power in commercial relations with non-German nations.

The roots of German backwardness, however, were neither solely nor primarily political. Germany's social structure was not yet geared to the needs of industrialization. The French occupation and domination of western German territories between 1790 and 1815 had led to a number of important institutional reforms, such as abolition of feudal restrictions on landed property, destruction of guild power, and reform of the commercial law. Such reforms had helped, but despite them the social and economic bonds of traditional corporate society remained strong in most of the German states. Until after 1848 the town and craft guilds, the landed aristocracy, the churches, and, not least of all, the government bureaucracies, restricted the mobility of resources so necessary to innovation and growth.

Nevertheless, substantial progress occurred between 1815 and 1870.

[1] Gerschenkron, *Economic Backwardness in Historical Perspective;* see also Veblen, *Imperial Germany and the Industrial Revolution.*

From 1815 to about 1842–43, and particularly in the 1830's, development was slow but perceptible. In Prussia, Saxony, and some other parts of Germany institutional and technical reorganization of agriculture was pronounced: commons and waste land were enclosed, crops such as turnips and potatoes began to be cultivated widely, and more efficient cultivation and breeding practices were introduced.[2] The manufacturing sector, particularly the textile industries, also grew in response to both foreign demand and the elimination of tariff barriers between most of the German states brought about by the *Zollverein,* created in 1834. Much of this growth was along traditional outwork lines, but considerable modernization also occurred, as is indicated by the growth of machine-making establishments in and around textile centers and by the increased use of steam power.[3]

This growth continued in the 1840's, but its impact upon the German economy was overshadowed by the spread of railroads. Railroad building in the 1840's marked a definitive turning point—some scholars call it the "take-off"—in the industrial development of Germany.[4] By conservative estimates, construction expenditures probably averaged around 20 million thalers per year during the 1840's—between 1 and 2 per cent of the estimated national income.[5] Moreover, railroad construction directly stimulated investment in ancillary branches of production, while the prospect of cheaper, more reliable transportation encouraged investment in other industries. Between 1850 and 1857, for example, 94 industrial joint-stock companies were founded in Prussia, with total paid-in capital of more than 84 million thalers. During the same period 61 such companies were founded in Saxony, with total paid-in capital by 1860 of roughly 9 million thalers.[6]

[2] Von Gülich, *Geschichtliche Darstellung,* IV, 343–4, 576–633.

[3] Ibid. 357, 432, 452, 472–4, 477, 560, 567–8. Benaerts, *Les Origines de la grande industrie allemande,* 374–8.

[4] Both Spiethoff and Schumpeter regarded 1842–43 as the critical turning point. Schumpeter, *Business Cycles,* I, 346–7, 350–51; Spiethoff, *Die wirtschaftlichen Wechsellagen,* I, 113–17; also, more recently, Hoffmann, "The Take-off in Germany," in Rostow (ed.), *Economics of the Take-off into Sustained Growth,* 95–118.

[5] The railroad investment estimates are based on data in von Gülich, *Geschichtliche Darstellung,* IV, 417; Kumpmann, *Reinischen Eisenbahn;* and von Mayer, *Geschichte und Geographie der deutschen Eisenbahnen,* I. The national income estimates are based on the uncertain assumptions that Prussia's share in the German national income was constant between 1830 and the early 1850's and that two-thirds of the increment to national income between 1830 and the 1850's was added in the 1840's. The data come from Käding, *Preussischen Finanzpolitik,* 83, 145–6; and Hoffmann, *Das Deutsche Volkseinkommen, 1851–1957,* 13–40. These estimates correspond closely to those presented by Hoffmann in his article cited in note 4.

[6] Blumberg, "Die Finanzierung der Neugründungen und Erweiterungen von Industriebetrieben in Form der Aktiengesellschaften währen der fünfziger Jahre des 19. Jahrhunderts in Deutschland, am Beispiel der preussischen Verhältnisse erläutert," in Mottek (ed.), *Studien zur Geschichte der industriellen Revolution in Deutschland,* 165–208.

TABLE VI.1

SELECTED INDICATORS OF GERMAN INDUSTRIAL GROWTH, 1840–70

		Pig Iron		Hard Coal		Steam Engines[a]	
Year	Railroads (kms.)	Output (tons)	Consumption Per Capita (kg.)	Output (mill. tons)	Consumption Per Capita (kg.)	No.	h.p.
1840	469	172,982	8.5	3.2	111		
1850	5,856	211,639	10.9	5.2	171	1,416[b]	26,354[b]
1860	11,088	545,299	19.3	12.3	337	10,113[c]	184,649[c]
1870	19,000	1,391,124	35.9	26.4	618		

[a]Includes *Zollverein* states. [b]1846. [c]1861.

Sources: Railroads; Benaerts, *Les Origines de la grande industrie allemande*, 319; Schumpeter, *Business Cycles*, I, 346–7, Coal and Pig iron: Arthur Spiethoff, *Die wirtschaftlichen Wechsellagen*, II, Tables 13 and 20, and accompanying "Erläuterungen zu den Tafeln." Steam Engines, Benaerts, ibid. 376-8.

Additional evidence of industrial progress is given in Table VI.1. It serves to support the argument that the foundations of German industrial power were laid in the period before 1870.

THE FINANCIAL STRUCTURE AND ITS EVOLUTION

Traditional Elements

The evolution of German financial institutions during the first half of the nineteenth century reflected the continued strength of "traditional society" and, perhaps, the roundabout channels by which industrialization proceeded in its early stages. This is well illustrated by the considerable importance attached at that time to the Prussian agricultural credit institutions, the *Landschaften.* Launched in the eighteenth century with the encouragement of Frederick the Great, they provided collective liability for the indebtedness of landed estate owners. They issued interest-bearing mortgage bonds (*Pfandbriefe*) guaranteed by the *Landschaften* and based on the value of the borrowing estates. After 1815, by which date the earlier restrictions on "bourgeois" ownership of aristocratic estates had been eliminated, there was an increase in the circulation of the *Pfandbriefe* and the corresponding flow of capital into Prussian—especially East Prussian—agriculture. In 1815 the value of all Prussian *Pfandbriefe* in circulation was reported as nearly 63 million thalers. In 1835 the circulation amounted to more than 100 million thalers— a sum much larger than the liabilities of any other Prussian financial institution and nearly equal to two-thirds of the total Prussian state debt. In subsequent decades this growth continued, though at a relatively slower pace.[7]

The weight of the past was also reflected in the preferred position which the German kingdoms and principalities continued to enjoy in the German capital markets, at least until around mid-century. Savers' confidence in the governments' abilities to extract revenues from their subjects was considerably greater than their confidence in the potential earning power of industrial companies.[8] In a sense this reflected a rational choice by savers

[7] Dieterici, *Handbuch der Statistik des Preussischen Staats,* 574–5; von Gülich, *Geschichtliche Darstellung,* II, 368; IV, 582–3. Until the 1840's interest rates on this type of debt tended to fall. Voye, *Ueber die Höhe der verschiedenen Zinssätze und ihre wechselseitige Abhängigkeit.*

[8] Particularly in view of foreign competition, especially British. In 1839 Christian Rother, a Prussian official, wrote, "The capitalists here are not inclined to pay industrial enterprises their proper due. Even the soundest of incorporation projects

and financial specialists among alternative investments. Investment in industrial enterprise did not appear to be very promising because of the lack of supporting enterprises and of a pool of technical skills, and because of the relatively undeveloped domestic market. Moreover, the framework of legal and political restraints placed by governments upon private enterprise inhibited the development of potentially rival borrowers. Governments deliberately retarded the growth of industrial borrowers by putting restrictions on joint-stock companies, limiting admission to formal stock exchange trading to certain kinds of securities, and restricting access to government funds. The success of German governments in raising funds during this period may be seen in the rise in the price of government securities and conversion of loans at reduced rates of interest in the 1820's and 1830's. The attractiveness of government securities to German savers was also reflected in the substantial placements of foreign government bonds in Berlin and Frankfurt during those years.[9]

The market for short-term capital to finance interregional and international trade represented a third traditional element in the evolving financial system of Germany. Through at least the first third of the century the accumulation of capital associated with trade was doubtless one of the most important financial aspects of Germany's economic development. Some historians have written of a "surplus" of capital in the trade sector for the 1820's and 1830's as revealed in falling rates of profit.[10] The situation has been contrasted with the 1840's, when railroad building and associated investment began to attract and provide more satisfactory employment for surplus capital, directly through the sale of railroad securities to merchants and indirectly through an induced increase in the volume of trade. The argument is to some extent buttressed by reference to the "German" balance of trade: generally active in the 1820's and 1830's, turning adverse in the 1840's.[11] In fact, it is virtually impossible to trace the flow of funds from trade to the new manufacturing and transportation sectors. The needs of all sectors grew substantially after 1840, and in any case it is diffi-

---

fail to attract interest. Rather than making funds available to industry, capitalists prefer to invest their fortunes in government securities or mortgages, and to enjoy the fruits of their investment with the greatest possible amount of peace and calm. The currently low interest rates seem associated only with the purchase of landed estates." Quoted in Blumberg, "Die Finanzierung . . . ," 167.

[9] Brockhage, "Zur Entwicklung des preussisch-deutschen Kapitalexports," 161, 164–71, 172–6; Spangenthal, *Die Geschichte der Berliner Borse,* 39–41; also the discussion and literature cited by Borchart, "Zur Frage des Kapitalmangels," 402–21.

[10] Von Gülich, *Geschichtliche Darstellung,* II, 436, 568.

[11] Hoffmann, "The Take-Off in Germany," in Rostow (ed.), *Economics of the Take-off into Sustained Growth,* 112.

cult to distinguish between "trade" and "industrial" capital in the economic sense of those terms.[12]

Despite such ambiguity, the existence of "trade capital" as well as the other traditional elements associated with agricultural and government finance suggests that a considerable "pre-industrial" accumulation of relatively liquid capital was at hand in the early stages of German industrialization. The problem of "capital shortage" faced by the German economy at that time was thus a relative one, more closely related to the distribution of the savings stream than to its aggregate size. This does not imply that no problem existed. In Prussia in the 1840's, for example, landed interests and elements of the bureaucracy strongly resisted what they felt was a significant transfer of capital from agriculture and government to industry.[13] This suggests that for certain purposes capital was readily available in Germany throughout the period. That it was not readily available for industrial purposes, at least until the 1840's, may indicate market imperfections on the supply side. It may also indicate that the demand for industrial capital was weak, however.[14] Both inferences are plausible. In assessing the performance of the German monetary system, therefore, both should be borne in mind.

Government Institutions

In a sense, government financial institutions should be included among the traditional elements of the German financial structure. Until the second half of the century at least, the state remained the instrument of conservative interests—in Prussia, the *Junker* class—with little interest in industrial development. Indeed, the states frequently supported policies which directly conflicted with the needs of industrialization.[15] The principal financial expression of this governmental orientation lay in official controls exercised over the money supply and over the award of charters for joint-stock com-

[12] The "industrial capital" of the period, after all, consisted to a large extent of raw and partially processed materials and goods in transit—employing trade capital. It may be that the sociological meanings of the terms provide more justification for their use than their economic content.

[13] Von Eichborn, *Soll und Haben,* 311; Kubitschek, "Die Börsenverordnung vom 24. Mai 1844 und die Situation im Finanz und Kreditwesen Preussens in den vierziger Jahren des 19. Jahrhunderts."

[14] This is one of the themes stressed by Borchardt in his excellent article, "Zur Frage des Kapitalmangels."

[15] For example, the early railroad policies in Prussia. See Eichholtz, *Junker und Bourgeoisie in der Preussischen Eisenbahngeschichte,* esp. chap. 2; see also Fischer, *Der Staat und die Anfänge der Industrialisierung in Baden, 1800–1850,* for a somewhat contrary view. Henderson, *The State and the Industrial Revolution in Prussia, 1740–1870,* must also be mentioned in this connection.

panies. (The financial implications of fiscal policy—that is, the management of the government's current account and its debt—are ignored here.) Specifically, most governments undertook increases and improvements in the coinage very cautiously, while government approval or support of the use of specie substitutes was severely restricted. Government authorization of joint-stock companies, whether for industrial, commercial, or financial enterprises, was similarly restricted until the North German Confederation enacted a free incorporation law in 1869.

Of greatest importance were measures and institutions related to the growth of the stock of currency. That stock included specie, government paper money, and banknotes. The growth of the money stock had an important influence on both the aggregate total and the composition of over-all spending in the economy. It may have had strategic indirect effects as well, by influencing the rate of growth of "money substitutes." Responsibility for the coinage in most German states rested ultimately with the ministries of finance or treasuries, though mints doubtless exercised some independence in such matters. In Prussia, the Treasury governed the introduction of new coin (and the attempted retirement of old) through government disbursements. It attempted to influence the composition of the coin circulation by making certain taxes payable only in certain types of coin.[16] The Treasury also was responsible for the circulation of government paper money, which it attempted to regulate through its revenues and expenditures.

Banks of Issue: Central Banking

The active role played by ministries of finance in most of the German states during the first half of the century mirrored the traditional predominance of fiscal concerns over the monetary and banking aims of governments. This interest perhaps explains the relative unimportance of banknote circulation in these years. Modern banks of issue first made their appearance in the 1830's. The first such German bank was the Bayerische Hypotheken-und Wechselbank (Bavarian Mortgage and Discount Bank), authorized by the Bavarian monarchy in 1835. The second was the Bank of Leipzig, founded in 1838 as the forerunner of the Bank of Saxony. From the standpoint of both contemporary and subsequent industrial growth, however, the importance of both of these banks was considerably less than that of the Prussian Bank, founded in 1846.

The Prussian Bank was a reorganized note-issuing joint-stock version of the old Royal Bank of Prussia. It took over all of the older institution's assets and liabilities, and a good deal of its operating procedures and

[16] Tilly, *Financial Institutions,* chaps. 2 and 3.

conservative viewpoint as well.[17] Like most such European banks it was privately owned, but bureaucratic control over its operations was closely maintained. The bank's capital was initially set at 10 million thalers, and its note-issuing rights limited to a maximum of 15 million thalers. In 1856 the growing circulation in Prussia of promissory notes issued by banks located outside Prussia led the government to remove the statutory limit upon its note circulation. This was supported by further legal measures which strengthened the demand for the bank's notes relative to other means of payments (for example, by making them acceptable for all payments to the government). By the end of the 1850's the bank's notes predominated in the paper money circulation of Prussia.[18]

Other Banks of Issue

The growth of the Prussian Bank did not satisfy all demands for new banking facilities. Entrepreneurs who were unable to obtain authorization for banks of issue within Prussia—or within Saxony, where similar conditions existed—founded them in other German states. Both Prussia and Saxony were partly surrounded by other German governments that willingly acceded to concession-seeking business groups' requests for bank charters. Beginning in 1847, with the establishment of the Dessauer Bank, located near both Prussia and Saxony, several banks of issue were set up in neighboring states. To facilitate the circulation of their notes they printed them in Prussian and Saxon denominations. Some of these banks, significantly, were founded by Prussian and Saxon entrepreneurs, such as the Bank für Süddeutschland in Darmstadt, established in 1855, and the International Bank in Luxembourg, established in 1856, both by the Prussian Rhenish financiers, Gustav Mevissen and the Oppenheims.[19] Many of the banks outside Prussia and Saxony neither issued thaler notes nor exhibited any recognizably close link to the financial demands of Prussian and Saxon industrial areas, but those that did were regarded as serious enough threats to the established issuing banks of Prussia and Saxony to cause the governments of those two states to enact laws in the 1850's forbidding the use of foreign banknotes. In 1856 the Prussian government also granted charters to seven new joint-stock banks of issue; it simultaneously expanded the Prussian Bank.

The approximate growth of the circulation of Prussian and German

[17] Niebuhr, *Geschichte der Königlichen Bank zu Berlin;* Tilly, *Financial Institutions,* chap. 3. A sound history of the Prussian Bank still remains to be written.

[18] Schauer, *Die Preussische Bank,* 41; Thorwärt, "Die Entwicklung des Banknotenumlaufs," 202–3.

[19] Tilly, *Financial Institutions,* chap. 3, and sources cited there.

banks of issue is recorded in Tables VI.4 and VI.5. Table VI.3 illustrates their over-all importance: there were 30 banks of issue in northern Germany (defined to include Frankfort/Main and all points north of it) in addition to the Prussian and Saxon banks, reporting paid-up capital and reserves of approximately 63 million thalers, a total note circulation of 60 million thalers, and total earning assets of nearly 150 million thalers. Though clearly important, such banks have generally been overlooked by historians, in part because, after the establishment of the German Empire, the *Reichsbank,* created in 1875 by conversion of the Prussian Bank, absorbed most of them.

Private Bankers

Private bankers constituted the most important class of German financial institutions between 1815 and 1870. They executed a substantial share of the economy's payments, provided a crucial link between savers and investment opportunities, and supplied entrepreneurial initiative. All three functions were related. Although the private bankers were prohibited from issuing banknotes or any other legally recognized media of exchange, they granted acceptance credits that in effect increased the quantity of the means of payment. Added to capital and deposits, this power of creating credit provided the basis of their entrepreneurial and investment banking activity. The role of private bankers as creators of credit, finally, was important because it weakened the effectiveness of government control over the money supply.

The evolution of German private banking after 1815 reflects the general pattern of economic development. From 1815 to about 1840 the most important private banking firms were concentrated in the older commercial and political centers of Germany: Hamburg, Leipzig, Berlin, and, above all, Frankfurt/Main. Smaller centers of trade and industry had their private bankers, but, with the exception of a few houses in Cologne, Augsburg, and Breslau, they were of purely local importance.[20] In contrast to English bankers, who came from a wide variety of occupations and professions, virtually all important (and most unimportant) German bankers were originally merchants.

The transition from merchant to specialist banker was connected not so much with the expansion of trade and industry as with the financial needs of European, and particularly German, governments. The most prominent banking firms—the Rothschilds and the Bethmanns in Frankfurt, the Schicklers in Berlin, Parish and Heine in Hamburg—owed their

[20] Von der Heydt-Kersten & Sons in Elberfeld was another exception; perhaps there were more, but the generalization is reasonably sound.

reputations and much of their wealth to successful operations in the government remittance and loan business.[21] During the decades after 1815 the contributions of private bankers in devising techniques for financing government operations were important, for these techniques later became useful in financing industrial development. These bankers converted short-term loans into long-term securities, placed such securities at a profit, and combined money and stock market operations in securities already placed.

The very success of the government loan business after 1815, in addition to the extra elements of risk and uncertainty stemming from the geographical separation of financial institutions from industrial centers, contributed to the reluctance of the German banking elite to finance new types of industrial activity. In view of the relative efficiency of other European (especially English) industrialists in the "growth" industries of the time, one has to admit that there was much wisdom and rationality in the "conservative" behavior of these private bankers.[22] In any case, whatever private bank lending for industrial purposes that was done before the 1840's was a relatively local phenomenon, confined to the nascent industrializing areas themselves. Significantly, the Rhenish bankers, unburdened—and unrewarded—by a tradition of government financial operations, provide the outstanding examples for this period.[23]

It is virtually impossible to trace the growth of German private banking in meaningful quantitative terms. In the present state of knowledge nothing at all can be said about Germany as a whole. By accepting certain official figures at face value, however, and by making a number of rather doubtful assumptions, it is possible to make some tentative statements for one important part of Germany, namely Prussia. Table VI.2 contains one kind of statement. If Berlin conditions may be taken as typical of Prussia as a

[21] In turn, much of their lending power was the result of the profitable mercantile and financial activities connected with government military needs during the Napoleonic Wars. See Schwarz, *Entwicklungstendenzen im deutschen Privatbankiergewerbe;* Lenz and Unholz, *Geschichte des Bankhauses Gebrüder Schickler,* 249–65; also Schnee, *Die Hoffinanz und der moderne Staat,* esp. vol. III, for the important role of the Jewish "court bankers" in the seventeenth and eighteenth centuries. This institution lost much of its importance in the nineteenth century, however.

[22] As many observers pointed out, most manufacturing operations that required more than negligible amounts of fixed capital could be launched and carried on much more cheaply and with less risk in England. Von Gülich, *Geschichte Darstellung,* II, 425ff; Banck, *Geschichte der sächsischen Banken,* 5; also *The Economist* (London), 31 May 1845, citing a comparative cost estimate.

[23] Krüger, *Kölner Bankiergewerbe;* Tilly, *Financial Institutions,* chaps. 6 and 7. As late as 1856, during the German-wide promotional boom, the *Frankfurter Aktionär* complained of the excessive timidity of Frankfurt bankers and compared them unfavorably with their Rhenish counterparts. *Der Frankfurter Aktionär,* 15 January 1856.

TABLE VI.2

ESTIMATED NUMBER OF PRIVATE BANKS AND UNINCORPORATED BANK-LIKE INSTITUTIONS IN PRUSSIA, 1820/21 TO 1861

Region	1820/21	1843	1849	1861
Rhineland	50	93	102	141
Berlin	60	80	107	165
Total, Prussia	330	424	439	642
Persons per institution	33,000	35,000	37,000	29,000

Sources: Benaerts, *Les Origines de la grande industrie allemande*, 136, 268; Tilly, *Financial Institutions*; Spangenthal, *Die Geschichte der Berliner Borse*, 7.

whole, then roughly 60 per cent of the number of institutions reported for the 1840's and later should be identified as full-fledged banks, a fact which should be borne in mind in any international comparison involving these figures.[24] The figures provide no more than an extremely crude index of banking growth. In terms of persons per bank, one might well conclude that there was almost no change at all during the period.

When one considers the period before the 1840's it is hard to distinguish between capital accumulation by private bankers and capital accumulation in trade or in the government and agricultural sectors served by trade and banking. That is, until the 1840's banking was in large measure a part-time business. Thereafter capital accumulation in banking was predominantly a matter of retained profits.

Evidence concerning the origins of bankers' capital resources is scarce.[25] Reliable estimates of average capitalization of private banking firms for this period are all but nonexistent. Figures covering Berlin bankers for the late 1850's suggest an average capital of around 400,000 thalers (£57,000, or 1,500,000 francs at then-prevailing exchange rates), and if one includes the other unincorporated institutions there, that figure falls to roughly 290,000 thalers.[26] Even the latter figure is probably too high for Prussia as a whole. According to an estimate made in 1845, the Rhineland, Prussia's most developed province, was equipped with a total private banking capital

[24] Benaerts, *Les Origines de la grande industrie allemande,* 268; "Verzeichniss der Banken, 1857 bis 1859," *Oppenheim Hausarchiv,* No. 93. This list for Berlin indicates that around 40 per cent of reported institutions were money changers and bill dealers, rather than full-fledged bankers.

[25] Tilly, *Financial Institutions,* chap. 4, summarizes most of the literature for Rhenish bankers.

[26] "Verzeichniss der Banken, 1857 bis 1859" *Oppenheim Hausarchiv,* No. 93.

of 20 million thalers.[27] This would imply (depending upon one's definition of "private banker") an average capital of between 200,000 and 300,000 thalers.

The Kreditbanken and Other Institutions

One of the most important financial developments before 1870 was the establishment of the corporate and quasi-corporate *Kreditbanken.* Their appearance deserves mention not so much because of their impact in this period, but because they were the forerunners of the German "great banks," which in subsequent years were the dominant financial institutions in Germany.[28]

The history of the German *Kreditbanken* begins in 1848 with the establishment of the Schaaffhausen'schen Bankverein in Cologne. The Bankverein, based on the illiquid remains of one of the Rhineland's oldest and largest private banking firms, Schaaffhausen and Company, must be regarded as a by-product of the Revolution of 1848 rather than as the first conscious step in the development of a new type of financial institution. It was, nevertheless, the first bank of its kind in Germany, and its success in subsequent years provided ample evidence of the utility of mixed banking in its joint-stock form.[29]

Prussia's conservative government chartered no more such banks until 1870, but the business demand for them, stimulated by the financial success of the French Crédit Mobilier after 1852, and coupled with the willingness of governments in other German states to grant liberal charters—at a price—led to the establishment of *Kreditbanken* outside Prussia in the 1850's. The first and most important example was the Bank für Handel und Industrie zu Darmstadt, or Darmstädter, founded by a syndicate of Rhenish and French financiers in 1853.[30] Others followed, but they were not all successful, for insofar as investment banking involved actual entrepreneurial activity and something more than mere stockjobbery, its success depended on finding combinations of resources and techniques which promised to be profitable in a real economic sense. Such combinations were not always present where the *Kreditbanken* operated. The pioneering Darmstädter

[27] Dr. Schulte, *Das Bedürfniss von Aktienbanken in Volkswirtschaftlicher Beziehung mit bosonderen Rücksicht auf die preussische Rheinprovinz,* 34.

[28] Contemporary theorists doubted whether they were banks at all. See Wagner, *Beiträge zur Lehre von den Banken,* 221. Later writers, however, concentrated their attention exclusively on the *Kreditbanken,* so important had they become. For example, see Riesser, *The German Great Banks.*

[29] Tilly, *Financial Institutions,* chap. 8; Koenigs, *Erinnerungsschrift zum fünfzigjährigen Bestehen des A. Schaaffhausen'schen Bankvereins.*

[30] Cameron, "Founding the Bank of Darmstadt."

itself ran into difficulties in the 1850's as a result of investments and promotions involving South German enterprises, and thereafter it restricted itself to operations involving first class securities.[31] Nevertheless, the banks were launched.

The possibility of founding joint-stock promotional banks in other German states did not remove the desire to introduce such institutions in Prussia itself. In the face of the government's refusal to charter banks as joint-stock companies, Prussian promoters during the 1850's turned to the *Kommanditgesellschaft auf Aktien,* the German name for the French *société en commandite.*[32] The first important *Kommandit* bank was the Disconto-Gesellschaft of Berlin. Founded originally in 1851 by David Hansemann, a Rhenish entrepreneur, on the model of the Comptoir d'Escompte, it was reorganized and enlarged in 1856 for mobilier-type operations.[33] Other such companies were soon established. In 1856 alone eight *Kommandit* banks were founded in Prussia, with a total nominal capital of roughly 70 million thalers, one-third of which was paid in during the same year.[34] Promoters in other parts of Germany imitated their Prussian counterparts, founding perhaps—exact figures are unavailable—an additional ten to twelve *Kreditbanken* in *Kommandit* form.

By the mid-1860's the position of joint-stock and *Kommandit Kreditbanken* was firmly established in Germany, though they had not yet attained the predominant position that they were to have following the free incorporation laws and promotional boom of the 1870's. Their quantitative importance toward the end of the period is summarized in Table VI.3, which also records some balance-sheet aggregates for other joint-stock banks as well. For Prussia, the total assets of the *Kreditbanken* must have been close to 10 per cent of what private bankers could command at that time.[35] The march of the *Kreditbanken* toward prominence had scarcely begun, but they were already an established institutional feature of the German financial scene.

The financial services provided by banking institutions were supplemented by the activities of insurance companies, savings banks, stock markets, and a host of other "auxiliary" individuals and institutions.

[31] Incidentally, this illustrates the limitations of such institutions as development mechanisms, a point also noted by Riesser, *The German Great Banks,* 66.

[32] See above, p. 106. It is interesting to note that August von der Heydt, Prussian minister of commerce and a former Rhenish banker, wished to enact laws making such companies subject to specific government charter, but his wishes were opposed by other members of the cabinet. Von Delbrück, *Lebenserinnerungen,* II, 82.

[33] Däbritz, *Gründung und Anfänge der Disconto-Gesellschaft;* Bergengrün, *David Hansemann.*

[34] Von Poschinger, *Bankwesen und Bankpolitik in Preussen,* II, 226–31.

[35] See below, p. 177, and note 65.

TABLE VI.3

ASSETS AND LIABILITIES OF PRUSSIAN AND OTHER NORTH GERMAN NOTE-ISSUING AND "CREDIT" BANKS, END OF 1865[a]

(million thalers)

		Assets			Liabilities			
Row	No.	Specie	Loans and Advances[b]	Total Assets	Curr. Acct.[c]	Accep-tances	Note Cir.	Cap.
1 Prussian Bank	1	61.8	19.3	177.8	17.0	–	125.2	20.7
2 Prussian banks of issue	7	4.2	6.0	24.2	7.3	–	7.2	9.7
3 Prussian credit banks	4	1.1	29.5	42.8	10.8	7.7	–	20.6
4 All N. German banks of issue	32	89.1	63.9	318.0	35.7	–	185.9	85.2
5 All N. German credit banks	10	4.1	48.1	86.3	20.3	11.6	–	46.0
6 All N. German banks	42	93.2	112.0	404.3	56.0	11.6	185.9	131.2
7 Row 6 minus Row 1	41	31.4	92.7	226.5	39.0	11.6	60.7	110.5

[a]"North German" defined as including Frankfurt/Main and all points north. [b]Figure is overstated in that it includes interbank loans. [c]Includes interbank loans.

Sources: Elster, "Die Banken Norddeutschlands im Jahre 1865 und während des Krieges 1866," *Zeitschrift des Königlich Preussischen Statistischen Bureaus*, VII (1867), 74–80; Annual Report of Bank for Commerce and Industry in Darmstadt, 1865 (Darmstadt, 1866).

Unfortunately, there is no space for a discussion of their development here, and the following generalizations will have to serve. The stock exchanges, of which the most important was Berlin's, assisted in the process of capital mobilization by broadening the market for securities and increasing the liquidity of security holders—including the banks. In Germany, however, the situation was unlike that in Britain and some other countries; the provision of promotional and placement facilities by bankers and banks, and their active role in managing the placement of securities which were eligible for formal quotation and trading, reduced the relative importance of the stock exchanges for channeling capital into industry.[36] The passive character of the stock exchanges is further reflected in the lag between the promotion and founding of industrial corporations and the appearance of their shares on the formal stock exchanges of Berlin or Frankfurt. Until the 1870's the bulk of such shares remained unquoted, and they moved

[36] In Germany, private bankers, and, subsequently, the *Kreditbanken,* supplied stockbroking services as well. Specialized stockbrokers have always been a rare breed in Germany.

within the financial world through the banking system. The major role of stock exchanges concerned government and other nonindustrial securities.

Insurance companies provided bankers and banks with additional financial resources, and in some cases were organized by bankers with this purpose in mind.[37] Savings banks also provided bankers with deposits, but, with one notable exception (David Hansemann's Aachen Association), the savings banks were government-administered, and their active business was confined to the acquisition of government securities and safe real estate mortgages.[38] Quantitatively, both the insurance companies and the savings banks seem to have been of minor importance when compared with the rest of the banking system. They were dependent upon voluntary savings to a much larger extent than banks and bankers were, and their development was thus a growth-induced rather than a growth-inducing phenomenon.

THE STOCK OF MONEY AND MONETARY POLICY

In Germany, as in other industrializing countries in the nineteenth century, government control over the money supply was an important policy aim. In Germany, as elsewhere, the aim was not fully realized. What are the general implications of this experience? To answer this question, three others must be asked. What was the state of the coinage and currency in these years? What measures were undertaken to control them? What is the evidence concerning the effectiveness of these measures and the institutions created to execute them?

Coinage

During the first half of the century the most important component of the stock of money was the coinage provided by the mints of the various German states. Most states were theoretically on a bimetallic standard, but in fact the silver standard prevailed. In any case, "cash" meant specie, whether gold or silver, and other means of payment were regarded as specie substitutes. This distinction was sharper in theory than in practice, but it was not wholly devoid of substance—a fact clearly revealed during the crises of 1830 and 1848, when holders of other forms of money tried to gain specie instead. In several parts of Germany, both the quantity and

[37] For example, the Aachen-Munich Fire Insurance Company, founded in 1825, and the Concordia Life Insurance Company, founded in 1853. Tilly, *Financial Institutions,* chap. 8.

[38] Klersch, *Die Sparkasse der Stadt Köln;* Kluitmann, *Geld- und Kapitalverkehr,* 20.

quality of metallic coins provided by the authorities were the objects of repeated complaints. In the case of Prussia, or at least certain parts of it like the Rhineland, it may be possible to speak of a "shortage of coin" directly related to the unwillingness of the government to provide it. One type of evidence is the frequency of the complaints, but this by its nature is difficult to evaluate. There would seem to be stronger evidence in the widespread use of foreign coins in the Prussian Rhineland, but this was to some extent counterbalanced by the circulation of Prussian coin outside Prussia. Matters are further complicated by the fact that in 1838 Prussia and several other North German states formed a union which agreed to employ the same types of coin, and in 1857 that union was expanded to include the South German states. It is thus virtually impossible to draw up a meaningful balance sheet.

Price fluctuations of different coins in circulation provide perhaps sounder support for the complaints about the instability of the payments media than the evidence underlying complaints about its over-all quantity. There was much fluctuation in the rates at which coins could be exchanged for one another. Contemporaries argued (as have more recent critics of international schemes for fluctuating exchange rates) that uncertainty about the value of different forms of money diminished business confidence, trade, and the level of economic activity. These criticisms had some merit. Such exchange rate instability was, however, at least in part, the necessary accompaniment of uneven regional economic development in the absence of developed and well-integrated banking facilities.[39]

In several German states, governments issued paper money, convertible and inconvertible. In Prussia this became an important part of the circulating media. (See Table VI.4.) In Prussia, moreover, the supply of government paper money might be characterized, like its official supply of coin, as inadequate for the demand. This claim would rest, once more, on evidence concerning the frequency of complaints and on the premium occasionally borne by such money relative to specie.[40] Prussian businessmen, however, used the paper money of their German neighbors, while the latter used Prussian money, so it is difficult to generalize. Some data on the approximate amount of such money in Germany as a whole is given in Table VI.5.

[39] Differences in the relative prices of different coins led to their transfer from one place to another and, where the denominator was merely a unit of account, represented capital flows induced by price differentials. See Tilly, *Financial Institutions,* chap. 2; also Schwann, *Ludolf Campenhausen als Wirtschaftspolitiker,* vols. II and III, for reprinted documents dealing with some of the manifestations of this problem in the Rhineland.

[40] Tilly, *Financial Institutions,* chap. 3.

TABLE VI.4

ESTIMATED STOCK OF CURRENCY IN PRUSSIA, 1835–65

(million thalers)

	1835	1845	1855	1865
Specie in circulation	105	110	115	155
Specie in banks	5[a]	12[a]	20[b]	70[c]
Government paper money	17	18	21	15
Bank notes	0	0	45[d]	130[e]
Total	122	128	181	300

[a]In Royal Bank of Prussia. [b]In Prussian Bank. [c]Prussian Bank plus six other Prussian banks of issue. [d]Total circulation of Prussian Bank plus estimated circulation of non-Prussian banks of issue *in Prussia*. [e]Total circulation of Prussian Bank and other Prussian banks of issue.

SOURCES AND PROCEDURES FOR TABLE IV.4

Specie: The estimate for 1835 is taken from Hoffmann, *Die Lehre vom Geld*, esp. 172–3, where an estimate applying either to 1835 or 1836 (it is not clear which) is given, based on Mint activity with adjustments for estimated exports of domestic coin and imports of foreign coin. The estimate for 1855 is based on data in Bergius, "Eine Deutsch oder Preussische Münzreform?," which utilize Mint statistics and adjustments for the continued export and import of coin. A figure for 1845 was obtained by averaging those reported for 1835 and 1855. Bergius' data for 1853 were carried to 1855 and to 1865 with the help of Mint data reported in Helfferich, *Beiträge zur Geschichte der deutschen Geldreform*, 99, and the assumptions that Mint additions to the stock of Zollverein coin between 1853 and 1870 took place at a constant annual rate. I have subtracted the specie holdings of the Prussian Bank from this total (Schauer, *Die Preussische Bank*, 41; Niebuhr, *Geschichte der Königlichen Bank*, 230–32).

Government paper money: Figures for all years are taken from Bergius, "Geschichte des Preussischen Papiergeldes." His figures, however, refer only to the non-interest-bearing portion of the Prussian national debt and do not take account of treasury notes held by the various government agencies—which may have been of considerable significance. On this point see Bergius, *Preussische Zustände*, 122.

Banknotes: The estimate for 1855 refers to and includes: (1) the average note circulation of the Prussian Bank as reported in Schauer, *Die Preussische Bank*, 41, and Thorwärt, "Die Entwicklung des Banknotenumlaufs in Deutschland," 202–3; (2) the estimated circulation in Prussia of non-Prussian banknotes, this statistic in turn based on estimates reported in Thorwärt, ibid. 200, and in Delbrück, *Lebenserinnerungen*, II, 29–32. The figure for 1865 is taken from the data presented by Elster, "Die Banken Norddeutschlands im Jahre 1865."

The importance of the Prussian Bank's note circulation as a part of the Prussian payments media cannot be doubted. In 1855 its notes represented more than 10 per cent of Prussia's estimated stock of currency. By 1865 the proportion was more than 40 per cent (see Table VI.3, p. 164). Its importance to the development of central banking controls is another matter, however. Some writers observed a "close" quantitative relationship

TABLE VI.5

ESTIMATED STOCK OF CURRENCY IN GERMANY, 1845–75

(million thalers)

	1845	1855	1865	1875
Specie in circulation	140[a]	180[a]	190[a]	460[b]
Specie in banks	15	30	85	203
Government paper money	24[c]	54	36	60
Bank notes	6	55	191	300
Total	185	289	415	820

[a]Estimated on the assumption that the Prussian ratio between bank and public holdings of specie also held for Germany as a whole. [b]Helfferich, *Beiträge zur Geschichte der deutschen Geldreform,* 99, 136. [c]Estimated on the assumption that the ratio of Prussian paper money circulation to the German total was the same as the ratio between Prussian coin in circulation and German coin in circulation.

Sources: As in Table VI.4 plus H. Paasche, "Die neueste Entwicklung der Banknoten- und Papier-geld-Zirkulation in den hauptsächlichsten Kulturländern der Gegenwärt," *Jahrbücher für National- Oekonomie und Statistik* (1878).

between the bank's circulation and the over-all level of financial activity.[41] From this they inferred that Prussian Bank lending and rediscounting activity "determined" the over-all rate of monetary expansion. They explained this by reference to the superior position which Prussian Bank notes appeared to occupy in the contemporary hierarchy of liquidity preference as the closest substitute for specie. This was explained, in turn, by the support of the Prussian government and the large accumulation of specie which stood behind the bank's notes. The Prussian Bank held the system's cash reserves, while credit creation by other financial institutions was believed to depend systematically upon the ease with which (or cost at which) they could call on those reserves if needed. In fact, the data are far too crude to support any hypothesis about causality. The available annual data on stock exchange prices, interest rates, and direct evidence on a handful of other financial institutions are hardly comprehensive enough to permit statistical testing. Moreover, such association as does appear suggests at the very most a conclusion of interdependence.[42] For a variety of reasons Prus-

[41] Speithoff, *Die Wirtschaftlichen Wechsellagen,* I, 32, 36, 114–23; Nasse, "Zur Banknoten- und Papiergeldfrage mit spezieller Beziehung auf den preussischen Staat."

[42] Spiethoff's figures actually show no more than this for the second half of the nineteenth century. Spiethoff, *Die Wirtschaftlichen Wechsellagen,* II, Tables 2–12. There is some evidence, moreover, that the level of Prussian Bank activity was not infrequently limited by the unwillingness of private bankers and others to borrow from it. Tilly, *Financial Institutions,* chap. 3.

sian Bank officials and their superiors in the government doubtless wanted to control the process of monetary growth, but it is impossible with present evidence to determine the extent to which they were successful in doing so, at least for the period before 1870.[43]

Some contemporary observers may have exaggerated the importance of the controls exercised by the Prussian Bank because they felt that its monopoly constituted an obstacle to the attainment of a more satisfactory rate of financial and economic development. They criticized the bank both in terms of its net aggregate contribution to the supply of money and the volume of credit and in terms of its lending policies. The relatively conservative specie reserve rules that it maintained—50 per cent of note liabilities was the normal minimum—limited its over-all expansion.[44] More important were rules governing the direction of its lending activity. It lent and discounted almost exclusively to private bankers or against a banker's signature. The one important exception to this practice, significantly, involved the lending and discounting services which the bank provided to *Junker* landlords and their commercial representatives in the eastern provinces of Prussia.[45] Given the bank's close ties with the government and its bureaucratic management, this may have been a wise and safe policy, but, as contemporaries observed, it made the bank a much poorer substitute for the privately run joint-stock banks of issue which it was in part designed to preclude. It did not reach as wide a range of borrowers as the joint-stock banks of issue would presumably have done. This meant that credit needed for new purposes or by new and unknown entrepreneurs was more difficult to obtain.[46]

The restrictiveness of Prussian Bank operations was reflected in the increased circulation of foreign banknotes within Prussia. According to contemporary estimates, in the 1850's this circulation exceeded that of the Prussian Bank. After 1856 the importance of foreign circulation shrank as a result of legal prohibitions and Prussian Bank expansion.[47] One might argue, however, that the impact of the outside issue was more permanent, because the Prussian Bank's expansion was a direct response to the competitive threat it had represented.

[43] Thorwärt, "Die Entwicklung des Banknotenumlaufs," 208, argued that the Prussian Bank began to operate effectively as a central bank as early as 1866.

[44] Schauer, *Die Preussische Bank,* 48. This cash reserve was extremely conservative by typical nineteenth-century standards.

[45] Ibid. 64–6.

[46] This was the view of *Der Frankfurter Aktionär,* Fritz Harkort, Gustav Mevissen, and many other contemporaries. Tilly, *Financial Institutions,* chap. 3.

[47] Von Delbrück, *Lebenserinnerungen,* II, 32; Thorwärt, "Die Entwicklung des Banknotenumlaufs," 200, 202.

Statistical Estimates

Estimates of the stock of currency for either Germany as a whole or for individual German states in this period are necessarily rough ones. The paucity and dubious reliability of available statistics are bad enough, but there are also problems in interpreting the statistics that are available (for example, determining whether reported circulation of government paper money included or excluded the holdings of government institutions themselves). The figures in Tables VI.4 and VI.5 must therefore be used with caution.

These tables suggest two important features: growth of the aggregate stock of currency and relative growth of the public's use of specie substitutes. The latter, more important phenomenon is reflected in the growing proportion of banknotes in the total stock of currency and in the accompanying shift in specie holdings from the public to banks. One must remember, however, that the tables describe only the stock of currency.[48] In fact, a number of financial instruments which served as substitutes for nominal types of money came into prominence during the period between 1815 and 1870. Consequently, no conclusions about the economic importance of currency should be drawn without reference to such money "substitutes" or to the institutions and techniques that facilitated their growth.

Money Substitutes and Credit Creation

Controls placed by governments on the nature and over-all quantity of the currency stimulated the development of other instruments for effectuating monetary exchanges. The earliest, and, for the period before 1870, the most important, were those supplied by private bankers. The effectiveness of private bankers as financial intermediaries grew with their own resources, but their major importance rested on their ability to mobilize the resources of others, especially by creating liabilities which served the functions of money. In many parts of Germany credit creation by bankers involved the use of bills of exchange and was already relatively well established before 1815. The German system of bill currency differed in an interesting and significant way from that of England and other areas where such existed, however. German businessmen made use of the *Trockenwechsel* ("dry

[48] The "stock of currency" can be defined here as the sum of outstanding or circulating specie, treasury notes, and Prussian Bank notes—even if the last were not always and by all people regarded as true "money."

bill"). Creditors did not draw these bills on debtors and then discount them with their bankers or pass them on in payment to other businessmen; instead it was customary for German merchants and industrialists to draw directly on their bankers, against either deposits or overdraft credit, and use the bills directly for payments with or without the banker's signature. The system thus resembled a modern checking system, except that the bills bore interest. As early as 1833 Fritz Harkort regarded it as one of the more obvious financial features of western Germany. In Silesia the von Eichborns of Breslau and other Breslau bankers had been providing local customers with a "banker's bill" currency since the eighteenth century. In commercial centers such as Berlin and Leipzig it was a familiar part of daily business.[49] This feature gave private bankers an important place in the economy. In addition, bankers provided *giro* services for payments involving two or more of their own customers, yet another possible means of credit creation, since bankers could create the balances they transferred.[50]

The liabilities that bankers created were redeemable in another monetary medium, usually specie; after 1848 treasury and Prussian Bank notes could sometimes be used for this purpose as well. In a technical sense this was the principal limitation on the bankers' credit-creating powers. One should add, however, that most liabilities of private bankers were not demand liabilities in the sense that banknotes were, because bills drawn against a bank account were usually payable at some time in the future. In the case of overdrafts, at least, bankers were generally advised as to each drawing.[51] This gave bankers greater flexibility with respect to their assets, but it limited the liquidity or spendability of their liabilities for those who held them. The interest they bore measured their degree of "non-moniness."

During the 1850's credit creation by means of bills of exchange drawn on bankers was supplemented and in part replaced by two developments: the growth of note issues, particularly around Prussia and Saxony; and the increasing use of bankers' acceptances. Through most of the 1850's note issues were the more important of the two, but acceptances gained importance in subsequent years. The guaranteeing signature of a banker gave greater currency to trade bills drawn between industrial or mercantile

[49] Harkort, "Plan einer Gessellschaft für die Eisenbahn," in Hermann, *Zeitschrift für das Lande zwischen der Weser und Maas,* 9 February 1833 (in *Stadt Archiv Barmen*); von Eichborn, *Soll und Haben,* 42–3, 46, 301; Schwarz, *Entwicklungstendenzen,* 30ff.

[50] *Giro* transfers involved payments made by one customer of a bank to another customer's account with that same bank.

[51] Tilly, *Financial Institutions,* chap. 5.

firms, and, more importantly, made them eligible for discount at the Prussian Bank, whose growing network of branches both stimulated and was stimulated by the use of acceptances.[52]

This practice linked bankers more closely to the discounting facilities of the Prussian Bank. In fact, to the extent that the volume of bankers' advances depended upon the subsequent substitution of banknotes for bankers' acceptances, the Prussian Bank held the private banking system's reserves. Contemporaries recognized this element of interdependence before 1870, and the simultaneous growth of Prussian Bank discounts and private bank acceptances confirm its importance. Yet, for reasons advanced earlier, the proposition that Prussian Bank policy effectively governed credit creation by private bankers cannot be demonstrated.

Credit creation by private bankers was clearly of great significance in Prussia before 1870. Table VI.6 presents some quantitative estimates of its importance. Comparison with Table VI.4 indicates that by mid-century, and possibly earlier, bankers' liabilities constituted the largest component in the monetary stock. Moreover, the proportion of entrepreneurial needs satisfied by the bankers—which was of greater relevance for industrial growth—was doubtless much higher.

Table VI.6 also includes the "monetary" liabilities of the *Kreditbanken* —of growing significance even before 1870. The experience of private bankers in developing money substitutes and employing the financial resources that they mobilized had lasting importance because they were able to use that experience when they established the operating procedures of the German *Kreditbanken*.[53] Spiethoff regarded the acceptance and current account liabilities of the *Kreditbanken* as the "note circulation of non-note-issuing institutions."[54]

Finally, Table VI.6 includes the interest-bearing liabilities of the *Landschaften*, the *Pfandbriefe*. There is an immense amount of evidence suggesting that these instruments, despite their relative large denominations, were widely regarded and used as currency, or at least as reservoirs of

[52] Ordinary current account credits with bankers could be drawn on in specie *or* other means of payment such as bills or drafts. Such credits involved interest charges or earnings; acceptance credits involved only a commission so far as the endorsing banker was concerned—usually around one half of 1 per cent—though the acceptances themselves of course bore interest.

[53] All banks provide credit and are in that sense, of course, "*Kreditbanken*." This term has been adopted here to refer to the corporate (*Aktiengesellschaften*) and quasi-corporate (*Kommanditgesellschaft auf Aktien*) banks which did not issue notes. This adoption signifies nothing besides dissatisfaction with all of the possible alternatives.

[54] Spiethoff, *Die Wirtschaftlichen Wechsellagen,* I, 36; also Riesser, *The German Great Banks,* 197–8, 211.

TABLE VI.6

ESTIMATED STOCK OF MONEY SUBSTITUTES IN PRUSSIA, 1835–65

(million thalers)

Supplied by:	1835	1845	1855	1865
Private bankers[a]	50	130	215	480
Kreditbanken	–	–	10[b]	20[c]
Landschaften[d]	100	110	125	125

[a]Their current deposit and acceptance liabilities. [b]Schaaffhausen'schen Bankverein (Cologne) and Discontogesellschaft (Berlin). [c]Schaaffhausen'schen Bankverein, Discontogesellschaft, Schlesischer Bankverein, Berliner Handelsgesellschaft. [d]Figures refer to outstanding *Pfandbriefe*.

SOURCES AND PROCEDURE FOR TABLE VI.6

Private Bankers. The estimates are based on the following assumptions and sources:

1. The current liabilities of the private bankers are defined as money substitutes.
2. The average of the estimated capital per banking firm for the Rhineland (all four years) and for Berlin (1857 or 1859) approximated that of all Prussian private bankers.
3. The ratio between the average capital per banker in Berlin and the average capital per banker in the Rhineland was constant over the period covered.
4. The ratio per firm of capital to current liabilities (excluding estimated savings deposits) for all Prussian private bankers in these years was the same as the ratio estimated for Rhenish bankers. That ratio was 1:1.4.
5. The estimated capital per firm was 100,000 thalers in 1835, 200,000 thalers in 1845, 300,000 thalers in 1855, and 500,000 thalers in 1865. The Prussian totals are obtained by multiplying the Rhenish totals by a coefficient relating the total number of Rhenish bankers to the total number of Prussian bankers.
6. Sources: Bankers' balance sheet information: Sal. Oppenheim jr. & Cie. (*Oppenheim Hausarchiv*, Nos. 85 and 90; Krüger, *Kölner Bankiergewerbe*, 65, 71); J. H. Stein & Co. (C. Eckert, *J. H. Stein*, 27, 83–4; Krüger, *Kölner Bankiergewerbe*, 58, 63); A. Schaaffhausen & Co. (Krüger, *Kölner Bankiergewerbe*, 53, 202–3; *HASK*, "Nachlass von Wittgenstein," No. 11); T. C. Sprenger & Co. (Kluitmann, *Geld-und Kapitalverkehr*, 106); W. T. Zurhelle & Co. (H. Bräutigam, *Das Bankiergewerbe des Regierungs-Bezirks Aachen*, 34); Nagel & Co. and Fischer & Co. (Poppelreuter and Witzel, *Barmer Bank-Verein*, 2, 22); Ludwig von Born & Co. (W. Däbritz, *Die Essener Credit-Anstalt*, 54–5); Johann Wichelhaus P. Sohn (R. Wichelhaus, *Bankhaus Johann Wichelhaus*, 63–9); von der Heydt-Kersten & Sohne (Kurzrock, *200 Jahre von der Heydt-Kersten & Sohne*). Capitalization estimates for the Berlin bankers are based on data in *Oppenheim Hausarchiv*, No. 93, cited in note 24, p. 161.

The Kreditbanken: Balance Sheet Information for 1855 and 1865: Berliner Handelsgesellschaft (R. Lüke, *Die Berliner Handelsgesellschaft*, 22 and Appendix 1); Disconto-Gesellschaft (Däbritz, *Gründung und Anfänge der Disconto-Gesellschaft*, Appendix; Däbritz, *David Hansemann und Adolph von Hansemann*); Schaaffhausen'schen Bankverein (Koenigs, *Erinnerungsschrift*, Appendix; Annual Reports, 1848–1869, in *Bibliothek der Industrie- und Handelskammer zu Köln*); Schlesischer Bankverein (Elster, "Die Banken Norddeutschlands," 74–80).

Landschaften. The data for the circulation of the *Pfandbriefe* are taken from Dieterici, *Handbuch der Statistik des Preussischen Staats*, 570–75. The *Pfandbriefe* circulation for 1865, however, simply repeats the figure given for 1859, and this may well mean that the total for 1865 is too low, because Landschaften net borrowing reportedly continued in these years (See Mauer, *Das Landschaftlichen Kreditwesen Preussens*.)

liquidity.[55] This was particularly true in Berlin and through the eastern provinces of Prussia, though their importance in this respect seems to have diminished in the second half of the century. They are included to round

[55] Some of the sources are von Eichborn, *Soll und Haben*, 287–8; *The Economist* (London), 3 July 1847; von Gülich, *Geschichtliche Darstellung*, IV, 583.

out the picture of the developing money "substitutes" and also to suggest that that development was by no means a monopoly of industrial needs.

INDUSTRIAL FINANCE AND THE ROLE OF THE BANKS

Money substitutes were developed to facilitate lending, particularly to industrial firms. What were the financial needs of German industry in this period? How and how well did banks satisfy those needs? What kind of evidence is there? These are the relevant questions.

The financial history of German industry between 1815 and the 1840's raises conceptual and statistical problems similar to those encountered in tracing the financial history of the English Industrial Revolution. During this period much industrial innovation and development in Germany took the form of step-by-step improvements and enlargements of capacity which could be financed internally out of profits accumulated in the hands of individual firms and entrepreneurs. Yet extensive use of credit—obtained from bankers, merchants, relatives, and friends—was nevertheless characteristic, for the accumulation of profits was irregular and did not always coincide with the appearance of investment opportunities. The utilization of bank or commercial credit in financing "normal" operations (e.g. the movement of raw materials from seaport towns to inland manufacturing centers) "freed" the resources of individual firms for the finance of Schumpeterian innovation.[56] Therefore the usual references to over-all gradual development and profit accumulation by no means settle the question of financing. After 1840 the ambiguity diminishes. The railroads, and a good deal of the heavy industrial enterprise which followed or accompanied their construction, involved external finance to a much larger extent than earlier types of business enterprise in Germany did. At this point, in Schumpeterian terminology, development, innovation, and credit creation clearly moved together.

Before the 1840's, however, the process of industrial development in Germany centered around the fortunes of business firms organized as private partnerships. Some qualification needs to be made here to take account of government-controlled mining operations, but even here the influence of private firms was significant, and, in terms of innovation and development, perhaps decisive. In the 1820's and 1830's the dependence of the growth industries, the textile industries above all, on private partnerships limited the development of a national industrial capital market. The German capital market at that time was a loosely connected series of local markets based on relatively personal and direct contacts between individual

[56] Schumpeter, *Business Cycles,* I, 292.

businessmen. Entrepreneurial and firm histories dealing with this era are virtually unanimous, and in most cases no doubt correct, in stressing the personal and intrafamilial character of industrial finance.[57]

This legal and financial framework, however, was considerably more flexible and conducive to growth than historians have generally recognized. Wholesale merchants and the larger manufacturing firms in most industries extended substantial credits to their customers. Evidence concerning the quantitative importance of such credit to the lender—it frequently amounted to as much as 50 per cent of a firm's assets—suggests, though it does not prove, the importance of intrabusiness finance for borrowers.[58] We do know, moreover, than in many industries the introduction of certain key innovations—for example, the steam engine—depended significantly upon the availability of business credit.[59]

The technical device that accompanied and facilitated the use of intrabusiness credit was the bill of exchange. By endorsement, a grantor of credit could pass a bill of exchange on to a third party. The practice could extend indefinitely, though six or seven endorsements per bill was probably typical.[60] Certainly during this period intrabusiness credit utilizing bills of exchange was for the most part used by those who knew each other personally, or who had personal connections, but it should be noted that the practice of endorsement, as well as the well-established legal and business traditions and rules regarding the use of bills of exchange, considerably widened the scope and effectiveness of personal connections as a basis for credit creation. The saying that the use of bills of exchange made every businessman a banker thus applied to German as well as to English experience.[61]

[57] See, e.g. Berdrow, *Friedrich Krupp, der Gründer der Gusstahlfabrik in Briefen und Urkunden,* 73, 146, 159, 201–2ff; Berdrow, *Alfred Krupps Briefe, 1826–1887,* scattered letters; Kluitmann, *Geld- und Kapitalverkehr,* 13, 20ff; Däbritz, *Bochumer Verein für Bergbau und Gusstahfabrikation,* 8–10, 45–6; see also Borchardt, "Zur Frage des Kapitalmangels," 414–16.

[58] Records for W. T. Rautenstrauch & Company, a Rhenish leather-goods firm, reflect this, but it was a large firm. Rautenstrauch Papers, *R-W Wa,* Abt. 9. Other company histories suggest the same.

[59] Berdrow, *Alfred Krupps Briefe, 1826–1887,* 22; Redlich, "The Leaders of the German Steam-Engine Industry During the First Hundred Years."

[60] This is the average number of endorsements found in a sample of roughly 150 bills of exchange used in the Rhineland, 1830–60. Protested Bills Registers, Selected Notaries, *Staatsarchiv Düsseldorf.* See also Tilly, *Financial Institutions,* chaps. 5 and 8, for further indications on the use of bills of exchange.

[61] Pressnell, *Country Banking,* 19. The use of bills of exchange is best documented for Rhenish Prussia (Tilly, *Financial Institutions,* chaps. 5 and 8), but von Gülich (*Geschichtliche Darstellung,* II, 558) believed that they were widely used all over Germany in the 1830's and 1840's.

Real estate mortgages were another capital-mobilizing device of some significance in the period before 1840 as well as after. As in most underdeveloped countries, real estate, improved and unimproved, was an attractive form of wealth. Titles to "immobile capital," to use the German term, offered greater security than more mobile forms of wealth, such as corporate stocks and bonds or the promissory notes of individual businessmen and firms. An industrialist who wished to finance expansion of one kind or another was able to secure credit—in some cases very substantial sums—by mortgaging his real estate. This real estate might be a workshop or a mill, but it might just as well be property—land or buildings, urban or rural—which had no direct commercial purpose whatsoever.[62] This was the main reason behind the repeated requests of Prussian business leaders in the 1830's and 1840's for the authorization of mortgage banks: not because of the importance of agricultural investment, though that was one motive, but because manufacturers and merchants used real estate as security for commercial and industrial loans on such a large scale. In 1847 an article in the Prussian *Handels-Archiv* reported that in the Rhineland alone 33.7 million thalers' worth of new mortgages had been registered in 1845, and 30.4 million thalers' worth in 1846. The article pointed out that a considerable share of these sums represented collateral for loans made to manufacturers and merchants.[63] The "monetization" of an illiquid form of wealth thus achieved was not as important or as thorough as that achieved by the *Pfandbriefe* and the *Landschaften* in eastern Prussia, but mortgages were clearly instruments of more than negligible proportions for industrial finance.

After 1840 such financial devices were improved, and they were increasingly used, but they were gradually overshadowed in importance by the organization of joint-stock companies and the mobilization of capital through the sale of shares and bonds.[64] Joint-stock companies were obviously dependent upon external financial sources. In general, however, such companies did not raise funds directly from the general public; they usually employed the services of financial intermediaries, mainly banks.

[62] The notarial files in the *Staatsarchiv Düsseldorf* contain many contracts dealing with such loans in the 1830's and 1840's. See also Tilly, *Financial Institutions,* chap. 6.

[63] *Preussische Handels-Archiv, 1846* (Berlin, 1847); also Cologne Chamber of Commerce Reports: 1845, 1846, 1847.

[64] The use of government securities as collateral for intrabusiness credit before 1840 should also be mentioned, along with bills of exchange and real estate mortgages, as a device which eased the capital-mobilizing problems of private partnerships.

Lending and Promotional Activity

What scattered evidence there is on Rhenish banking conditions suggests that in the Rhineland bankers' advances and loans outstanding amounted to between 30 and 35 million thalers in the 1840's, between 50 and 60 million in the 1850's, and between 120 and 130 million by the 1860's.[65] Generalized for Prussia as a whole, this sample estimate suggests the following total of outstanding bankers' advances and loans: 100 to 120 million thalers in the 1840's; 140 to 160 million in the 1850's; and close to 400 million in the 1860's. The figures for the 1840's and 1850's might be compared with an estimate of the total value of working and fixed capital in the *Zollverein's* textile industry at mid-century: 190 million thalers.[66]

Most credit extended by private bankers (and by the *Kreditbanken* that followed them) was ostensibly short term in nature, because that form of credit was in the banking tradition, and because working capital—relative to fixed capital—was of great importance in the German economy before 1870.[67] It is important to emphasize the flexibility of bankers' policies in this respect, however. They frequently found themselves financing the accumulation of fixed capital. During the 1830's, for example, the Rhine-Ruhr iron and machinery works, the Gutehoffnungshütte, began a large-scale modernization program financed in part with credit obtained from its two bankers, A. Schaaffhausen and von der Heydt-Kersten and Sons. Between 1829 and 1839 a net credit balance with its bankers was converted into a debit of nearly 100,000 thalers. In the 1840's the Gutehoffnungshütte reaped the benefits of its investment, and by 1849 it again had credit balances.[68] More examples could be cited, but unfortunately no quantitative generalization is possible. Joint-stock companies permitted bankers to be still more flexible, for the possibility of funding current debt by means of new securities was greater for such companies than for private partnerships.

[65] This estimate is based on the balance sheet data for eight Rhenish bankers over the period 1820–70, cited in the Sources to Table VI.4, and on the data on Cologne bankers given in Krüger, *Kölner Bankiergewerbe,* 16, 23, 32, 46, 48, 53, 58. These data suggest a ratio of capital to current assets between 1:1 and 1:2. These ratios are assumed to hold for Prussia as a whole.

[66] Borchardt, "Zur Frage des Kapitalmangels," 404.

[67] The reader is reminded once again of the difficulty in distinguishing between short-term and long-term credit. Maintenance and even growth of an outstanding debit balance over long periods of time, if accompanied by increased turnover, might not represent long-term credit at all. Bankers themselves indicated their expectations in this regard by levying annual commissions based on an annual turnover of four or five times the amount of debit. Tilly, *Financial Institutions,* chap. 6.

[68] Woltmann and Frölich, *Die Gutehoffnungshütten, Oberhausen, 1810–1910,* 55–6.

In the 1840's the Rhenish Railway Company regularly owed its bankers between 300,000 and 400,000 thalers (at one point the company owed the Oppenheims of Cologne alone more than 300,000 thalers); by this means the company's construction program was carried forward. By 1845, however, a bond issue had converted this debt into a substantial deposit balance.[69] In 1855 the failure of one stock issue and the brighter prospects for another led Sal. Oppenheim Jr. and Cie., von der Heydt-Kersten and Sons, and the Schaaffhausen'schen Bankverein to extend to the Stolberg Zinc Mining Company a total current account credit of 700,000 thalers.[70]

The flexibility of bankers' credit policies was related in an obvious way to the investment banking functions they performed. Their relatively large capitals and close links with the capital market enabled them to regard the debit balances of corporate customers with some degree of equanimity and permitted them to provide debt-funding facilities directly. The unique feature of German "mixed" banking lay in the directness of the funding operation. Unlike the English bankers, the German bankers regarded the funding operation as one of their major responsibilities. In Schumpeter's words, they ". . . provided machinery to do this themselves. They took care of the necessary issues of stocks and bonds, thus helping the enterprise to redeem its short debt and providing it with additional means. In order to effect this they were ready to take these stocks or bonds for their own account, not only if they were unable to place them, but in the ordinary course of their business routine. . . . When eventually they placed the securities acquired, they again financed the private investors so that, temporarily at least, the transaction often meant no more than a shift in assets." [71] Schumpeter's description of this type of business concerned the mature form developed by the German "great banks" at the end of the nineteenth century, but all of its essential elements were present in some degree in the practice of the private bankers before 1870.

German investment banking also had an entrepreneurial element of considerable importance. In some instances the bankers initially perceived new opportunities for investment and suggested methods of exploiting them. More important, however, were entrepreneurial tasks that were allied directly with financial ends. Frequently, interested bankers obtained government approval and support for the projects of others. Then they had to create a market for the new securities. Finally, it was essential for them

[69] Kumpmann, *Rheinische Eisenbahn,* 423–6; General Balances, Rheinische Eisenbahn Gesellschaft, 1842–45, *Historisches Archiv der Stadt Köln* (Cologne), R.E.G.

[70] Krüger, *Kölner Bankiergewerbe,* 221–3; Cameron, *France and Europe,* 380; Blumberg, "Die Finanzierung . . . ," 203, indicate that such examples were widespread.

[71] Schumpeter, *Business Cycles,* I, 349.

to insure that the policies, financial and otherwise, of enterprises newly created or enlarged would continue to favor, or at least not interfere with, their own banking interests.

The first significant examples of German investment banking are found in connection with railroads. From the beginning Rhenish bankers were engaged in the organization and financing of the Rhenish Railway Company—which was at its inception in 1837 the largest enterprise in Germany of its kind. Their current account advances and brokerage services kept the company afloat throughout the difficult early years of the 1830's and 1840's. They rewarded themselves with promotional and stockjobbing profits while maintaining their positions of influence within the company by holding or obtaining voting rights over significant blocs of its shares, and by occupying strategic positions upon its board of directors.[72] This pattern was repeated in the development of other railroads. Leipzig bankers played a leading role in organizing and financing the first Saxon railroads, the Leipzig-Dresden and Magdeburg-Leipzig lines.[73] In Silesia banker participation was less marked, but the von Eichborns and other Breslau bankers did engage in railroad organization and finance, serving, like their colleagues in the West, as influential directors of the local companies.[74]

Bankers in the Rhineland, Saxony, Silesia, Berlin, and elsewhere were concurrently engaged in founding insurance companies, and, by assuming leading roles in their direction, they linked those companies closely to their own financial and entrepreneurial aims. In similar fashion they took the lead in founding joint-stock banks.[75]

Private bankers, finally, were successful in promoting and organizing manufacturing companies in the Rhenish-Westphalian area and in Silesia. The Kölner Bergwerksverein (1849), the Hörder Bergwerks- und Huttenverein (1852), the Phönix (1852), the Stolberg Zinc Co. (1852), the Bochumer Verein (1855), the Kölnische Maschinenbau, A. G. (1856), are all examples of enterprises promoted by Rhenish bankers. In the 1850's and 1860's Berlin bankers entered the field as well. In Silesia von Eichborn and Company was financially involved in a number of mines and metalworking enterprises, though its connections with joint-stock organizations were limited mainly to a small number of textile firms.[76]

The over-all quantitative impact of the banker's role should not be

[72] Kumpmann, *Rheinische Eisenbahn; Oppenheim Hausarchiv,* Nos. 159–60; also cited in Tilly, *Financial Institutions,* chap. 7.

[73] Benaerts, *Les Origines de la grande industrie allemande,* 270.

[74] Von Eichborn, *Soll und Haben,* 307–8.

[75] Ibid. 312–13; Banck, *Geschichte der sächsischen Banken,* 9–14, 28; Tilly, *Financial Institutions,* chaps. 7 and 8.

[76] Von Eichborn, *Soll und Haben,* 316.

exaggerated; the manufacturing sector, in contrast to railroads, was not dominated by joint-stock company organization. Nevertheless, joint-stock companies possessed the most modern equipment and organization in almost all branches of manufacturing. In the production of pig iron, for example, a handful of joint-stock companies produced most of the output as early as the 1850's.[77] Moreover, there was a stronger element of entrepreneurship and risk-bearing involved in promoting and placing manufacturing companies' securities than railroad securities, at least by the 1850's. Most railroad securities could be admitted for trading on the stock exchanges by mid-century, while the securities of most manufacturing companies had to be placed privately until the 1870's. It was doubtless more difficult for the financial community to form an opinion about the merits of the securities of manufacturing concerns than it was to judge the different railroad securities; moreover, the latter frequently bore guaranteed interest and dividends for a stated number of years, in many cases guaranteed by the government itself. The securities of manufacturing companies bore no such guarantees; they represented, in short, capital which was more pronouncedly risk capital. Thus the techniques and devices utilized by German bankers in placing these securities were important, not only to the enterprises involved, but also because they gave both bankers and investors experience in handling a new kind of financial asset.[78]

SUMMARY AND CONCLUSIONS

The foundations of German industrial development were laid in the Railway Age. The minimum necessary capital in the characteristic growth industries of the period was typically in excess of the financial resources of individual entrepreneurs. From about 1840, one may speak of a relative scarcity of savings available for industrial purposes in Germany. Accumulated savings were at hand, particularly in the trading sector, but powerful institutional mechanisms were necessary to attract them into industrial employment. These mechanisms were in large part provided by the banking system.

Before 1870 private banks, which were substantial centers of mercantile capital accumulation in themselves, were the most important institutions for capital mobilization in Germany. German private bankers were among the first European financial institutions to combine "commercial" and "in-

[77] Blumberg, "Die Finanzierung . . . ," 190–91.

[78] Ibid. 185–7, for indications on "risk" securities placed in the 1850's alone. His estimates suggest that close to 100 million thalers' worth of such securities involving Prussian and Saxon companies were placed between 1850 and 1857.

vestment" banking functions—"mixed banking" as it came to be called. It had two aspects: first, the entrepreneurial or promotional aspect, by which bankers, by organizing new enterprises and identifying them with their own credit standing, succeeded in attracting savings which would not have been made available to new enterprises directly; and, second, the funding aspect, by which current or short-term credits created by the bankers (in their more conventional "commercial bank" capacity) could be more readily converted into long-term investments. It is very important to note that the contribution of German bankers to the mobilization of capital operated not only on the supply side but on the demand side as well; by organizing and allying themselves so closely with industrial enterprises, bankers strengthened and in part represented the demand for investment funds.

Entrepreneurial or mixed banking involved credit creation. The forms of credit creation in Germany differed from those in England and several other countries, however. Germany relied much less on banknote issues—except temporarily in the 1850's—and demand deposits. Instead, German banks and bankers utilized bills of exchange, acceptances, and *giro* transfers to create credit. A number of factors contributed to this situation, but the most important influence was government policy.

The *Junker*-oriented government of Prussia pursued restrictive monetary policies in several respects. Most importantly, it proved unwilling to permit the proliferation and growth of privately run banks of issue. Its answer to the demands for expanded note circulation (and the means of credit creation this implied) in the 1840's was the reorganization of the old Royal Bank of Prussia into a modern central bank of issue, the Prussian Bank. After 1846 this bank possessed a virtual monopoly of note issue in Prussia, a monopoly it gradually extended over the rest of Germany in the 1860's and afterward.

The expansion of the Prussian Bank (in terms of enlarged note circulation and number of branches) in the 1850's and 1860's was a major factor behind the growing use of bank acceptances as a means of credit creation in the business community. Its importance, however, should not obscure the essentially restrictive role it played in Prussian and German financial development. Its virtual monopoly of issue was restrictive in the general sense that its specie reserves were much higher relative to its note circulation than was common among other banks of issue at that time. It was also restrictive in the kinds of collateral it required and the types of lending it carried out: it scrupulously avoided risk and dealt with no borrowers who could not have obtained funds from private bankers. In short, it did not meet the range of needs that a competitive, privately controlled system of banks of issue might have.

The most visible and important consequence of the Prussian Bank's policy was in shaping the forms of credit creation that became dominant in Germany. In the 1850's its policies encouraged the use in Prussia of banknotes issued in German states on Prussia's borders. More importantly, throughout the period its policies strengthened the development of credit creation employing varieties of bills of exchange, drafts, and *giro* facilities. These money substitutes activated deposits or overdraft credits created by bank lending. Businessmen used such substitutes to settle payments among themselves on a very large scale. For a wide range of transactions, they were practically identical with money. It is true that to some extent their circulation and use depended on the availability of specie, government paper money, and Prussian Bank notes, because there were times and places in which "money substitutes" were unsuitable, and because the former served in part as the cash reserve to which the expansion of money substitutes was tied. Nevertheless, the degree of elasticity in the use of such substitutes was one of the facts which most struck contemporary observers. Barring wholesale breakdowns in confidence, restriction of the conventional currency supply led to the increased use of substitutes.[79]

One final aspect of the use of money substitutes deserves mention. The development of such substitutes as liabilities by German private bankers and banks was related to their active business, i.e. their promotional and investment banking activities. Bills and acceptances were much less likely to involve sudden and unforeseen demands on bankers' resources than were the promissory notes payable at sight which were used by other banking systems. This went well with lending and investment policies which could —and did—involve substantial accumulations of relatively illiquid assets. One might therefore conclude that the Prussian government's policies contributed—albeit unwittingly—to an institutional development which was on other grounds congenial to German development needs.

[79] Wagner, *Beiträge zur Lehre von den Banken,* 200–202; also von Poschinger, *Bankwesen und Bankpolitik in Preussen,* II, 160–61.

VII
RUSSIA
1860–1914

by Olga Crisp

A conscious process of modernization of the Russian economy started on the morrow of Russia's defeat in the Crimean War. Thereafter it was pursued more or less assiduously by the government, depending upon the personalities and the views of the official personages involved, finance ministers in particular. The main motive behind the decision to modernize was the awareness that, because of the technological progress made by other European powers, Russia could no longer maintain its status as a great power without developing a modern industrial economy. Other motives were also important, such as the government's dependence on foreign credits and the attendant fears of state bankruptcy, and a concern for social stability which made even reactionary provincial governors anxious to provide industrial employment in areas with land shortage.

In the developments that followed the state played a paramount part, both directly and indirectly. This was partly due to age-old traditions, but was mainly a matter of necessity because of the sluggishness of the business community. Modernization was identified with industrialization; only after 1905 was there also a concerted, government-directed policy to modernize agriculture. The two outstanding policy makers of this period, Reutern in the 1870's and Witte in the 1890's, both wished to leave the task of developing the economy to private capital and initiative, with the state encouraging them and removing obstacles. In practice things worked differently.

The accent in the government's development program was on speed, and, in view of the slow pace of domestic capital accumulation, a special set of favorable conditions had to be created. The country's commercial, monetary, and budgetary policies in their mutual interdependence were part of the framework intended to assure a steady influx of foreign capital.

Between 1856 and 1914 Russia made substantial progress in overcoming its backwardness. This was reflected in the rapid growth of a modern transport system, the emergence and expansion of mining, metallurgical, and textile industries equipped with modern technology,[1] the creation of a fairly advanced and flexible credit system, and a moderately wide money market.

After the 1880's the rate of growth in industry was sustained on a fairly high level on the average, the rates being quite impressive by any standards for the latter part of the 1890's and from 1910 to 1913, as indicated below.

Annual Rate of Industrial Growth (*in per cent*) [2]

1885–1889	6.10
1890–1899	8.03 (nearer 9 per cent 1894–1899)
1900–1906	1.45
1907–1913	6.25 (7.5 per cent 1910–1913)
1885–1913	5.72

The weight of agricultural production relative to the total remained very high, however. Agricultural production grew at a lower rate than industry, thereby reducing the growth rate of national income. Given a rapidly increasing population, income per capita remained low in comparison to that in the major European countries and the U.S., as shown below:

Gross National Product per Capita (*in rubles*)

	1897 [3]	1913
U.S.	346	682.2
Great Britain	273	460.6
France	233	—
Germany	184	300.4
Russia	63	101.4 [4]

Industry developed mainly under the aegis of large-scale firms, either joint-stock companies or so-called "share associations." According to Strumilin's 1926 estimate, corporate industry in Russia accounted for two-thirds of the total capital in industry by 1900.[5] A more recent authoritative computation puts the proportion of corporate capital invested in industro-

[1] See Table VII.1.

[2] Gerschenkron, "The Rate of Growth of Industrial Production in Russia since 1885," 149.

[3] Prokopovich, "Ueber die Bedingungen der industriellen Entwicklung Russlands," 25.

[4] Kondrat'ev (ed.), *Mirovoye khozyaystvo 1913–1925,* 168.

[5] Strumilin, *Ocherki sovetskoy ekonomiki,* 69.

TABLE VII.1

SELECTED INDICATORS OF RUSSIAN ECONOMIC DEVELOPMENT, 1860–1913

	1860	1870	1880	1890	1900	1910	1913
1. Population (in millions)	74.1	84.5	97.7	117.8	132.9	160.7	175.1 (1914)
2. Pig iron (mill. poods)	20.5	21.9	27.4	59.6	179.1	185.8	283.0
3. Coal (mill. poods)	28.5	42.3	200.8	367.2	986.3	1,526.3	2,200.1
4. Railways (thous. km. end year)	1.6	10.7	22.9	30.6	53.2	66.6	70.2
5. Gold (thous. kg.)	24.5	35.5	43.2	39.4	39.3	57.3	59.4
6. Consumption of cotton (mill. poods)	2.8	2.8	5.7	8.3	16.0	22.1	25.7
7. Imports (mill. rubles)	159.3	335.9	622.8	406.6	626.3	1,084.4	1,374.0
8. Exports (mill. rubles)	181.3	359.9	498.6	692.2	116.2	1,449.0	1,520.0
9. Budget revenue (ordinary, mill. rubles	407.6 (1861)	480.5	651.0	943.7	1,704.1	2,780.9	3,417.3
10. Budget expenditure (ordinary, mill. rubles)	413.7	481.7	694.5	877.8	1,599.1	2,473.1	3,094.2

SOURCES FOR TABLE VII.1

1. P. A. Khromov, *Ekonomicheskoye razvitiye Rossii v XIX-XX vekakh*, Moscow-Leningrad, 1950, Table 4, 453–5.
2. "Narodnoye Khozyaystvo," St. Petersburg, 1914, 372. One pood equals 36 lb.
3. & 5. Khromov, ibid.
4. "Mirovyye ekonomicheskiye krizisy 1848-1935 gg," M.-L., 1937, 517.
6. For 1860, 1870, 1880, M. Tugan-Baranovsky, *Russkaya fabrika, v proshlom i nastoyashchem*, Moscow, 1934, 244; for 1890–1913, P. I. Lyashchenko, *Istoriya narodnogo khozyaystva SSSR*, 2 vols., II, M.-L., 1952, 414–15.
7. & 8. 1860–1900, V. I. Pokrovsky (ed.), *Sbornik svedeniy po istorii i statistike vneshney torgovli*, vol. I, St. Petersburg, 117, 141; Khromov, ibid. 487.
9. & 10. "Ministerstvo Finansov," 2 vols., St. Petersburg, 1902, I, 623–3, II, 640–49; Khromov, ibid. 269.

commercial companies at 74 per cent of the total in 1900; it was 86 per cent by 1914.[6]

Little reliable information is available on noncorporate industry, which consisted of a variety of small concerns, workshops, associations known as *artyels,* and several million *kustars,* or cottage workers. Though noncorporate industry was losing ground insofar as capital was concerned, it was

[6] Shepelev, "Aktsyonernoye uchreditel'stvo v Rossii," 156.

still very significant socially and, except in the textile industry, it probably largely satisfied consumer demand, especially in the countryside.[7]

In the older industries, such as textiles and food processing, corporate industry mainly took the form of "share associations"; i.e. their shares were registered and could not be sold to third parties without the consent of the other partners, who had the right of prior purchase. The denominations of shares were from 5,000 to 10,000 rubles. The majority of firms, especially in Moscow, were family partnerships. Their legal position was similar to that of joint-stock companies: both required sanction of the appropriate government department before incorporation.[8]

The newer industries, e.g. mining, metallurgy, and machine construction, had in the majority of cases developed from the start in the form of joint-stock companies. By 1914 the largest amount of capital was invested in the group of industries comprising heavy and light metallurgy, metal goods and machine construction (858.6 million rubles), mining (791 million), and textiles (713.0 million).[9]

Parallel with the increasing weight of corporate industry went the increase in the average capital per company, rising nearly threefold from 1861 to 1917. By 1911, 309 concerns, with a capital of over 2,000 million rubles each, represented 22.3 per cent of all concerns and owned two-thirds of the total capital.[10]

THE FINANCIAL STRUCTURE AND ITS EVOLUTION

The history of Russian banking from the beginning of organized banking in the 1750's to the 1860's is an uninspiring recital of the vicissitudes of a small variety of government-organized and government-operated banking institutions which in the main confined their activity to granting long-term credit on mortgages of landed estates, or rather of their serf working force. The position was somewhat different in the Polish and Baltic regions, but

[7] According to Khromov, "small industry" accounted for 32 per cent of the total value of industrial output in 1913 (*Ocherki ekonomiki Rossii perioda monopolisticheskogo kapitalizma,* 60). The larger firms of noncorporate character were known as "mercantile houses." By 1 January 1914 there were 7,980 mercantile houses, with a capital of 390.3 million rubles. Most of them (77.6 per cent of the number, 57.2 per cent of the capital) were engaged in commerce only. Of the 42.8 per cent of the capital that went into industry as well, 19.2 per cent went into food processing.

[8] Shepelev, "Aktsyonernoye uchreditel'stvo v Rossii," 135, n. 6.

[9] See Table VII.2. In addition, debenture capital was 238.7 million rubles, 1 January 1914. Shepelev, "Aktsyonernoye uchreditel'stvo v Rossii," Table 6A.

[10] See Table VII.3.

TABLE VII.2

DISTRIBUTION BY INDUSTRY OF COMMERCIAL-INDUSTRIAL* COMPANIES IN RUSSIA

(1 January)

Branches of Industry	1861		1875		1881		1893		1900		1908		1914	
	A	B	A	B	A	B	A	B	A	B	A	B	A	B
I Industrial companies	54	34.5	232	193.7	356	330.8	414	501.8	960	1,507.8	1,014	1,694.8	1,621	3,223.6
Mining	–	–	21	32.5	31	48.2	45	97.9	83	274.1	168	492.9	271	791.0
Metallurgical, mechanical, including construction	2	1.2	17	28.1	30	39.8	38	40.6	210	486.0	156	305.1	262	858.6
Processing of mineral products	3	0.7	5	0.9	11	5.0	9	8.1	65	61.6	54	46.7	92	124.0
Chemicals	3	1.5	14	8.2	25	13.6	17	16.0	69	69.4	74	103.1	107	153.8
Processing of fibers	25	24.6	59	55.6	93	112.4	136	219.6	226	384.1	237	486.5	315	713.0
Food processing	10	2.2	87	57.8	132	92.6	124	90.8	217	160.7	234	184.6	373	389.6
Processing of animal products	3	1.2	7	2.2	10	5.4	10	8.1	11	9.9	17	21.5	34	43.4
Timber processing	1	0.1	3	0.5	4	0.8	13	6.6	25	18.7	30	24.5	83	67.4
Paper, printing	7	3.0	19	7.9	20	13.0	22	14.2	54	43.3	44	29.9	84	82.8
II Commercial concerns	6	8.1	15	17.3	16	18.3	18	36.0	49	51.1	76	99.8	214	203.0
Total	60	42.6	247	211.0	372	349.1	432	537.9	1,009	1,588.9	1,090	1,794.6	1,835	3,426.6

A = Number of companies. B = Capital in millions of rubles.

*As a large number of industrial companies also sold their own production, Shepelev included them into a compound group, singling out (under II) those specifically formed for purpose of commerce, without industrial output of their own.

TABLE VII.3

RUSSIAN COMPANIES ACCORDING TO THE SIZE OF THEIR SHARE CAPITAL IN 1911

	Up to 500		From 501 to 1,000		From 1,001 to 2,000		From 2,001 to 5,000		From 5,001 to 10,000		Over 10,000		Total	
	A	B	A	B	A	B	A	B	A	B	A	B	A	B
I Industrial concerns	360	124.0	344	264.1	226	352.1	200	653.3	75	540.5	23	346.1	1,228	2,280.1
Mining and metallurgical	31	11.4	50	40.7	38	59.7	58	193.1	37	263.9	17	238.1	231	806.9
Metal products and machine construction	58	19.6	41	30.7	19	29.2	22	73.5	10	62.4	1	30.0	151	245.4
Brick and cement industry	22	7.0	24	17.0	8	10.6	10	25.1	1	5.0	–	–	65	64.7
Chemical	36	12.2	18	13.2	15	23.5	8	24.7	2	15.0	1	18.0	80	106.6
Textile	36	14.7	75	59.7	68	109.2	72	245.6	19	152.6	3	45.0	273	626.8
Food-connected	107	37.2	104	77.2	48	70.9	20	57.3	4	25.6	1	15.0	284	283.2
Meat products	15	5.0	5	4.1	7	11.4	5	16.9	1	6.0	–	–	33	43.4
Timber products	26	8.2	10	8.2	9	15.5	3	11.0	–	–	–	–	48	42.9
Paper, printing	29	8.7	17	13.3	14	22.1	2	6.1	1	10.0	–	–	63	60.2
II Commercial concerns	63	19.7	53	44.9	31	47.4	5	16.1	6	50.4	–	–	158	178.5
Total	423	143.7	397	309.9	257	399.5	205	669.4	81	590.9	23	346.1	1,386	2,458.6
As percentage of total	30.4	5.8	28.8	12.5	18.5	16.2	14.8	27.3	5.9	24.1	1.6	14.1	100	100

A = Number of companies. B = Capital in millions of rubles.

Source: Shepelev, ''Aktsyonernoye uchreditl'stvo v Rossii,'' Table 7, p. 157, based on the ''Statistical Yearbook for 1914,'' St. Petersburg, 1914, pp. 306–7.

in Russia proper the twenty-odd banking institutions classed as private by the Law Code of 1857 had a combined capital of only 500,000 rubles. The only bank with the specific purpose of granting commercial credit was the government-owned State Commercial Bank, which was founded in 1817. Notwithstanding the bank's substantial resources, and its ability to attract large deposits, which showed the availability of savings, the structure of its assets reflected the stagnation of business life and the inertia of the business community.

There is no satisfactory analysis of the credit organization before 1860, and this is not the place to attempt it.[11] One can only tentatively suggest some causes for the inadequate development of private banking before 1860. These were the general slackness of the economy; the slow process of urbanization; underdeveloped market relations due to the prevalence of subsistence agriculture and poor transport facilities; lack of private initiative; the legal disabilities affecting the Jews, who elsewhere were among the most energetic promoters of credit institutions; the prevailing anticommercial mentality of the population; the lack of adequate laws and judicial procedures for the enforcement of credit claims in the face of a very low level of commercial ethics; and the tendency of the authorities to interpret any form of activity that implied compensation for risk-taking as usury. In addition, government-sponsored banking institutions failed to stimulate the economy for a number of reasons: banks were generally regarded as weapons against usury rather than as channels of credit for stimulating commercial turnover or the improvement of the gentry estates; the laws restricted the right to borrow against bills to registered members of the merchant class only; borrowers had to comply with bureaucratic supervision and a multiplicity of annoying regulations; the government had relatively small resources which it could put at the disposal of the banks; and, at that time, the government played an insignificant part in the economy.

It was characteristic of the manner in which changes took place in Russia that in undertaking to set up a new credit system the old one was almost completely dissolved. This was in part a necessity because of the critical situation of the State Commercial Bank after the Crimean War. In part, however, the dissolution of the existing network was prompted by the desire to start anew on a quite different basis. One Russian authority, Migulin, maintained that "doctrinaire" considerations were the dominant ones, and

[11] For a recent detailed but analytically disappointing history, see Borovoy, *Kredit i banki v Rossii, 1650–1861*. See also Pogrebinsky, *Ocherki finansov dorevolyutsyonnoy Rossii,* 37–42; Rozhkova, "Ekonomicheskaya politika pravitel'stva," 363–6; Migulin, *Nasha bankovaya politika.* Shepelev, "Arkhivnyye fondy aktsyonernykh bankov," 58–105.

that the financial position was not beyond repair.[12] A special committee of enquiry set up to consider the nature of the credit system to be created expressed itself against state banks and suggested that the central bank then under consideration should be a joint-stock bank modeled on the Bank of England, but the system that emerged had a very large element of state participation and control in it.[13] At that stage it was necessity more than tradition or ideology which dictated this course.

The credit structure of Imperial Russia even in 1914 was still fairly simple and the variety of financial intermediaries as yet very restricted. At the apex stood the State Bank with a monopoly of issue. It was under the direct supervision of the State Council and under the immediate jurisdiction of the Finance Ministry. Though its credits were increasingly reaching the economy through the medium of other financial institutions, the State Bank continued right up to 1914 to grant credits directly to several branches of the economy.

Directly connected with the State Bank were the state savings banks, the balances of which were on deposit with it. The Peasants' Land Bank and the Land Bank for the Nobility, founded in 1882 and 1885, respectively, were creations of the State Bank, as was the Zemstvo and Urban Bank, founded in 1912. The State Bank had also important interests in the Russo-Chinese Bank, founded in 1895, and in the Loan and Discount Bank of Persia, founded in 1894, which had the aim of furthering Russian interests in China and Persia, respectively.

The most important channel through which credit flowed into the economy were the joint-stock commercial banks. On the lower rungs of the commercial credit ladder were the municipal banks and the mutual credit associations. After 1905 a variety of co-operative banks rapidly expanded in the rural areas. They were grouped under the general heading of small credit institutions. Long-term mortgage credit was provided in 1914 by 56 institutions, of which two were state-owned, one was a zemstvo (district council) bank, and ten were private joint-stock land banks. The remainder belonged chiefly to the co-operative banks of land and property owners.

Tables VII.4 through VII.8 present a summary quantitative view of the evolution of the commercial credit system from 1875 to 1914. The pages

[12] Pogrebinsky, *Ocherki finansov dorevolyutsyonnoy Rossii,* 42–5; Migulin, *Nasha bankovaya politika,* 91–2.

[13] A memorandum of the Finance Ministry, published 1 September 1859, stressed the need for a "correct credit organization as the most vital condition of national development. The urgency of a suitable credit organization is most pressing because of the revival of industrial entrepreneurship, anticipated construction of railways and other improved means of communication, and in view of the great economic reform under consideration for the majority of the agricultural population." Borovoy, *Kredit i banki v Rossii, 1650–1861,* 279.

TABLE VII.4

THE RUSSIAN COMMERCIAL CREDIT SYSTEM, 1 JANUARY 1875 AND 1881

(million rubles)

Credit Institutions	Discount Operations		All Discount & Loan Operations		Main Assets		Net Worth		Current Accounts and Deposits		Main Liabilities	
	Absol.	%	Absol.	%	Absol.	%	Absol.	%	Absol.	%	Absol.	%
1875												
State Bank	71.0	14.5	116.5	15.4	127.4	14.0	23.0	13.2	224.7	30.0	278.7	26.5
Joint-stock banks	243.0	49.7	374.5	49.6	515.4	56.4	108.3	62.3	299.3	40.0	510.0	48.5
St. Petersburg banks only (excl. Volga-Kama)	27.8	5.6	61.9	8.0	93.6	10.1	36.2	21.8	53.3	7.1	103.7	9.9
Mutual credit societies	85.4	17.4	136.9	18.2	140.4	15.3	23.5	13.5	110.6	14.7	128.1	12.2
Municipal banks	89.9	18.4	127.1	16.8	130.3	14.3	19.1	11.0	115.2	15.3	134.3	12.8
Total	489.3	100.0	755.0	100.0	913.5	100.0	173.9	100.0	749.8	100.0	1,051.1	100.0
1881												
State Bank	101.4	21.2	225.0	27	253.2	26.1	28.3	15.5	223.3	29.8	341.2	31.8
Joint-stock banks	146.2	30.6	261.0	31.3	354.9	36.5	97.0	53.1	206.8	27.6	359.5	33.3
St. Petersburg banks only (excl. Volga-Kama)	18.0	3.8	50.1	6.0	86.1	8.9	39.2	21.5	44.5	5.9	101.4	9.4
Mutual credit societies	96.3	20.2	145.2	17.4	148.1	15.3	23.1	12.6	112.9	15.1	136.0	12.6
Municipal banks	133.7	28.0	202.7	24.3	215.7	22.1	34.2	18.8	206.2	27.5	240.4	22.3
Total	477.6	100.0	833.9	100.0	971.9	100.0	182.6	100.0	749.8	100.0	1,077.1	100.0

Source: Gindin, *Kommercheskiye Banki*, 66.

TABLE VII.5

THE RUSSIAN COMMERCIAL CREDIT SYSTEM, 1 JANUARY 1893

(million rubles)

Credit Institutions	Discount Operations		All Discount & Loan Operations		Main Assets		Net Worth		Current Accounts and Deposits		Main Liabilities*	
	Absol.	%	Absol.	%	Absol.	%	Absol.	%	Absol.	%	Absol.	%
State Bank	83.5	20.1	160.1	19.8	213.6	19.2	29.1	12.0	226.5	30.5	455.5	33.0
Joint-stock banks	195.1	47.0	420.1	52.1	645.7	58.6	152.0	63.0	313.1	42.1	661.8	47.8
St. Petersburg banks only (excl. Volga-Kama)	42.7	10.3	123.3	15.3	230.3	20.8	66.3	27.4	56.2	7.5	215.0	15.3
Mutual credit societies	81.7	19.6	129.2	16.0	136.9	12.4	26.8	11.0	115.4	15.4	142.2	10.3
Municipal banks	55.4	13.3	98.0	12.1	109.9	9.8	33.8	14.0	90.0	12.0	123.8	8.9
Total	415.7	100.0	807.4	100.0	1,106.1	100.0	241.7	100.0	745.0	100.0	1,383.5	100.0
Increase or Reduction compared with 1881												
State Bank	−17.9	−17.0	− 64.9	−29.0	− 39.6	−16.0	0.8	3.0	3.2	1.0	114.5	34.0
Joint-stock banks	48.9	33.0	159.1	61.0	290.8	82.0	55.0	56.0	106.3	51.0	302.3	84.0
St. Petersburg banks only	24.7	137.0	73.2	146.0	144.2	166.0	27.1	69.0	11.7	26.0	113.6	112.0
Mutual credit societies	−14.6	−15.0	− 16.0	−11.0	− 11.2	− 8.0	3.7	14.0	2.5	2.0	6.2	5.0
Municipal banks	−78.3	−59.0	−104.7	−52.0	−105.8	−49	−0.4	− 1.0	−116.2	−56.0	−116.6	−48.0
Total increase or reduction	−61.9	−13.0	− 26.5	− 3.0	134.2	14.0	59.1	32.0	− 4.2	− 1.0	306.4	29.0

*Included are the balances of the Treasury and of the state savings banks, of which the State Bank held 200.1 million rubles in 1893, as against 89.7 million in 1881.

TABLE VII.6

THE RUSSIAN COMMERCIAL CREDIT SYSTEM, 1 JANUARY 1900

(million rubles)

	Discount Operations		All Discount & Loan Operations		Main Assets		Net Worth		Current Accounts & Deposits		Main Liabilities		Main Liabilities Excl. Treas. Accts.	
Credit Institutions	Absol.	%	Absol.	%	Absol.	%	Absol.	%	Absol.	%	Absol.	%	Absol.	%
State Bank	226.9	26.7	379.6	25.3	431.1	21.6	53.1	12.3	195.7	18.6	865.7	36.6	248.7	15.6
Joint-stock banks	447.0	52.7	802.3	53.5	1,219.0	61.3	302.3	70.0	585.8	56.0	1,157.1	48.9	1,157.1	65.1
St. Petersburg banks only (excl. Volga-Kama)	115.5	13.7	217.1	14.5	469.0	23.3	140.8	32.5	150.4	14.4	450.2	18.7	450.2	25.4
Mutual credit societies	102.4	12.2	202.7	13.5	211.7	10.6	37.6	8.7	168.1	16.1	205.8	8.8	205.8	11.6
Municipal banks	70.2	8.4	113.8	7.7	127.8	6.5	38.9	9.0	97.0	9.3	135.9	5.7	135.9	7.7
Total	846.5	100.0	1,498.4	100.0	1,989.6	100.0	431.9	100.0	1,046.6	100.0	2,364.5	100.0	1,747.5	100.0
Increase or Reduction Compared with 1893														
State Bank	143.4	172.0	219.5	137.0	217.5	102.0	24.0	81.0	−30.8	−13.0	410.0	89.0	−7.9	−3.0
Joint-stock banks	251.9	129.0	382.2	91.0	573.3	89.0	150.3	99.0	272.7	85.0	495.3	75.0	495.3	75.0
St. Petersburg banks only	72.8	170.0	93.8	76.0	238.7	101.0	74.5	111.0	94.2	168.0	235.2	109.0	235.2	109.0
Mutual credit societies	20.7	25.0	73.5	57.0	74.8	55.0	10.8	40.0	52.7	46.0	63.6	45.0	63.6	45.0
Municipal banks	14.8	27.0	15.8	16.0	17.9	16.0	5.1	15.0	7.0	8.0	12.1	10.0	12.1	10.0
Total increase	430.8	104.0	691.0	84.0	883.5	80.0	190.2	79.0	301.6	41.0	881.0	71.0	563.1	47.0

Based on *Yezhegodnik Ministerstva Finansov*, St. Petersburg, 1902, here reproduced from Gindin, *Kommercheskiye Banki*, 104.

TABLE VII.7

THE RUSSIAN COMMERCIAL CREDIT SYSTEM, 1 JANUARY 1908

(million rubles)

Credit Institutions	Discount Operations		All Discount & Loan Operations		Main Assets		Net Worth		Current Accounts & Deposits		Main Liabilities		Main Liabilities Excl. Treas. Accts.	
	Absol.	%	Absol.	%	Absol.	%	Absol.	%	Absol.	%	Absol.	%	Absol.	%
State Bank	230.4	20.0	540.6	25.8	638.5	22.6	55.0	10.8	282.4	18.7	694.8	24.5	337.4	13.7
Joint-stock banks	687.7	60.0	1,199.6	55.1	1,742.8	61.8	353.0	69.1	896.4	59.0	1,678.1	59.8	1,678.1	68.3
St. Petersburg banks only (excl. Volga-Kama)	341.9	29.7	613.1	28.5	982.5	34.7	204.2	40.0	442.1	29.1	971.0	34.5	971.0	41.0
Mutual credit societies	158.3	13.7	273.0	12.7	288.9	10.2	54.6	10.7	228.7	15.0	283.3	10.0	283.3	11.5
Municipal banks	72.2	6.3	138.7	6.4	153.5	5.4	48.1	9.4	111.4	7.3	159.5	5.7	159.5	6.5
Total	1,148.6	100.0	2,151.9	100.0	2,823.7	100.0	510.7	100.0	1,518.9	100.0	2,815.7	100.0	2,458.3	100.0
Increase or Reduction Compared with 1900														
State Bank	3.5	1.0	161.0	42.0	207.4	48.0	1.9	3.0	86.7	44.0	–170.9	–20.0	88.7	36.0
Joint-stock banks	240.7	54.0	397.3	49.0	523.8	43.0	50.7	17.0	310.6	53.0	521.0	45.0	521.0	45.0
St. Petersburg banks only	226.4	197.0	396.0	183.0	513.5	109.0	63.4	45.0	291.7	193.0	520.8	115.0	520.8	115.0
Mutual credit societies	55.9	55.0	70.3	35.0	77.2	36.0	17.0	44.0	60.6	36.0	77.5	38.0	77.5	38.0
Municipal banks	2.0	3.0	24.9	22.0	25.7	20.0	9.2	24.0	14.4	15.0	23.6	17.0	23.6	17.0
Total increase	302.1	36.0	653.5	44.0	834.1	42.0	78.8	18.0	472.3	45.0	451.2	19.0	710.8	43.0

Based on "Yezhegodnik Ministersva Finansov," 1869–1915 for the appropriate years, here reproduced from Gindin, *Kommercheskiye Banki*, 142.

TABLE VII.8

THE RUSSIAN COMMERCIAL CREDIT SYSTEM, 1 JANUARY 1914

(million rubles)

Credit Institutions	Discount Operations		All Discount & Loan Operations		Main Assets		Net Worth		Current Accounts and Deposits		Main Liabilities	
	Absol.	%	Absol.	%	Absol.	%	Absol.	%	Absol.	%	Absol.	%
State Bank	416.2	15.6	1,071.4	20.2	1,179.4	16.4	55.0	5.0	277.1	7.6	1,283.2	18.5
Joint-stock banks	1,564.7	58.5	3,188.3	60.0	4,913.8	68.0	845.6	76.1	2,575.7	70.7	4,632.1	66.9
St. Petersburg banks only (excl. Volga-Kama)	804.9	30.2	1,821.9	34.3	3,156.6	43.7	506.8	45.7	1,592.9	43.6	2,994.3	43.2
Mutual credit societies	563.2	21.2	843.9	15.7	865.0	12.2	150.5	13.5	595.0	16.3	745.5	10.8
Municipal banks	126.1	4.7	5,330.6	4.1	244.8	3.4	59.7	5.4	198.4	5.4	258.1	3.8
Total	2,670.2	100.0	5,330.6	100.0	7,203.0	100.0	1,110.8	100.0	3,646.2	100.0	6,918.9	100.0
Increase compared with 1908												
State Bank	185.8	81.0	530.8	98.0	540.9	85.0	–	–	–5.3	–2	588.4	84.0
Joint-stock banks	877.0	127.0	1,988.7	166.0	3,171.0	182.0	492.6	133.0	1,679.3	187.0	2,954.0	176.0
St. Petersburg banks only	463.0	136.0	1,208.8	198.0	2,174.1	222.0	302.6	147.0	1,150.8	260.0	2,023.3	208.0
Mutual credit societies	404.9	256.0	570.9	209.0	576.1	199.0	95.9	175.0	366.3	160.0	462.2	163.0
Municipal banks	53.9	75.0	88.3	64.0	91.3	60.0	11.6	24.0	87.0	76.0	98.6	62.0
Total increase	1,521.6	132.0	3,178.7	147.0	4,379.3	155.0	600.1	117.0	2,127.3	140.0	4,103.2	146.0

Source: Grindin, *Kommercheskiye Banki*, 203.

that follow supplement that summary with some of the more relevant institutional details.

The State Bank

The State Bank, founded in 1860, had to assume the payment of interest and the refund of deposits of the pre-reform government-owned banking institutions, a task which seriously deflected it from serving the economy until well into the 1880's.[14] Until 1897 the State Bank was not a bank of issue. Paper currency was issued on the basis of a law of 1843 by the State Printing Office, and was carried out solely on the demand of the government. However, the notes issued and their redemption fund were entered in a special section of the balance sheet of the Bank, and that part of it which was not secured by the fund was reckoned as the debt of the Treasury.

Until the 1890's the State Bank held approximately 30 per cent of the current accounts and deposits of the whole commercial credit system, which it attracted by offering high interest rates. The Bank's own capital grew as well, from the initial 15 million rubles derived from the resources of the liquidated banks to 25 million in 1879 and to 50 million in 1892. Its reserve capital grew to 5 million in 1893. Its network of branches expanded from 47 in 1875 to 89 in 1893, not counting the offices in the two capital cities, St. Petersburg and Moscow.[15]

Though the State Bank was an integral part of the financial structure of the state, it was not, even at this early stage, simply an instrument of the Treasury. The Treasury had its current account with the Bank and employed the Bank for issuing and subscribing to state loans and short-term treasury bonds. The Bank also paid the interest and amortization of the state debt. During the 1870's, as a consequence of the Russo-Turkish War, the debt of the Treasury to the Bank on account of note issues increased very substantially.[16] In the course of the 1880's the debt of the Treasury began to decrease. The issue of notes almost ceased, and gold stocks, thanks to special buying and loans, grew appreciably. Until 1894, when the ruble finally became stabilized, the State Bank was effectively used for the purpose of counteracting the adverse effects of currency fluctuations. In addition to its purely financial and monetary role, it did play—though more

[14] Gossudarstvenny Bank, *Kratkiy ocherk deyatel'nosti s 1860 po 1910 g.*, 105–6. The liquidation of the old banking institutions absorbed 60 million rubles annually on the average.

[15] Mukoseyev, "Money and Credit," 362–3. See Table VII.9, based on Gindin, *Russkiye kommercheskiye banki*, 442–3.

[16] The debt of the Treasury on this account was 480 million rubles on 1 January 1880, 350 million in 1882; only in 1888 was it finally liquidated. Pogrebinsky, *Ocherki finansov dorevolyutsyonnoy Rossii*, 120–21.

TABLE VII.9

THE RUSSIAN CREDIT NETWORK

(1 January)

Banking Institutions	1875	1881	1893	1900	1908	1914
State Bank						
St. Petersburg	1	1	1	1	1	1
Moscow	1	1	1	1	1	1
Provinces	47	55	89	112	114	135
Additional Treasury offices performing simple banking operations	–	–	–	600	700	791
Savings banks	72	76	2,439	4,781	6,710	8,553
Total excl. Treasury offices and savings banks	49	57	91	114	116	137
St. Petersburg joint-stock commercial banks						
St. Petersburg head office	5	5	10	10	11	13
Local branches	–	–	–	3	7	22
Moscow	1	1	4	7	12	26
Provinces	19	19	24	84	225	495
Abroad	–	–	2	19	25	31
Total St. Petersburg banks	25	25	40	123	280	587
Moscow banks						
Moscow head offices	4	3	4	4	5	8
Local branches	–	–	–	–	2	3
St. Petersburg	–	–	–	1	1	5
Provinces	2	1	7	25	42	134
Abroad	–	–	1	8	4	3
Total Moscow banks	6	4	12	38	54	153
Provincial banks						
St. Petersburg	1	1	2	2	1	1
Moscow	–	–	–	1	–	–
Provincial head offices	30	25	26	29	23	29
Provincial branches	26	13	34	124	74	58
Total provincial banks	57	39	62	156	98	88
Total joint-stock commercial banks						
Head offices	39	33	40	43	39	50
Local and other branches	49	35	74	274	393	778
Total	88	68	114	317	432	828
Mutual credit societies						
St. Petersburg	2	3	2	3	7	29
Moscow	2	2	2	1	1	10
Provinces	80	97	97	113	296	1,069
Total	84	102	101	117	304	1,108

TABLE VII.9 (cont.)

THE RUSSIAN CREDIT NETWORK

(1 January)

Banking Institutions	1875	1881	1893	1900	1908	1914
Urban banks	235	281	242	241	267	317
Total all banks	456	508	548	789	1,119	2,390
Of which:						
St. Petersburg	9	10	15	20	28	71
Moscow	8	7	11	14	21	48
Provinces	439	491	519	728	1,041	2,237
Abroad	–	–	3	27	29	34

In addition, Treasury offices and savings banks as above under State Bank.[a] One banking office per 56,500 people in 1914 (excluding savings banks). If the savings banks are included the proportion is 1:15,300.

[a] In 1911 the State Bank began a program of building its own elevators and grain stores. Those situated at a distance from branch offices had the right to grant loans against grain. By 1914 it had 9 such sections. It also had 45 settlement sections.

effectively from the mid-1880's onward—an important part in directing and controlling all the credit and financial relations of the country.

The currency reform of 1897 converted the State Bank into a central bank by making it the only bank of issue in Russia. The introduction of the gold standard also required the Bank to redeem the government paper currency. At the beginning of this operation the quantity of notes in circulation had reached 1,068.8 million rubles, while the entire stock of gold belonging to the Bank and the Treasury, reckoned in terms of the new currency unit, amounted to 1,131.7 million rubles. To carry out the exchange of notes the Treasury transferred to the Bank 862.5 million rubles in gold, and the remaining debt of the Treasury was gradually redeemed. It was extinguished by April 1900.[17] From then until the outbreak of war in 1914 the notes of the Bank were convertible into gold on demand.

The liabilities of the State Bank (other than note issues, which, except during the autumn harvest, did not vary greatly) consisted mainly of Treasury deposits both on current account and in special deposits. After 1893 the Bank also held the current accounts of the state and private railways. Private deposits and current accounts, which had run to large amounts, fell off after interest on them was first reduced and then eliminated in the 1890's. At the same time there was a noticeable development of con-

[17] Mukoseyev, "Money and Credit," 363–4.

ditional current accounts (*giro* accounts) introduced in 1895 and reformed in 1900. They were designed to form a basis for the clearing house operations of the Bank. The Bank did not charge any commission on such operations.

The discount rates of the State Bank were regulated by the 1894 statutes. A minimum was laid down for bills up to three months, which rose progressively for bills of longer duration. In 1910 a flat rate was introduced.

Throughout the period under consideration the State Bank continued to act as a large-scale commercial bank granting direct credit to the public. Even when intermediary banking institutions took over the bulk of transactions the State Bank continued to advance credits to areas or industries which the other credit institutions left unattended or insufficiently served: small and medium concerns, small towns in depressed areas, etc. It did so by carrying out banking operations of all kinds on a very large scale. This was possible because there were a large number of provincial branches and because several hundred local Treasury offices were utilized for carrying out simple banking operations. In the earlier stages, the confidence of the public, still shy of private banks, enabled the Bank to attract more private deposits than all joint-stock commercial banks together.

After 1897 the most important factor in the State Bank's operations was the availability of large Treasury balances. The Bank still provided credit directly on a large scale, but increasingly it relied on intermediaries, mainly banking institutions. Direct credit fell from 45.5 per cent in 1909 to 23.5 per cent in 1913. In January 1914 42.5 per cent of the Bank's aggregate discount and loan operations were with private commercial banks, against only 7.8 per cent in 1893.[18] At the beginning of 1914 the balances of the Treasury represented 70 per cent of the Bank's total resources, which had increased threefold since 1893, when they already accounted for 44 per cent of the Bank's resources.[19]

Joint-stock Commercial Banks

The first joint-stock commercial bank ("commercial" being their official designation) was the St. Petersburg Private Commercial Bank, founded in 1864. The state provided half of its initial capital, taking 40,000 shares for 1 million rubles. It renounced its right to dividend during the first ten years if the dividend did not exceed 5 per cent.[20] Until 1870, however, the number of joint-stock banks remained small.

[18] Based on Mukoseyev, "Money and Credit," 373, and on Gindin, *Russkiye kommercheskiye banki,* 45, 189.

[19] See Table VII.10, based on *Ocherki istorii Leningrada,* II, 84.

[20] Migulin, *Nasha bankovaya politika,* 101.

TABLE VII.10
EVOLUTION OF DEPOSITS OF THE RUSSIAN STATE BANK, 1 JANUARY 1875–1914

(million rubles)

Year	Treasury Deposits	Current Accounts of Savings Banks	Private Deposits Long-term	Private Deposits Current	Private Deposits Together	Total
1875	30.3	0.7	92.5	132.2	224.7	255.7
1876	48.2	1.0	94.6	166.9	261.5	310.7
1877	60.0	0.1	95.6	134.0	229.6	289.7
1878	38.8	0.5	106.1	159.5	265.6	304.9
1879	30.3	1.0	115.7	142.3	258.0	289.3
1880	42.1	0.8	124.5	100.3	224.8	267.7
1881	88.9	0.8	123.5	99.9	223.4	313.1
1882	69.5	0.4	124.1	105.0	229.1	299.0
1883	58.4	0.2	135.8	123.9	259.7	318.3
1884	78.8	0.5	145.4	119.3	264.7	344.0
1885	65.9	0.8	155.0	135.7	290.7	357.4
1886	71.8	0.5	174.8	144.9	319.7	392.0
1887	117.0	1.4	171.4	116.6	288.0	407.3
1888	167.1	1.5	166.6	97.0	263.6	432.2
1889	185.0	1.5	164.2	85.3	249.5	436.0
1890	162.0	2.7	161.1	63.5	224.6	389.3
1891	199.6	3.7	158.4	75.5	233.9	437.2
1892	204.1	17.9	148.4	83.4	231.8	453.8
1893	147.7	52.4	159.8	66.7	226.5	426.6
1894	172.0	74.3	135.3	72.0	207.3	453.6
1895	331.2	50.7	128.7	69.0	197.7	579.6
1896	323.6	46.7	117.6	68.2	185.8	556.1
1897	332.4	27.9	109.6	89.7	199.3	559.6
1898	419.1	73.0	91.8	114.0	205.8	697.9
1899	471.5	8.3	86.6	117.6	204.2	684.0
1900	594.0	23.0	83.3	112.3	195.6	812.6
1901	479.8	23.9	72.6	95.0	167.6	671.3
1902	499.3	54.4	68.3	115.6	183.9	737.6
1903	354.0	114.5	58.9	198.6	257.5	726.0
1904	553.6	69.7	52.7	178.3	231.0	854.3
1905	351.2	43.7	53.0	202.1	255.1	650.0
1906	289.8	–	59.5	204.3	263.8	553.6
1907	301.2	36.4	66.2	183.0	249.2	586.8
1908	357.4	51.3	64.1	167.0	231.1	639.8
1909	433.4	52.0	57.5	252.2	309.7	795.1
1910	427.2	37.7	55.9	217.8	273.7	738.6
1911	651.2	24.0	48.9	212.4	261.3	936.5
1912	857.0	18.3	38.6	219.7	258.3	1,133.6
1913	872.9	15.1	33.9	232.1	266.0	1,154.0
1914	951.2	13.9	28.5	234.6	263.1	1,228.2

In the meantime Russian contacts with foreign money markets and bankers were being established through the flotation of government and government-guaranteed loans abroad and through foreign participation in Russian railway construction. This speeded up the development of the private banking system in Russia. The good dividends distributed by the first few banks gave a further impetus. Government encouragement—especially on the part of finance minister Reutern, who was convinced of the advantage to the economy of private business and credit, and of the ability of Russian industry to interest foreign banks—accounted for accelerated growth. A number of German and Austrian banks participated in the share capital of several banks in St. Petersburg and in the Polish and Baltic regions.

On the whole, however, private initiative was not easily aroused. This was particularly so in Moscow. Encouraged by the director of the Moscow branch of the State Bank, V. A. Kokkor'ev, a merchant who had made a fortune in tax farming, managed to get 113 Moscow merchants and cotton mill owners to subscribe 2.2 million rubles for the Moscow Joint-Stock Commercial Bank. It took two years to agree on the statutes, during which time nearly half the merchants who had originally promised to subscribe withdrew. They feared that they might "offend the authorities" and thereby prejudice their chances in any future transactions with government departments. Thus the initial capital of the bank upon opening in 1866 was only 1.2 million rubles. Nevertheless, the finance minister was delighted, and sent a telegram announcing the opening by the State Bank of a credit up to 1 million rubles for rediscounting bills, and an open credit on securities.[21] By 1873 there were 33 joint-stock banks and 49 branches in the provinces.

The slump of 1873 and difficulties connected with the Russo-Turkish War of 1877–78 led to the collapse of six of the newly created banks.[22] The State Council began to fear "too much competition" among banks, as well as the effect of bank failure upon public opinion, and began to restrict new promotion. Only during the 1880's, when finance minister Bunge, concerned about the depressed state of business, intervened forcibly with the State Council, did the Council allow further bank promotion. Each individual case had to be considered on its own merits, however, and promotion was liable to prolonged bureaucratic delay. Laws regarding the minimum size of the capital, the stipulated ratio of liabilities to the bank's own resources, etc., also worked in this direction. Government policy was thus partly responsible for the small number and early concentration of capital in a few banks.[23]

[21] Akademiya Nauk SSSR (ed.), *Istoriya Moskvy,* IV, 208.

[22] Shepelev, "Arkhivnyye fondy aktsyonernykh bankov," 18.

[23] Ibid. 61–2.

In 1900 there were 43 joint-stock commercial banks, of which six accounted for 46.6 per cent of the total liabilities.[24] Of these six, three had resources of 100 to 150 million rubles each, and the remaining three had between 60 and 75 million.[25] By 1908 the six largest accounted for 51.7 per cent of total liabilities. From 1909 to 1913 the aggregate liabilities of all joint-stock commercial banks nearly trebled, the six largest increasing their share to 55.3 per cent of the total. Of the 50 banks that existed in 1914, banks with liabilities under 100 million rubles accounted for only 17 per cent of the total, against 71 per cent in 1900.[26] The greater concentration of banking during this period was connected with the increased promotional activity of the banks and the special relations that developed between the largest Russian banking houses and foreign banks.

Before 1890 the largest bank was the Volga-Kama, which, with its vast network of branches, reached into the most remote centers of European Russia. Although it was a St. Petersburg bank, it differed in character from other banks there. It was connected with commercial credit in the strict sense of the word, and in that it resembled Moscow banks. (It was founded by a Muscovite.) Unlike the Moscow banks, however, which gradually became banks of a regional rather than a national character, the Volga-Kama was much more comprehensive in geographical coverage. The second largest joint-stock bank was the Moscow Merchant Bank, which was connected with the Moscow textile interests.

By 1900 the Volga-Kama still held first place, but the Moscow Merchant Bank had fallen to fifth. Between 1909 and 1914 the Volga-Kama dropped to sixth and the Moscow Merchant to eighth place. In 1914 the five largest banks in order of their importance were the Russo-Asiatic Bank, founded in 1910 through the amalgamation of the Northern Bank, which had been founded in 1902 by the French Société Générale, and the politically compromised Russo-Chinese Bank; the St. Petersburg International, with strong German connections, run by the brilliant Rothstein who had assisted Witte in effecting currency reform; the Azov-Don, run by Kamenka, which was closely connected with the new industries in the Dnieper Basin; the Russian Bank for Foreign Trade, known for its British connections; and the Russian Commercial and Industrial Bank. Seventh was the Siberia Commercial Bank, run by the capable and spirited Soloveychik, who had refused to amalgamate his bank with the Russo-Chinese Bank; and ninth was the

[24] Gindin and Shepelev, "Bankovskiye monopolii v Rossii nakanune velikoy oktyabrskoy sotsyalisticheskoy revolyutsii," 21.

[25] Ibid.

[26] Ibid.

Moscow-United Bank, founded in 1910 by the amalgamation of three small banks by the Union Parisienne.[27]

Municipal Banks

The municipal banks were organs of the municipal administrations, which were given limited self-government in the 1870's.[28] They accepted both current account and time deposits. They granted short-term credit, made loans to municipalities and district councils, and also granted loans secured by real estate. They engaged in pawnbroking business as well. The minimum capital of a municipal bank was 10,000 rubles. The total liabilities could not exceed ten times the ordinary stock and reserve capital jointly. Liquid assets had to represent at least 10 per cent of total liabilities.[29]

In 1881 municipal banks accounted for 22 per cent of the assets and liabilities of the commercial credit system, but many failed during the depression of the 1880's. By 1893 the assets and liabilities of the municipal banks represented only 10 and 9 per cent, respectively. After 1908 they resumed growth, but they continued to decline in relative importance, so that by 1914 they accounted for not more than 3.4 per cent of the aggregate assets and 3.8 per cent of the aggregate liabilities of the commercial credit system.[30]

In general these banks were located in towns with poorly developed trade, where they were the sole credit institutions. It was to such towns, often situated in depressed agricultural areas—the *mestechka,* proverbial for the lethargy of their business—that the State Bank turned its attention shortly before the war. As much as 30 per cent of these banks' assets took the form of long-term loans secured by urban property.[31] Many of the credits were granted to government officials, who often borrowed on second and third mortgages on their houses; the banks frequently were unable to foreclose on bad debts because of the depressed state of the market.

[27] See Table VII.11. The Volga-Kama Bank and the Moscow Merchant Bank, though they took sixth and eighth place by size of assets, are here listed separately to emphasize the different nature of their activities as compared with the rest, in which contacts with foreign banks and issues on behalf of industrial concerns played a large part.

[28] The first of these banks was founded in 1809.

[29] Mukoseyev, "Money and Credit," 385.

[30] See Tables VII.4 through VII.8, pp. 191–5.

[31] Atlas, *Natsyonalizatsiya bankov v SSSR,* 17.

TABLE VII.11

THE ACTIVITY OF THE TWELVE LARGEST RUSSIAN JOINT-STOCK BANKS, 1 JANUARY 1914

(million rubles)

Bank	Bills & Goods Credits	Transactions in Guaranteed Securities	Transactions in Unguaranteed Securities	Other Correspondents[a]	Main Assets	No. Branches	Total Net Worth	Deposits and Current Accounts	Liabilities to Correspondents[b]	Main Liabilities	Rediscount and Redeposit
1. Russo-Asiatic	258	42	280	92	672	102	78	367	184	629	63
2. St. Pet. Intntl.	144	40	199	105	488	56	79	265	118	462	21
3. Azov-Don	173	28	168	29	398	73	92	206	90	388	8
4. Foreign Trade	187	33	108	103	431	76	67	227	107	401	9
5. Main Ind. & Comm.	178	25	83	90	376	111	44	193	127	364	41
6. Bank of Siberia	116	19	81	21	237	57	36	164	46	246	7
7. United of Moscow	143	12	52	17	224	80	35	117	52	204	54
8. St. Pet. Loan & Disc.	42	13	93	18	166	6	30	63	70	163	4
9. St. Pet. Priv. Comm.	65	6	82	21	174	1	44	52	74	170	7
10. Comm. Bank in Warsaw	49	8	31	73	161	12	32	55	69	156	7
Total	1,355	226	1,177	569	3,327	574	537	1,709	937	3,183	221
In % of aggregate balance of all joint-stock banks	62	60	73	78	68	74	64	66	77	69	66
11. Volga-Kama Bank	179	40	82	20	321	60	38	246	31	315	11
12. Moscow Merchant	147	25	55	4	231	20	30	164	21	215	14
Total 12 banks	1,681	291	1,314	593	3,879	654	605	2,119	989	3,713	246
Per cent of all commercial banks	77	76	81	81	79	84	72	82	82	80	73

[a] Mainly industrial concerns or banking syndicates. [b] Mainly foreign banks.

Source: Grindin, *Kommercheskiye Banki*, 381.

The Mutual Credit Societies

The mutual credit societies were institutions of a co-operative character. Their capital was composed of members' subscriptions and served as security for the societies' operations. Liability of a member for the society's business was ten times the amount of his contribution. As a rule no outside resources were attracted and credits were granted to members only. No individual member could receive a credit larger than ten times his entry fee.

The societies conducted all types of short-term credit operations. Several of them, especially in the two capitals, owned very large resources and closely resembled joint-stock commercial banks. The majority, however, operated in the provinces. They granted credits of less than 100 rubles (about £11) to their members, for the most part small shopkeepers and artisans, who were unable to obtain credit from the joint-stock banks.[32] They frequently operated in areas where the joint-stock banks had no branches. They weathered the difficult years of crisis and depression much better than the municipal banks, and they developed with a spurt during the pre-1914 boom (1908–14), when they grew fourfold in number, mainly in the provinces but also in the two capitals. During the prewar boom the assets of the societies increased by nearly 200 per cent and their liabilities by 163 per cent.[33]

By 1914 there were 1,108 mutual credit societies. On 1 January 1914 they accounted for 12.2 per cent of the aggregate assets and for 10.8 per cent of the liabilities of the commercial credit system. They greatly benefited from increased credit from the State Bank.[34]

Other Banks of Private Commercial Credit

Not enough is known about the so-called banking houses or offices that are sometimes known as "bourse banks." Several of them emerged in the first half of the nineteenth century, mainly in the Baltic and Polish regions; they were merchant firms that had turned to banking activities. New ones gradually made their appearance throughout the period, especially during the promotional booms of the early 1870's, and from 1908 to 1914.[35]

It is difficult to assess the role of these offices in banking activities, as

[32] Mukoseyev, "Money and Credit," 383. The first society was founded in 1864.

[33] See Table VII.8, p. 195.

[34] See Table VII.8, p. 195; Atlas, *Natsyonalizatsiya bankov v SSSR,* 17.

[35] The assets and liabilities of the bourse banks are not included in our tables on the evolution of the commercial credit banks. *Ministerstvo finansov, 1802–1902,* II, 77.

they were registered as commercial firms. It is known that they were very active in stock exchange speculation. The largest among them amalgamated with or were absorbed by joint-stock banks, or turned themselves into joint-stock banks. For the period 1903 to 1914 several such cases are known. The Yunker Banking Office became the Moscow Industrial Bank, Ryabushinsky and Brothers became the Moscow Bank, and Wavelberg became the St. Petersburg Bank of Trade and Industry.[36] Several went into liquidation; a few turned into commission offices undertaking all manner of bourse and commercial transactions. Some of them specialized in currency exchange, but this line became much less profitable once the ruble became stabilized and the State Bank concentrated the bulk of foreign exchange transactions in its hands. On 7 July 1914 the assets of the banking offices amounted to 117 million rubles, about half the assets of municipal banks; their deposits amounted to 88 million rubles.[37]

Small Credit Institutions

The small credit institutions in Russia were comprised of a variety of popular co-operative banks which served rural districts. The majority of them fell roughly into two main types: loan and saving co-operatives and credit societies. The co-operatives served both peasants and rural cottage workers, and even urban craftsmen, while the credit societies served peasants only. There were also differences in the composition of their capital: in the societies it was made up from deductions from profits, while in the co-operatives it consisted of members' fees. In both types the members were mutually liable for their obligations. A portion of their working capital consisted of subsidies from the Treasury.[38]

After 1905 the small rural banks grew very quickly; there was undoubtedly a connection between the expansion of the co-operative movement and the dissolution of the compulsory rural communal organization after the Revolution of 1905. In that year, after 50 years of authorized existence, there were only 1,629 credit societies and loan and saving co-operatives in the whole of Russia.[39] In 1910 a special department was organized in the State Bank for the provision of credit to them. In addition, credits at a maximum interest of 2 per cent were granted from the deposits

[36] Atlas, *Natsyonalizatsiya bankov v SSSR,* 18.

[37] Ibid. See also Shepelev, "Aktsyonernoye uchreditel'stvo v Rossii," 162. Shepelev gives a list of the bourse banks with dates of foundation and capital (pp. 174–6). The majority, judging by the names, seem to have been Jewish firms; most had a rather small capital.

[38] Atlas, *Natsyonalizatsiya bankov v SSSR,* 22; Mukoseyev, "Money and Credit," 386.

[39] Atlas, *Natsyonalizatsiya bankov v SSSR,* 22.

of the state savings banks through the medium of the State Bank for the formation and increase of the capital of small credit institutions. Operations of this type developed very radiply.[40]

The societies and co-operatives advanced money to peasants, as individuals or in groups, for periods up to twelve months against personal or material security or against sureties of third parties. If the bank had long-term deposits, they could loan for periods up to five years against material or personal security. In addition to credit for the purchase of land, cattle, agricultural equipment, and fertilizers, for renting land and the erection of buildings, loans were also granted for the purchase of goods for sale.[41]

Many co-operatives not only undertook sales of agricultural produce for their members, they also traded on behalf of nonmembers on a commission basis, and on their own account. Some of the societies had their own grain stores to which members could deliver their grain, the societies seeing to it that it was dispatched either to more distant markets in the grain-deficit areas or to the ports, and sold when the market was good. Some societies succeeded in bypassing all intermediaries and even formed county and district committees for the purpose of joint sales of peasant produce, thereby freeing the peasant from the necessity of selling in the glutted autumn market to monopolistic merchants who could dictate the price.[42] The trading activities of the co-operatives were especially well developed in the southern and eastern districts of Russia, and they dealt in other agricultural products as well as in grain.[43]

The transactions of small credit banks are shown in Table VII.12.[44]

The Moscow Narodny Bank, founded in 1912, became the central credit institution of the co-operative banks. By 1917 it had 14 branches in Russia and commission agencies in London and New York. All co-operatives and their regional unions held shares of the Moscow Narodny Bank.[45] The credit co-operatives also received short-term credits from the Joint-Stock Commercial United Bank in Moscow.[46] The development of the rural co-operative movement was among the most promising of the social

[40] *Ocherk razvitiya deyatel'nosti gosudarstvennykh sberegatel'nykh kass,* 41.

[41] Of the credits granted in 1913, 21.6 per cent were for the purchase of cattle, 19.3 per cent for renting land, 6.8 per cent for buying land, 11.2 per cent for buildings, 5.5 per cent for the purchase of seeds, 3.4 per cent for agricultural equipment, 3 per cent for the hire of labor, and 22.6 per cent for various other purposes. Atlas, *Natsyonalizatsiya bankov v SSSR,* 22. An item of 6.6 per cent seems to be missing.

[42] Katzenellenbaum, *Kommercheskiye banki i ikh torgovo-kommissyonnyye operatsii,* 7.

[43] Dikhtyar, *Vnutrennyaya torgovlya v dorevolyutsyonnoy Rossii,* 159–60.

[44] Mukoseyev, "Money and Credit," 386.

[45] Atlas, *Natsyonalizatsiya bankov v SSSR,* 23.

[46] Ibid. 22.

TABLE VII.12

ACTIVITY OF SMALL RUSSIAN CREDIT BANKS, 1 JANUARY 1910–1914

Year	No. Institutions	No. Participants (1,000's)	Operations (million rubles) Advances	Own Re-sources	Deposits	Borrow-ings
1910	9,978	4,644	213.0	75.0	144.2	24.9
1911	11,567	5,578	279.2	87.0	198.8	37.7
1912	13,627	7,095	389.8	109.0	284.7	58.9
1913	15,979	9,008	524.7	130.0	365.0	105.4
1914	17,933	10,678	673.0	157.7	466.0	128.0

phenomena of peasant Russia. Unfortunately it was cut short by the Bolshevik Revolution, which substituted compulsory co-operation, in spirit not unlike the fiscal commune abolished by Stolypin's reforms of 1906–11.

Chattel credit was served by a number of pawnshops, of which two were state-owned, 18 joint-stock, and 105 municipal.[47] The assets of the pawnshops were 68.2 million rubles in 1914, their liabilities 91.3 million.[48]

State Savings Banks

Although legislation introducing savings banks goes back to 1841, there were only two such banks in 1862. Until the 1880's development was very slow. The expansion of the savings banks owes much to the drive initiated by finance minister N. K. Bunge. In 1881 he raised the interest rate on deposits to 4 per cent. In 1884 the State Bank was authorized to open savings banks in each agency of the State Bank without waiting for the initiative of urban or rural councils. Bunge also prepared the plan for the introduction of Post Office savings banks, whereby the rural population would be reached. These were introduced in 1889, and they led to a vast increase in savings, which continued even after interest was reduced to 3.6 per cent.[49] Table VII.13 shows the evolution of savings in the state savings banks.[50]

The breakthrough occurred, as with so much else, under Witte in the 1890's. Witte substantially simplified the opening of new banks and at the

[47] Dikhtyar, *Vnutrennyaya torgovlya v dorevolyutsyonnoy Rossii,* 163.

[48] Mukoseyev, "Money and Credit," 38.

[49] *Ministerstvo Finansov, 1802–1902,* II, 53–5; Pogrebinsky, *Ocherki finansov dorevolyutsyonnoy Rossii,* 121–3.

[50] *Otchety gosudarstvennykh sberegatyel'nykh kass,* etc., 16.

TABLE VII.13

GROWTH INDICATORS OF STATE SAVINGS BANKS IN RUSSIA, 1870–1914

(million rubles)

Year (1 Jan)	No. of Banks	No. of Books (1,000's)	Balance of Money Deposits	Balance of Deposits in Securities
1870	64	67	4.8	–
1880	75	97	7.6	–
1890	871	638	111.3	–
1900	4,781	3,145	608.3	90.0
1910	7,051	6,940	1,282.9	279.0
1911	7,365	7,436	1,396.8	287.0
1912	7,705	7,973	1,503.0	300.0
1913	8,005	8,455	1,594.9	318.0
1914	8,553	8,992	1,835.4	349.0

same time offered the depositor many important facilities. The most important factor in encouraging savings, however, was the stabilization of the currency under Witte from 1894 onward.

Depositors could purchase securities through the banks without commission by means of their deposits. By 1912 2.5 per cent of all savers held securities. For some of the savers the purchase of securities was a means of continuing saving beyond the statutory maximum on deposits, which was 1,000 rubles for individuals and 3,000 rubles for institutional savers. However, the majority of those who purchased securities were small-scale savers.[51] The average deposit in 1912 was 182 rubles; the average for rural savers was 190 rubles, for urban savers, 173 rubles. The poorest elements —peasants and cottage workers, industrial workers and craftsmen, domestic servants and minor public servants—accounted for over 60 per cent of all books and 55 per cent of the deposit balances, the average deposit in this class being 166 rubles.[52]

Life insurance through the savings banks was introduced in 1905. Less than 13,000 people were insured in 1912; nearly a quarter of those insured, the highest proportion for any group, were government officials.[53]

The deposits in the state savings banks were an important element in the development of a capital market in Russia. It was in large part owing to them that the Imperial Government could begin to issue loans internally

[51] *Ocherk razvitiya deyatel'nosti gosudarstvennykh sberegatel'nykh kass,* 34.
[52] Ibid. 39.
[53] Ibid. 36–7.

from the 1890's onward. Furthermore, they were of great assistance in temporarily accommodating government securities before their firm placement, whether abroad or in Russia. Until 1910 savings banks deposits were invested in securities (chiefly state funds), mortgages, and railway loans guaranteed by the government.[54] In 1912 the proportions were 39.2 per cent in state funds, 38.2 per cent in mortgage bonds, and 22.6 per cent in guaranteed railway bonds.

Mortgage Banks

In 1914 long-term credit operations on real estate were conducted by 56 institutions. Two were state banks for particular classes—the Peasants' Land Bank, founded in 1882, and the Land Bank for the Nobility, founded in 1885—one was a zemstvo (district council) bank, and ten were joint-stock banks. The remainder were chiefly the co-operative banks of land and property owners.[55]

The rise in agricultural prices and the growth of the urban population led to an expansion of long-term mortgage credit, especially after 1906. Table VII.14 shows the development of the indebtedness of rural and urban real estate.[56]

On 1 January 1914 mortgage bonds represented nearly one-quarter of the total value of all Russian securities, 5.3 billion out of 21.6 billion, and nearly 38 per cent of the total value of securities held domestically. Only 5 per cent of the mortgage bonds were in foreign portfolios. From 1908/9 to 1914 mortgage bonds absorbed a larger proportion of domestic capital than any other type of security. Of the 5.3 billion rubles in mortgage bonds only 1,690 million were mortgages on urban properties.[57]

FUNCTIONS OF THE MAIN INSTITUTIONS OF COMMERCIAL CREDIT

The State Bank

The active work of the State Bank was based on the provisions of new statutes issued in 1894, three years before the introduction of the gold

[54] For example, on 1 January 1901, from the total balance of 752 million rubles, 637 million were invested in government bonds, of which 37 per cent were government-guaranteed railway bonds. Lyashchenko, *Istoriya narodnogo khozyaystva SSSR,* II, 155; *Ocherk razvitiya deyate'nosti gosudarstvennykh sberegatel'nykh kass,* 44–5; Mukoseyev, "Money and Credit," 390.

[55] Atlas, *Natsyonalizatsiya bankov v SSSR,* 21.

[56] Mukoseyev, "Money and Credit," 387.

[57] Atlas, *Natsyonalizatsiya bankov v SSSR,* 21.

TABLE VII.14

LEVEL OF REAL ESTATE DEBT IN RUSSIA, 1870–1913

(million rubles)

	Rural Real Estate	Urban Real Estate	Total
1870–79	353.7	218.5	572.2
1880–89	776.5	416.1	1,192.6
1890–99	1,246.4	620.6	1,867.0
1900–1909	2,123.7	1,168.6	1,392.3
1 January			
1910	2,773.1	1,265.2	4,038.3
1911	3,051.7	1,393.7	4,445.4
1912	3,300.2	1,496.8	4,797.0
1913	3,478.8	1,642.6	5,121.2

standard. Though there was an awareness that the 1894 statutes, as interpreted by contemporary orthodox financiers, were incompatible with the new role of the State Bank as a central bank of issue, those statutes were in force throughout the period under consideration.[58]

The statutes were prepared under the active leadership of Professor A. I. Antonovich of Kiev, a convinced supporter of the policy of financing intensive economic growth through paper issues. He was critical of the 1860 statutes of the State Bank, which allowed only discounting of commercial bills, because he felt that they did not correspond to the specific character of Russian economic life. He spoke of "currency of honesty and intelligence" which could be used as collateral. S. Y. Witte, who took office as finance minister in August 1892, was greatly impressed by Antonovich, whom he brought to participate in the special committee set up to reconsider the role and functions of the State Bank.[59] Initially, under Antonovich's influence, Witte even contemplated discontinuance of his predecessors' work of preparing for the introduction of the gold standard. Ultimately, however, he decided that, given the unhappy history of Russian currency and the pressing need for foreign capital, a currency based on gold was more likely to further his plans for activating the economy.

[58] Gindin, "Neustavnyye ssudy gosudarstvennogo banka i ekonomicheskaya politika tsarskogo pravitel'stva," 90; Pogrebinsky, *Ocherki finansov dorevolyutsyonnoy Rossii,* 125ff.

[59] A special committee under the chairmanship of Witte sat from 1892 to discuss means of reforming the policy of the State Bank in the direction of more active credits to industry. *Ministerstvo finansov, 1802–1902,* II, 48; Pogrebinsky, *Ocherki finansov dorevolyutsyonnoy Rossii,* 177.

The main aim of the statutes was to increase credit to all branches of the economy where private credit was deficient. The Bank could discount not only six-months' bills but also in certain circumstances those running up to nine and 12 months, and not only bills based on commercial transactions but also those for "industro-commercial purposes." The most characteristic innovation of the statutes was the industrial loan on a *solo* bill secured by real estate, agricultural or factory equipment, "respectable guaranty," or "other credit-worthy security." The aim of such credits was not only "provision of working capital but also of industrial equipment." The maximum credit to any one industrial concern could not exceed 500,-000 rubles. While original credit for this purpose could only be granted for 12 months, the statutes allowed for renewal upon expiry. Similar loans could be granted to agricultural producers, artisans, *kustars,* etc.

The 1894 statutes also authorized the Bank to grant credits on goods and on commercial paper for five to 15 months with right of renewal for a further three months upon expiry. In certain specified cases the goods could remain in store with the debtor, and could even be passed on for manufacture or processing. The statutes envisaged opening up special accounts for bills and securities, the supply of working capital to country and municipal authorities, and grants of credit through a variety of intermediaries.[60]

In practice, the State Bank did not develop its operations on the scale envisaged by the statutes, though the substantial increase in discount and loan operations and especially its credit to industry during 1893–96, as well as loans to estate owners, greatly contributed to the boom of the 1890's. There was in particular an increase in advances against goods. The introduction of the gold standard in 1897 forced the Bank to restrict its program temporarily, but this retrenchment was not felt acutely in the economy because these were years of unprecedented expansion in connection with railway construction and large-scale foreign capital imports directly into industry. Furthermore, as the Bank no longer had to advance credit to the Treasury and to the state mortgage banks, it was able to increase its ordinary commercial operations.[61]

When the recession came in the autumn of 1899 the State Bank began to apply in practice the provisions of the 1894 statutes, stepping up its advances on non-guaranteed securities especially. Even during the years when the State Bank acted more on the lines of an orthodox bank of issue, its promotion of the Russo-Chinese Bank and of the Chinese Eastern Railway Company, and its subsidies to the Loan and Discount Bank of Persia, were significant departures, even though they were measures which the Bank

[60] *Ustav gosudarstvennogo banka po offitsyal'nom izdaniyu 1895 g.*

[61] Gindin, *Istoricheskiye zapiski,* vol. 35, p. 91, and Mukoseyev, "Money and Credit," 362.

carried out on behalf of the government in accordance with the government's program of what Witte termed "peaceful economic penetration" into colonial territories.[62] During the recession the State Bank also advanced direct credits to industrial undertakings on a large scale. These were known as "infra-statutory" loans and they needed the sanction of the finance minister in each case. These loans will be discussed later in another connection.

Viewing the over-all lending policy of the State Bank after 1897, it can be seen that commercial discounting represented on the average only 50 per cent of its activity, against 70 to 90 per cent of that of the Bank of France and the Reichsbank. The average duration of bill discounts was 43.68 days, as against 15 to 20 days in France and Germany. About 50 per cent of the bills discounted were one to three months' bills; 30 to 40 per cent were three to six months' bills. A large proportion of discounts applied to securities.[63] The Bank also made loans of various terms and designations —industrial, agricultural, on bonds, and on goods. Loan operations on goods took the form of pledging agricultural and industrial products for terms up to nine months, of metals up to 15 months. Loans secured by various commercial documents, such as bills of lading and railway duplicates, were usually of three months' duration. Loans with securities as collateral (mortgage bonds were a very popular collateral) were granted up to nine months, or special current accounts were opened. Loans to small industrial concerns, agriculturalists, artisans, and small traders were advanced on bills with one signature for terms up to 24 months if secured by movable or immovable property, or a guaranty of other persons already enjoying credit.

Somewhat similar in character were the loans to small rural co-operative banks. They were issued on the security of bills for periods up to 12 months. In addition to these different kinds of credit, the State Bank after 1911 undertook the construction of grain elevators for the improvement of the grain trade in the country. Grain stored in these elevators could be pledged at the Bank.[64]

Thus the State Bank continued to play an important part in supporting the credit organization of the country even during the latest phase of the period under consideration, i.e. during 1908–14, when the private credit organizations were much stronger. It acted not merely as a clearing house for all kinds of settlements and as a keeper for the national reserves, but as an active credit institution which compensated for the weaknesses of the Russian money market.

[62] Crisp, The Financial Aspect of the Franco-Russian Alliance, 356–83; Anan'ich, "Uchetno-Ssudnyy bank Persii v 1894–1907 g.," 274–315.

[63] Mukoseyev, "Money and Credit," 367–8, 371.

[64] Ibid. p. 372; *Ocherki istorii Leningrada,* III, 88.

The State Bank was able to continue its active credit policy after the introduction of the gold standard because of the manner in which the reform was implemented and because of the special budgetary and foreign exchange policies which were followed to assist its operation. According to the 1897 reform, the laws governing note issues of the State Bank required 100 per cent backing of notes over and above 600 million rubles, up to which amount 50 per cent backing was required. The inelasticity of the country's monetary system as established in 1897 was the subject of much contemporary criticism. The Council of the State Bank, and the Finance Committee responsible for over-all financial policy, made no attempt to allay this criticism by drawing attention to the operations of the State Bank, because they themselves adhered to orthodox concepts of what the policy of a bank of issue should be. Even the more adventurous spirits, like Witte, preferred not to attract any publicity that might damage the very delicate and sensitive pattern of monetary and credit relationships that was gradually evolving.[65]

Russia was not yet ripe for the adoption of the system current in other countries, where, in addition to gold, first class securities were used as cover for note issues. The Russian government, in order to secure the necessary elasticity of the system, maintained gold reserves far in excess of legal requirements and refrained from fully exercising its right to issue uncovered notes. The Russian ruble was thus more in the nature of a gold certificate than a banknote. The maintenance of this large gold reserve was a luxury for a country so deficient in capital. It was thought necessary, however, because Russia was a large-scale debtor.[66] Russia had always had a balance of payments problem and was exposed to gold drains continually, not just during periods of economic and political crisis. The large gold reserve, especially the gold balances of the Russian Treasury and of the State Bank held abroad, helped to maintain the stability of the exchange rate. Furthermore, because most exports were of agricultural products, Russian export earnings had a seasonal character, and the government found it necessary to pay close attention to that fluctuation, as it also affected the stability of the exchange rate. The large gold balances also added to Russia's financial prestige and enabled Russian financial authorities to choose the most propitious moment for seeking foreign credits.[67]

Side by side with the accumulation of the gold reserve went another process, an integral part of the first—namely, the stabilization of the budget. Witte followed a policy, which was continued by his successors (except

[65] Gindin, *Istoricheskiye zapiski,* vol. 35, p. 93.

[66] For the history of the monetary reform of 1894–97, see Crisp, "Russian financial policy and the gold standard at the end of the nineteenth century."

[67] Verstrate to Delcassé, 19 June 1900, Archives Nationales, Paris, F30 335.

during the Russo-Japanese War and the Revolution of 1905), of accumulating large budgetary surpluses from year to year. These were the so-called "Treasury Balances," which were kept on Treasury account with the State Bank and represented a very substantial proportion of the resources not only of the State Bank but also of the joint-stock banks. After the monetary reform, had there been no government deposits to be drawn upon, the State Bank would have been forced to reorganize its credit policy completely, in the direction of strictly short-term operations with full security. Because of the 100 per cent gold cover for banknotes and the appearance of a stable source of funds for credit operations in the form of Treasury balances, the character of banking operations did not change after 1897, except for a short interval, in the direction of more orthodoxy. On the contrary, the Bank was able to assume the role of an economic development agency in accordance with the objectives of the government in the economic field.[68]

There was undoubtedly a danger that, with political complications, public deposits might suddenly be withdrawn and the State Bank would be deprived of the larger part of its working capital. (Treasury deposits exceeded the Bank's total authorized fiduciary issue of 300 million rubles.) The upheaval of 1905–7 also proved the Bank's inability to attract private deposits to compensate for the withdrawal of Treasury balances. This indicates that, in Russia's circumstances, political stability was a *sine qua non* for the success of her measures of modernization.

Though the quantity of currency in circulation more than doubled between 1897 (when the gold standard was introduced) and 1914, from 1,133.8 million rubles to 2,281.6 million, this obviously was not sufficient to meet the demand for money of a rapidly expanding economy in which whole regions, theretofore almost self-sufficient, were being drawn into the sphere of money exchange.[69] The various transfer and clearing operations introduced by the State Bank went a long way to offset the demand for currency. The opening of banking operations in the branches of the State Treasury led to a very large turnover in book transfers and in bills of exchange which had to be sent to other towns for payment. The introduction of postal money orders in 1906, the organization of clearing houses in the principal commercial and industrial centers, the creation of a special clearing house for the railways, and the opening of special current accounts for railways worked in the same direction.[70] During the first decade after

[68] Gindin, *Istoricheskiye zapiski,* vol. 35, p. 93.

[69] Mukoseyev, "Money and Credit," 359. On 1 January 1912 the quantity of coins and notes in circulation was only 34 francs per capita in Russia, as against 75 in Germany and 230 in France; Epstein, *Les Banques de commerce russes,* 45. Epstein estimated that in 1907 the deposit-transfer operations of Russian banks meant a saving of 400 million rubles in monetary tokens; ibid.

[70] Mukoseyev, "Money and Credit," 378.

the introduction of the gold standard the proportion of specie in circulation was kept high in order to induce public confidence in the new monetary system. After 1906 the ratio of specie to total money in circulation fell from 54.6 per cent on 1 January 1906 to 27.1 per cent on 1 January 1914.[71]

The Functions of Private Commercial Banks

Municipal banks and mutual credit societies, although the mainstay of small business in providing commercial credit, played a relatively minor role in the progress of industrialization. The nature of their operations reflected the weakness and lack of initiative of small business, especially outside the main urban centers. While they provided short-term commercial credit by discounting bills and promissory notes, they devoted relatively large resources to credits secured by real property. On 1 January 1914, the mutual credit societies had outstanding credits secured in this fashion of 56 million rubles and the municipal banks 87 million rubles, compared with 563 million and 126 million, respectively, devoted to discount operations.[72] Furthermore, loans to individuals rather than to business represented a large part of the credits granted. The setbacks that they suffered during the early stages of their activity were, for both the bank directors and the public, an object lesson in the very delicate task of rational utilization of commercial credit.[73]

The relative weakness of the municipal and mutual credit banks was a reflection of the underdevelopment of small urban centers and of the provinces in general. It was consistent with the pattern of Russia's industrialization, which on the whole proceeded from above, first affecting certain key industries and regions and only very slowly percolating into others.[74] The expansion of railways and improvements in the agricultural sector contributed to a quickening tempo of economic life in the provincial towns, but, given the size of the country, areas removed from the main trunklines remained untouched by these new developments.

Thus it was left mainly to the joint-stock commercial banks to perform the most important functions of providing short-term credit for all branches of the economy as well as long-term credit to industry for the acquisition of fixed capital. The joint-stock banks also engaged in promotional activity on

[71] Based on Mukoseyev, "Money and Credit," 359–60.

[72] Based on Atlas, *Natsyonalizatsiya bankov v SSSR,* 17; Gindin, *Russkiye kommercheskiye banki,* 271.

[73] Epstein, *Les Banques de commerce russes,* 16.

[74] By 1900 58 per cent of the factory workers were concentrated in the St. Petersburg and Moscow regions. Lyashchenko, *Istoriya Narodnogo khozyaystva SSSR,* II, 159.

an appreciable scale. Until the 1890's almost all the funds that flowed into the joint-stock banks were utilized in the form of discounts, advances on goods, and credits *en blanc* to industrial and commercial firms whose activities were almost entirely based on credit. "Aucune entreprise," wrote the experienced E. Epstein, "industrielle ou commerciale, la plus grande comme la plus petite, ne pouvait pas se passer d'avoir recours au crédit, sur la plus grande échelle." [75]

Commerce in particular resorted to intensive use of credit. Merchants bought goods from producers and wholesalers with promissory notes or bills drawn by their suppliers and, in very rare cases, with cash obtained from banks by discounting promissory notes. In consequence, almost all commercial bills and notes accumulated in the banks.[76] In the 1890's the general progress of the Russian economy, connected mainly with railway construction, and the substantial increase in the resources of the joint-stock banks, which increase was partly a consequence of this general improvement and partly a result of the policy of the State Bank of encouraging the flow of deposits into the joint-stock banks, enabled the banks to turn to other forms of credit. Nevertheless, as late as 1914 discounts and advances against commercial bills and notes represented a very important though declining proportion of their total assets, and bills of exchange discounted with the banks seemed to have increased at a greater rate than the estimated commercial turnover.[77] According to Gindin the relative importance of the joint-stock banks in discounting bills of exchange rose from 30 per cent in 1881 to 47 per cent in 1893, 52 per cent in 1900, 54 per cent in 1908, and over 58 per cent in 1914.[78]

The role of the joint-stock banks in making advances on goods was even greater. The State Bank and the joint-stock commercial banks were the only banking institutions granting such credit. Until about 1905–6 the State Bank took first place; then it was overtaken by the joint-stock banks. The State Bank tended to concentrate on rediscount and direct credit on goods to specific sectors and areas. The joint-stock banks' credits against goods applied to a greater variety of merchandise. All evidence seems to indicate that commerce in general was well served by the banks, though certain

[75] Epstein, *Les Banques de commerce russes,* 32.

[76] Ibid. According to Gindin (*Russkiye kommercheskiye banki,* 274), banking credits covered 46 per cent of the value of bills of exchange in circulation in 1901, 49 per cent in 1908, and 70 per cent in 1914.

[77] While in the whole commercial credit system discount and loan operations and advances against goods had increased in the same proportion as other assets in 1908–14, i.e. 2.5 times, in the joint-stock banks discounts and goods advances increased only 2.5 times while total assets rose 2.8 times. On the other hand, in the provincial branches the relative weight of credits against bills and goods had risen.

[78] See Table VII.8.

regions were neglected, as is shown by Agahd's biting criticism of the joint-stock banks' activities in the Far East.[79]

There was a tendency among Russian economists to blame the joint-stock banks for the backward commercial structure and habits of the country and for the failure to wrest Russian foreign trade, especially import trade, from foreign firms. This criticism seems to be only partly valid. The banks did reduce the hold of large-scale monopolistic merchant firms considerably. They did not, however, reduce the many intermediate stages through which a commodity passed before it reached the final consumer. This was partly a matter of transport facilities and partly a matter of organization. With regard to foreign trade, the joint-stock banks could, given the experience and information available to them through their foreign branches, advise Russian merchant firms on foreign markets, sources of supply, etc., but the business of selling or buying was primarily that of the merchants. It would appear that the joint-stock banks were blamed for what were essentially shortcomings of the Russian merchant class. Indeed, where the joint-stock banks took upon themselves direct trading activities or when they undertook selling and buying on a commission basis, they were very successful indeed.[80]

Joint-stock Banks and Industry

The credit policy of the joint-stock banks with respect to industry falls into two periods. From the 1860's until the 1890's the joint-stock banks mainly provided working capital by discounting bills of industrial firms and by advancing documentary credits for the importation from abroad of machinery, raw cotton, chemical products, etc. There was an essential difference between the commercial bills and the majority of industrial bills offered for discount. Commercial bills represented almost exclusively bills drawn by the firms' suppliers, while bills (really promissory notes) presented by industrialists bore two signatures: the first, that of the firm to whom credit was granted, and the second, that of one of the directors of the same concern, as a personal guarantee. In certain industries, such as textiles or

[79] Agahd, *Grossbanken und Weltmarkt,* 112ff.

[80] Katzenellenbaum, *Kommercheskiye banki i ikh torgovo-komissyonnyye operatsii,* 81. In 1909 one-third of all grain exports from Nikolayev was effected by banks directly, *viz.,* the St. Petersburg International, the Northern, and the Bank for Foreign Trade. The banking houses built stores, branch lines, etc. Similar activities were followed in the ports of Odessa and Kherson. Southern branches of joint-stock banks traded in coal and exported cocoons to Italy and France, *viz.,* the Russian Bank for Foreign Trade, The Russo-Asiatic, the Bank of Siberia, and the Azov-Don. The Russian Bank for Foreign Trade and the St. Petersburg International concentrated in their hands almost the entire sugar export.

sugar, where the director was the principal or even the sole owner of the concern, his signature was even more important than that of the concern itself. This special character of industrial bills was due partly to the fact that the purchase of raw materials did not coincide in time with the firm's receipt of cash or bills for the products sold. Furthermore, the most important purchasers usually did not pay in bills, but by bank drafts, for which their accounts were debited on the basis of contracts with the banks.[81]

From the 1890's onward, at first gradually, and then on an increasing scale, the joint-stock banks added to their existing activities a new branch—namely, provision of fixed capital for the formation of new concerns or the redevelopment of old ones. In this way the largest joint-stock commercial banks added investment banking, on an appreciable scale, to their ordinary deposit banking business. Most of the St. Petersburg banks were of this "mixed" Continental type, except the Volga-Kama Bank, which for this reason is listed separately in the statistical tables showing the evolution of the assets and liabilities of Russian commercial banks. The Moscow joint-stock commercial banks, on the other hand, tended to be of the "English" type, advancing (in principle) only short-term, strictly commercial credit.

Like the majority of textile firms in the Moscow region, the banks there were unincorporated share companies. The directors of the banks were all local textile manufacturers and merchants. The directors of the St. Petersburg banks included retired government officials of high standing, promoters of railway companies, stock exchange dealers, and a few rich landowners.[82] The largest Moscow bank, the Merchant Bank of Moscow, was, from its foundation in the 1870's to its dissolution in 1917, the property of 50 families. The number of partners changed only with changes in family membership through death or marriage. The membership of the board was remarkably stable; only one man held the post of chairman from 1891 to 1917.[83]

In the financial practice of the Moscow banks, credits to commerce and industry by bill discounts took first place, while in St. Petersburg, except for the Volga-Kama Bank, they represented only half of the banks' total operations. Advances on securities, if practiced at all, as during the depression of the 1880's, were very sparing and were granted on security of state bonds and state-guaranteed bonds in the main. Industrial shares ac-

[81] This is the view expressed by Epstein; Gindin maintains that until well into the 1890's even the so-called "commercial" bill was more in the nature of a promissory note, in which what mattered was the ultimate solvency of the debtor, not prompt repayment. Bills tended to be renewed repeatedly upon expiry.

[82] Akademiya Nauk SSSR (ed.), *Istoriya Moskvy,* IV, 213.

[83] Ibid. 215.

counted for a very small fraction of the total, and the advance, when given, was not more than 50 to 60 per cent of the market value. St. Petersburg advanced 70 to 80 and even 90 per cent of the market value.[84]

A study of the Moscow Merchant Bank shows that it kept aloof from lucrative contacts with founders of private railway companies (railways were a favorite form of investment of St. Petersburg banks). It even voted against participation in the capital of the government-sponsored Russo-Chinese Bank, as "money will get stuck for six months." [85] It also refused to take an interest in the officially supported Loan and Discount Bank of Persia.[86] On the other hand, as early as 1873 the Moscow Merchant Bank granted loans against the shares of large Moscow firms, officially for nine months but in practice for several years. During the crisis of 1899–1901 large credits were granted to manufacturing firms, mainly in Moscow, on security of shares or by continuous renewing of bills.[87] After 1907 there was an increase in industrial credits and a change in their form. In addition to credits granted against shares and debentures of large Moscow concerns, the bank's branch in Kiev made loans to sugar refineries against *solo* bills plus additional security of shares. Substantial credits were also advanced through the bank's St. Petersburg, Rostov, and Kiev branches on security of municipal property by discounting finance bills without additional security.[88]

A distinguishing feature of these credits, compared with similar operations by St. Petersburg banks, was the fact that they were not used for fixed capital but used to supplement the working capital of concerns. The credits were given, in accordance with the bank's charter, for nine months, but many of them through frequent renewal were held for five or six years. The nature of the industries that Moscow banks served may also explain the difference in practice between the Moscow and the St. Petersburg banks. The Moscow banks served the textile and sugar refining industries, in which working capital represented a high proportion relative to fixed capital, whereas the St. Petersburg banks served the mining, metallurgical, and similar industries, in which working capital, in contrast, represented a low proportion relative to fixed capital. Furthermore, the textile mills of the Moscow region developed gradually over a fairly long period, and

[84] Ibid. Out of 12.4 million rubles lent in 1890 against securities, only 150,000 were credits against industrial shares.

[85] Ibid.

[86] Anan'ich, "Uchetno-Ssudny bank Persii v 1894–1907 g."

[87] Akademiya Nauk SSSR (ed.), *Istoriya Moskvy,* IV, 216. The Moscow banks were also reluctant to join the "Red Cross of the Bourse." Gindin, "Moskovskiye banki v period imperializma (1900–1917)," *Istoricheskiye zapiski,* vol. 58, p. 41.

[88] Gindin, *Istoricheskiye zapiski,* vol. 58, pp. 41, 43.

firms could rely on their own internal accumulations for fixed capital requirements.[89]

Another distinguishing feature of the Moscow banks was that they made no attempts to control or to interfere with the running of any concern to which credits were granted. Bank representatives did not as a rule sit on boards of the industrial firms; on the other hand, the majority of the borrowers did hold shares in or were directors of the Moscow banks. As industrialists they did not want bank interference. As bankers they knew their credits to be so secure that intervention was superfluous. The intimate connection between Moscow banking and industrial interests meant that the banks were in fact associations of several manufacturing concerns, and the firsthand knowledge of the credit standing of the firms made it possible for the banks to lend in this manner. Moscow banks also did not as a rule branch out; they operated within fairly closely knit communities, and did business with firms of long standing and solid reputation.[90]

Unlike the Moscow banks and the Volga-Kama Bank of St. Petersburg, all other large joint-stock banks engaged in transactions with nonguaranteed securities on a significant scale. The St. Petersburg banks were most active in this respect. In 1893 they accounted for 37 per cent of the value of transactions on nonguaranteed securities of all joint-stock commercial banks; by 1914 they accounted for 76 per cent.

Gradually these joint-stock banks evolved a mechanism for financing industry. This mechanism is reflected in Table VII.15.[91] The "special current accounts (Onkol')" and the "correspondents' *loro*" (items 3 and 4 in Table VII.15), were most significant, and they provide a key for understanding the mechanism. Through the special current accounts the banks opened credits to private investors to enable them to acquire shares which a given bank had issued, or had placed in association with other banks in so-called "syndicates," on behalf of various industrial concerns. Credits given directly to a concern under a bank's patronage (i.e. a concern for which the bank made an issue) are chiefly reflected in item 4, "correspondents' *loro*." Even when concerns were connected with the banks in this way (*Konzernunternehmung* was the term used in German banking parlance to describe financing of this type), the banks tended to advance short-term credits to them on security of their shares rather than by discounting bills or lending against goods. This can be seen in items 5 and 6, which show the limited credits granted in the two latter fashions.

The placing of securities through special accounts reflected the narrow-

[89] Ibid. 43.

[90] Ibid. 44.

[91] Table VII.15 is based on Gindin, *Kommercheskiye banki,* Table 34.

TABLE VII.15

RUSSIAN JOINT-STOCK BANKS' ACCOUNTS OF NONGUARANTEED SECURITIES[a] AND ACCOUNTS "LORO" ON BILLS AND GOODS

(million rubles, 1 January)

Designation of Account	1895	1900	1908	1914
1. Banks' own nonguaranteed securities				
St. Petersburg banks	6.6	20.0	17.8	91.7
Volga-Kama	0.9	1.4	1.5	3.1
Moscow banks	1.4	3.7	3.2	20.6
Provincial banks	6.0	12.3	10.6	21.3
Total	14.9	37.4	33.1	136.7
2. Loans on nonguaranteed securities				
St. Petersburg banks	0.8	1.7	2.1	12.8
Volga-Kama	1.9	2.8	2.4	2.6
Moscow banks	6.7	11.7	6.0	11.9
Provincial banks	8.6	14.4	4.4	3.7
Total	18.0	30.6	14.9	31.0
3. Special current accounts under nonguaranteed securities ("Onkol' ")				
St. Petersburg banks	57.0	69.8	85.8	534.5
Volga-Kama	16.8	36.0	26.8	70.5
Moscow banks	20.3	30.7	27.0	137.4
Provincial banks	25.8	42.0	28.5	67.4
Total	119.9	178.5	168.1	809.8
4. Correspondents' "loro" secured by nonguaranteed securities				
St. Petersburg banks	26.8	70.1	27.6	589.6
Volga-Kama	0.5	1.2	0.8	5.4
Moscow banks	1.6	2.9	1.6	31.7
Provincial banks	4.3	7.7	8.5	14.9
Total	33.2	81.9	38.5	641.6
Total on accounts with nonguaranteed securities				
St. Petersburg banks	91.2	161.6	133.3	1,286.6
Volga-Kama	20.1	41.4	31.5	81.6
Moscow banks	30.0	49.0	37.8	201.6
Provincial banks	44.7	76.4	48.7	107.3
Total	186.0	328.4	251.3	1,619.1
5. Correspondents' "loro" secured by bills and commercial bonds				
St. Petersburg banks	9.0	35.1	75.4	219.5
Volga-Kama	0.5	2.7	5.4	9.9
Moscow banks	0.4	1.8	0.5	9.6
Provincial banks	13.2	19.2	35.4	79.7
Total	23.1	58.8	116.7	318.7

TABLE VII.15 (cont.)

RUSSIAN JOINT-STOCK BANKS' ACCOUNTS OF NONGUARANTEED SECURITIES[a] AND ACCOUNTS "LORO" ON BILLS AND GOODS

(million rubles, 1 January)

Designation of Account	1895	1900	1908	1914
6. Correspondents' "loro" secured by goods and commercial documents				
St. Petersburg banks	6.5	12.6	49.5	54.1
Volga-Kama	–	0.9	0.7	1.3
Moscow banks	4.5	5.8	7.2	6.5
Provincial banks	2.2	7.5	6.3	16.1
Total	13.2	26.8	63.7	78.0

[a]Nonguaranteed securities were shares and bonds, the interest payment of which was not guaranteed by the government, in contrast to government-guaranteed securities, among which were the majority of railway bonds, the mortgage bonds of the Peasants' and Nobles' Land Banks, and a small number of railway shares.

ness of the Russian capital market and the preference shown by the investing public for fixed income securities such as mortgage bonds and those emanating from or guaranteed by the government. The banking houses were therefore performing an important function in accustoming the public to invest in shares through the "Onkol' accounts" and thereby contributing to the formation of a stock market.

It is evident from Table VII.15 that the mechanism here described did not evolve fully before 1908, and that its heyday came during 1908–14. The placing of industrial shares through "Onkol' accounts" started in the 1890's.[92] It would appear that, with the recession of 1899, the joint-stock banks found themselves with holdings of industrial securities that immobilized a large proportion of their resources. The banks immediately stopped all further credits to industry, but this did little to solve their predicament, as foreign banking houses, the French in particular, drastically cut their short-term credits, both to Russian firms directly and to Russian banks. There were no buyers for industrial shares either in Russia or abroad.[93]

The banks' survival and ultimate growth were mainly due to prompt action on the part of the State Bank, which adopted a very liberal policy of advances to joint-stock banks on the nonguaranteed securities owned by the banks themselves. To enable the banks to attract more deposits, Witte

[92] The State Bank had encouraged investments in industry by the joint-stock banks. The Charter of 1894 was partly motivated by the "passive" attitude of the joint-stock banks in this respect. Gindin, *Istoricheskiye zapiski,* vol. 35, p. 88.

[93] *Ocherki istorii Leningrada,* III, 95.

instructed the State Bank to reduce interest payments on its private deposits and to cease payments on current accounts. The State Bank was authorized to accept for rediscount bills up to eight months' duration.

Upon the initiative of the State Bank, and with its capital, a special banking syndicate was set up, with the object of purchasing securities of "sound" concerns to prevent their further depreciation and to allay panic. This so-called "Red Cross of the Bourse" was in operation throughout the worst period of the crisis, and it proved a very effective weapon. In particular it helped to raise morale in a society in which, as the prerevolutionary expert on Russian banking, I. I. Levin, expressed it, "the industrial psychology of the nation was still in its infancy." The "Red Cross" was resurrected again in 1912 to allay panic connected with the disturbed international situation.[94]

Both the State Bank and the Treasury substantially increased their deposits in private banks and in the banks' foreign branches, and continued to maintain them on a high level, except during the Russo-Japanese War and the Revolution of 1905. Finally the State Bank applied on a large scale the so-called "infrastatutory loans" to industrial concerns directly. Such loans required the special sanction of the finance minister and were entered on special accounts of the State Bank. These loans, given to "sound" firms in temporary difficulties, reached very large dimensions.[95] The essence of the infrastatutory loans from the point of view of the banks lay in freeing a portion of their immobilized resources. The credits of the State Bank enabled the industrial concerns involved either to resume their normal payments or to effect a partial settlement with their creditors immediately and pay the balance, under government supervision, within a specified time.[96]

On the whole, thanks to the timely intervention of the State Bank, both the banks and industry weathered the drastic withdrawal of foreign credits which followed the crisis. Partly because of the need to cope with the new situation arising from the withdrawal of foreign credits, and partly because the banks had on their hands the large blocks of industrial shares,[97]

[94] Gindin, *Kommercheskiye banki,* 195.

[95] Gindin, *Istoricheskiye zapiski,* vol. 35, pp. 95ff. The wording of the Imperial Consent to this effect (12 November 1899 O.S.) was that the State Bank could "accept as security and also acquire with special permission in each case, in departure from the Statutes, the unrealized debenture capital of such joint-stock companies, whose viability is beyond doubt. . . ." This meant, in effect, aid to leading metallurgical and machine-building concerns which might be in difficulty because of the cessation of foreign credits. "Unrealized" meant "not realized abroad."

[96] Ibid. 116.

[97] Thus in 1898 in the St. Petersburg International Bank one-quarter of all securities held were shares and bonds of industrial concerns; in the Discount and Loan Bank the proportion was 53.3 per cent and in the Commercial and Industrial Bank as much as 62.2 per cent. *Istoriya Leningrada,* III, 95.

they began to take a much more direct interest in industrial firms, and began to reorganize them, giving them greater efficiency and better technological equipment.[98] Short-term foreign credits resumed as soon as the situation became stabilized, but direct foreign investments in Russian industry practically ceased. They were resumed only after 1908, and then in a radically different form.

A further evidence of the government's solicitude for the joint-stock banks was shown when it took over the two weakest ones to prevent them from declaring bankruptcy and thereby weakening the standing of private banking in general. This policy of the State Bank, which was of great importance in strengthening banking in Russia, had its obvious dangers. It encouraged favoritism, graft, and bureaucratic intervention. It also could, and on occasion did, encourage improvidence and a claim on government assistance when things went wrong. It was, however, consistent with the Russian government's determination to modernize the economy speedily; it was also consistent with Russia's reliance on foreign capital.[99]

Industrial Finance after 1908

After 1908 a change took place in the pattern of industrial investment. Foreign financiers, having sustained serious losses on their direct investments in Russian industry during the slump because of their abysmal ignorance of Russian conditions, began to realize that in a country like Russia direct investment in industry was fraught with dangers. They also became aware, through their experience in the slump, that behind the Russian joint-stock banks stood the Russian Treasury with its enormous resources.[100] Consequently there was a growing tendency on the part of foreign bankers, the French in particular, to acquire shares of Russian joint-stock banks, either by purchase, or by participation in new issues of their capital, or by taking part in the financial reorganization of the weaker ones (including the two banks under the patronage of the State Bank).[101] By 1916 foreign partici-

[98] For example, steam horsepower in the factory industries in St. Petersburg grew from 69,949 h.p. in 1894 to 134,634 in 1908 and to 216,835 in 1913. Ibid. 13.

[99] Gindin, *Istoricheskiye zapiski,* vol. 35, gives a detailed analysis of infrastatutory credits to industry. He makes it quite clear that Russian liberals had completely misunderstood Witte's policy in this respect, seeing in it simply a manifestation of autocratic and bureaucratic arbitrary intervention; ibid. 124. Other Soviet historians see in Witte's policy simply a manifestation of an "alliance between tsarist autocracy and monopoly capitalism."

[100] Crisp, "French Investment in Russian Joint Stock Companies, 1894–1914," 87–8.

[101] Archives Nationales, F30 336, Banque de l'Union, "Procès verbal de l'Assemblée Générale . . . du 8-4-1910"; Ronin, *Inostrannyy kapital i russkiye banki,* 67, 70.

pation in the capital of the ten largest joint-stock commercial banks, aggregating 420 million rubles, accounted for 45.1 per cent of the total. Of the 189.7 million rubles invested by foreigners, 50.5 per cent was French, 37.1 per cent German, 9 per cent British, and 3.4 per cent other nationalities.[102]

In addition to acquiring bank shares, French banking houses, especially the Banque de Paris et des Pays Bas, the Société Générale, the Union Parisienne, and the Crédit Français, began to form syndicates with Russian joint-stock banks for joint financing of Russian industrial concerns. It is clear from the contracts consulted that the aim of the French banks was to delegate to the Russian banks the tasks of seeking out investment opportunities, acquiring concessions from the government where appropriate, and taking the general responsibility for the practical side of the business arrangement in Russia. The French banks for their part undertook to underwrite the capital for the ventures and (very important from the Russians' point of view), to place the shares on the French market.[103] Placing industrial shares was still a prolonged and laborious business in Russia; moreover, the Russian banks, which were usually allowed about one-third of the underwriting profits on issues, could count upon higher profits when shares were sold on the Paris market. Therefore Russian banks tended to introduce Russian shares on foreign markets, even though they could have placed them domestically, and even though such shares were subsequently purchased by Russians.[104]

The French passed on responsibility for the industrial firms to the Russians and thereby secured participation in business which the Russian government by preference entrusted to Russian banks. During the period 1908–14 the French were attracted by the Russian armaments industry, shipbuilding, and the debentures of the private railway companies, 23 of which had been authorized by the Russian government. Russian banks in conjunction with foreign banking houses raised practically all of the capital for these companies, as well as new capital for the large old companies which had survived the nationalization of the lines during the 1890's.[105]

The usual procedure was for a Russian bank to buy up the concession from the original founder by offering him a place on the board, or by acquiring concessions in the name of bank directors. (By law a company

[102] See Table VII. 16.

[103] Archives Nationales, "Reconstruction de la Banque de Commerce Privée de St. Petersburg, 26–12–1909."

[104] Agahd, *Grossbanken und Weltmarkt,* 113; Solov'yova, "K voprosu o roli finansovogo kapitala v zheleznodorozhnom stroitel'stve Rossii nakanune pervoy mirovoy voyny," *Istoricheskiye zapiski,* vol. 69, p. 199.

[105] Ibid. 177, 183.

TABLE VII.16

FOREIGN PARTICIPATION IN RUSSIAN JOINT-STOCK BANKS, 1916–17

(million rubles)

Bank	Capital	French Absol.	French %	German Absol.	German %	British Absol.	British %	Other Absol.	Other %	Total Foreign Absol.	Total Foreign %
First group											
1. Russo-Asiatic	55	36	65.4	2	3.6	4	7.2	1.5	2.7	43.5	79.0
2. United	40	18	45	1	2.5	0.5	1.2	0.5	1.2	20	50
3. St. Pet. Priv. Comm.	40	22.8	57	0.2	0.5	0.2	0.5	–	–	23.2	58
4. Russo-French, Moscow Priv. Comm., & Rostov-Don Merchant	35.5	14	39.4	–	–	–	–	–	–	14	39.4
Total	170.5	90.8	53.2	3.2	1.8	4.7	2.7	2.0	1.1	100.7	59.6
1-3 only	135.0	76.8	56.8	3.2	1.8	4.7	2.7	2.0	1.4	86.7	64.4
Second group											
5. Russian Bank for Foreign Trade	60	–	–	24	40	–	–	–	–	24.0	40.0
6. St. Pet. Intntl.	60	1	1.66	20	33.3	0.5	0.8	2.5	4.1	24.0	40.0
7. Warsaw Comm.	20	–	–	6	30	–	–	–	–	6.0	30.0
8. St. Pet. Loan & Discount	30	–	–	4	13.3	–	–	–	–	4.0	13.3
9. Four Polish and Baltic banks	35	–	–	11	31.4	–	–	–	–	11.0	31.4
Total	205.0	1	0.4	65	31.7	0.5	0.8	2.5	2	69.0	33.6
5-8 only	170			54	31.7					58	34.1
Third group											
10. Azov-Don	60	10	16.6	8	13.3	2	3.3	2	3.3	22	36.7
11. Bank of Siberia	20	4	20	4	20.0	–	–	–	–	8	40.0
Total	80	14	17.5	12	15	2	2.5	2	2.5	30	37.5
Fourth group											
12. Russian Comm. & Indust.	35	4	11.5	1	2.8	10	28.5	–	–	15	42.8
13. Anglo-Russian	10	–	–	–	–	8	80	–	–	8	80.0
Total	45	4	8.8	1	2.2	18	40	–	–	23	51.0
Grand total	500.5	109.8	21.9	81.2	16.2	25.2	5	6.5	0.1	222.7	44.4
The 10 largest only (1-3, 5-8, 10-11, 12)	420	95.8	86.2	70.2	16.7	17.2	4	6.5	1.5	189.7	45.1
In % of total foreign participations	–	50.5%		37.0%		9.0%		3.4%		100%	

Based on V. Ol', *Inostrannyye kapitaly v Rossii*, Petrograd, 1922, 146–250.

could not be a promoter of another company.) Second, a technical committee was set up, or, if the issue in question was on behalf of an already existing company or a reorganized concern, expert opinion was enlisted. Third, a financial syndicate was organized. Sometimes the technical committee and the banking syndicate were set up simultaneously, as was the case with the project for the electrification of the Moscow horse-tramcar service.[106]

Enumeration of the various investment projects considered and implemented in this way would take too much space. Suffice to say that there was large-scale financing in various branches of industry, municipal services, railway construction, etc.[107] Share issues of Russian railway companies did not attract the banks greatly because there was no market for them before the line was in operation and had proved profitable; only then could the banks introduce the "matured" shares to quotation. To encourage Russian joint-stock banks to undertake share issues of railway companies, the government had to agree to guarantee 3 per cent interest on the shares during construction.[108] On the whole the initiative with regard to railway financing came from foreign banks. The Russian banks were interested, however, in securing profitable "railway deposits" which they were allowed in proportion to their share in the syndicate. In this way, as the funds for construction were utilized gradually over four to five years, substantial deposits were put at the disposal of the banks.[109] Eighty per cent of the debentures for construction were raised in France alone. The British, through a firm of brokers, C. P. Crisp & Co., took up debentures of several railway companies.[110]

Excepting railways, armament works, and shipbuilding, the tendency of Russian banks was to finance business by means of financial reorganization, or by enlarging the capital of existing companies, or by transforming individually owned firms into companies. Shepelev estimates that out of some 1,087 companies that commenced activity during 1910–1913 only 30 per cent by number and 35 per cent by capital were entirely new. During the

[106] Ibid. 183; Shatsillo, "Formirovaniye finansovogo kapitala v sudostroitel'noy promyshlennosti Yuga Rossii," in *Iz istorii imperializma,* 26–56.

[107] See Crisp, "French investment in Russian joint stock companies, 1894–1914," 184; Solov'yova, "K voprosu o roli finansovogo kapitala v zheleznodorozhnom stroitelstve Rossii nakanune pervoy mirovoy voyny," *Istoricheskiye zapiski,* vol. 69, p. 184; Gindin and Shepelev, "Bankovskiye monopolii v Rossii nakanune velikoy oktyabrskoy sotsyalisticheskoy revolyutsii," 45, appendices, tables 3–5; Sidorov, "O strukture promyshlennosti Rossii v kontse XIX v.," *Istorcheskiye zapiski,* vol. 69, p. 271.

[108] Solov'yova, "K voprosu o roli finansovogo kapitala v zheleznodorozhnom stroitelstve Rossii nakanune pervoy mirovoy voyny," *Istoricheskiye zapiski,* vol. 9, p. 185.

[109] Ibid.

[110] Ibid. 191. For example, Kakhetya, North Caucasus, Fergana, Armavir-Toapse.

same period only 49 per cent of the total net capital issued on behalf of joint-stock companies (railway companies excluded) was on behalf of newly formed companies.[111]

Looked at from this angle, the entrepreneurial activity of the joint-stock banks seems to have been restricted to the most profitable kind of business and/or that involving the least risk because of its connection with the government. There is voluminous evidence, however, showing the expansion of banking activity involving innovation and risk. For example, the region of the Urals was stagnant throughout the nineteenth century, and "the renaissance of the Urals," as contemporaries called it, was in part a result of the activities of the banking houses. Inadequate transport was among the factors which caused stagnation in the Urals, and the banks, seeing a potential market, undertook railway construction in this region.[112] Joint-stock banks also branched out into financing cotton growing, ginning, and its transportation to the cotton mills, thus freeing cotton growers from dependence on a few monopolistic firms. They thus contributed to the increase in the proportion of home grown cotton used for manufacture.[113] Furthermore, the joint-stock banks were closely connected with the glass and cement industries, which, during the building boom associated with Stolypin's land reforms, 1906–11, registered the highest rates of growth of all Russian industries.

Nevertheless, there is evidence, confirmed by the recurrent clamor for special industrial banks, that smaller concerns and those in light industry did not get enough credit from the joint-stock banks. This was in part due to the manner in which the joint-stock banks granted credit. They usually gave credit by discounting finance bills guaranteed by persons of standing or enjoying credit with the banks. Such credit was usually not accessible to the smaller concerns, unless they were among the circle of concerns under banking patronage, i.e. those connected through issues.[114] A further criticism that was commonly leveled at the credit mechanism devised by the joint-stock banks was that they favored issues where ordinary credits would have sufficed because they could make bigger profits and because such issues gave them control over the concern. There were complaints that banks ran

[111] Shepelev, "Aktsyonernoye uchreditel'stvo v Rossii," 145.

[112] Solov'yova, "K voprosu o roli finansovogo kapitala v zheleznodorozhnom stroitel'stve Rossii nakanune pervoy mirovoy voyny," *Istoricheskiye zapiski,* vol. 69, p, 200.

[113] Epstein, *Les Banques de commerce russes,* 31–2. By 1914 64 per cent of the demand for raw cotton was met from domestic sources.

[114] Gindin, *Russkiye kommercheskiye banki,* 294ff. In all projects for the setting up of special banks to grant credits to particular industries or regions, there is expressed the demand for government assistance, whether by way of direct participation or by way of subsidies. Ibid. 314–15.

the firms, interfering with every detail and ordering business managers about "as if they were bank officials." [115]

The joint-stock banks were able to engage in promotional activities because of the special nature of the resources of the Russian credit system. In the earliest stages, when current accounts were still underdeveloped, this was a reflection of the backwardness of the system. Later, however, when relatively long-term resources, such as the banks' own capitals and time deposits, were on the increase, current accounts grew as well (from 300 to 500 million rubles from 1893 to 1900, to 900 million in 1908, and to 2,425 million in 1914).[116] Funds which in other countries went directly into securities or into savings banks in Russia went into commercial banks. Deposits in savings banks during the latest phase increased by only a slightly higher amount than those in the joint-stock banks, and were less than deposits in the commercial credit system.[117]

Even deposits in current accounts—according to Epstein—represented a profitable investment of capital in Russia. This is confirmed by the restricted turnover of the current accounts. In 1913 the average turnover was 23 times in the State Bank, which paid no interest on current account deposits, but it was only six times in provincial banks, seven times in Moscow banks, and under ten times in St. Petersburg banks. Therefore the *de facto* long-term capital resources were much larger than the banks' own capital and time deposits together.[118] It was the structure of the banks' liabilities which enabled the banks to concentrate their funds in relatively illiquid assets with less than the usual risk inherent in the resulting immobilization of banking funds.

A further factor in the same category was the large relative weight of Treasury funds in the totality of banking resources. The Treasury funds available to joint-stock banks via the State Bank have already been mentioned. Large Treasury funds were also available directly to the joint-stock banks. A large proportion of the gold balances of the Treasury which were on the accounts of the Credit Office of the Finance Ministry did not pass through the State Bank accounts at all. Some were deposited by the Credit Office in foreign branches of Russian banks, where they were entered into "Correspondents' Account." The Treasury charged only 3 per cent interest on the foreign balances, which were *de facto* long-term. Then there were

[115] Ibid.

[116] See Tables VII.4 through VII.8 and Table VII.17, and Gindin, *Russkiye kommercheskiye banki,* 245.

[117] Gindin, *Russkiye kommercheskiye banki,* 244.

[118] Ibid. During 1912–13 the average rate paid by joint-stock banks on current account deposits was 3.87 in St. Petersburg, 4 per cent in Moscow, and 4.64 per cent in the provinces. The average yield of the 4 per cent government *Rente* was only 4 per cent.

TABLE VII.17

GOLD HOLDINGS OF THE RUSSIAN GOVERNMENT ABROAD, 1 JANUARY 1902–1914

(million rubles)

Year	State Bank	Treasury	Total
1902	27	81	108
1903	58	138	196
1904	167	186	353
1905	146	204	350
1906	206	47	253
1907	296	134	430
1908	213	63	276
1909	139		305[a]
1910	237		551.8
1911	213		638.9
1912	176.2		627.7
1913	226.2		634.1
1914	167.7		635.3

[a]From 1909 onward data are taken from A. I. Bukovetskiy, "Svobodnaya nalichnost' i zolotoy zapas," 368–70.

Source: Archives Nationales F30 329, Affaires Etrangères aux Finances, 23 February 1913.

the "railway deposits," of which the joint-stock banks held over 336 million rubles on 1 January 1914.[119] Altogether, out of the aggregate amount of resources in the commercial credit system, 6.9 billion rubles on 1 January 1914, 1.5 billion rubles were Treasury funds of one kind or another.[120]

A lion's share of long-term deposits in general and of Treasury funds in particular went to St. Petersburg joint-stock banks. They also had at their disposal short-term credits of foreign banks. Table VII.18 shows the availability of funds emanating from the State Bank, the Treasury, and the foreign banks to joint-stock banks.[121] Altogether the resources of the joint-stock banks in 1914 reached 4.9 billion rubles, accounting for 68 per cent of the resources of the commercial credit system.[122]

[119] Crisp, "Some problems of French investment in Russian joint stock companies, 1894–1914," 234.

[120] See Table VII.8.

[121] *Vestnik finansov,* No. 6, 1928. The figures given here differ slightly from those given in my article quoted above (n. 119), which were reproduced from a different source. A more recent work by A. I. Bukovetsky, "Svobodnaya nalichnost' i zolotoy zapas," in *Monopolii i inostrannyy kapital v Rossii,* 365, gives somewhat different figures again.

[122] See Table VII.8.

TABLE VII.18

FINANCIAL RATIOS IN RUSSIA ON 1 JANUARY, 1914

(million rubles)

Gross national product		11,805.0
Principal assets of the commercial credit system[a]		7,203.0
Ratio to GNP: 0.61		
Assets of other financial institutions[b]		8,041.2
Total assets of all financial institutions		15,244.2
Ratio to GNP: 1.29		
Specie in circulation[c]		616.9
Paper currency in circulation[c]		1,664.7
	Total	2,281.6
Income velocity of specie and currency		5.19

[a]The State Bank, joint-stock banks, mutual credit societies, and municipal banks; see Table VII.8, p. 195.

[b]Bourse banks, savings banks, small credit institutions, mortgage banks, and pawnshops.

[c]From Katzenellebaum, S.S., *Russian Currency*, 6, and Raffalovich, *Russia: Its Trade and Commerce*, 359.

The concentration of relatively long-term resources in the banks was in a sense of reflection of economic backwardness. The funds which in other countries were used by the private investor to purchase securities directly were at the disposal of the banks because the Russians preferred depositing their funds in banks to holding securities. The banks used these funds, together with others, for the widening of their "Onkol' " operations, whereby they assisted and encouraged other private investors to buy industrial securities issued by them.

A further point should be made. Though the resources of the commercial banks reached 6.9 billion rubles in 1914,[123] the effectiveness of those resources was much less in Russia than a similar amount would have been in a more developed country, because of the slower circulation of goods, longer tenor of bills, and less developed clearing operations. Therefore more credit was required for the realization of returns on goods in Russia than on goods of the same value elsewhere.[124]

[123] Ibid. Bourse banks with 88 million rubles' deposits are not included.

[124] Epstein, *Les Banques de commerce russes,* 74. On the other hand, Epstein demonstrates how, under the influence of a wide network of bank branches and of improved means of transportation, the bill of exchange penetrated gradually to the small commercial firm, and how its tenor gradually diminished.

Average Value of Commercial Bills

1860–1879	1,866 rubles
1880–1884	1,769 "
1885–1889	1,071 "
1890–1894	777 "
1895–1899	582 "
1900–1904	475 "
1905–1909	428 "

CONCLUSION

In a final assessment of the role of banking in the industrialization of Russia, it must be stressed that the development of the Russian banking system was itself part of the industrialization process. Banking had to be brought into being, and not just adapted and expanded to serve new needs as was the case in most of Western Europe. E. Epstein, the Russian expert, even goes so far as to claim that, while elsewhere banking was the product of economic evolution, in Russia economic evolution was the product of banking.[125] Though this assertion is exaggerated, it nevertheless remains true that in many spheres of economic activity in Russia the banker was the initiator and not simply the servant.

As many contemporary underdeveloped areas are in a position similar to that of Russia in 1860, the Russian experiment may be highly relevant. On the other hand, Russia was unique in having "a very rich state in a very poor country," and once the state set itself the task of making the country richer it could mobilize enormous resources for the job. The banks undoubtedly succeeded in mobilizing vast resources previously lying idle or used less productively; however, the first spurts of industrialization, and the investments connected with them before 1890, took place largely independently of the Russian banking system. A high proportion of investment in the railway system was financed by the state, either directly through the budget or indirectly by guaranteeing interest payments on railway bonds issued abroad. Banks were instrumental in this, but they were foreign banks in the main until well into the 1890's. Moreover, the new growth industries —the oil industry in Baku, the iron industry in Krivoy Rog, the coal mining industry in the Donetz Basin, the metallurgical industry in Russian Poland —all came into being through direct foreign investment, which had begun in the 1870's but which fully evolved only during the 1890's.

On the other hand, from the very start of their activity both the State

---

Average Duration of Commercial Bills

1860–1874	156 days
1875–1879	138 "
1880–1884	149 "
1885–1889	149 "
1890–1894	137 "
1895–1899	109 "
1900–1904	96 "
1905–1909	92 "

[125] Ibid. 50.

Bank and the joint-stock banks, especially the latter, and, within their sphere of activity, the municipal banks and the mutual credit societies as well, did provide working capital for industry. Furthermore, from the 1890's onward both the joint-stock banks and the savings banks began to play a more active part, the joint-stock banks by making advances not only against state securities and state-guaranteed securities but also against shares and debentures of industrial concerns, the savings banks by accommodating state securities' issues before final placement.

In the 1890's the joint-stock banks began to contribute to the widening of the capital market by operations with dividend-bearing securities through the "Onkol' " accounts. The St. Petersburg Bourse, though its importance as a market for Russian securities was undoubtedly growing, especially during the years 1908–14, still played a secondary role to the Paris Bourse, and even to that of Brussels; moreover it leaned heavily on the St. Petersburg banks, whose creation it largely was. A large number of Russian securities, though quoted in St. Petersburg, were involved in active dealings only in foreign bourses.[126] The Paris, Brussels, and other foreign bourses had established their position with regard to Russian securities in the 1890's and earlier, while St. Petersburg began to gain strength in the 1900's. Even so, the preference of the Russian public for mortgage bonds, and the large issues of those bonds during 1906–14 in connection with Stolypin's land reform, meant that foreign investment in Russian industrial securities represented a higher proportion relative to their total investment during this period than domestic holdings did.[127] Gindin estimates that, by 1 January 1914, out of a total of 21.6 million rubles (nominal) of Russian securities, 7.8 billion, or over 36 per cent, were held abroad. This proportion rises

[126] Of the 28 types of shares of metallurgical and construction works quoted in Paris, 25 were among the most active; of these only 14 were quoted in St. Petersburg. The shares of coal mines in the Donetz Basin and the Dombrova Basin in Russian Poland had dealings in Paris only. Of the 17 types of securities of metallurgical firms quoted in Brussels, only seven were also quoted in St. Petersburg. Brussels had a practical monopoly of dealings in shares of tramcar-transport in Russian towns. The London stock exchange was gaining importance during 1909–13, in connection with oil, copper, and gold-mining. The Berlin bourse continued to maintain its role in dealings in shares of electrical and chemical concerns. The Amsterdam bourse was important for Russian government stock. The Moscow bourse dealt mainly in bonds issued by the government, railway companies, and mortgage bonds. The shares of the Moscow textile firms were not quoted on the bourse.

[127] The total increase in the value of securities held domestically during 1908–14 was 3,687 million rubles; of these only 1,175 million rubles were shares and bonds of joint-stock companies. Foreign holdings increased by 1,373 million, of which 990 million, or 72 per cent of the total, were shares and bonds of companies. Based on Ol', *Inostrannyye Kapitaly v Rossii,* here reproduced from Gindin, *Russkiye kommercheskiye banki,* 239.

to over 47 per cent if one excludes mortgage bonds, for which there was practically no market abroad.

According to Gindin's estimates, foreign holdings of Russian securities accounted for

48.7 per cent of state and state-guaranteed bonds
39.4 per cent of shares of joint-stock companies
55.3 per cent of debentures of joint-stock companies
74.0 per cent of municipal bands
5.0 per cent of mortgage bonds.

The 13,775 million rubles of securities estimated to be in Russian portfolios were, according to Gindin, distributed in the following proportions:

State & railway bonds ....38.4 per cent
Municipal bonds .... 2.2 per cent
Mortgage bonds ....37.7 per cent
(urban property ....12.2 p. c.)
Shares and debentures of
joint-stock companies ....21.7 per cent [128]

After 1908 a preponderant proportion of foreign investment in Russian industry entered Russia through the St. Petersburg joint-stock banks, as did short-term credits from abroad. It can be argued that French banking houses would not have resumed their investment activities in Russia had it not been for the Russian banking houses which were prepared to shoulder responsibility. On the other hand, Russian joint-stock banks, because the State Bank assured their liquidity, could act as promoters and even engage in entrepreneurial activity, which was still inadequate in Russia. Behind the State Bank stood the Treasury with its vast resources and still vaster potential, and with an extremely elastic fiscal system—if one ignores the fact that political instability was likely to prejudice its effectiveness. As Agahd expressed it so graphically: "Between the [Russian] industrial share and the Paris bank is the *giro* of a St. Petersburg bank; between a St. Petersburg bank and the Paris bank is the *giro* of the Russian Finance Ministry." [129]

Furthermore, the imaginative use of the gold balances of the Treasury and the State Bank abroad, whereby the exchange rate of the ruble could

[128] Based on Gindin, *Russkiye kommercheskiye banki,* Tables 38 and 39. Crisp, *The Financial Aspect of the Franco-Russian Alliance,* gives somewhat different estimates of foreign holdings of Russian securities. Here, for the sake of consistency, Gindin's estimates, based partly on Ol', *Inostrannyye Kapitaly v Rossii,* are given.

[129] Agahd, *Grossbanken und Weltmarkt,* 111.

be kept stable, reassured the foreign investor.[130] There was also in these holdings an excellent standby in the event of pressure on the ruble or on Russian credit. Special financial operations by the State Bank, such as forward buying of foreign currency, bills, or checks in rubles, with promise of repayment of the same sum in foreign currency at a fixed time, acted in the same way. They insured the rate of exchange and allowed foreign banks to open credits to Russian banks and concerns without any risk of loss arising from variations in the rate of exchange. The purchase and sale by the State Bank of foreign bills and checks at its major branches, both actually in the market and for delivery at a stipulated future date, and its purchase at the agencies of the State Bank abroad of bills paid to the credit of Russian exporters, offering them the right to receive the equivalent in rubles at any branch of the Bank, facilitated Russian settlements with foreign countries and strengthened the position of the Russian money market.

Of inestimable importance in enabling the credit system to play its part was the alertness of the State Bank (with the Finance Ministry behind it) in averting disaster, the flexibility of the Bank's lending policy, and the Bank's awareness of the weakness of the credit structure and readiness to fill the gaps left unattended by other banking institutions. With some reservations, it can be said that the Russian State Bank played the role that, in E. Nevin's opinion, should be played by a central bank in an underdeveloped territory.[131] Within limits it provided direct finance of development; it certainly provided indirect finance and it provided the financial infrastructure. Like Nevin's central bank, the Russian State Bank held a certain proportion of its assets externally "in order to guard against contingencies involving an external drain of funds." [132] Unlike Nevin's model, in which the central bank does not engage in ordinary commercial banking because of the risk of compromising the bank's moral position,[133] the Russian State Bank was a large commercial bank, until the 1890's the largest, and up to a point it competed with private banks in attracting deposits. Both the public and the business community apparently found its moral position beyond reproach.

Opposition to and a certain self-consciousness about the unorthodox policies of the State Bank, especially after it became a bank of issue, came from people who felt that the departure from the current practice of major banks of issue was an admission of inferiority. The financial authorities

[130] During the Agadir crisis in 1911 the Russian Finance Minister thought it advisable to increase the foreign balances in order to prevent withdrawals of credits from the St. Petersburg banks.

[131] Nevin, *Capital Funds in Underdeveloped Countries: The Role of Financial Institutions,* 40–44.

[132] See Table VII.19.

[133] Nevin, *Capital Funds,* 34–5.

TABLE VII.19

SOME SOURCES OF RUSSIAN JOINT-STOCK BANK FUNDS, 1 JANUARY 1910–1914

(million rubles)

Year	Debt to State Bank	Railway Deposits	Treas. Deposits in For. Brs. of Rus. Banks	Total Govt. Funds	Foreign Credits	Total
1910	61.6	52.8	76.4	190.8	209	399.8
1911	208.7	154.9	155.5	519.1	268	787.1
1912	378.4	130.7	226.1	735.2	446	1,181.2
1913	386.6	221.5	191.5	799.4	500[a]	1,299.4
1914	386.6	333.6	202.6	924.8	546	1,470.8

[a]Estimated.

Source: *Vestnik Finansov*, No. 6. 1928.

themselves, except for a few bold spirits like Witte, were shamefaced about it.

The large proportion of resources taken up by mortgage credit was a negative feature of the Russian capital market, especially as, to judge by literary evidence, the credits obtained by estate owners were used for conspicuous consumption, often outside Russia. It could also be argued that the availability of credit for land purchase kept peasants on the land who would have otherwise looked for other sources of income, and thus easy credit impeded urbanization. The agrarian problem was not one which could be approached from a strictly economic point of view, however, at least where short-term measures were concerned.[134] The interrelated complex of measures and policies followed after 1906 augured well for the solution of the agrarian problem. From the point of view of industrialization, there is much evidence that mortgage bonds were used as collateral when obtaining loans for industrial purposes. This was widespread prior to the 1890's

[134] This also applies to the contemporary situation: "agricultural credit cannot be judged by economic standards alone." Nevin, *Capital Funds in Underdeveloped Countries: The Role of Financial Institutions,* 83–4.

and continued throughout that decade, especially where Moscow banks were concerned. Furthermore, many landowners used the funds they obtained by mortgaging their estates to buy shares of joint-stock companies as well as government bonds. Finally the land banks contributed to a redistribution of real wealth and rendered it more liquid.[135]

A final point must be mentioned. The Russian experiment in modernization had, after some hesitation, been made not by using money inflation, but, on the contrary, by using a very rigid system of note issue. Russia's earlier unhappy experience with paper currency would have been reason enough to impose rigid checks upon an improvident government, but as already explained, there were valid reasons—connected in the main with the need for foreign credits—why Russia should have adopted the system it did. The generous provision of means of payments via the credit system corrected the inadequacies of the currency supply.

It may be appropriate to sum up by paraphrasing Nevin: solvency and sound finance cannot be provided by statute. Whatever the statutory provisions, central bank credit will be misused unless the bank exercises good judgment and the government uses wise abstention. Otherwise the central bank will become the milk cow of an improvident government.[136] On the whole, during the period under consideration, and especially after the 1880's, both the State Bank and the Imperial Government acted with wisdom and restraint. There were departures from this line: the State Bank was used indirectly to finance Russian adventures in the Far East and in Persia. The lack of parliamentary representation before 1906 and the circumscribed competence of the Duma after 1906 were serious drawbacks. The large foreign debt and the government's intense concern for its financial reputation abroad, however, had a very salutary restraining effect upon government action and upon officials responsible for financial policy.

[135] Before the 1890's, when the joint-stock banks were still weak, raising a mortgage was a fairly common means of obtaining credit for fixed capital, or even for operating purposes; e.g. the Bryansk Company. See also Epstein, *Les Banques de commerce russes,* 44.

[136] Nevin, *Capital Funds in Underdeveloped Countries: The Role of Financial Institutions,* 39–40.

VIII
JAPAN
1868 – 1914

by Hugh T. Patrick

Thus far Japan is the only non-Western nation that has succeeded in achieving sustained industrialization and economic growth. Moreover, this was accomplished without Japan having any special advantages; at the beginning of modernization Japan was a densely populated, low-income country with a rather meager natural resource base. Concomitant with industrialization Japan developed a comprehensive and relatively efficient financial system, combining traditional institutions with the systematic and pragmatic adaptation of various Western models. For these reasons the Japanese case is of particular interest in this study.

The period treated is from 1868 to 1914.[1] The initial date is not of major importance in our analysis, because during the early years of the Meiji Era [2] there was great political and economic turmoil, confusion, and change. This turmoil, though perhaps an essential ingredient in the breakthrough of new ideas and new leaders, contributed little directly to economic growth. The beginning of World War I inaugurated major changes in Japan's industrial structure, and the period between World War I and World War II, while very important for changes in and continued development of the financial structure, represents the country at a later phase of economic growth. Moreover, by World War I the over-all institutional and operational framework of the financial system was already well established.

I am particularly indebted to Pong S. Lee and Yoshiko Kido, who served as my research assistants, and David Ebel, who computed certain background statistical materials, for their aid in the preparation of this essay.

[1] This period may be subdivided according to various criteria. For a division into three subperiods based on criteria of over-all financial policy, see Patrick, "Financial Policy in Meiji Japan."

[2] The Meiji Era (1868–1912) is virtually identical with the period covered here.

THE SETTING

In 1868 Japan was a country of about 33 million people, with a predominantly agrarian economy and a relatively low per capita income, long isolated from major world forces, with what has been characterized as a strong feudal tradition, and a domestic political muddle. The Tokugawa system had gradually decayed, and had been overthrown by a group of administrative, middle-level samurai [3] and certain opposition daimyo who had the objective of restoring the Emperor to power, at least nominally. The Meiji Restoration thus brought control of the country under the political oligarchy of a relatively young and ambitious group of samurai. Their domination lasted throughout the entire period. For about a decade this new government was neither stable nor in full control of the society and economy. Before anything else it had to achieve a stable revenue source and to reduce substantially the traditional daimyo and samurai consumption claims upon agricultural production. (It accomplished the first by an agricultural land tax, and the second by capitalizing annual stipends at low rates into government bonds, with low yields.) Meanwhile it could not risk alienating any of the major groups—daimyo, samurai, peasants, merchants, and artisans—sufficiently to provoke them into violent opposition to its consolidation of power. The ways in which these aims were achieved had important implications for the early development of Japan's financial system.

The political oligarchy initially was convinced that Japan was in great danger of foreign attack and military and economic penetration. This apprehension was not unreasonable, since Japan had been forcibly opened to foreign trade and intercourse, and the spectacle of increasing intrusion into China by Western powers suggested that Japan too might suffer the same fate. Accordingly, national security was a pre-eminent goal throughout the period. At first this was defensive, but later it became expansionist in concept. The government realized that a strong industrial base had to be built, not only to make Japan "modern," but also to support an adequate military force; from the beginning, therefore, it placed considerable emphasis on economic development. At the same time, a relatively high and increasing proportion of government expenditures went to support the growing military apparatus.[4] Because of this, and because of the policies promot-

[3] The military class which, during the long period of peace, had assumed the expanding bureaucratic and administrative functions of running the Tokugawa system under the daimyo (feudal lords).

[4] Between 1880 and 1910 the proportion of GNP devoted to military and war-related expenditures approximately doubled every decade, rising from 2.6 per cent in 1880–89 to 11.3 per cent in 1900–1909. Cf. Emi, *Government Fiscal Activity and Economic Growth in Japan, 1868–1960,* esp. chap. 3, and Table Al, pp. 140–41.

ing economic growth, the government, despite the orthodox conservative principles it professed, in practice tended to maintain high levels and rates of growth of aggregate demand, especially in war periods—the Satsuma Rebellion in 1877, the war with China in 1894–95, and the 1904–5 war with Russia. Further, the early foreign domination of international trade and its financing, shipping, and insurance was gradually eliminated as the government encouraged domestic entrepreneurs to take over these functions.

In general, the government conceived its function in the economic sphere to be the establishment of an institutional framework conducive to economic growth. It utilized the private market mechanism to allocate resources and to attain other objectives (e.g. income distribution), exerting its influence through the market via tariffs, subsidies, differential tax rates, guaranteed purchases or dividend rates, and the like, rather than replacing the market by government planning or production. The government was particularly vigorous in establishing a new and modern financial system.

A major issue in the analysis of Japan's economic development, especially for the formative years, is the determination of the main locus of the impetus to sustained growth. There are two prevailing views. The first may be characterized as "growth-from-above." This argument contends that economic growth resulted primarily from central government policies and from the efforts of a relatively small number of industrialists who established large-scale enterprises, epitomized in the *zaibatsu* [5] conglomerates. These enterprises utilized modern Western technology and relatively capital-intensive techniques of production. The other view is a reaction to this; it may be termed "growth-from-below." It argues that the former view overemphasizes the contribution of government and large-scale enterprise to increases in output, and that proper emphasis should also be placed on the contribution of the myriads of smaller rural and urban enterpreneurs who used more labor-intensive methods of production that embodied relatively simple improvements in technology, who acted in response to opportunities for profit, and who were relatively independent of the government.

While the difference in the two positions is primarily one of degree, it is significant. Of particular relevance here is the fact that analysis of the relationship of the financial system to economic growth is considerably influenced by the attitude toward the impetus to growth. The "growth-from-above" position emphasizes the importance of the establishment of the national banks, the role of government banks and other financial institutions, and the emergence of the *zaibatsu* banks. The "growth-from-below"

[5] The term *zaibatsu* (literally, "financial clique") is used so loosely that it frequently simply connotes "bigness." A common and useful explanation is that a *zaibatsu* was a conglomerate of horizontally and vertically related enterprises in mining, industry, finance, and commerce under a single family's ownership and control.

position stresses these less, and instead places more emphasis on the financing of small-scale economic activity in industry and agriculture. I shall stress in this essay the earlier importance of the financing of agricultural and small-scale industrial production (especially the processing of primary products), and the later, increasing importance of relatively large-scale, Western type of enterprise.

The standard estimates suggest that Japan achieved a growth rate of real national income of about 4 per cent between 1878 and 1914.[6] Growth was not smooth; it was subject to considerable cyclical fluctuation. The pattern of growth fits the classical case: initial production of agricultural goods mainly; industrialization based first on light consumer goods industries, gradual diversification, and eventually (but mainly during and after World War I) increasing emphasis on heavy industry; and an increasing role of foreign trade in a free economy, with specialization based on evolving dynamic comparative advantage.

Manufacturing output rose from 10.5 per cent of national income in 1878–82 to 21.3 per cent in 1908–12, which was still less than primary sector production. Factory production (with factories defined as plants with five or more production workers), which initially was very small, by 1914 was 52 per cent of total manufacturing (the other being household industry), and 10.8 per cent of national income.[7] Most of Japan's light industry developed at first in response to the demand of home markets; i.e. it was import-competing. Later, light industries expanded their capacity and improved their productivity to the point where Japan could rely increasingly upon exports of light manufactured goods. This phase really did not reach fruition until World War I, however. The cotton textile industry, the first modern industry to develop, and the largest industry throughout the period, is a case in point. The value of exports of cotton yarn did not surpass imports until 1897, and that of cotton fabrics did

[6] Ohkawa *et al., Growth Rate*. The Ohkawa estimates of Meiji growth, notably the agricultural sector, have been attacked as excessive; see Nakamura, "Agricultural Production in Japan, 1878–1922," and Oshima, "Government Revenues and Expenditures in Meiji Economic Growth." On the other hand, recent evidence suggests that industrial production has been underestimated; Shionoya, "Waga Kuni Kogyokan no Nibumon Pattern" ("The Two-Sector Pattern of Japan's Industrialization"). For analysis of the role of the financial system, the implications are: (1) that financial intermediation in agricultural production was even more important than realized for mobilizing surplus production and for encouraging the switch from subsistence production to production of cash (and export) crops, while less important in encouraging increases in output per se, and (2) that the financial system was even more successful than previously recognized in transferring resources to be used for industrialization.

[7] Ohkawa *et al., Growth Rate,* 26, 79–80, 247.

not do so until 1909.[8] While by the late 1890's a peak of some 40 per cent of yarn production was exported, this amounted to only 10 per cent of total exports. Cotton fabrics were even less important until World War I and thereafter; at best less than 20 per cent of production was exported, less than 5 per cent of total exports.[9]

Thus, during most of the period, Japan's exports consisted mainly of raw and semi-processed primary products—silk, tea, rice, coal, copper. Imports, which initially were manufactured consumer goods, gradually shifted in composition, with increasing proportions of investment goods and industrial raw materials. While Japan at first had substantial problems in shifting from complete autarky to virtually complete free trade, as the adjustment proceeded trade grew rapidly—at an average annual rate of 7.5 per cent between 1880 and 1913.[10]

Exports were very important for Japanese growth. They provided an addition to aggregate demand and, more important, a means both for paying for the imports necessary for the growth process and for obtaining the gains from international specialization in production. In this respect the agricultural sector made a major contribution to the beginning of Japan's modern growth process, before modern industry could take over the leading role. Special emphasis should be placed on silk, both because it constituted about one-third of total exports over the period and because it represented an effective utilization of the existing resources in agriculture combined with simple technological improvements and small additions of capital. Cocoon raising and silk-reeling became important, small-scale rural activities.[11] Thus, just as the development of the cotton spinning and weaving industry typifies Japan's early modern industrial effort, so the growth of the silk industry represents the contribution of traditional resources to growth. Accordingly, the financing of these industries will be considered in order to provide insights into the role of the financial system in providing growth.

Japan's growth was based upon increases in the quantity and, especially,

[8] Seki, *The Cotton Industry of Japan,* Appendix Tables 8–9, pp. 304–7. In the case of fabrics, the volume of exports exceeded imports a few years earlier, because of the lower average quality of exports.

[9] Ministry of Finance, *Dainihon Gaikokuboekinempyo* (*Annual Statistics of Foreign Trade in Japan*), as provided in Shinohara, "Economic Development and Foreign Trade in Pre-War Japan," in Cowan, *Economic Development of China and Japan,* 227.

[10] Cf. Lockwood, *Economic Development of Japan,* 312.

[11] On the surface it is surprising that Japan did not carry the processing of silk beyond the yarn to the weaving stage in greater quantity; raw silk exports were always substantially greater than silk fabric exports. The main reason for this relative lack of development was that the United States constituted the major market for Japanese silk, and it imposed high protective tariffs against silk fabrics, but not against yarn.

improvements in the quality of the factors of production. The population and the labor force grew relatively slowly, slightly more than 1 per cent a year. Given the large pool of low productivity labor, the early and continued emphasis by the government on improving the quality of labor through education was of major importance.[12] The rate of investment increased somewhat throughout the period, but was rather lower than might be expected.[13] In part this increased investment rate resulted from a redistribution of income from the daimyo and the samurai to the central government and to landowning farmers with higher marginal propensities to save. One of the functions of the financial system early in the Meiji Era was to mobilize this newly created saving for productive purposes. Nonetheless, the fact that increases in the supplies of labor and capital were relatively limited suggests that sustained growth was due more to other forces. In part the economy took up some of the slack of inefficient allocation and utilization of the initial stock of labor and capital. More important, probably, were improvements in technology. In industry, transportation, communications, electric power, and other sectors there occurred the major introduction and adaptation of Western techniques (significantly more advanced than the Japanese), usually embodied in the machinery used in these sectors.

THE FINANCIAL STRUCTURE AND ITS EVOLUTION

Between 1868 and 1914 Japan's financial system, originally based on essentially traditional institutions, developed rapidly into a modern, pervasive, variegated system, providing a wide spectrum of financial services.[14] By

[12] See Japan, Ministry of Education, *Japan's Growth and Education.* See also Emi, *Government Fiscal Activity and Economic Growth in Japan, 1868–1960,* 124–31, and, for a more critical view, Oshima, "Government Revenues and Expenditures in Meiji Economic Growth." By 1875 50 per cent of young boys and 19 per cent of young girls were enrolled in school; in 1895 the respective percentages were 77 and 44, and in 1905, 98 and 93.

[13] In 1887–96, excluding military goods, gross domestic fixed capital formation was 7.9 per cent of GNP, and its net counterpart 4.5 per cent of NNP; by 1907–16 the respective figures were 10.4 per cent and 6.2 per cent. These represent some underestimation, however, since self-produced agricultural investment is not included. Computed from Rosovsky, *Capital Formation in Japan,* Tables 1, 3, 5, pp. 2, 9, 15. On the other hand, the composition of investment shifted radically from uses for traditional purposes to uses for purposes of modern industrialization. Ibid. 16–19.

[14] For useful descriptions in English of the Meiji financial system, its policies, and its development, see Sakurai, *Financial Aspects of Economic Development of Japan;* Matsukata, *Report on the Adoption of the Gold Standard in Japan;* "Banking in Modern Japan," *Fuji Bank Bulletin.* A standard Japanese source is Akashi and Suzuki,

World War I Japan had virtually all the types of financial institutions that it has today, though of course there has been substantial modification in the structure and role of the system as the economy has continued to develop. This financial development was not automatic or simple; there was considerable experimentation in modern institution-building. Moreover, many commercial banks and other financial institutions evolved from their counterparts in the Tokugawa Era.

The Traditional Structure

The Meiji economy inherited considerable financial expertise, though with a rather traditional, commercial orientation, from the Tokugawa period. The range of institutions included houses that specialized in exchange and banking; those that combined exchange business with merchant operations, silversmiths, warehousing, and financing of inventories; and firms that handled government funds, pawnshops, individual moneylenders, and rotating credit associations (*mujin*). Many of these institutions, especially the smaller ones, continued their traditional activities in their traditional forms throughout the Meiji period, and, indeed, into the present time. Others evolved into modern, Western-style banks, savings banks, and other financial intermediaries.

These institutions had developed relatively early. By the end of the seventeenth century a credit system had evolved from money changers, merchant financiers, and financiers of daimyo, which was "not inferior to those existing in Europe at that time." [15] While retail transactions were settled only in currency—a custom which has continued to the present—these incipient bankers provided the major medium of exchange for wholesale transactions, as well as short-term credit by means of commercial bills secured by rice or specie. They accepted deposits, but only from credit-worthy merchants, and issued deposit receipts in small denominations which circulated in commerce. The main financial center, and the major commercial city, was Osaka, which was on a silver standard. An important exchange business devel-

Nihon Kinyushi (*Financial History of Japan*), vol. I, *Meiji Hen* (*Meiji Period*). Particularly useful analyses are provided in Kato, *Hompo Ginko Shi Ron* (*A History of Japanese Banks*), and Asaqura, *Meiji Zenki Nihon Kinyu Kozoshi* (*A History of the Japanese Financial Structure in the Meiji Era*). The major statistical sources used in this chapter are Ministry of Finance, *Financial and Economic Annual of Japan,* various issues; Toyo Keizai Shimposha, Oriental Economist Publishing Co. (ed.), *Meiji Taisho Kokusei Soron* (*Survey of the State of the Nation in the Meiji-Taisho Periods*); Bank of Japan, Statistics Department, *Historical Statistics of Japanese Economy.*

[15] From p. 342 of Crawcour's excellent article, "The Development of a Credit System in Seventeenth Century Japan."

oped between Osaka and Edo (Tokyo), the administrative capital, in part because in Edo gold was the standard coin. In addition to the exchange business among the many types of coins and daimyo paper notes, and the financing of commerce (especially trade in rice by daimyo, who had collected it as a tax in kind), many of the largest urban financial houses became increasingly involved in lending for consumption to daimyo and high-level samurai. Financing was also relatively well developed in smaller cities and rural areas, but ties were not as close to the Tokugawa aristocracy, and funds were used mainly for agriculture; the financial units were smaller and their activities more nearly resembled moneylending by individuals.

Although there was considerable continuity of financial institutions and family fortunes and activities associated with them, most of the largest and richest Tokugawa urban merchant-banking houses did not long survive the Meiji Restoration.[16] Those which dealt most closely with the government and the daimyo clans had become the most firmly ensconced in the Tokugawa economic system, and apparently they were unable to adapt from the rather static conditions of middle Tokugawa to the vastly different circumstances of late Tokugawa and early Meiji. Any but the most agile traditional mercantile-financial houses were likely to be hurt by rapidly changing political conditions and institutional arrangements. For example, the merchants in Osaka suffered great losses, first from the change in the domestic silver-gold exchange rate of between 5 and 10 to 1 to the world exchange rate of about 15 to 1, and second from the 1869 decision of the new government to have all silver contracts voided and rewritten in terms of gold. Moreover, many merchants lost considerable wealth by the repudiation of their loans to daimyo made prior to 1844, and by the assumption by the new central government of loans made to daimyo between 1844 and 1871, which were paid off in long-term government bonds bearing a zero interest rate. Only two or three of the major financial houses of the Tokugawa period continued to thrive in modern Japan, notably Mitsui and Sumitomo, and Sumitomo developed into a *zaibatsu* more on the basis of its rich copper mines than on its financial activities.

In terms of the development of Japan's modern commercial banking system, the Tokugawa financial heritage manifested itself early in the Meiji period in the rapid growth of quasi-banking companies (*ginko ruiji kaisha*) and of private banks. They differed in that the latter are defined as concentrating solely on a banking business, while the former engaged in the multiple functions of trade, and even production, as well as finance. Quasi-banks accordingly more closely resembled their Tokugawa precursors than did private banks, which together with the national banks became the foundation of the commercial banking system.

[16] See Hirschmeier, *Origins of Entrepreneurship in Meiji Japan,* chap. 1, pp. 6–7.

Quasi-banks [17] operated mainly in rural areas and port cities. They were established by relatively small to medium-sized merchants, landowners (richer farmers), and moneylenders. Their size varied considerably, but on the average their capital was much smaller than the average capital of private banks, as is indicated in Table VIII.1. Official statistics seriously underestimate the number and total amount of loans of quasi-banks, and therefore their importance, as has been well documented by Asakura for specific prefectures.[18] This is especially true of those relatively more advanced rural areas which produced large surpluses of cash crops. Their own capital was apparently considerably more important than deposits.

Quasi-banks lent mainly to finance the production and the domestic and foreign trade of such cash crops as rice, silk, and tea, and the processing of agricultural goods, such as silk reeling, sake brewing, and production of agar-agar. Usually financing was directly linked with trade and, in some cases, production; the lender sold supplies to producers on credit, bought the crop, and arranged for its shipment to final markets. While comprehensive data are not available on the size of quasi-bank loans, they probably were somewhat in excess of quasi-bank capital. Loans were usually short-term, to finance working capital requirements, and interest rates were high.[19] It appears that close ties existed between some quasi-banks and private or national banks. Executives of the latter in some cases ran quasi-banking companies for purposes of money-lending and/or getting ownership of land by charging extremely high interest rates, using funds borrowed from their banks.

Asakura argues that the substantial increase in tenant farming, from 31 per cent of the total land at the beginning of Meiji to 40 per cent in 1887 and 46 per cent in 1913, was in substantial part due to the activities of quasi-banking institutions, whose owners were able to gain possession of considerable land through their multiple activities. It is notable that the number of quasi-banking institutions developed very rapidly during the depression period of the early 1880's. In many cases this appears to have been the result of individual lenders establishing formal institutions and companies as means of collecting debts or of taking possession of land

[17] Asakura, *Meiji Zenki Nihon Kinyu Kozoshi,* 263ff. An important implicit thesis of his study is that until the 1890's quasi-banks and rural banks were of major importance in financing primary sector production (which provided most of the increase in output) and simple, small-scale processing of agricultural and other primary products; Asakura, however, places more emphasis on such finance in transferring land to large landowners and to merchants.

[18] Ibid. 187, 205–24. See also Ouchi and Kato, *Kokuritsu Ginko no Kenkyu* (*Studies on National Banks*), esp. chap. 6, Table 6.

[19] Asakura suggests that interest rates were commonly up to 60 per cent a year, and that probably they were seldom less than 20 per cent or so. Ibid. 263.

TABLE VIII.1

NUMBER, TOTAL PAID-IN CAPITAL, AND AVERAGE CAPITAL OF NATIONAL BANKS, PRIVATE BANKS, AND QUASI-BANKS IN JAPAN, 1873–1899

(capital in thousand yen)

	National Banks			Private Banks[b]			Quasi-Banks[d]		
Year End	No.	Total Cap.	Avg. Cap.[a]	No.	Total Cap.	Avg. Cap.	No.	Total Cap.	Avg. Cap.
1873	1	2,441	2,441.0	0	0	0	c	c	c
1874	4	3,432	858.0	0	0	0	c	c	c
1875	4	3,450	862.5	0	0	0	c	c	c
1876	5	2,350	470.0	1	2,000	2,000	c	c	c
1877	26	22,986	206.4	1	2,000	2,000	c	c	c
1878	95	33,596	167.8	1	2,000	2,000	c	c	c
1879	151	40,616	151.9	10	3,290	329.0	c	c	c
1880	151	43,041	168.1	39	6,280	161.0	120	1,211	10.1
1881	148	43,886	177.3	90	10,447	116.1	369	5,894	16.0
1882	143	44,206	184.5	176	17,152	97.5	438	7,958	18.2
1883	141	44,386	189.7	207	20,487	99.0	573	12,071	21.1
1884	140	44,536	192.2	214	19,421	90.8	741	15,142	20.4
1885	139	44,456	193.0	218	18,750	86.0	744	15,397	20.7
1886	136	44,416	197.0	220	17,959	81.6	748	15,391	20.6
1887	136	45,839	207.5	221	18,896	85.5	741	15,112	20.4
1888	135	46,878	216.8	195	15,790	81.0	711	14,408	20.3
1889	134	47,681	224.5	218	17,432	80.0	695	14,421	20.7
1890	134	48,645	231.7	217	18,976	87.4	702	14,512	20.7
1891	134	48,701	232.1	252	19,796	78.6	678	13,827	20.4
1892	133	48,326	231.1	270	22,856	84.7	680	13,944	20.5
1893	133	48,416	231.7	604	31,030	51.4	–	–	–
1894	133	48,816	234.8	700	37,411	53.4	–	–	–
1895	133	48,951	235.8	792	49,967	63.1	–	–	–
1896	121	44,762	224.5	1,005	88,970	88.5	–	–	–
1897	58	13,630	112.6	1,217	149,286	122.7	–	–	–
1898	4	390	97.5	1,444	189,440	131.2	–	–	–
1899	0	0	0	1,561	209,973	134.5	–	–	–

[a] Excluding the Fifteenth National Bank, which had a capital of 17.8 million yen.

[b] Reclassified as "ordinary banks" in 1893.

[c] Unknown.

[d] The official statistics exclude a large number of quasi-banks, especially smaller ones; this classification was ended in 1893.

Source: Quasi-banks and private banks prior to 1893· Asakura, *Meiji Zenki Nihon Kinyu Kozoshi*, 187; other: Tokyo Keizai Shimposha, *Meiji Taisho Kokusei Soran*, 5, 7, 10.

that had been under mortgage, since as individuals they found it difficult to collect debts owed them.

Such quasi-banks, due to their very heterogeneity and large number, have quite disparate histories. Under the banking law that went into effect in 1893, quasi-banking institutions as a class were not recognized; they had to become either ordinary banks or ordinary companies if they wanted to continue their corporate form. Some had earlier evolved into private banks, and many others became ordinary banks under the new law, as can be seen (Table VIII.1) from the large increase in number of ordinary banks and the decrease in average size of their paid-in capital. Many simply re-established themselves as business corporations but continued to carry on their lending activities with their other business.

The Government's Concept of the Financial System

We should not put too much emphasis on the role of the government in the establishment and development of Japan's financial system, since it was mainly through the initiative of profit-minded individuals that most Japanese financial institutions were born. Indeed, an extremely important feature dominating governmental policy throughout this period was its explicit advocacy of a private, competitive, laissez-faire banking system. At the same time the government attached great importance to a modern banking system and provided considerable incentives to encourage financial entrepreneurship. To the extent that private banking did not meet all the requirements for growth, however, the government was quite willing, even anxious, to create special institutions to meet particular needs.

Government interest in the domestic transplantation and adaption of advanced Western financial institutions was highly developed from the beginning of the Restoration. As is true in many underdeveloped countries today, Japan's leaders wanted forced-draft development of the economy and of the financial system, rather than tolerating evolutionary growth at a more deliberate pace. At the beginning, however, the government had little knowledge of the West, and proceeded on an *ad hoc* and somewhat haphazard basis. The initial experiments in institution-building reflected more a faith in the efficacy of Western financial institutions than an understanding of their appropriate operations. This was illustrated in the establishment of the national banking system and its short-lived predecessors, the eight government-sponsored "exchange companies."

Mitsui, Ono, and other wealthy merchants, on the basis of their experience with the exchange companies, were willing to set up banks on the Western model, with, of course, the expectation of substantial government deposits and business. At the same time, the government was searching for the appropriate Western banking system to adopt in order to accumulate mercantile capital for industrialization and to provide for orderly development of the currency system while solving the problem of inconvertible government currency circulation. Two alternating proposals were considered in late 1871 and early 1872.

The first proposal was that Japan adopt the American national banking system, with government bonds to constitute the collateral for the issuance of national banknotes. The government bonds would be issued in redemption of the government's inconvertible currency. Critics argued that the American model would not solve the currency problem, but would only result in another form of inconvertible paper currency; they recommended instead the adoption of the British model, with a central bank which would have the sole power of note issue and which would hold reserves in specie. Other banks would be ordinary commercial banks. In this way a convertible currency system could be achieved. The American model, supported more by powerful leaders than by rigorous analysis of its applicability, was accepted, though with some modification.[20] This model was not successful, and it became essentially inoperative several years later when national banks were given the right to issue inconvertible banknotes.

The government's concept of what constituted a proper financial structure took shape gradually.[21] This view envisaged an amalgam of the British and the Continental systems, with specialized classes of institutions carrying on specific types of financial activities. Commercial banks were to finance the needs of trade and the working capital of industry, mainly from funds provided by deposits. Savings banks were to collect the savings of low-income groups, and were accordingly to pursue conservative policies to protect their depositors. The central bank was to serve as the government's fiscal agent and financier, to control the money supply, and to serve as lender of last resort for the banking system. Specialized banks under government auspices were to assist in financing foreign trade and fixed investment in agriculture and industry, in encouraging the inflow of foreign portfolio capital, and in developing the northern island, Hokkaido, and the colonies of Taiwan and Korea. Relatively less emphasis was placed upon the development of a broad long-term capital market in equities and bonds as the means for transferring individual saving to productive investment.

This governmental approach to a comprehensive financial structure—specific types of financial institutions for specific functions—reflected the basic views of Masayoshi Matsukata. Matsukata, as government adviser, minister of finance, and eventually prime minister, was the architect of

[20] Adams, *A Financial History of Modern Japan,* 9.

[21] In the following I rely heavily on Kato, *Hompo Ginko Shi Ron,* esp. pp. 79–83, 169–74.

Japanese fiscal and monetary policy between 1881 and the turn of the century. In an 1881 memorial to the emperor he enunciated his basic program, advocating the establishment of a central bank, and urging that an industrial bank and a savings bank be created to supplement the inadequate private financial system. In his own thinking Matsukata differentiated between commercial capital, which was liquid and had high turnover, and agricultural and industrial capital, which was of a fixed nature. He felt that since the functions of these different kinds of capital were different, so too should be the institutional sources of their financing and the kinds of collateral used. He feared that otherwise there would be a confusion in sources and uses of funds, and abuses in the uses of funds lent.

Of course the actual flows of funds through the economy were never so segregated as Matsukata had envisaged, nor did banking develop along narrowly defined lines. The use of specific types of collateral for loans did not mean that the funds were actually used by the borrower for the expected purposes. For example, loans on inventories or on farm land did not necessarily mean the financing of working capital or land improvements. Nor did loans to particular classes of borrowers. Some rich farmers used borrowed funds to establish small processing plants, and some merchants used them to purchase land. This makes it difficult to trace financial intermediation activities through to actual real expenditures. Morever, the thinking of the times frequently confused the development of financial capital with that of real capital formation.

Until the end of the century Matsukata was too busy setting up the convertible currency system, establishing the central bank, arranging for the orderly ending of the national bank system, financing the Sino-Japanese War, and pushing Japan onto the gold standard to implement his vision of special long-term credit banks. Moreover, though bills to establish such banks were introduced in the early and mid-1890's, the opposition of private financial interests delayed the passage of these bills.

The consequence of the government's interest in Western financial models was the eclectic borrowing of what were considered the most appropriate aspects of the best Western institutions: the American national banks; the Belgian central bank; and the French Crédit Foncier and Crédit Mobilier. The commercial bank system, influenced by the high repute of British banking, by English banking adviser Alexander Allan Shand, and by the establishment of the Bank of Japan with a monopoly of note issue, eventually moved toward the English model. This model continued to be dominant in government and private thinking for a long time, although, as so often happens in Japan, financiers responded pragmatically, and without great concern, to opportunities and to particular characteristics of the Japanese economy that happened to be inconsistent with their ideal model.

Growth of the Money Supply

While the government placed considerable emphasis on the development of a modern banking system, initially it had to be even more concerned with the development of a unified, convertible currency system, especially since currency was virtually the sole component of the money supply.[22] At the time of the Meiji Restoration a bewildering variety of Tokugawa gold, silver, and copper coins, differing in purity, weight, and nominal value, circulated with daimyo paper money and merchant-issued notes at fluctuating relative rates. In this chaotic situation the Restoration government issued inconvertible paper currency, initially as the main means of financing its expenditures, and again in 1877 to finance extraordinary military expenditures for the Satsuma Rebellion. Inconvertible national banknotes provided a further complication after 1876. The persistent import surplus, combined with paper money issue, resulted in a major outflow of specie.

There were two problems to be solved: the establishment of a national currency, and the achievement of convertibility for that currency. The first was accomplished within a few years by reminting Tokugawa coins, and by replacing daimyo paper money with government notes. The war-induced inflation of 1877–81 produced a situation in which inconvertible government and national bank paper money circulated at a substantial discount relative to specie. The Matsukata reform of the early 1880's established par between the two by 1886, when Bank of Japan convertible notes began to circulate, replacing inconvertible paper money.

The Matsukata reform had two components: deflation by increasing government revenues and reducing expenditures, and institution-building. In the latter category was the establishment of the Bank of Japan as the central bank in 1882. The Bank of Japan Act was a direct outgrowth of Matsukata's memorial of the previous year. The government investigated the various European models, and, under the advice of Leon Say, settled on the Belgian central bank as the latest and most modern.

The Bank of Japan was set up as a private joint-stock company, but half of the capital was subscribed by the government, which also had the right to appoint the governor and other officers and to supervise its policies, activities, and administration. Perhaps because it was created, full-blown, under the instigation and control of the Minister of Finance, rather than evolving, the Bank of Japan always remained rather subservient to the Treasury. Its objectives, as defined in the enacting law, were to serve as government fiscal agent, to smooth out seasonal and regional flows of funds, to finance international trade and handle specie reserves, and to control the

[22] The following discussion is based on Patrick, "Financial Policy in Meiji Japan."

issuance of currency. To achieve this final objective it was given the monopoly of note issue. Accordingly, the systems of (inconvertible) note issue by the government and by the national banks came to a legal end. Since the Bank of Japan was not initially endowed with specie reserves, it was several years before it could begin the issue of convertible notes as circulating currency.

Although it had taken a severe deflation and depression to put the domestic currency system in order, the monetary authorities realized early that the money supply, which was based on full convertibility to specie, might well be too inelastic to stimulate the growth of the economy and to meet extraordinary government financial requirements. To overcome this difficulty they authorized the Bank of Japan in 1888 to issue currency in excess of stipulated specie reserve requirements. The Bank of Japan also actively supported the banking system, both as a lender of last resort in crises and as a continuous supplier of loans to banks.[23] In accepting as loan collateral bank bills which had corporate stock as collateral, the Bank of Japan also in effect made commercial bank lending for the financing of productive fixed investment feasible by guaranteeing commercial bank liquidity. Although the central bank and the government at times in the next forty years allowed the discipline of the specie standard to manifest itself in reducing the money supply, when it came to the choice between severe depression or fiduciary money issue, the latter, more elastic route was usually taken. This is well indicated by the preliminary estimates of the growth of the money supply, given in Table VIII.2.

The generally expansive government fiscal policy, abetted by the Bank of Japan's active accommodation of both the government and the commercial banks, meant that the inflationary tendencies of the early years continued over the long run as well. On average the inflation was mild, however; prices rose most in wartime, and there were occasional brief deflationary spells. The attendant balance of payments difficulties that accompanied ample increases in money and generally faster price rises in Japan than in the rest of the world were met in a variety of ways. Until 1882 the main method was to use up the accumulated stock of gold and silver. While most of the import surplus did not represent capital goods, at least it did give the government time to consolidate its position while postponing facing up to the balance of payments. From the mid-1880's until 1897, and especially in the early 1890's, the balance of payments pressure was eased by having a *de facto* depreciating exchange rate, since Japan was in practice on the

[23] Especially between 1890 and 1900, when loans from the Bank of Japan ranged between 10 and 18 per cent of the sum of commercial bank deposits and net worth; thereafter they declined to between 2 and 6 per cent. See Yoshino, "Waga Kuni Shichu Ginko no Obaaron ni Tsuite" ("Overloan of Commercial Banks in Japan"), 1–39.

TABLE VIII.2

PERCENTAGE GROWTH RATE OF THE STOCK OF MONEY IN JAPAN, 1875–1914

	Growth Rate Per 5-Year Period (%)	Ratio of Money Supply to National Income
1875–80	17	35[b]
1880–85	–31	26
1885–90	31	23
1890–95	65	24
1895–1900	46	24
1900–1905	42	24
1905–10	32	26
1910–14[a]	3	23

[a] Four-year period.

[b] For 1875–80 money supply may be overestimated and national income underestimated.

Sources: Patrick, "Financial Policy in Meiji Japan," and Ohkawa, *Growth Rate*.

silver standard while the world price of silver relative to gold declined by almost half. The past depreciation was accepted when Japan went onto the gold standard in 1897, with the yen valued at one-half the former (nominal) gold yen price. Thereafter, until the beginning of World War I, Japan relied heavily on foreign portfolio capital inflows to finance a substantial current account deficit in the balance of payments; foreign investment equaled approximately one-half of net domestic capital formation (excluding military) between 1904 and 1913.

Three general points can be made about the behavior of the money supply over this period. First, it responded on the whole quite flexibly to the needs of growth—in the first few years overly so. Secondly, available data [24] indicate that by the early 1880's the money supply became an approximately constant proportion of national income in current prices. (See Table VIII.2.) This seems to have occurred surprisingly early in Japan's modern economic development. It suggests that the economy was quite highly monetized

[24] Recently published data suggest that the ratio of money to national income declined somewhat (income velocity rose) between 1875 and the early 1890's, and was constant thereafter until the beginning of World War I, when it began to decline again (until 1940). See Fujino, *Nihon no Keiki Junkan* (*Business Cycles in Japan*), pp. 209–15 and Charts 12-1 and 12-2. A more detailed discussion of Fujino's as yet unpublished data appears in Hoekendorf, "The Secular Trend of Income Velocity in Japan, 1897–1940." Fujino notes a substantial rise in deposit turnover which economized on the amount of money held; in addition, national income for the early period may be underestimated.

from an early stage, and that other financial assets developed rather quickly as substitutes for money as a store of wealth. Thirdly, the money supply economized increasingly on the stock of specie as a circulating medium, thereby freeing it to finance an import surplus. Circulating specie constituted 75 per cent of the money supply in 1868; by 1881 it was down to 20 per cent, where it remained until declining further with the rapid growth of deposit money after the turn of the century. While at first the decline was due to the outflow of specie and the creation of inconvertible paper, the fact that the ratio remained low once convertibility between paper notes and coins was restored, and again when the shift to the gold standard was made, indicates that there was a general public willingness to accept other monetary forms in its stead. In the early years the substitute was primarily paper currency. With the expansion of the number of banks, commercialization of the economy, and development of the banking habit, deposit money became increasingly important—from about 7 per cent of the money supply in 1881, to 31 per cent in 1898, and to 44 per cent in 1914.

Origins of the Commercial Banking System: National Banks

The National Banking Act, on the American model, was promulgated in 1872. Of national bank capital 60 per cent was to be held in government bonds yielding 6 per cent. The national banks could issue an equivalent amount of banknotes, which were in effect an interest-free source of funds. The remaining 40 per cent of the capital was in specie to provide a reserve for the redemption of banknotes, which were convertible into gold upon request.

Although the government anticipated that these terms would provide sufficient profit inducement, in fact the national banks so established were not very successful. In part this reflected their ignorance of Western-style banking. More important was the tendency for the public to mistrust the banknotes and to present them for specie. Without full public confidence in the ability of the banks to maintain currency convertibility, the national banks were never able to circulate their notes in large quantities, and this reduced profits substantially. Moreover, the 6 per cent yield on the government bonds was considerably below the short-term market rates of interest of 10 to 15 per cent.

Accordingly, only four national banks were established during the three-year period 1873–1876. Of these the most important was, and continued to be, the First National Bank (Dai-ichi Ginko).[25] The First National Bank provides an illuminating case study of the extreme importance of close ties

[25] The national banks were named in numerical sequence when they received their charters.

with the government for large-scale banks and financial groups.[26] The bank was founded in July 1873, by the joint subscription (under government prodding) of the rival financial houses of Mitsui and Ono, both of which were serving as government fiscal agents and were threatened with loss of government business if they did not participate co-operatively. They each purchased 1 million yen of the bank's share issue, and a further 440,800 yen was obtained from public subscription, the first in Japan. In the first several years government deposits were an extremely important source of funds, amounting to about one-half of total deposits and somewhat larger than paid-in capital. Its loans were mainly used to finance rice speculation, the silk trade, urban real estate, and mining, and were made in large part to Mitsui and Ono interests.

Management of the bank was assumed by Eiichi Shibusawa, who resigned as deputy minister of finance (a position he had achieved through ability at a relatively early age) to take the post. Shibusawa, who became the outstanding financial and industrial entrepreneur of the Meiji period, was a romantic-type entrepreneur of great charm, ability, and a certain measure of unscrupulousness. He was a protégé of several of the most important members of the political oligarchy. Somehow within a few years Shibusawa succeeded in wresting control of the First National Bank completely away from Mitsui and Ono and in making it his own organ. His qualities and connections typify the requisites for success as a leading businessman early in the Meiji period: entrepreneurial ability, experience, and vision of an industrial Japan, extremely close relations with top government officials, and access to large amounts of funds.

In 1874 the government suddenly announced that its fiscal agents would have to provide liquid collateral equal to the government deposits they held. Ono, unable to do so, was forced into bankruptcy (as were several other major Tokugawa financial houses), and simply disappeared. Shibusawa had been tipped off in advance, so the First National Bank was able to seize Ono's real assets, which were serving as collateral for loans from the bank, before Ono's other creditors could, and the Ono portion of the capital was written off the bank's books to cover the remainder of its debts.

Mitsui escaped the same fate because it had even closer ties with the government than Ono.[27] It learned of the impending collateral requirement

[26] The following is based heavily on Ouchi and Kato, *Kokuritsu Ginko no Kenkyu,* chap. 1, and Choi, "Shibusawa Eiichi and his Contemporaries." A somewhat more laudatory view of Shibusawa appears in Hirschmeier, "Shibusawa Eiichi and Modern Business Enterprise."

[27] Mitsui had given financial support to the Restoration group even before they achieved final victory over the Tokugawa Shogun, and it received extremely favorable treatment from the government from then on. Mitsui served as government fiscal agent and banker in the early years, received government deposits for its bank, was

sufficiently in advance to be able to improve its liquidity position. Moreover, the government did not enforce its requirement that Ono and Mitsui be jointly responsible for the government funds each had. With the Ono shares eliminated, Mitsui came to own some 80 per cent of the bank's stock.

Shortly thereafter, in late 1874, Mitsui proposed making the First National Bank a branch of its own financial house. Shibusawa strongly opposed this, and he was able to obtain the support of top-level officials in the Ministry of Finance. The Mitsui House did not fight, because it was afraid it would hurt its own long-run interests of maintaining close connections with the government. In this crisis Shibusawa dramatically asserted his power and control, and Mitsui influence in the First National Bank waned thereafter, although it continued to own a majority of the stock for a number of years. In 1876 Mitsui was finally able to set up a private bank under its own control.

By 1876 the difficulties of the national banking system were all too evident. The four national banks petitioned the government to allow their bank notes to be convertible into (inconvertible) government paper money rather than into specie. Just at this time the government was devising its program to capitalize the hereditary pensions of the samurai and the feudal lords. Changing the collateral requirements for banknote issue seemed a convenient way to handle several problems simultaneously: to help the dispossessed but still powerful aristocracy, to build a strong national banking system, to provide funds for industrial purposes,[28] and to maintain the value of the immense supply of government pension bonds to be issued.

Accordingly, the national bank law was amended in August 1876 to allow banks to hold 80 per cent of their capital in government bonds and the remaining 20 per cent in government paper currency rather than in specie. The national banks could issue banknotes up to 80 per cent of paid-in capital. They were convertible only into inconvertible government notes. These much more liberal terms, combined with the large issue (174 million yen) of government hereditary pension bonds, provided tremendous profit incentives to establish national banks. One indication of the responsiveness of many Japanese to profit opportunities is that almost 150 national banks

able to purchase government enterprises when they were sold (in part because it had sufficient resources and was willing to take the risk), and even got Bank of Japan special discounts (at the insistence of the Ministry of Finance) in the 1890 crisis when the Mitsui Bank (discussed below) was under special pressure.

[28] Matsukata later scored the simplistic views of government officials on the effects on hereditary pension bond issue. "It was believed that . . . the economic market would be supplied with the much needed capital in the form of banknotes. It is needless to notice that these ideas were based on the erroneous notion that capital and currency were interchangeable terms." Matsukata, *Report on the Adoption of the Gold Standard in Japan,* 25.

were established between 1877 and 1879, and they issued large amounts of banknotes.[29] Expansion was so rapid that the government in 1878 set a ceiling on national banknote issue of 34 million yen and, following the establishment of the One Hundred and Fifty-third National Bank in Kyoto in 1879, chartered no more national banks.

The standard interpretation has been that the national banks were dominated by the samurai and daimyo, since they provided the major source of capital, in the form of government bonds. They did indeed own most—initially more than three-quarters—of the national bank shares. However, Asakura cites numerous cases in which national banks were established on the initiative of wealthy merchants and landlords, who provided the 20 per cent cash portion of capital. Between 1880 and 1896 the proportion of national bank stock held by samurai declined from 31 per cent to 19 per cent, while that held by commoners rose from 24 per cent to 39 per cent. While banks were often founded with a large number of samurai small stockholders, they were soon bought out by members of the merchant-landowner-financier group. Stock ownership in each bank gradually became concentrated into the hands of relatively few individuals.

While the average size of national banks was considerably larger than that of private banks or quasi-banks (see Table VIII.1, p. 248), most were rather small. Some 39 per cent had an initial paid-in capital of less than 100,000 yen, another 34 per cent had between 100,000 and 200,000 yen, and only two banks were capitalized at more than 1 million yen—the First National Bank and the Fifteenth National Bank.[30]

The Fifteenth National Bank was unique. It was established by some 480 daimyo and court families.[31] Not until 1891 were commoners allowed to purchase the bank's shares, and then only a limited amount. The bank's paid-in capital (17.8 million yen) was approximately 40 per cent of the total capital of all national banks. Its note issue (16.7 million yen) [32] was nearly half of total national banknote issue. Apparently its immediate purpose was to make a 15 million yen loan at 5 per cent to the government to

[29] For details on the relative importance of the different kinds of currency in circulation, see Patrick, "Financial Policy in Meiji Japan," Table 1. Approximately one-fifth of hereditary pension bonds were used directly as national bank capital.

[30] Kato, *Hompo Ginko Shi Ron,* 33.

[31] Some 294 of the poorer nobility, allotted 13 per cent of the stock, were unable to raise the cash portion of the payment; they were accordingly lent funds by the Ministry of the Imperial Household for this purpose. The Ministry subsequently received loans from the bank sufficient to cover its loans to the bank's stockholders. A few rich nobles refused to join. Cf. Ouchi and Kato, *Kokuritsu Ginko no Kenkyu,* chap. 3.

[32] As a special concession it was allowed to use bonds and to issue notes in excess of the standard 80 per cent limitation.

assist in putting down the Satsuma Rebellion. Inasmuch as the government could have issued its own paper notes without paying interest, this was a further means by which the government bought off the daimyo. Continued coddling was evident in subsequent government relations with the Fifteenth National Bank.[33] Interest from the pension bonds and the government loan, coupled with a policy of paying out all earnings, permitted annual dividend payments of 10 per cent of paid-in capital, a reasonable yield then.

The national banks in the early years relied on government funds for 25 to 35 per cent of total deposits. Private deposits, especially from individuals not directly connected with the bank, grew relatively slowly, as might be expected in the early stages of the development of a financial system. The growth in deposit money was almost entirely for business use, since individuals continued to use currency for retail transactions. The slow growth of deposits combined with privilege of note issue meant that national bank loans were always substantially larger than deposits.

The elimination of the privileged status of national banks was foreshadowed in 1881, when Matsukata, who was dedicated to the idea of establishing a central bank, became minister of finance. He had the National Banking Act amended to limit the charters of the national banks from 30 to 20 years and to prohibit renewal, to end their privilege of issue, and to provide for gradual, orderly redemption of their notes. With national bank expansion halted, it was only a matter of time—their charters expired in the late 1890's—until they were amalgamated into the ordinary bank system.

Aside from their regular banking activities, which were scarcely different from those of other banking institutions, the national banks did make several unique contributions to the development of Japan's commercial banking system. They provided the first sustained, successful experience in modern banking techniques. They set the pattern of unit banking, and were relatively well dispersed throughout the country. They made modern banking, and, by extension, modern enterprise generally, a highly respectable and even prestigious occupation; this probably resulted in part from continuing general respect for the nobility and samurai.

The national banking system had a significant role in popularizing important Western business institutions, notably the corporate form of business organization. The national banks were the first to adopt the joint-stock form

[33] For example, when the government first wanted to repay the loan, it did not because the bank objected on the ground that it could not adequately loan out so much money elsewhere. Later, when the bank had to begin redemption of its banknotes and was in difficulties, the government repaid 5 million yen in cash to be used to retire its banknotes, and replaced the 10 million yen portion of the loan with special bonds carrying a (then unduly high) rate of 7.5 per cent. The bank's annual interest income from the government thus remained at 750,000 yen. Kato, *Hompo Ginko Shi Ron,* 118.

with limited liability. Thereafter the corporate form was utilized not only in the establishment of almost all modern enterprises in Meiji Japan, but also in many cases was grafted onto the existing, traditional forms of industrial, commercial, and financial organization. For example, by 1896 2,585 joint-stock companies, 1,666 limited partnerships (half in commerce), and 344 ordinary partnerships were officially registered. Of their total net worth of 472.6 million yen, joint-stock companies accounted for 90.1 per cent, limited partnerships only 6.6 per cent, and ordinary partnerships 3.3 per cent.[34] In addition, the national banks introduced the first modern book-keeping system, including depreciation accounting.[35] These techniques spread not only to other financial institutions but to new industrial enterprises as well.

Origins of the Commercial Banking System: Private Banks

Early Meiji was characterized by a diversity and rapid growth of financial institutions. This proliferation ranged from a relatively few, extremely large banks, to numerous small banking and quasi-banking institutions. Unit banking predominated, though relatively close relationships developed among different types of financial institutions. Continuity with Tokugawa experience was a dominant feature for those institutions that were not national banks. The private banks are the most important case of evolutionary development; they show the grafting of Western banking techniques and forms of organization onto traditional sources of capital and institutional arrangements.

Private banks were on the average considerably larger and more modern in their characteristics than the quasi-banking institutions, but they were smaller than the national banks. (See Table VIII.1, p. 248.) The founders were almost all from the merchant-landowner-financier group, but were usually among their wealthier elements, especially in rural areas. The largest, most important private banks were established in urban areas by the wealthiest mercantile-financial houses. The private banks ranged widely in size—from a few with capital of more than 500,000 yen to many small banks with a capital of 10,000 or 20,000 yen—and they ranged correspondingly in their activities and roles in the economy. Some of the earliest private banks were established by industrialists as a means of obtaining funds (from deposits of individuals) to finance their activites; an example is the Nada Shogyo Ginko in Hyogo Prefecture, set up by local sake brewers. This

[34] Ministry of Finance, *Financial and Economic Annual of Japan,* VIII (1908), 89.

[35] Takatera "Early Experiment of Depreciation Accounting in National Banks, 1875–1879," 50–70.

characteristic was increasingly important in the establishment of private, and later of ordinary, banks—especially as the deposit habit (mainly time deposits) became more developed.

The beginning of private banks can be formally dated from 1876, when the Mitsui House received permission to use the word *ginko* (bank) in separating its financial activities from its commercial activities. *Ginko* was a new term, invented to mean Western-style bank; it had been applied first to the national banks. It had a strongly favorable connotation, indicating privileged status and power. During the 1870's numerous quasi-banks requested authorization to use the term *ginko*. Several years after Mitsui received permission to establish a private bank, this privilege was extended to other applicants, and the number of private banks grew rapidly in the early 1880's. (See Table VIII.1, p. 248.)

By far the largest of the private banks was the Mitsui Bank, which started with an initial capital of 2 million yen, four times that of any of the other private banks. Several other large mercantile houses also established banks with capital ranging from 200,000 to 500,000 yen. In the Tokugawa Era Mitsui had become one of the largest mercantile and financial houses. In the Meiji Era it became pre-eminent. Given its extremely close relations with the government, combined with its large fortune amassed over time, it is not surprising that the Mitsui House grew through its financial and industrial activities into the largest *zaibatsu* in Japan. It diversified first into mining (the Miike coal mines became a major source of Mitsui profits to finance expansion in the late Meiji period), then, in the late 1880's, into cotton textiles, and, as profits accumulated, into one industrial sector after another. Its entrepreneurial leadership was provided by a series of men, unrelated to the Mitsui families, who were brought up through the ranks and given authority. Its growth was substantially enhanced in the mid-1880's and later by its ability to utilize its financial institutions—especially the Mitsui Bank—to collect private individual deposits and to channel them to the purchase and development of new enterprises in the rapidly expanding sphere of Mitsui influence.

The national banking system has been proclaimed the major modern financial innovation promoting early Japanese growth. A great deal of emphasis in the analysis of the financial system has been placed on the development of the national banks. However, their importance relative to private banks and quasi-banks and the uniqueness of their over-all role in the growth of the economy has been exaggerated. Data on loans by type of financial institution are poor until the late 1880's. Still, it seems likely that by 1883 or so the amount of private bank loans outstanding was approximately equal to that of national banks. When the loans of quasi-banks and savings banks are added, the total was probably considerably greater than national bank loans until the late 1880's.[36]

Granting that the national banks were unique in their right of note issue and source of capital, in other respects they were quite similar to private banks. Both classes of banks had a wide range in size and in location. The merchant-landowner-financier group were the source of promotional and entrepreneurial incentive for many national banks as well as for all the private banks. And the sources of deposits and the lending behavior of both classes of banks were virtually identical.

Thus the dichotomy drawn between national and private banks does not have much economic meaning. A more useful distinction can be made between large banks, located in the largest cities, and small banks, located mainly in smaller towns. The large banks tended to receive most of the government's deposits and to serve as its fiscal agents, though certain smaller banks that were located in important regional commercial centers also obtained government support. In the first years, until the late 1880's, the lending behavior of large banks was not so different from that of the smaller banks. Thereafter, their roles diverged as the large banks assumed the major role in financing large-scale industrial development.

Aside from the Fifteenth National Bank loan to the government we do not have detailed data on the uses to which banks put their funds in the early years. To some extent they purchased the hereditary pension bonds which, due to their large supply and inadequate interest income, the great majority of poorer samurai were forced to sell at discounts of up to one-third. The most successful speculator in such government bonds was Zenjiro Yasuda, who, starting with literally nothing, founded the fourth largest *zaibatsu,* concentrating primarily upon finance.[37] Yasuda began by speculating in monies at the end of Tokugawa and the beginning of Meiji, and within a decade built his assets from 25 yen to more than 1 million yen. He joined in establishing the Third National Bank under the amended regulations in 1876, and became its president. He also converted his exchange company into the private Yasuda Bank in 1880. These two banks obtained government deposits, bought government bonds at a discount, and made large profits when the price of the bonds returned to par in the mid-1880's. The Yasuda Bank, which was at the apex of the group of banks controlled by Yasuda, was alone among the large banks throughout this period in developing a sizable structure of interrelated banks through merger or the establishment of branches, "daughter" banks, or other affiliates under its control.

[36] For estimates based on extrapolation of results of regression analysis, see Hoekendorf, "The Secular Trend of Income Velocity in Japan, 1879–1940," 206–13.

[37] Cf. "Banking in Modern Japan," *Fuji Bank Bulletin.* The Fuji Bank is the postwar successor of the Yasuda Bank.

By 1908 Yasuda's *zaibatsu* directly controlled eleven banks, three insurance companies, three railroads, a construction company and an electric power company.

In general, however, national and private bank purchases of government bonds and private (equity) securities were considerably less important than their lending activities. Most of their funds tended to flow to the traditional sectors of agriculture and commerce, although the financing of production for export was a new use. This was particularly true of the smaller national and private banks in the more rural areas; they were akin to quasi-banks in their size and activities. The larger banks, notably in Tokyo and Osaka, had a somewhat wider range of activities, including real estate financing and the handling of government tax revenues. But they also channeled their funds mainly to traditional sectors, by direct loans, by lending to smaller, rural banks and quasi-banks, and by using the rural institutions as intermediaries for loans to farmers for such purposes as the payment of taxes. This structure of loans reflected the high profit opportunities in traditional sectors, where interest rates normally ran from 10 per cent up, coupled with relatively unprofitable prospects for large-scale modern enterprises. The first major case of an industrial loan, and it was exceptional, was Shibusawa's loan from the First National Bank to help finance the establishment of the Osaka Spinning Company in 1882.[38] Even so, most of the First National Bank's loans continued to be used for the financing of commerce, especially rice and silk.

Growth of the Commercial Banking System

By the mid-1880's Japan had a well-established commercial banking system based upon the twin foundations of national banks and private banks. It thus was relatively well prepared for Japan's first major industrial spurt, which began in the late 1880's and continued until the turn of the century. Concomitant with that industrial development the commercial banking system also entered a period of rapid growth and full flowering. Between 1888 and 1901 the number of banks rose almost sixfold, their net worth quadrupled, loans increased sixfold and deposits multiplied some 7.5 times.

[38] The immediate success of this company probably had the most significant demonstration effect of any enterprise established in Japan. It was a purely private, merchant-capitalized venture. It succeeded where earlier government and private cotton spinning enterprises failed because of its large scale (10,500 spindles instead of the previous maximum of 3,000), use of steam power (rather than water), advanced Western machinery (although the failures also used such machinery), and two shifts (20–22 hours operation a day) of female labor. Its high profitability encouraged other members of the urban merchant-landowner-financier group to establish first cotton spinning and then weaving enterprises, from 1886 on.

TABLE VIII.3

GROWTH OF JAPANESE COMMERCIAL BANKS, 1888–1914*

Year	Number of Bank Offices: Head Office	Branches	Total	Bank Offices per 10,000 Pop.	Net Worth (million yen)	Avg. Net Worth (1,000 yen)	Deposits (million yen)	Loans & Advances (million yen)
1888	346	197	543	.139	74.5	215.3	58.9	99.6
1889	352	205	557	.141	79.5	225.9	65.5	115.8
1890	351	203	554	.139	85.1	242.5	58.9	117.0
1891	386	257	643	.160	90.1	233.4	64.9	123.4
1892	403	253	656	.162	89.7	222.6	88.2	117.0
1893	678	318	996	.244	98.3	145.0	98.3	139.6
1894	833	371	1,204	.293	118.1	141.8	116.2	170.0
1895	925	457	1,382	.333	123.8	133.8	159.3	245.1
1896	1,126	590	1,716	.409	176.9	157.1	203.7	351.8
1897	1,281	717	1,998	.477	200.6	156.6	263.3	435.1
1898	1,448	913	2,361	.551	210.6	145.4	288.8	441.1
1899	1,561	1,069	2,630	.606	237.7	152.3	392.3	573.1
1900	1,802	1,374	3,176	.724	272.4	151.2	436.8	653.2
1901	1,867	1,457	3,324	.749	290.6	155.7	450.2	628.4
1902	1,841	1,470	3,311	.737	303.8	165.0	536.7	687.4
1903	1,754	1,441	3,195	.702	303.5	173.0	566.2	715.3
1904	1,708	1,404	3,112	.675	308.4	180.6	605.3	720.7
1905	1,697	1,415	3,112	.668	316.8	186.7	692.5	783.7
1906	1,670	1,476	3,146	.669	329.8	197.5	1,033.8	1,093.0
1907	1,658	1,611	3,269	.689	375.8	226.7	944.3	1,100.3
1908	1,635	1,648	3,283	.685	394.4	241.2	938.1	1,085.5
1909	1,617	1,645	3,262	.672	408.7	252.8	1,054.4	1,111.5
1910	1,618	1,700	3,318	.675	421.5	260.5	1,185.7	1,234.3
1911	1,615	1,782	3,397	.681	443.3	274.5	1,256.2	1,377.2
1912	1,621	1,946	3,567	.705	481.2	296.9	1,357.3	1,504.7
1913	1,616	2,097	3,713	.724	518.7	314.8	1,443.5	1,649.9
1914	1,595	2,173	3,768	.724	537.9	337.2	1,519.8	1,713.8

*Commercial banks include private banks between 1888–1892, and ordinary banks thereafter, and national banks until their final elimination in 1899.

Source: Ministry of Finance, *Financial and Economic Annual of Japan*, various issues, and those cited in Table VIII.1.

(See Table VIII.3.) Industrialization and the increase in governmental expenditures related to the Sino-Japanese War made financial intermediation profitable as the demand for financial services grew rapidly.

The main institutional feature of the evolution of the financial structure was the codification and unification of the commercial banking system under the Bank Act of 1890, which took effect in 1893. By this law private banks and quasi-banking companies had to change into "ordinary banks" or lose their banking status. This resulted in a major conversion of small-sized institutions into banks as well as a shift by private banks to ordinary bank status. (See Tables VIII.1 and VIII.3.) Moreover, national banks, aside from those which had earlier merged or closed, began to change to ordinary banks in substantial numbers from the end of 1896, when their charters started to expire. By 1899 no national banks remained. The three classes of commercial banking institutions—national, private, and quasi-bank—had been amalgamated into one.

Interestingly, the new bank law did not set any minimum bank size. The government defended this as providing free competition, despite the continuing protests of the various city and national bankers' associations, which were controlled by the larger banks. Many new banks were founded; the total reached a peak of 1,867 in 1901. As a result, unit banking continued to predominate in Japan until after World War I. At the same time, the use of branch offices developed quite rapidly, particularly from the late 1890's, so that the total number of bank offices rose steadily throughout the period, with the number of branch offices exceeding head offices from 1908 on.

The 1890 law also limited bank loans and discounts to a single customer to 10 per cent of the bank's capital. Bankers and industrialists objected vigorously to this provision, particularly since many banks were developing close relations with specific industrial entreprises. They were able to put sufficient pressure on the government so that the 10 per cent restriction was removed in 1895. Since that time there has been no statutory limit on the proportion or amount of a bank's loans to a single customer. The subsequent rapid expansion in the number of banks was due in large part to industrialists setting up or getting control of banks to finance their enterprises.[39] This may have fostered industrial development. It definitely fostered the development of certain individual enterprises and of the *zaibatsu;* the Mitsubishi and Sumitomo *zaibatsu,* for example, transformed their finance departments into banks in 1895. It also made the monetary crises that usually accompanied recessions more severe because banks, particularly smaller ones, were more susceptible to failure.

Thus smaller banks were hard hit by the recessions of 1901 and 1907 when monetary crises and runs on some banks occurred. In such crises larger banks grew at the expense of smaller ones as individuals rushed to switch their deposits to what they regarded as, and therefore made, safe institu-

[39] The role of the *kikan ginko* (literally, "organ bank," meaning the bank as an organ of industrial enterprise) is repeatedly emphasized in Kato's writing. He points out (*Hompo Ginko Shi Ron,* 144) that only a handful of banks had no special ties to specific enterprises. Sometimes there enters into the Japanese discussion of the point the implication that most banks were "organs" of the *zaibatsu* combines; this, however, was true for only a relatively few, though large, banks. (This is inherent in the very definition of *zaibatsu,* as is discussed in the next section.)

tions. Following the small bank failures of 1901 the government shifted its policy somewhat, using suasion (but not legislation) to encourage banks to have a minimum capital of 250,000 yen. This naturally met with strong opposition from smaller bankers, and it was not successful. The government did discourage the establishment of new banks and encouraged mergers (take-overs) of smaller banks by larger ones. After 1901 the number of banks declined gradually, average net worth increased steadily, and deposits and loans continued to grow rapidly. (See Table VIII.3.)

The commercial banking system grew not simply in the number of bank offices, but also in relation to population and in regional coverage. The number of bank offices per 10,000 persons in 1880 was only 0.08 (0.11 if quasi-banks are included). Fifteen years later the ratio had risen to 0.33, and by 1910 to 0.68. Bank offices were dispersed throughout the country, not solely in the largest urban centers. Smaller towns and rural areas obtained banking services from local banks or branches of large urban banks such as the First National and Mitsui; this was particularly true of agricultural areas producing commercial crops, notably silk, tea, and rice. This development of banks where market circumstances seemed feasible meant that less commercialized areas, and those more sparsely populated, received fewer banking services per capita. Indeed, in a frontier region such as Hokkaido the provision of banking services came mainly from governmental initiative.

The development of the banking system surely improved the interregional flows of funds and reduced regional disparities in interest rates. Unfortunately, no comprehensive data on these points are available. Yet even by 1914 financial markets were far from perfect. In that year the average (mean) commercial bank discount rate by prefecture was 11.46 per cent; the lowest was 9.36 per cent and the highest 15.23 per cent (excluding Hokkaido, where it was 19.26 per cent). Major financial centers were much more closely related. The differences in lending rates in Tokyo and Osaka apparently were quite narrow by the turn of the century, and have remained so, despite considerable fluctuation in the absolute levels.

The sources and uses of bank funds changed gradually but substantially. Government deposits became relatively much less important (7.3 per cent of total ordinary deposits in 1893, 1.1 per cent in 1903, and less thereafter). Private deposits grew even more rapidly than bank paid-in capital and reserves [40] as individual savers became increasingly attracted to holding their savings in financial rather than real form. Large banks lent increasingly for large-scale industrial purposes and reduced their support of agriculture and

[40] The ratio of deposits to net worth for commercial banks was 0.8 in 1888, 1.0 in 1893, 1.4 in 1898, 1.9 in 1903, 2.4 in 1908, and 2.8 in 1913.

small-scale enterprises. These sectors were accordingly financed mainly by smaller banks and by traditional financial institutions.

The Special Banks

We have already noted that Matsukata, the architect of Japan's modern financial system, conceived of a variety of banking institutions to specialize in different aspects of finance. His first step was to establish the Bank of Japan. His second was to gain control over and to strengthen a specialized foreign exchange bank, the Yokohama Specie Bank.

The Yokohama Specie Bank opened in 1880 to finance foreign trade, to provide a more efficient market for foreign exchange, and to end the domination of these activities by the foreign banks operating in port cities. This delineation of functions may be in part a restrospective rationalization, since the establishment of the Yokohama Specie Bank was another example of the machinations of the time. This is charmingly described in the official history of the bank.[41]

> The original plan for the establishment of the bank was worked out by Mr. Hayashi (one of the promoters of the bank), Mr. Nakamura (the first president of the bank) and twelve others, with a view to retrieving the fortune of the Maruya Firm (run by Mr. Hayashi). They concocted various schemes, dabbled in speculation in silver money, and after failing in all their trials to save the firm, planned to set up a small bank with a capital of 200,000 yen or 300,000 yen, half in silver money and half in paper money, and lend this money to the traders and speculators of the port at daily interest. Mr. Hayashi consulted Mr. Fukuzawa, his friend, about this plan. Mr. Fukuzawa's adequate and wise advice improved the plan and made it feasible. Then Nakamura took it to Marquis Okuma (Minister of Finance) through Mr. Fukuzawa's recommendation. Fortunately, Marquis Okuma not only approved the plan but gave every assistance possible. The result was that a big bank with a capital of 3,000,000 yen was set up.

Though the Yokohama Specie Bank was of private origin, within a decade it became in effect a government bank. The government initially provided one-third of the capital and up to three-quarters of the deposits. The bank suffered major losses in its early operations, and in the process of repeatedly bailing it out the government assumed complete control.

When the Bank of Japan was established, there was some uncertainty whether it would supersede the Yokohama Specie Bank by developing its own foreign exchange business in addition to managing the domestic cur-

[41] As quoted in Kato, "Development of the Monetary System," 205.

rency system. The Ministry of Finance persisted in its view of specialized institutions for specialized functions on an independent basis. Moreover, the government came to appreciate increasingly the importance of exports and export promotion for growth. Accordingly, in the late 1880's the Ministry forced through an agreement whereby the Bank of Japan would not engage in foreign exchange business, would provide cheap deposits to the Yokohama Specie Bank, and would rediscount its foreign exchange bills at preferentially low interest rates. The Yokohama Specie Bank thereafter not only came to dominate the financing of foreign trade, but was able to subsidize export industries by making them loans at low interest rates.[42]

The keystone in Matsukata's system was the creation of special banks to provide long-term finance for private and local government fixed investment in agriculture, industry, electric power, and transportation. From the beginning of the 1890's the government repeatedly attempted to establish such special banks, but it encountered vigorous opposition from private financial leaders, and was unable to get enabling legislation through the parliament until 1897.[43] Within the next five years, the government founded the Hypothec Bank of Japan (Nippon Kangyo Ginko), its 46 affiliated prefectural Agricultural and Industrial Banks, the Hokkaido Colonial Bank (Hokkaido Takushoku Ginko), and the Industrial Bank of Japan (Nippon Kogyo Ginko). Of these by far the most important were the Hypothec Bank and the Industrial Bank.[44]

The banks were organized on the joint-stock principle, with the stock subscribed by private investors. The government guaranteed dividends at 5 per cent for ten years. More important, the special banks were regarded as public service institutions, so they came under the effective policy control of the Ministry of Finance, which appointed their officers and directors. The major source of loanable funds were bank debenture issues, which were authorized in amount up to five (later ten and then fifteen) times the paid-in capital. A relatively small proportion of these bonds were purchased by domestic private financial institutions or individuals. Most were purchased

[42] Sakurai, *Financial Aspects of Economic Development of Japan,* 76–7.

[43] The government's rationale in setting up special banks was not so much that entrepreneurs were starved for funds for productive fixed investment as that the national and the ordinary banks, in providing such financing, were in fact industrial rather than commercial banks. This was considered (by the government anyway) as an improper function for the commercial banking system.

[44] A description of the institutional features of special banks appears in Sarasas, *Money and Banking in Japan,* 234–78. I exclude the establishment and operations of the Bank of Taiwan and the Bank of Korea as colonial central banks, inasmuch as they had little direct influence on financial and economic development in Japan proper during this period. Also excluded from the following generalizations are the Bank of Japan and the Yokohama Specie Bank.

by the Ministry of Finance Deposit Bureau, which used postal savings deposits and any surplus government funds. Almost all special bank loans were long-term, though the special banks were allowed to make short-term loans and discounts in limited amounts. The interest rates on loans were low (6 to 9 per cent) relative to comparable rates of other financial institutions. The special banks grew rapidly; by 1914 their loans amounted to 26 per cent of commercial bank loans, indicating an important but not paramount role.

The Hypothec Bank was the largest of these banks; as late as 1914, its issues of debentures and its loans constituted more than half the total for all special banks. The bank had some success in selling small-denomination debentures with lottery features to rural and other individual savers. It was modeled after the French Crédit Foncier, lending primarily for land improvement and nonresidential construction. To this end it accepted, in theory, only immovable property—land and buildings—as collateral, though in practice it was somewhat more liberal.[45] Whether or not the Hypothec Bank could also make loans to industry was initially somewhat ambiguous, but this issue was immediately resolved when the bank made most of its first loans to support the Osaka textile and other industries in the 1898 crisis, using government funds. Thereafter the Hypothec Bank made substantial loans to the cotton textile and other light industries.

According to the distribution of its loans by stated purpose, between 1897 and 1914 slightly more than 40 per cent of the Hypothec Bank's loans went to agriculture, an equivalent proportion to industry, and somewhat less than 20 per cent to local governments.[46] Most loans to local governments, at least in the early years, were for such agricultural purposes as local irrigation. Agricultural loans were used mainly for such land improvements as irrigation and drainage, purchase of fertilizer, and the straightening of borders and consolidation of plots (which was a major governmental land reform program in the early years of this century). Some land reclamation was also financed by Hypothec Bank loans. Relatively little went for the purchase of agricultural machinery. A considerable share of the loans made to farmers was probably used for industrial enterprises for re-lending to poorer farmers at higher interest rates.[47] This resulted from the policy of making the minimum size of loan relatively large.[48] Matsukata felt, probably

[45] The government had initially proposed that the Hypothec Bank also make loans on securities as collateral, but the parliament objected on the ground that this would provide too much competition for ordinary banks. Kato, *Hompo Ginko Shi Ron,* 176. See also Sakurai, *Financial Aspects of Economic Development of Japan,* 80–81.

[46] Computed from Hypothec Bank, *Nippon Kangyo Ginko Shi* (*History of the Hypothec Bank of Japan*), 171, 236, 310.

[47] Kato, *Hompo Ginko Shi Ron,* 181.

[48] In rural areas the Hypothec Bank was called the "village headsman's bank."

correctly, that richer farmers would use funds more productively and would be safer risks.

The Industrial Bank, long proposed by the government on the model of the French Crédit Mobilier, finally began operations in 1902. It had three major purposes: to provide long-term loans to modern industries, to promote the inflow of foreign portfolio capital while avoiding foreign control of domestic industries, and to develop a market for corporate and local government bonds by creating the appropriate institutional arrangements. Industrial Bank debenture issues and domestic loans were quite limited until shortly before World War I; they were always less than those of the Hypothec Bank for industrial purposes. Most of its loans went to heavy industry—shipbuilding, iron and steel, chemicals, and machinery manufacture—and to electric power generation. Its initial portfolio operations were less than successful. During the Russo-Japanese War it made loans (on government orders) to domestic gold mines, which later could not be repaid. It also suffered losses from the postwar decrease in value of the securities it held. By 1913 the Industrial Bank's reserves had been completely depleted, and it had to be shored up with loans from the government, the Bank of Japan, and the Yokohama Specie Bank.[49]

The Industrial Bank's major contributions prior to World War I lay in its successful development of a debenture-issuing market and in its attraction of foreign portfolio capital. Business corporate financing by bonds was severely hampered by legal restrictions and lack of underwriting facilities and other institutional arrangements until 1905, when new legislation and the guidance of the Industrial Bank allowed a somewhat wider use of corporate debentures. Between 1890 (when the first private bonds were issued) and 1901 the value of bond issues amounted to only 26 million yen. Growth thereafter was rapid, as indicated in Table VIII.4. For the period 1902–1913 21 per cent of corporate domestic bond issue was for marine transport, 20 per cent for railroads, 16 per cent for textiles, and 15 per cent for electric machinery and power.[50] The Industrial Bank's direct underwriting role for domestic corporations was limited, mainly because large banks and securities dealers became active in providing these services.

Japan's reliance on foreign capital inflow after 1901 has already been alluded to. By 1913 total foreign portfolio indebtedness, which had been only 195 million yen in 1903, amounted to 1,970 million yen, equivalent to 46 per cent of national income. Most (1,599 million yen) was central government debt, in which the Industrial Bank had no underwriting role.

[49] "Banking in Modern Japan," *Fuji Bank Bulletin,* 60–61.

[50] Data on corporate and other bond issue, both domestic and foreign, are derived from Industrial Bank, *Nippon Kogyo Ginko Gojunen Shi* (*Fifty Year History of the Industrial Bank of Japan*), 87–97.

TABLE VIII.4

TOTAL CORPORATE AND LOCAL GOVERNMENT BOND ISSUE, AND UNDERWRITING BY THE INDUSTRIAL BANK, JAPAN, 1902–1913

Bond issue by:	Amount (million yen)	Share Industrial Bank Underwriting
Domestic corporations[a] (in yen)	152.9	8.4%
Domestic corporations[a] (denominated in foreign currency)	19.8	0
Special corporations[b] (in yen)	49.3	7.3
Special corporations[b] (denominated in foreign currency)	156.0	87.5
Local government bonds (denominated in foreign currency)	177.6	79.6

[a]Nonfinancial enterprises; i.e. excludes bonds issued by special banks.

[b]The South Manchuria Railroad Co. and the Oriental Development Co., semigovernmental firms for foreign expansion whose bonds were guaranteed by the government.

Source: Derived from Industrial Bank, *Nippon Kogyo Ginko Gojunen Shi* (*Fifty-Year History of the Industrial Bank of Japan*), Tables 43, 45, 52.

As indicated in Table VIII.4, its main function was to underwrite and sell abroad the bond issues of local governments, the South Manchuria Railroad, and the Oriental Development Company. These two companies used their funds for direct investment in Korea, Manchuria, and China; of 294.4 million yen in foreign portfolio capital underwritten by the Industrial Bank, 46 per cent was exported as semigovernmental direct investment.

The Industrial Bank's induction of foreign portfolio capital was not limited to its underwriting activities. Of the bank's paid-in capital of 17.5 million yen, 7.5 million yen was raised in the London market in 1906. Foreign subscribers purchased 19.5 million yen [51] (24 per cent) of the 82.5 million yen in Industrial Bank debentures issued between 1902 and 1913. Further, the Industrial Bank facilitated some foreign purchase of yen-denominated bonds.

While the special long-term credit banks did come to be an important source of loanable funds, they did not seriously hamper the growth of the

[51] These bonds, issued in sterling in New York and London under guarantee by the government, were re-lent to the Korean government. The Deposit Bureau purchased 55 per cent of the Industrial Bank debentures, and the general public (including private financial institutions) purchased only 21 per cent. Ibid. Tables 41–2, pp. 84–5.

private financial system. In fact, the re-lending of government-collected funds for private corporate investment and the induction of foreign capital encouraged a more rapid rate of growth of the economy, from which private financial institutions benefited through increased deposits and demands for their loans.

Other Financial Institutions

Between 1875 and 1914 a number of other modern financial institutions were created, though they remained less important than the commercial and special banks. (See Table VIII.5, p. 273.) The most important as mechanisms for collecting individual savings were the postal saving system and savings banks.

The postal savings system was established in 1875 (only ten years after the first such system was established in Great Britain), as a convenience to small savers. After a slow start postal savings experienced rapid growth between 1883 and 1889, when they almost equaled bank time and savings deposits, and again between 1904 and 1913, when they increased sixfold. Their early growth attests to the widespread nature of the savings habit and the frugality of even low-income groups in Japan, and to the increasing tendency of individuals to hold whatever wealth they had in financial form. The funds so accumulated were transferred, after 1885, to the Ministry of Finance Deposit Bureau, which used them mainly to buy government bonds and, after the Russo-Japanese War, special bank bonds.

Savings banks began operations in the early 1880's, but really grew as a class only after the Savings Bank Law went into effect in 1893. By 1897 their deposits exceeded those of the postal system, and they continued to grow more rapidly thereafter since they paid substantially higher interest rates on deposits. Many savings banks evolved from the traditional rotating credit co-operatives (*mujin*); many others were created by ordinary banks as deposit-collecting organs for them.[52]

Life insurance companies began operations in 1886, but they grew slowly, and even by 1914 they represented only a small share of total financial claims. In terms of insurance services, marine and fire insurance companies started earlier and grew more rapidly, concomitant with the growth of foreign trade.

The first securities market opened in Tokyo in 1878, and it was soon followed by exchanges in other cities.[53] These markets embodied many of the characteristics of commodities exchanges (notably rice), from which

[52] Arai, *Development of Local Banking in Japan,* 38.

[53] See Adams, *A Financial History of Modern Japan,* chaps. 1–2.

TABLE VIII.5

TOTAL ASSETS OF JAPANESE FINANCIAL INSTITUTIONS

(in million yen and per cent of total

	1876		1885*		1900		1905		1913	
	Amt.	%	Amt.	%	Amt.	%	Amt.	%	Amt.	%
Commercial banks	26	100	106	57.4	835	62.7	1,063	47.1	2,152	52.8
Special banks			19	10.1	76	5.7	148	6.6	553	13.6
Savings banks			3[c]	1.6	82	6.2	148	6.6	361	8.9
Financial institutions[b] for small business							1		38	0.9
All banks—Subtotal			128	68.1	993	74.6	1,360	60.3	3,104	76.2
Bank of Japan			51	27.1	312	23.4	814	36.1	673	16.5
Postal savings and life insurance			9	4.8	24	1.8	53	2.4	205	5.0
Life insurance					3[a]	0.2	28	1.2	90	2.2
Total	26	100	188	100	1,332	100	2,255	100	4,072	99.9
Ratio to national income (%)	10.[c]		30.		66.		102.		96.	

*For 1885, paid-in capital, reserve funds, and deposits are used as an estimate of assets, so some understatement results.

[a] Paid-in capital only; for later years includes premium reserve fund.

[b] Excluding the large and important number of quasi-banks and other traditional financing institutions.

[c] Crude estimate.

Sources: Bank of Japan worksheets and Ministry of Finance, *Financial and Economical Annual of Japan*, III, 1903. National income: Ohkawa, *Growth Rate*.

they evolved. Most transactions were term (or "futures"), with very little expectation of actual delivery. There was no protection of ordinary investors. Thus the markets were almost entirely speculative, with very little public participation. They dealt at first in government bonds and the shares of the companies forming the exchange, and later in railroad, textile company, and other shares. Even though brokers eventually appeared, securities markets remained pre-eminently speculative and private in nature until after World War II.

THE ROLE OF THE BANKS

Implicit in the discussion of the previous section is some evaluation of the contribution of the banking system to Japan's early industrialization and economic development. This contribution can be traced in several areas: an adequate monetary system and a comprehensive financial structure were developed, industrial enterprise was promoted and entrepreneurial activity in industry stimulated, and funds to finance productive investment were provided. These aided economic growth in that through them a more efficient allocation of an initial capital stock and of net additions to capital (i.e. investment) was achieved, and incentives to save, invest, and work were provided.[54]

After initial difficulties Japan developed a satisfactory system of currency and money supply before industrialization got underway in the late 1880's.[55] With the substitution of paper currency, and later of deposits, for circulating specie, the real cost of supplying money was substantially reduced. Control over the money supply was vested in a central bank which had both the right of fiduciary issue and (under Treasury pressure) a rather expansive attitude. Its active support of the banking system enabled banks to pursue a vigorous policy of lending and deposit money creation. Thus, although there were occasional panics and liquidity crises—which cyclically were quite important—the secular trend was toward growth of the money supply and a mild inflationary tendency.

While the evolving structure of Japan's banking system has already been delineated, we have yet to assess its role in financing economic activities. Aggregative measures of the role are provided in Tables VIII.5, VIII.6, and VIII.7. The entire financial system grew rapidly, both absolutely and

[54] See Chapter I; see also Patrick, "Financial Development and Economic Growth."

[55] Some economists have argued that such monetary reform was a major cause of the immediately subsequent industrial spurt, though no close analysis of the nature of the causal relationship has been made. I think this view considerably overstates the actual case.

TABLE VIII.6

RATIO OF JAPANESE BANK LIABILITIES* TO NATIONAL INCOME

	Commercial Bank Liabilities / National Income	Special Bank Liabilities / National Income
1878–82	15.5%	0.6%
1883–87	23.1	3.5
1888–92	21.7	1.9
1893–97	27.1	2.3
1898–1902	34.6	6.0
1903–7	43.4	9.3
1908–12	47.2	13.0

*Liabilities are the sum of net worth, bank note issue, deposits, and special bank debenture issue. Special banks include the Yokohama Specie Bank, The Hypothec Bank and its affiliates, the Industrial Bank, and the Hokkaido Colonial Bank. Private bank deposits for 1878–86 are rough estimates.

Sources: Ministry of Finance, *Financial and Economic Annual of Japan*, various issues; Asakura, *Meiji Zenki Nihon Kinyu Kozoshi*; Hoekendorf, "The Secular Trend of Income Velocity in Japan, 1879–1940"; Ohkawa, *Growth Rate*.

relative to national income (Table VIII.5,), and banks were of overwhelming importance in that system.

The increasing role of commercial banks and special banks is suggested particularly by the growth of their total liabilities (assets) relative to national income (Table VIII.6). No contradiction exists between the increases in this ratio and the relatively stable, even declining, ratio of money supply to national income noted earlier (see Table VIII.2, p. 254). Bank demand deposits were substituted for currency. Perhaps more important, bank time and savings deposits grew rapidly, as substitutes both for money and for tangible assets. An important characteristic of individual savers in Japan has been that, once knowledge of and confidence in the banking system was developed, they have tended to hold their wealth increasingly in financial form, particularly in time and savings deposits.

Economic development brought with it both increased saving and investment rates and a widening divergence between the distribution of aggregate saving and investment. Data are not available for early years, nor for self-invested agricultural savings, but by World War I the transfer of personal saving to finance corporate and government investment was certainly very important: 63.5 per cent of national saving was done by the personal sector between 1908–1917, but personal real investment was only 21.1 per cent of the total; the corporate sector saved 11.8 per cent and invested

TABLE VIII.7

RATIOS OF ISSUANCE OF PRIMARY SECURITIES AND INDIRECT FINANCE IN JAPAN

Year	Primary Securities Outstanding[a] / National Income	Indirect Finance Unadjusted[b] / Primary Securities: Total	Monetary Inter-mediaries[c]	Other Inter-mediaries	Indirect Finance Adjusted[d] / Primary Securities
1878–85	.92	.44			.42
1886–92	.88	.68	.42	.07	.66
1893–1901	1.09	.47			.52
1902–8	1.67	.29	.21	.08	.54
1909–14	2.04	.46	.28	.18	.56

[a] For final year of period; e.g. 0.92 for 1885.

[b] Net purchases of primary securities by financial institutions, including foreign purchase.

[c] Monetary intermediaries including the Bank of Japan, ordinary (commercial) banks, and savings banks.

[d] Adjusted net of foreign purchase of primary securities.

Source: Ott, "The Financial Development of Japan, 1878-1958," Tables 4, 6, 9.

33.9 per cent; and the government saved 24.7 per cent and invested 45 per cent.[56]

The gap between savers and investors was met by financial intermediation, principally by banks. Issues of both primary securities [57] and indirect financial claims increased rapidly.[58] The increase in the proportion of outstanding primary securities (mainly government bonds and corporate loans, shares, and bonds) to national income (Table VIII.7, column 1) reflects the growth of the modern industrial sector and the corporate form of organization, as well as the growth of government debt. From the beginning a fairly high proportion of primary securities was purchased by financial intermediaries, mainly the banking system,[59] except during the first decade of the twentieth century when the government and the semi-governmental corporate enterprises relied heavily on the sales of bonds to foreigners.

[56] Emi, "An Approach to the Measurement of National Saving in Japan, 1878–1940," Tables 11 and 12.

[57] Using the Gurley-Shaw terminology; see their "Financial Intermediaries and the Saving-Investment Process."

[58] Ott, "The Financial Development of Japan, 1878–1958."

[59] As is discussed below, indirect finance is underestimated since banks financed a substantial proportion of individual purchases of corporate stock issues.

The timing of the development of a country's banking system relative to its first industrialization spurt is significant in analyzing the contribution of the banking system to industrialization. Often the development of the financial system is "demand-following," in that modern financial institutions, their financial assets and liabilities, and other financial services are created and grow in an evolutionary manner in response to the demands for these services by investors and savers during the process of industrialization. Under these circumstances finance, while perhaps very important, is basically permissive and accommodating in nature.

In the Japanese case, the early development of the banking system was "supply-leading"; that is, it was created in advance of the industrial demand for its loans and other financial services, and also in advance of the demand of individual savers for monetary and time deposits. This was achieved by *de facto* government subsidies combined with the responsiveness of entrepreneurs to the profit opportunities offered by banking. Subsidization initially consisted of the national bank right of note issue at zero cost. (This, rather than any newly arisen expectation of making loans for industrial purposes, as is occasionally alleged, was the prime cause of the rapid growth of the number of national banks in the late 1870's.) The government also subsidized certain (mostly large) national and private banks by entrusting to them government deposits and many of its fiscal activities. Since the growth of private deposits initially was slow, note issue and government deposits were important supplements to paid-in capital as sources of bank funds.[60]

In the absence of any large-scale industrial demand for funds, the banking system initially concentrated its funds on financing agriculture, domestic commerce, and foreign trade. However, once the industrialization spurt began in the late 1880's the banking system was able and willing to provide the necessary financing. Interest rates were perhaps high (8 to 12 per cent) compared to those of other countries, but they were lower than interest rates of traditional Japanese financial institutions As Japan was a capital-scarce

[60] The Japanese literature on this phase of Japanese banking emphasizes the fact that banks engaged in overloan (i.e. made loans in excess of deposits) and that they therefore had the characteristic of moneylenders (e.g. they lent their own capital) rather than of "true commercial banks" (which made loans out of deposits). Implicit in this discussion is some criticism of the early development of Japanese banking as not being "modern," or as not conforming to Western (or Marxist) prototypes. From the viewpoint of the contribution of financial institutions to economic development such emphasis seems misplaced. In an economy where currency rather than demand deposit forms the bulk of the money supply, where the time or savings deposit habit is not well formed (or other financial or real assets are more attractive), and where the asset portfolios of banks consist mainly of loans because securities supplies are limited (or have unattractive terms), it is virtually inevitable that loans will exceed deposits. Under these circumstances this is a good rather than a bad thing.

country the marginal efficiency of investment came to be quite high once initial developmental hurdles were overcome. It appears that in modern Japan availability has always been rather more important than the interest cost of funds. Also important is the fact that the banking system was the locus of much of the early promotional and entrepreneurial talent which initiated the industrial spurt.

In part because of the prestige attached to the national banks, bankers in Meji Japan had particularly high status. Hirschmeier classifies eight of the first 20 outstanding entrepreneurs of Meiji Japan as bankers initially.[61] With only one exception these men engaged not only in banking but in industrial promotion. Accordingly they were extremely influential in the establishment and encouragement of a large number and wide variety of early large-scale industrial enterprises. Shibusawa is the best example of the creative entrepreneur operating from a banking base. Banks and bankers could play a major entrepreneurial role in part because they were relatively unhobbled by restrictive traditional or Western conventions (such as the dogma of loans for commercial purposes only). They were abetted in risk-taking by the Bank of Japan's policy of discounting loans collateralized by corporate stock, which thus imparted liquidity to longer-term assets.

Later, once the industrial spurt was well under way, the entrepreneurial flow reversed its direction: businessmen founded or obtained control of captive banks in order to obtain funds cheaply and readily for their own use. As the economy grew, the industrial demand for bank funds and other financial services caught up with and outstripped supply. With this, the impetus to growth of the financial system tended to shift from supply-leading to demand-following, and accordingly its role became relatively more growth-accommodating and less growth-inducing. This did not occur in all industrial sectors at the same time. A sequential shift in the financing of different industries from supply-leading to demand-following evolved in essentially the same pattern as the sequential development of the industries themselves. It appears that by the mid-1890's finance had moved to a demand-following basis in such light industries as cotton spinning and weaving (which had early comparative advantage because of the opportunities of combining modern technology with relatively labor-intensive factor proportions) and in railroads (which had early government subsidization). However, in heavy manufacturing industries, electric power, and other sectors where factor proportions tended to be much more capital-intensive, financing continued on a supply-leading basis until World War I (and later in some cases), with funds provided by the special banks as well as by direct government investment or subsidy payments.

[61] Hirschmeier, *Origins of Entrepreneurship in Meiji Japan,* 248–9. For a discussion of the role of banks and bankers in industrial promotion, see chaps. 6 and 7.

Financing of Agriculture and Small-scale Industry

Data on the flow of funds through financial institutions to final spenders are not available, so the general trends in the financing of investment (or consumption) by banks and other financial institutions can be determined only indirectly. Some information is available on collateral provided and on the stated purpose of loans, mainly those by special banks after 1897. But caution should be used in interpreting these data; divergences between indicated and actual uses of funds can be wide. For example, we have noted that some loans to rich farmers (with land as collateral) were diverted for use in financing industrial enterprises, probably small-scale processing of agricultural commodities.

It is clear that until the late 1880's most bank loans financed domestic and foreign trade, small-scale units of production in agriculture and processing industries, and, to some extent, the consumption of poor samurai and poor farmers (who, respectively, used pension bonds and land as collateral). Loans for agriculture were used mainly to finance the production, processing, and distribution of cash crops. Silk is an outstanding example. The opportunities provided to farmers by the strong export demand for cocoon and raw silk, the productive responsiveness of large numbers of farmers, and the efficiency of the financing mechanism in accommodating these activities, are indicative of the importance of an increasingly monetized agriculture for growth.[62] It is not surprising that the largest number of private banks and quasi-banks—and the most active—were found in the relatively advanced agricultural regions and in port cities.

The financing of productive investment in the first years of Meiji was carried on pre-eminently by individual moneylenders. As modern financial institutions were created they too apparently became primarily involved in financing production in traditional sectors. Asakura attributes a major role to quasi-banks and smaller private and national banks in rural areas and foreign trade ports. The larger, urban banks assisted in this finance. Bank funds typically passed through several hands—from larger to smaller financial institutions—before being lent to the final spender. There were several channels. Quasi-banking institutions borrowed funds from banks and re-lent them for productive purposes. Members of the merchant-landowner-financier group borrowed from banks or quasi-banks, and in addition to engaging in their own productive activities re-lent to others.

As the economy evolved, particularly in the late 1880's, when industry

[62] Fujino (*Nihon no Keiki Junkan,* 404–8) documents the activity of national banks in financing both cocoon production and silk reeling.

TABLE VIII.8

DISTRIBUTION OF LOANS OF ORDINARY AND NATIONAL BANKS, JAPAN, 31 DECEMBER 1894

	Number	Amount (yen)	Per Cent
A. By Occupation of Borrowers			
Agricultural	110,673	15,412,960	12.5
Industrial	7,207	1,701,188	1.4
Commercial	74,843	50,407,117	40.8
Local bodies	1,267	10,955,077	8.9
Miscellaneous	25,611	35,527,859	28.7
Companies	2,267	8,484,437	6.9
Unaccounted		1,000,000	0.8
Total	221,868	123,528,640	100.0
B. By Nature of Collateral			
Government bonds	4,846	3,962,718	3.2
Shares	18,649	42,969,570	34.8
Grain	10,249	5,022,333	4.1
Land	76,620	16,908,562	13.7
Houses	5,201	1,447,203	1.2
Land with houses	16,219	5,696,659	4.6
Fertilizers	993	1,080,385	0.9
Miscellaneous	17,219	11,295,626	9.1
Credit	71,872	35,145,584	28.5
C. By Term			
Within one month	7,183	4,060,017	3.3
Above one month, but below three months	17,509	11,388,762	9.2
Above three months, but below six months	54,704	25,458,417	20.6
Above six months, but below one year	93,430	32,798,053	26.6
Above one year	49,042	49,823,391	40.3
D. By Number of Renewals			
Not renewed	179,483	100,512,945	81.4
Renewed once	21,317	11,968,445	9.7
Renewed twice	10,842	6,012,397	4.9
Renewed three times	7,526	3,784,929	3.1
Renewed more than four times	2,700	1,249,924	1.0

Source: Soyeda, "A History of Banking in Japan."

began to be important, the large urban banks tended to alter their lending emphasis from the financing of agricultural activities and commerce to the new industrial enterprises. By the end of 1894, agriculture apparently received only a small proportion of the loans of ordinary and national banks, though commerce continued to be very important. (See Table VIII.8.)

The growth of the modern banking system relative to traditional financial institutions, coupled with its increasing emphasis on provision of funds for industrial purposes, inaugurated a change in the allocation of saving, and thereby resources, away from traditional sectors to new, modern sectors. Modern financial institutions—banks, savings banks, and postal savings—directly siphoned off agricultural saving to industry, so that the agricultural sector was probably a net saver (savings greater than investment). To the extent that traditional financial institutions tended more than banks to make loans directly or indirectly (by financing the purchase of land) for consumption expenditures, this shift increased the rate of saving and thereby investment in the economy. At the same time the structure of aggregate investment was drastically altered. The use of farm land as collateral for loans actually applied to industrial investment suggests that the marginal efficiency of investment was higher in manufacturing than in agriculture.

With the shift in emphasis of the larger members of the banking system toward industrial finance, agricultural and small-scale industrial units fared relatively less well. They continued to rely primarily upon individual moneylenders and moneylending companies. Of course smaller banks, particularly those established early or in rural areas, perforce found their main customers among small-scale enterprise and farmers rather than among the larger industrial enterprises. The respective roles of smaller rural banks and the larger urban banks accordingly tended to diverge. This was more a matter of degree than of kind, especially since many of the small as well as larger banks that were set up in the 1890's had close industrial ties. Part of the difficulties that the agricultural sector suffered in the early decades of this century can be attributed to the relative de-emphasis of the organized financial system in providing agricultural credit, despite the activities of the Hypothec Bank. As is indicated in Table VIII.9, the great preponderance of agricultural credit in 1914 was provided by the unorganized financial sector, notably companies and individuals. The banking system, including the special banks established to finance agriculture, held only 28 per cent of total agricultural debt.

Bank Financing of Modern Industrial Enterprise

Comprehensive data are not available on the sources of funds for new industrial enterprises or for their subsequent growth in the first years of

TABLE VIII.9

DISTRIBUTION OF AGRICULTURAL DEBT OUTSTANDING BY LENDER AND TYPE OF COLLATERAL, JAPAN, 1912

Lender	Real Estate Collat-eral	Other Collat-eral	No Collat-eral	Total	Non-Agri. Borrowers Using Real Est. Coll.
Hypothec, Hokkaido, and Agri. & Indust. banks	16.8%	0.1%	4.5%	10.3%	11.0%
Ordinary banks	19.9	31.3	11.9	17.6	35.3
Insurance companies	–	0.3	0.1	0.1	1.3
Credit co-operatives	1.1	2.5	5.4	2.9	0.4
Moneylending companies and individuals	26.5	18.7	12.6	20.3	19.5
Pawnshops	–	11.9	4.3	1.3	–
Merchants	–	–	–	1.7	–
Rotating credit co-ops	–	–	21.8	8.4	–
Individuals	35.8	30.5	37.5	36.2	32.0
Others	0.6	4.8	2.0	1.6	0.7
Total per cent	99.9	100.1	100.1	100.4	100.2
Total amount in million yen	377.9	79.1	289.1	746.0	489.7

Source: Calculated from Asakura, *Meiji Zenki Nihon Kinyu Kozoshi*, Table 109, pp. 360–61, derived from Ministry of Finance study.

industrialization. On the basis of available evidence the following generalizations are plausible.

Initial capital came primarily from stock subscription by members of the wealthy merchant-landowner-financier group and, in some instances (notably railroads), by the aristocracy. However, it appears that most individual subscriptions to new corporate stock issues were financed to a considerable degree by loans from commercial banks. Table VIII.8 shows that corporate shares constituted the predominant form of collateral for bank loans, and that 40 per cent of bank loans were for a term of more than one year.[63] For banks in large cities, notably Tokyo and Osaka, which were the new industrial centers, the proportion of stock in collateral was considerably higher. The opportunity to borrow from a bank was accorded particularly to

[63] Data for the period 1893–1914 indicate that most of the time land was the most important form of collateral, with corporate shares close behind; together they were well over 70 per cent of all collateral provided. See Kato, *Hompo Ginko Shi Ron*, Table 52, pp. 136–7.

the bank's stockholders; in some cases they even used their shares in the bank as collateral.[64] Indeed, it is not clear whether the decision to invest in a new enterprise was made by stockholders or by the bank, even though this financing route was used. From the viewpoint of stockholders this was a particularly opportune route for bank funds to be channeled into an enterprise. The possibilities of gain from success would accrue directly to the stockholders, while the bank would have some commitment to provide working capital funds sufficient to keep the enterprise prospering.

The aristocratic Fifteenth National Bank provides an illustration of this mechanism of finance. The nobility had early been interested in railroad investment; they had seen its success in Europe and the United States and were confident of sufficient government subsidies. At the bank's stockholders meeting in 1881 it was decided to finance the proposed Japan Railroad Company. It was agreed that the stockholders would purchase the railroad shares, using funds borrowed from their bank. These loans were at an interest rate somewhat below the 10 per cent dividend rate of the railroad (payment of which was 38 per cent covered by government subsidies [65]), and were renewed. The stock in the railroad constituted some 90 per cent of the collateral of the bank's non-government loans until 1890.

Stockholder reliance on bank loans to finance their stock purchases meant that stockholders were anxious to have dividend payouts at least sufficient to cover the interest charges on the loans. In the early years companies had profit rates which were only equal to (and in some instances less than) the loan interest rate, so profits tended to be paid out fully. This also coincided with the relatively short-run time horizons of many investors (against which Shibusawa, for example, frequently inveighed), who preferred to receive profits as income rather than plow them back as retained earnings. Retained earnings in most industries thus apparently were an insignificant means of financing expansion until after the Russo-Japanese War, when in more profitable, better established, labor-intensive industries expanding profits and changed attitudes resulted in a higher proportion of retained earnings.

How then did enterprises, once established, finance their expansion? We have noted that corporate bond issues were virtually nonexistent before 1905; they remained relatively unimportant until the 1920's. Industrial enterprises relied on two main sources of funds: new capital stock issues, sold mainly to existing stockholders; and short-term and long-term loans from banks. It is not clear which was more important in the early years, but

[64] Ouchi and Kato, *Kokuritsu Ginko no Kenkyu,* chap. 2, Table 19.
[65] Ibid. chap. 3, Table 6.

by the turn of the century bank loans were clearly the major source.[66] For example, the Industrial Bank's data indicate that for a total of 247 million yen in industrial funds supplied to main industrial corporations between 1897 and 1913, 57.5 per cent was from bank loans, 32.4 per cent from new stock issue, 6.5 per cent from corporate debenture, and 3.6 per cent from internal reserves.[67] With no legal constraints on how much could be lent to a single company, banks tended to concentrate their loans to relatively few enterprises. We do not know the extent to which banks made term loans explicitly to finance fixed investment. Nonetheless, there probably was an increasing tendency to renew short-term loans upon maturity, so that in addition to financing working capital needs bank loans to some extent financed fixed investment by related industrial enterprises.

Stockholder purchase of additional stock issues for enterprise expansion also was financed to a considerable extend by further bank loans. A system developed whereby subscription to newly issued shares was paid on an installment basis.[68] In addition, the policy of high dividend payout did not mean a complete loss of funds for industrial purposes, since part was probably used to finance not only the purchase of additional shares in the same company but also the establishment of new enterprises through stock purchases by the dividend-recipient owners of already established enterprises.

Thus it appears that the banking system, through its loans to enterprises and to individuals who then subscribed to new share issues, was the principal source of funds for Japanese industrialization throughout this period. In the absence of a well-developed capital market to transfer individual saving directly to industrial enterprise, with the high business reliance on external sources of funds, and with savings held increasingly in time de-

[66] Corporate stocks issue and loans accounted for virtually all net issue of primary securities throughout the period, except for the war periods when central government bond issues were substantial. This occurred particularly during and following the Russo-Japanese War, when many government bonds were sold abroad. Cf. Ott, "The Financial Development of Japan, 1878–1958," 125, 129.

[67] Industrial Bank, *Nippon Kogyo Ginko Gojunen Shi,* 38. The source of data and extent of coverage are not clear. The cotton textile industry was then still the largest, and it appears that that industry—or at least part of it—was not included, since their retained earnings were much higher after 1905. Nonetheless, Emi estimates ("An Approach to the Measurement of National Saving in Japan, 1878–1940") that between 1903 and 1912 corporate saving was only 3.6 per cent of national saving.

[68] Yoshino lists this—the dominance of financial institutions over securities issue—as one of the three major characteristics of the early Japanese financial system; the others were the close interrelationship between fiscal and monetary authorities and activities, and the reliance of both fiscal authorities and commercial banks on Bank of Japan credit. Cf. Yoshino, *Waga Kuni Kinyu Seido to Kinyu Seisaku* (*Japan's Financial System and Monetary Policy*), 1–18.

posits, financial intermediation by banks was a vital force for industrial growth.

Data on the financing of the cotton spinning industry between 1900 and 1914 provide some illustration of these generalizations. It is unfortunate that earlier data are not available, since cotton spinning was not only the first but also, together with cotton weaving, by far the largest modern industry to develop prior to World War I. The following quotation from a contemporary observer writing in 1913 suggests the pattern of this industry's financing.[69]

> Before the Russian War a majority of the mills paid out most of their semi-annual profits as dividends, and whenever the tide ebbed many were stranded for lack of working capital. Many of the shareholders then, and even today, owned many more shares than their financial status warranted. They borrowed money on stock with which to buy more, and then borrowed on this to increase their holdings still further. Any decrease in the market quotations for mill shares meant that they had to put up more collateral with the banks, hence they exerted strong pressure on the directors to pay as large dividends as possible, not only for the sake of the money received, but to keep up the value of the shares.

Though we know that spinning companies were very profitable during the 1890's, almost all profits were paid out as dividends, since in 1900 outstanding reserve balances amounted to only 3.5 million yen, less than 9 per cent of paid-in capital.[70] However, the years 1905–7 were exceptionally prosperous, so that spinning firms were able to maintain the dividend rate while adding substantially to reserves. After 1910 industry policy on dividend payout changed, and increased emphasis was placed on retaining earnings. During the period 1905–14 the net increase in funds available totaled 101.1 million yen; of this 32 per cent came from increases in reserves, 47 per cent from additions to paid-in capital, and 21 per cent from loans and debenture issues.[71] Additions to reserves and capital stock issue were just sufficient to cover the increase in fixed real capital of 74.1 million yen, which suggests that cotton spinners had to rely substantially, both directly and indirectly, on bank credit for working capital. The instrument mainly used was the bill of exchange, drawn by the raw cotton importer on the spinner; the bills were then discounted by banks.

[69] Clark, *Cotton Goods in Japan,* 219.

[70] Arai, *Development of Local Banking in Japan,* 26–7.

[71] Toyo Keizai Shimposha, Oriental Economist Publishing Co. (ed.), *Meiji Taisho Kokusei Soran* (*Survey of the State of the Nation in the Meiji-Taisho Periods*), 609. This may understate short-term loans.

Finally, it is often asserted in the Japanese literature that the pattern of the development of the Japanese banking system, in particular the ties of large banks with specific entrepreneurs and large enterprises, was the major cause of the *zaibatsu* form of industrial organization. There is some truth in this assertion. It is tied to the further assertion that during this period the banking system was increasingly dominated by the "Big Five" banks (Mitsui, First, Mitsubishi, Sumitomo, Yasuda). Each of these assertions merits brief examination.

The *zaibatsu* conglomerates were innovation-oriented, major importers of Western technology, who plowed back profits into expansion and diversification, and generally reaped the benefits of economies normally external to the individual firm. They also eventually formed objectionably great concentrations of wealth and of economic and political power.

The story of the financing of *zaibatsu* expansion, and the role of the *zaibatsu* financial institutions, has not been fully unraveled, but it is clear that the *zaibatsu* banks and related financial institutions (notably insurance companies) became of major importance in transferring funds among affiliated enterprises and in collecting private individual savings to finance *zaibatsu* investment. It appears the most successful *zaibatsu* (as measured by size) were those which has their own strong banks. This not only made available a cheap source of funds, but perhaps more important, enabled a *zaibatsu* with its own bank to withstand (and even benefit from) the pressures of sporadic depressions and crises. Those with less close banking connections were placed in more exposed positions, resulting in some cases in bankruptcy and take-over by other *zaibatsu*. Or, as in the case of the Okura *zaibatsu,* expansion could not be financed without loss of control.

However, during this period a one-to-one correspondence did not exist between the largest banks and their membership in the *zaibatsu*. Further, the assertion that the Big Five banks dominated the banking system prior to World War I is belied by the facts. While between 1897 and 1912 the Big Five share in total commercial bank net worth increased from 6.5 to 12.5 per cent (due to policies of high retained earnings), and their proportion of total loans rose from 12.6 to 17.7 per cent, deposits remained a constant 20.5 per cent and security holdings declined from 33.1 to 20.6 per cent.[72] These shares are not overwhelmingly large—certainly not enough to assert that the Big Five were then paramount in the banking system. The Fifteenth Bank, not even included in this group, at the beginning of World War I still had a larger net worth than any other bank, though by

[72] Over the period the relative positions among the Big Five shifted; Dai-ichi grew relatively rapidly, as did the newly established Mitsubishi and Sumitomo, while Mitsui and Yasuda declined somewhat. Mitsui Bank remained the largest of the five. Kato, *Hompo Ginko Shi Ron,* 45, 140–41.

the end of the War it had been outstripped. The emphasis on the Big Five appears in part to be retrospective, an attempt to push back the pre-eminence which they undoubtedly achieved in the late 1920's and the 1930's to the period before World War I.

Of the six largest banks in the Meiji Era, five were large when they started—the First, the Fifteenth, and the Mitsui banks at the beginning of the development of the modern financial system, and the Mitsubishi and Sumitomo banks somewhat later. Yasuda grew from nothing, through shrewd management, high retained earnings, and merger. There were other quite large urban banks which followed these several routes to success. In general, the large banks were increasingly important in financing the early and continued development of large-scale enterprise, with the notable exception of the Fifteenth Bank.

We can distinguish four different patterns of relationships of the six largest banks with the *zaibatsu* industrial conglomerates. In the first category, the bank was at the core of the *zaibatsu,* not only in terms of organizational structure and supply of funds but also in serving as a font of promotional activity. The Mitsui Bank can be so classified. In the second, the bank, while an important component, was set up by an already established *zaibatsu,* to handle the financial side of its activities; its role thus was demand-following and accommodating. This was true of the Mitsubishi and Sumitomo banks. In the third, the bank was important as a supply-leading industrial promotor and lender, but was not incorporated into the *zaibatsu* industrial conglomerate structure of ownership and control. This was true of the First and Yasuda banks. While Shibusawa promoted the foundation of a number of new enterprises, he never fully welded them into a lasting conglomerate. Yasuda had close ties with certain *zaibatsu,* especially Asano, but mainly through financing rather than through control by ownership. In the fourth category, the bank had no specially close relationship with a major industrial group, either ownership, promotional, or lending. Probably the only member of this category, among not only the top six but also a wider definition of large banks, was the Fifteenth Bank, which was an historical oddity. Despite its immense paid-in capital and favored political position, because of its conservative, traditionalistic outlook the Fifteenth Bank never played as great a developmental role as might have been anticipated. It did not attempt to collect deposits for a number of years; by 1890 they amounted to only 5 per cent of net worth, and had been received only from nobility and the Japan Railroad Company. Lack of vigor in both collecting deposits and extending loans made for slow growth and diminishing power. It inevitably remained a large bank, and continued to be highly respected, but it never came close to achieving its potential.

CONCLUSION

Between 1868 and World War I Japan developed an extensive, variegated, sophisticated, modern financial system, well structured to meet the needs of economic development. It had the banking system as its core and dominant component. This was accomplished more by forced-draft than by evolution, through a combination of governmental encouragement and of entrepreneurial response by the many Japanese who established financial institutions. The government provided a setting conducive to the growth of the economy and of finance by giving high priority to economic development, by an expansive fiscal policy, by accommodating legislation, and by creating a unified, acceptable currency system such that the money supply could elastically respond to the needs of the economy as determined by the monetary authorities. In the latter part of this period the government also established special banks to make long-term loans for agricultural and industrial fixed investment and to tap foreign and domestic sources of portfolio capital.

The role of the government should not be overemphasized, however. Given the generally favorable economic environment, financial and general economic development in Meiji Japan should be attributed primarily to the private individual response to profit (and status) incentives to increase output. The ordinary banking system, for example, developed along the lines that private entrepreneurs determined rather than according to the (idealized) British model the government desired. That is to say, the banks did not concentrate on short-term, self-liquidating commercial loans. Instead, because of their close ties with industry and industrialists, banks and bankers until late in this period increasingly served the function of industrial banks, providing funds for fixed investment as well as for working capital. The occasional problems of illiquidity and bank runs were met by shoring up defenses as best one could (it was usually the smaller rather than the larger banks that failed), and by running to the acquiescent Bank of Japan for help. Such an approach to banking no doubt was in the long run much more conducive to industrial growth, and it is just as well that the government did not transplant and impose the narrow view of commercial banking.

Though the financial system was good, it was not ideal. Institutions were not perfectly devised, and there were a variety of constraints on preferences which distorted the allocation of funds from what might have been an even more optimal allocation. In terms of access to funds, and in terms of relatively low interest rates, the government always had preferential treatment. Large-scale industry and public utilities (transportation, electric power, etc.)

were next in line at the credit window of the financial system. This enabled them to grow rapidly and to provide the industrial and infrastructural foundations for a modern, developed, growing economy. Consequently, small-scale enterprise and agriculture were the residual claimants upon funds for investment. Even so, these sectors at least were able to provide substantial increases in the output of commercial crops and processed and manufactured goods which were the major exports during this period. The financing thereby of imports essential for industrial growth should not be slighted. Whether the small-scale, and less well organized, financial structure for agriculture and small industry can be regarded as adequate depends upon one's evaluation of the total performance of these sectors during this first phase of Japanese growth.

IX
CONCLUSION

by Rondo Cameron

It is not the purpose of this book to derive, on the basis of historical experience, a model of the "one best" banking system for all times and places, or even for all countries in the early stages of industrialization. On the contrary, our study shows the wide range of variability of successful systems; the system that "works" or is "best" in one place and time may not work successfully in another.[1] In every case the financial system is related to and must grow out of the distinctive legal, social, and political traditions and the objective economic conditions of its specific environment. The Japanese case is especially revealing: Japan deliberately attempted to imitate first the American banking system, then, disillusioned with that, the English banking system. What actually resulted was a system that in many respects was uniquely Japanese, consonant with other Japanese institutions and traditions. On the other hand, it is true that nations in the early stages of industrialization face many similar problems. Although the solutions to those problems may differ according to circumstances, there are certain common features in all successful solutions that deserve further study as possible keys to an understanding of the process of development. Moreover, some solutions are more successful than others.

In the historical cases reviewed in this book the banking systems of Scotland and Japan appear to have represented the best adaptations of structure and function to the growth requirements of their particular economies. Those of Belgium, Germany, England (the last two *in spite of* official pol-

[1] H. C. Wallich, "Comparison of Monetary Systems," 2: "The behavior of money is determined by the kind of economy in which it circulates. Monetary phenomena are not the same in a highly developed and in a significantly underdeveloped economy. They differ also depending upon the relative importance, within any type of economy, of the balance of payments, the public sector, and the private sector." Much the same is true of banks, the most important money-creating institutions.

icy), and Russia (after about 1890) qualify in one way or another as "moderately successful." Only the French banking system gets definitely unfavorable marks, although even it had some points in its favor.

Admittedly, such judgments are impressionistic and partly subjective. Lacking generalized, unambiguous criteria by which to measure the performance of banking systems, they cannot be otherwise. The basic criterion employed above is the contribution the banking system made to industrialization and over-all development, but the evidence is neither complete, precise, nor unambiguous. Moreover, the banking system is by no means the only, or necessarily the most important, element in national economic development, and, unfortunately or not, other things do not remain equal. It is conceivable that a nation with a theoretically perfect banking system (if such existed) might have a lower rate of growth than one with a less highly developed banking system but more favorable conditions among the other elements of growth. Such unruliness and apparent paradoxes are unavoidable when one moves from the realm of pure theory to those of history and policy.

In this chapter we shall first summarize and synthesize the preceding case studies in order to make clear the objective evidence (such as it is) for the judgments above. In so doing we shall attempt to distill from the evidence some generalizations of more nearly universal applicability concerning the role of banks in the early stages of industrialization, answering insofar as possible the questions raised in Chapter I. Finally we shall essay a few tentative remarks on the applicability of those generalizations to contemporary underveloped economies.

FINANCIAL STRUCTURE AND FUNCTION

Both theoretical reasoning and the historical evidence suggest that the banking system can play a positive, "growth-inducing" role as well as responding passively to the demand for financial services. According to Professor Hicks,

> The beginning of a process of expansion (pretty much, I suppose, what Rostow means by "take-off") might occur because of real factors (inventions and the like) raising the real (prospective) rate of profit. But it might also occur because of financial improvements, diminishing the size of our "gap" [between the rate of return on real investment and the return received by holders of idle balances]; thereby permitting access to funds, for improvements which could have been made earlier, if the necessary funds had been forthcoming. It is not savings only that

> are required, but a channel of communications between potential savings and potential real investment.[2]

Moreover, the potential role of the financial system is greater in cases of derivative or imitative industrialization (i.e. in every case since England's original industrial revolution) because of the relative ease with which financial innovations can be introduced and the relative amenability of the banking system to sensible policy measures. For this reason the banking system should be of particular interest to policy makers in developing nations. It also helps to explain the paradox of Professor Gerschenkron's "advantages of backwardness."

Whether in fact the banking system actually plays the growth-inducing role that is theoretically possible depends upon its structure and behavioral characteristics. To review briefly the theoretical considerations in Chapter I from a slightly different standpoint, the financial requirements for industrialization can be conveniently summarized under three major headings: (1) the accumulation of capital; (2) the mobilization of capital; and (3) the efficient utilization of capital. (This classification can, of course, be applied to any economy, not only to those undergoing industrialization; but the precise nature of the problem will differ for underdeveloped and highly industrialized economies.) In addition, a fourth requirement is closely related: the necessity for an extensive monetization of the economy to alter the flow of resources from production directly to consumption to the more roundabout but productive channels of specialization, exchange, and markets. Financial institutions are especially concerned with the second of these requirements, and if they fail to function satisfactorily in that respect they can effectively prevent any significant degree of industrialization. This appears to have been the fate (not to the exclusion of other causes of backwardness) of portions of the Austro-Hungarian Empire and the countries of Mediterranean Europe in the nineteenth century, as well as of Russia before 1890 and (to some extent) of France and Germany before 1850. The role of financial institutions is not restricted to the mobilization of capital, however. They can facilitate its accumulation by stimulating saving and by serving as vehicles for the introduction of capital from abroad, as well as by "forcing" society to save by putting newly created money in the hands of entrepreneurs. Responsibility for the efficient utilization of capital lies primarily with nonfinancial entrepreneurs, but financial institutions exercise a large measure of discretion in the selection of investment alternatives and—potentially, at least—in the follow-up supervision of the productive processes in which the capital is employed. Finally, as the chief

[2] Hicks, *Capital and Growth,* 290n. Hicks also states that "I am prepared to believe that this last point has considerable historical significance."

dispensers of money in recent times, banks have played a major role in the monetization of the economy.

To repeat, the effectiveness with which an actual financial system discharges its functions depends in large measure on its structural characteristics. The following summary of the historical cases is intended to highlight structural features which are especially favorable or unfavorable.

The Legal Status of Banking

The legal status of banking as an industry varied considerably in the countries constituting our sample, but in every case banks were subjected to greater restriction and regulation than other forms of business enterprise.

Bankers had the greatest liberty in Scotland. There were two well-established chartered banks there before the onset of industrialization, and eventually Scotland obtained five chartered banks before the middle of the nineteenth century. Their larger size may have been related to their special legal status, but other than that it is difficult to see what privileges their charters conferred. Apart from the restrictions on small notes (less than £1) that prevailed from 1765 to 1797 and again after 1829, no legal obstacle prevented private individuals, partnerships, or unregistered joint-stock companies (without limited liability) from setting themselves up as bankers before 1845. It is clear that many did so, adding a degree of competition not to be found in any other country. (A few American states for short periods in the first half of the nineteenth century present the only comparable examples.) Although some private bankers did not issue their own notes, most did. Freedom of issue was evidently a greater inducement to enter banking than the privilege of incorporation, for no new banks were set up in Scotland after 1845, when incorporation remained a simple matter of registry but new note issues were prohibited.

English banking benefited from freedom of entry, but in other respects was severely hampered by restrictive legislation. Until 1826 the privileges of the Bank of England effectively prevented any but very small partnerships (fewer than seven persons) from engaging in banking operations. Freedom of note issue enticed many entrepreneurs into banking, giving England one of the highest banking densities in the world, but the restrictions on size doomed the English system to instability and periodic breakdowns. After 1826 the authorization of joint-stock banks eliminated the artificial limitation on size, but concurrent developments, which culminated in the Bank Act of 1844, imposed new restrictions on note issues and freedom of entry without remedying the instability of the system.

France, as the country most encumbered by restrictive legislation on banking, stood at the opposite extreme from Scotland. Until 1863 the privilege of incorporation was reserved to a very few institutions specially chartered and regulated by the state. Even more harmful to the development of banking, the right of note issue was similarly restricted until 1848, when it was conferred on a single monopolistic institution. Moreover, France did not grant legal recognition to checks until 1865. As a result, and in spite of vigorous efforts at financial innovation to surmount the obstacles imposed by legislation, the French banking system exhibited—with a few notable exceptions—very little of the vigor associated with free competition.

Belgium was unique in the combination of competition and monopoly imposed by legislation. Until near the end of the period of industrialization covered in this volume, the privilege of incorporation for banks was reserved to institutions specially chartered by the state. On the other hand, the Belgian government was somewhat more liberal in granting charters of incorporation than the French. (Private banks existed, but they were relatively unimportant.) Nevertheless, Belgium had only two banks that gained national significance before 1850. The resulting cutthroat competition led the government to confer a monopoly of issue on a single state-controlled institution in 1851. Thereafter the Belgium banking system evolved a variety of highly specialized institutions with relatively little competition among them.

Germany presented a kaleidoscopic spectacle. In all states the right of note issue—if it existed at all—was restricted to institutions chartered and usually controlled by the governments. Joint-stock banks were similarly restricted until 1848—even longer in Prussia, with minor exceptions. Private banks existed in considerable numbers, but without the right of note issue or legal recognition of checks they were obliged to develop novel financial techniques which in subsequent years made Germany a leader in industrial finance through the banking system.

The legal status of banking in Russia shows the continued primacy of the state both as regulator and direct participant in the economic system. The government itself assumed the responsibility for the issue of paper money until 1897, when it gave a monopoly of issue to the state owned and operated State Bank. At the same time, the government made a deliberate effort to enlist private enterprise in filling out the financial structure—subject, however, to continued paternalistic supervision. The poor results of the government's encouragement in the early years appear to have been due primarily to the backwardness and sluggishness of the private business community—itself in part a product of a long tradition of paternalism—requiring the authorities to assume a more direct role than they apparently intended in order to achieve their goals. Nevertheless, the omnipresent influence of the state and the formidable bureaucratic processes involved in chartering and operating ordinary commercial banks should not be overlooked as factors in the slow development of the financial system. When, in the 1890's and afterward, joint-stock commercial banks began to play a prominent role in the economy, they did so frequently with the assistance, both financial and technical, of foreign banks—again with government encouragement.

Japan exhibited a number of similarities to Russia in this respect, with the significant difference that private entrepreneurs in Japan responded far more vigorously to their opportunities to establish privately owned banking companies. Whether the pecuniary incentives were higher in the case of Japan, or whether other factors, such as some special quality of the Japanese entrepreneurial mentality, were more important is difficult to test; but the rapid growth of national banks after the liberalization of charter provisions in 1876 argues for the former. Whatever the motivation, the decision to charter a number of banks of issue using government bonds as partial backing for the issues proved to be a stroke of genius, even though it was subsequently revoked. Apart from its favorable political effects (including the value it imparted to government bonds), it undoubtedly hastened the formation of banks and accustomed the public to using bank money, thereby preparing the way for ready acceptance of the Bank of Japan's convertible notes as well as the deposit money of ordinary commercial banks. This instance fully verified Bagehot's prescription for habituating the population to the use of bank money.[3]

This brief survey of the legal status of banking seems to indicate that, for a country in which the banking system is but little developed, the right or privilege of note issue is one of the most effective means both of eliciting a rapid growth in the number of banks and of habituating the public to the utilization of financial intermediaries. To that extent, for reasons already indicated, it is (or was) favorable to development. Historically, free incorporation seems to have been less of an incentive to potential bank entrepreneurs than freedom of issue, but the limitation of corporate charters certainly discouraged the formation of new banking enterprises where such limitations were in effect. Other restrictions associated with the limitation of corporate charters tended to make the banking system weaker and more unstable. The prohibition or lack of clear legal recognition of financial assets other than specie and banknotes inhibited the growth of currency substitutes, thereby hampering the ability of the banking system to gain control of the idle financial resources of the society. On the other hand, where legislation or accepted custom permitted the use of deposits, bills of exchange, and similar assets as means of payment, the banking system was able to secure control of a larger fraction of the society's resources and could therefore exert greater leverage in the process of development.

[3] See above, p. 127.

Quantitative Aspects of Financial Structure

1. *Density*. The "density" of financial institutions is significant primarily in terms of their accessibility, but it also has an important bearing on the degree of competition in banking. Utilization of bank facilities, whether by borrowers or lenders (depositors), is costly in terms of time and convenience (witness the popularity of "drive-in banking" and "bank-by-mail" schemes in the United States), in addition to being costly in terms of the interest paid by borrowers, and the gap between cost and benefit is considerably less than infinity. Other things being equal, the larger the proportion of the population that has access to bank facilities (and the larger the share of financial assets passing through the hands of bankers), the more effectively the banking system can discharge its functions.

Density can be measured in various ways: number of offices per unit of area or per number of inhabitants, value of assets per number of persons or as a percentage of income payments, etc.[4] Any single measure of density is by itself inadequate, however. The number of offices per unit of area or inhabitants says little about the volume of bank resources available to service the area or its inhabitants. The ratio of bank assets to area or population does not tell us whether or not the assets are in fact available to the entire area and its population. Ideally one would like to be able to measure regional as well as national variations in density. Unfortunately, for the historical cases in hand we do not even have statistics to make all of the international comparisons we should like. Moreover, there are serious conceptual difficulties involved in the international comparisons because of differences in currencies and fluctuations of exchange rates and price levels. The difficulties are especially serious in comparisons of two or more countries in different chronological periods. In spite of these difficulties, it may nevertheless be worthwhile to try to distinguish significant variations, bearing in mind the inherent limitations of the concept and its measures.

The simplest measure of banking density is one which relates the number of institutions or offices to area. If distances between centers of population were great and communications facilities poor there would be a special advantage in a high banking density, but in fact those are precisely the circumstances in which density is likely to be lowest. Thus the ratio of bank offices to territory is not likely to be very significant for purposes of economic analysis. At the ends of the respective periods of interest in this volume Japan had the highest geographical density of bank offices, 26.4 per thousand square miles of territory. England and Wales also had a relatively high density—almost 19. The figure for Scotland was 12.8; it is probable

[4] Cf. Goldsmith, *Financial Intermediaries*, 5.

that Belgium was in the same range, Germany somewhat lower. France in 1870 had only 2.2 offices per thousand square miles. Because of Russia's vast extent of thinly populated territory, its figure is so small as to be almost entirely meaningless. (For some modern comparisons, for what they are worth, the United States in recent years has had about seven offices per thousand square miles, England and Wales about 170.)

These figures clearly suggest that geograpical density of banks is related to the geographical density of population. Accordingly, a somewhat more significant measure of density relates bank offices to total population. The actual index used here is constructed as follows:

$$\frac{\text{no. of bank offices} \times 10{,}000}{\text{total population}}$$

We arbitrarily define a ratio over 1.0—that is, more than one office per 10,000 inhabitants—as "high." A ratio between 0.5 and 1.0 is "moderate," whereas one below 0.5 is "low." A ratio of less than 0.1 is "very low." Unless otherwise indicated, the index refers to commercial banks only, excluding saving banks, mortgage banks, etc. Banks of issue are included if they did a significant amount of business with the general public, but not if they functioned principally or exclusively as central banks.

For England in 1750 the index was about 0.0625. Of course, when the total number of banks is small the index has very little significance. Most of the banks, in fact, were located in London; there were not more than a dozen in the rest of the country. By 1785 the density had more than tripled, raising the index to about 0.21. At the beginning of the nineteenth century every county but one in England and Wales had at least one bank, and the index stood at 0.48. By this time the inclusion or exclusion of London's banks and population made very little difference in the index, indicating a fairly widespread network. The index remained almost stable until the crisis of 1825–26, then rose rapidly again with the growth of joint-stock banks to a maximum for the entire period of about 0.77 at the end of the 1830's. (For modern comparisons, the banking density in England and Wales in 1960 was 2.2. In the United States in 1957 it was 1.27; it had reached a maximum of 2.94 in 1920).

Scotland shows both a relatively high initial density and a high rate of increase. Already in 1750 its index stood at approximately 0.1. It rose rapidly to about 0.3 in the 1770's, and to 0.58 in 1800. By 1845, when its index stood at 1.4, Scotland had almost twice the banking density of England and, overall, probably the highest for any country at a comparable stage of development. In the latter part of the nineteenth century the Scottish index rose to about 3.3.

France, on the other hand, shows one of the lowest banking densities of any developed country. In 1800 the index was less than 0.025. As late as 1840 it was still less than 0.1, or "very low," and had risen only to 0.12 in 1870. Even in the twentieth century, in spite of the spread of great banking chains, France had an unusually low density. In 1960 the index stood at about 0.67, lower than England in 1840. (The 1960 index figure does not take into account the several *banques d'affaires* or the numerous branches of the Bank of France, all of which performed some commercial banking functions.)

For the other countries, except Japan, we have insufficient data for even this simple measure. For Belgium in the early 1830's the index was approximately 0.22. For subsequent years the lack of information on private banks and branches of joint-stock banks makes it impossible for us to compute an index, but it is probable that if we could it would register 0.5 or more. The Prussian figures show surprisingly little variation during the period in question, falling slightly from 0.3 in 1820–21 to 0.27 in 1849, then rising to 0.34 in 1861. It is likely that an all-German index would be higher than this, especially in the 1860's. After 1870, of course, with the formation of joint-stock banks and the spread of branch banking (the latter less pronounced than in Britain or France, however [5]), the density increased substantially. Russia in 1914 had some 900 joint-stock bank offices, about 1,100 mutual credit societies, and perhaps 500 municipal banks, giving an index of approximately 0.17. If one includes branches of the State Bank, which also conducted some commercial bank operations, the index is slightly higher.

Japan experienced an extremely rapid increase in banking density, especially if one includes the officially registered quasi-banks. In 1876 the index was approximately 0.01; by 1884 it had risen to 0.32. It remained relatively stable in that range until 1895, when it again rose rapidly with the spread of branch banking. In 1901 the index reached a maximum of 0.77, then fell off slightly to 0.75 in 1914. Over-all, the Japanese index rose more than twice as rapidly as the English; in less than 30 years it reached the same point that the English had taken almost 100 years to reach.

Some measure of the geographical distribution of bank offices with respect to population would be more relevant than either a strict area or population ratio in discussing the adequacy of banking facilities. Only for England do we have reasonably precise data. (See map, Chart II.2, p. 28.) These indicate that, at the beginning of the nineteenth century, England was already well served by banks, in the sense of convenience of location. By 1841 not only were there more banks, they were also more uniformly distributed through the country with respect to both area and population. In fact, the areas with the smallest population densities had the highest ratios

[5] Reisser, *The German Great Banks,* 685–8, 695.

of banks to people. In Scotland, too, although the figures are less precise, there is no doubt that the country was well covered. Naturally the largest concentration of bank offices was in the heavily populated industrial belt between the firths of Forth and Clyde; but by the 1820's every town or village of as many as 1,000 inhabitants—and some smaller—had at least one office, even in the Highlands. Towns of 5,000 to 10,000 typically had three or four offices. In 1836, when the North of Scotland Banking Company was established in Aberdeen, then a city of 50,000, the city already had two local banks, each with several branches in the immediate area, and four branches of Edinburgh banks.[6] More extreme examples could be cited.

In Belgium in 1833, in addition to the Société Générale and its five branches, there were 84 private bankers. These provided reasonably good coverage of the main commercial and industrial centers, though without more information on the size and nature of the operations of the banks it is difficult to form a judgment about their effectiveness. In subsequent years there is no doubt that coverage increased in both depth and breadth; in the second and third quarters of the century private bankers flourished most, and there was also a growth in the numbers and branches of joint-stock banks; but precise figures are not available.

France suffered from financial overcentralization as well as political overcentralization. The large number of private bankers in Paris had relatively few counterparts in the provinces. Most major commercial centers had one or two, sometimes more, full-time bankers; but until after midcentury the majority of financial transactions in the provinces was probably handled by merchants or tax officials who were part-time bankers at best. So important a city as the port of Le Havre depended principally on agents of Paris bankers for financing its commerce.[7] Several important industrial centers, such as St. Étienne and Mulhouse, apparently had no banks at all until after 1850.

The largest concentrations of private bankers in Germany were naturally to be found in the larger commercial and administrative centers, but owing to the greater importance of these centers in Germany than in France the result was a more comprehensive coverage of the country. By means of correspondent relationships among the bankers, including those with part-time bankers in the smaller centers, each region of the country maintained financial contact with the others directly, instead of by way of a single major financial center as in France. The dearth of financial institutions in Russia outside the two major cities of St. Petersburg and Moscow, and the efforts of the government to counteract it, have already been discussed;[8]

[6] Keith, *North of Scotland Bank,* 15.

[7] Gille, *Banque et crédit,* 64.

[8] See above, p. 186.

nothing further need be added. Taking into account the quasi-banks and similar small credit institutions, the Japanese banking system was apparently relatively well dispersed in accordance with the density of population.

2. *Relative size of the banking sector.* The ratio of bank assets to national income might be regarded as simply another measure of banking density. The importance of this ratio is considerably greater than that of other measures of density, however, in that it also measures the size of the banking sector relative to the whole economy. (Ideally, perhaps, the best measure of size would be the ratio of assets in banking to total assets—financial and nonfinancial.[9] In the present state of our knowledge, however, the computation of such ratios is out of the question.) In a sense, the relative size of the banking sector, although not an infallible indicator, is the best practical measure of its efficiency in the performance of one of its two essential functions: securing control of disposable funds for investment.

Table IX.1 presents in summary fashion some of the relevant statistics that have been worked up in earlier chapters regarding the relative size of the banking sector in the different countries, plus a section on the United States to lend additional perspective. The specific figures and ratios are subject to all the reservations and qualifications mentioned previously. Despite the inevitable inaccuracies and crudeness, the table reveals some hitherto unsuspected patterns of indubitable significance.

Not much weight can be attached to international comparisons of bank resources per capita, except perhaps for comparison of Scotland with England and Wales and of Belgium with France, because of the problems of price fluctuations and exchange rate variations. (Price indices appropriate for the deflation of these series to permit valid comparisons do not exist.) The growth of bank resources per capita in Scotland was very much more rapid than in England. Although starting from farther behind, by 1800 Scottish banks controlled a larger fraction of national wealth in relation to population than did the English, and that in spite of substantially lower average incomes in Scotland. By 1845 the ratio was about two and one half times that of England. A similar result emerges in the comparison of France and Belgium. The two banking systems were on a par with respect to resources per inhabitant in the 1830's, but Belgium soon pulled ahead. By 1860 the Belgian banks commanded almost twice the resources per capita as those of France, and in the 1870's more than two and a half times as much. It is tempting to push the comparisons further, but more can be learned from studying the ratio of bank resources to national income.

Column 5 of Table IX.1 indicates a surprisingly wide range in the ratio

[9] See Goldsmith, *Financial Intermediaries;* Kuznets, *Capital in the American Economy,* esp. chap. 6; Gurley and Shaw, "The Growth of Debt and Money in the United States."

TABLE IX.1

COMPARATIVE FINANCIAL RATIOS

(1) Year	(2) Total Bank Resources	(3) Resources per Capita	(4) National Income	(5) (2) ÷ (4) × 100
		A. England and Wales		
	(£ million)	(£)	(£ million)	(per cent)
1775	20.5	2.7	135.0	15.2
1800	54.8	6.0	196.7	27.9
1825	80.0	6.2	270.0	29.6
1844	139.0	8.4	403.8	34.4
		B. Scotland		
1750	0.6	0.5	a	6.0
1800	13.25	8.3		41–69[a]
1845	60.0	21.9		89.6
1865	77.2	24.2		80.0

[a]See note on sources.

(1) Year	(2) Total Bank Resources	(3) Resources per Capita	(4) National Income	(5) (2) ÷ (4) × 100
		C. France		
	(million francs)	(francs)	(million francs)	(per cent)
1800	102.	4.	7,400(1801)	1.5
1830	576.	18.	9,600	6.0
1840	948.	28.		
1850	1,236.	35.	13,800(1847)	9.1
1860	2,250.	62.	19,300(1859)	11.6
1870	3,744.	101.	24,000	15.6
		D. Belgium[b]		
1825	81.	21.		
1830	63.5	16.	1,000–1,200	5.–6.
1835	102.7	25.		
1845	331.	78.		
1850	225.	51.	1,600–1,700	13.–14.
1860	584	115.		
1875	1,323	249.	3,200–3,300	40.–42.

[b]Joint-stock banks only.

(1) Year	(2) Total Bank Resources	(3) Resources per Capita	(4) National Income	(5) (2) ÷ (4) × 100
		E. Russia		
	(million rubles)	(rubles)	(million rubles)	
1914	7,203 (comm. banks only)	41.	11,805	61.
1914	15,244 (all fin. inst.)			129.

TABLE IX.1 (cont.)

COMPARATIVE FINANCIAL RATIOS

(1) Year	(2) Total Bank Resources	(3) Resources per Capita	(4) National Income	(5) (2) ÷ (4) × 100
		F. Prussia		
	(million thalers)		(million thalers)	
1855	270		1,530	17.6
1865	610		1,960	31.1
		G. United States		
	($ million)		($ billion)	
1871	2,003	49.	GNP 6.71 (1869–73)	29.8
1884	4,221	76.	11.3 (1882–86)	37.5
1894	7,291	103.	13.6 (1892–96	53.5
1899	10,679	104.50	17.3 (1897–1901)	62.0
1900	10,011	103.10	NNP 15.8 (1897–1901)	63.3
1922	47,267	429.00	67.9	69.8
1929	65,621	540.00	95.8	68.5
1939	64,997	495.00	83.3	78.0
1952	188,603	1,219.00	323.0	58.5
		H. Japan		
	(million yen)	(yen)	(million yen)	
1878–82	107.5	2.9	667	16.1
1883–87	161.6	4.2	607	26.6
1888–92	191.3	4.8	809	23.6
1893–97	355.4	8.5	1,208	29.4
1898–1902	802.7	18.3	1,978	40.6
1903–7	1,328.6	28.5	2,522	52.7
1908–12	2,026.2	41.2	3,366	60.2

SOURCES FOR TABLE IX.1

A. Table II.1.

B. Table III.1; national income estimated as on p. 94, with the range in the ratio for 1800 depending upon whether one takes a high, low, or medium estimate of relation of Scottish to English per capita income.

C. Tables IV.1 and IV.2.

D. Table V.1. National income estimated on the assumption that per capita incomes in Belgium and France were approximately equal.

E. Table VII.10.

of bank resources to national income. The countries with the highest ratios at the end of the period investigated (and the highest growth rates within it) were also the countries that experienced the most rapid spurts of industrialization. Scotland is outstanding both for the very high ratio it achieved and for the rapidity with which it grew. Japan and Russia, both latecomers among the industrial nations, achieved a relatively high ratio in a very short time. (Lack of national income data for Russia inhibits the comparison, but one can infer a high rate of growth in the ratio from the fact that assets of the commercial banking system grew from less than 1 billion rubles in 1875 to more than 7 billion in 1913.) Although the Belgian ratio stood at less than 50 per cent in 1875, it should be remembered that the Belgian figures for bank assets refer to joint-stock banks only. It is quite likely that if private banks could be included the ratio would be in the vicinity of 60 per cent. In any case, the Belgian ratio is remarkable for the rapidity of its rate of increase, especially from 1850 to 1875. Given the fact that in each of these cases the main outlines of the banking system and the principal banking institutions had been established prior to the onset of rapid industrialization, the pattern strongly suggests a major role for the banking systems as determinants of that rapid industrialization.

The French ratio is remarkable for its very slight development even by 1870, leading one to suspect the figures on which it is based. If they are not wildly inaccurate, however, the weak and tardy development of the banking structure which they depict may very well hold the key to understanding the peculiar pattern of economic development in France. That is to say, the monetary and banking policies of the French government, which repressed and retarded the free development of the banking system, must bear a large share of the responsibility for the relatively slow progress of industrialization.

Comparable data for Germany are unfortunately not available. The Prussian data, such as they are, indicate that Prussia achieved a financial capability by 1855 that France had not yet achieved in 1870, and by 1865 was as highly developed financially as England in the 1830's or the United States in the 1870's. This suggests that private bankers in Prussia before

---

F. Tables VI.4 and VI.6; national income from W. Hoffmann, *Deutsche Volkseinkommen*, p. 186. Figures for bank resources do not include equity capital or liabilities of the *Landschaften*. Inclusion of the latter would raise the ratios to 29 per cent in 1855 and 45 per cent in 1865.

G. 1871–1899: U.S. Bureau of the Census, *Historical Statistics of the United States, Colonial Times to 1957* (Washington, D.C., 1960), Series A-2, F-1, and X-21 ("all banks—total assets or liabilities"). 1900–1952: net national product as above, series F-6; bank resources from Raymond Goldsmith, *Financial Intermediaries*, Table A-2, "operating commercial banks—total assets."

H. Tables VIII.5 and VIII.6, Ohkawa, *Growth Rate*, and Bank of Japan, *Historical Statistics*.

1855 were unusually successful in circumventing the restrictions placed on the monetary and banking systems by official policy, but it is also significant that the rapid growth in the ratio between 1855 and 1865 corresponds in timing with both the liberalization of Prussian banking and monetary policy and with Prussia's first spurt of rapid industrialization. In terms of the general relationship between banking and industrial growth, it is also significant that the period after 1870, when Germany achieved its highest industrial growth rates of the century, was also a period of virtually complete freedom (except for note issue) for German banks.

England might in some respects be considered the "normal" case, with the others constituting variations or extremes. Although the English series stops in 1844, other data suggest that the ratio continued to rise gradually during the century, probably reaching 50 or 60 per cent at the beginning of the twentieth century. In the 1920's the ratio of the assets of London clearing banks to United Kingdom national income was approximately 50 per cent, and England and Wales accounted for approximately 85 per cent of United Kingdom income. The United States, which we have not considered in previous chapters for the reasons indicated in Chapter I, might also be considered a "normal" case. Projecting the United States series backward requires somewhat more daring and imagination, but it is not inconceivable that the ratio for the United States in 1800 was less than 5 per cent, and that it attained perhaps 15 or 20 per cent in the 1830's. It seems likely that in the cases of England and the United States the banking systems were essentially passive or permissive, responding fully to the demand for financial services but not inducing growth directly. (This generalization should be accepted very tentatively for the United States pending further study. Certainly there were periods in American history—the 1830's and possibly the period from about 1885 to 1929—when the banks played a more positive, active role.) If so, this may help explain why English and American banking theorists generally deprecate the contribution of banks to industrial growth.

These findings are broadly consistent with those of Goldsmith in his study of financial structure in developed economies, which deals primarily with the twentieth century.[10] Goldsmith chose to relate financial assets to national wealth rather than income, and included savings banks along with commercial and central banks. The results of his computations are presented in Table IX.2. If the proportion of national wealth to national income is on the order of four or five to one, then the ratios are closely comparable to what might result from a projection of the series in Table IX.1 They show that France closed the gap somewhat between 1870 and 1912—as one would

[10] Goldsmith, "Financial Structure and Economic Growth in Advanced Countries," in Abramovitz (ed.), *Capital Formation and Economic Growth.*

TABLE IX.2

BANK ASSETS AS PER CENT OF NATIONAL WEALTH

Country	Date	Bank Assets as Per Cent of National Wealth
United States	1912	16
Germany	1913	14
United Kingdom	1913	12
France	1913	10

Source: Goldsmith, "Financial Structure and Economic Growth in Advanced Countries," in Abramovitz (ed.), *Capital Formation and Economic Growth*, Table 9, p. 151.

expect from the widespread development of branch networks by the large Paris joint-stock banks—but still lagged behind the industrial leaders. Goldsmith's data, like those of Table IX.1, also suggest a fairly close correspondence in rank order between the rates of growth of the banking system and the rate of industrial growth.

The empirical relations indicated in Table IX.1 prompt a number of questions. What are the determinants of the ratios of column 5 and their rates of growth? Is there an "optimal" growth path that the ratio should follow in the course of development? Is there a practical ceiling on it, or can it continue to rise indefinitely? Do the ratios reveal—or conceal—any causal relationships between financial development and industrial growth?

One obvious determinant of the relative size of the banking sector is the extent to which bank liabilities fulfill the role of money. The contrast is striking in the cases of Scotland and France, and explains much of their deviation from the mean. The same factor helps to explain the rapid growth of English banking before 1800, Belgian after 1850, and Japanese after 1875. The use of bank liabilities as money in these cases (except for Belgium) is, in turn, related to the question of freedom of note issue. In almost every case the most rapid expansion of the banking system occurred during the phase when banknotes constituted the most important liabilities of the banks. (Even Belgium is not exceptional in this respect.) In most countries deposits subsequently assumed greater importance, but it is also worthy of note that demand deposits were most widely used in countries that had previously become accustomed to the note issues of competing independent banks. The public of countries with monopolistic issuing agencies evidently regarded banknotes as a form of fiat money; in any event, they did not develop the "banking habit" to the same degree as did the public in countries in which relative freedom of banking prevailed. The consequence of this may be observed in France and Germany, where the general public still makes relatively infrequent use of checks.

The "latecomers" to industrialization (at least in the cases considered here) typically not only demonstrated a higher rate of industrial growth, but also a more rapid growth of the banking sector. This is consistent with the hypothesis of the "advantages of backwardness" of Professor Gerschenkron.[11] Just as underdeveloped nations have the option of adopting the most modern technological devices, they have the option of adopting the latest and/or most efficient techniques of banking—and at considerably less real cost. This was obviously important in the cases of Japan and Russia, as well as in Germany in the 1850's and 1860's. (Though they are outside the range of this study, the Scandinavian countries also benefited from the banking experience of other countries, especially that of France and of Germany.)[12]

Another factor of considerable importance in the cases of Russia and Japan was the role of government. Government initiative and desire to industrialize have frequently been cited as contributory factors in the rapid industrialization of those two countries. It is important to recognize, therefore, that government influence was exercised in large part through the banking system. In addition to such measures as governmental presure on the central banks to lend liberally in periods of financial strain of crisis, government deposits accounted for a substantial part of the total resources of the banks in countries in which private resources were extremely limited. Unlike the governments of some contemporary underdeveloped countries, who use the money-creating facilities of the banking sector as an alternative to taxation, the governments of Russia and Japan transferred resources obtained by taxation to the banking system. In effect, they used a combination of the tax power of the state and the specialized talents of bankers to shift resources from consumption to production.

The question of an "optimal" growth path is difficult to answer. If the banking system expands its loans and liabilities too rapidly it may generate inflationary pressures, which, especially if the economy is relatively open to foreign competition or is tied to an international monetary standard, may cause balance of payments problems that will result in setbacks to the effort to industrialize. At one time or another all the countries in our sample experienced such strains as a result of too rapid expansion on the part of banks: for example, Scotland in the 1760's leading up to the crisis

[11] *Economic Backwardness in Historical Perspective,* esp. pp. 11–16.

[12] This was brought out by Professor Hildebrand at the Bellagio conference mentioned in the Preface. See also Cameron, *France and Europe,* 129, 164–5, 490–91.

of 1772; England in 1825 and 1836; France in 1837; Belgium in 1838; Germany in the 1850's and again in 1872–73; Japan in 1881–82; Russia in 1900–1901. (Not all financial crises resulted from such expansion; essentially noneconomic events were responsible for the crises of 1797 and 1848, among others. Still others were propagated internationally, and had little if anything to do with bank expansion in certain of the affected countries.) Russia was persistently hobbled in its effort to industrialize by balance of payments problems; Japan solved similar problems by *de facto* depreciation. Thus it is possible for the banking system to expand too rapidly. On the other hand, it can certainly expand too slowly. The "optimal" rate of expansion would seem to be that which is consistent with the full employment of resources, reasonable price stability, and the ability of the economy to absorb and utilize technical innovations; unfortunately, such criteria cannot be specified in advance or generalized to cover all situations.

It is tempting, nevertheless, to conceive of a theoretically optimal long-term path of bank expansion. It would probably resemble a logistic curve, rising rapidly at first owing to the monetization of the subsistence sectors of the economy, the substitution of bank liabilities for commodity money, and the existence of banks as the sole or only significant institutions capable of supplying external finance for industry and commerce. Subsequently the rate of expansion would drop off (relative to the economy as a whole, at least) as business firms become able to supply more of their own financial needs by retained earnings, and as other financial institutions arise to compete with the banks for the investable funds of surplus spending units. The growth of non-bank financial intermediaries might eventually reduce the relative share of banks in total assets; both Goldsmith and Gurley and Shaw have noted this fact in highly developed economies, especially in the United States.[13]

Chart IX.1 shows how actual performance might compare with the hypothetical optimum. The data come from column 5 of Table IX.1, but the time scale is a composite one. This introduces an element of arbitrariness to match the crudeness and incompleteness of the data; if different "time-zeros" were chosen the chart would convey a slightly different impression (e.g. if t_0 for the U.S. were 1789 or 1865 instead of 1800), but the individual growth rates are not affected. As it is, the following "time-zeros" have been selected:

England	1750
Scotland	1750
France	1800

[13] Goldsmith, "Financial Structure and Economic Growth in Advanced Countries," in Abramovitz, *Capital Formation and Economic Growth;* Gurley and Shaw, "Financial Aspects of Economic Development," and other writings (see List of Works Cited)

Belgium	1800
Prussia	1800
United States	1800
Russia	1860
Japan	1870

The "curves" for Japan and Scotland come closest to the hypothetical optimum. (Selecting the median estimate for per capita income of Scotland in 1800 appears to give the line a constant slope; a higher or lower estimate would show more of a curve, but a logistic curve can easily be fitted to the three fixed points. The ratio for 1865, not shown in the graph, is actually lower than that for 1845, probably indicating a leveling of the curve in the years before 1845.) This accords with other evidence on the efficacy of the Scottish and Japanese banking systems, and thus supports the notion of a theoretical optimum. The data for Belgium and the United States, as well as that for Prussia and Russia, could also be fitted to a logistic curve, but the first two in particular seem to have suffered a long delay before beginning their financial "take-offs." The appearance could be the result of the arbitrariness of the "time-zeros." On the other hand, it is likely that the United States, at least, had already completed one cycle, with a sharp rise in the 1830's—the heyday of wildcat banking—and a leveling off before or during the Civil War. A similar, though more muted, phenomenon appears to have occurred in England: there was a sharp rise in the ratio associated with the growth of country banking; a leveling off after the Napoleonic Wars, perhaps indicating a saturation point for banknote issues; and a renewed rise with the advent of deposit banking on a large scale. The French data give only the barest hint of following a logistic pattern, and that at the very end of the period under consideration. The evidence presented in Chapter IV, of the desire of the French business community for increased banking facilities in the 1820's, 1830's, and 1840's, indicates that the French curve, too, might have followed the theoretical optimum but for the artificial restrictions imposed upon the banking system.

3. *Size and concentration of bank power*. The issue here is the size of the individual bank unit, and the degree of concentration of assets within the banking sector. Is there an optimal size or an optimal degree of concentration or dispersion? The question is obviously related to that of branch vs. unit banking, and to the degree of competition within the banking sector, both to be discussed below. Here we indicate merely the trends in the experience of the countries studied. Since in most cases our estimates of total resources in banking were based on estimates of the average size of the estimated number of banks, there is little point in breaking the aggregates down to obtain the original estimates. The best we can do with this

CHART IX.1

BANK ASSETS AS PER CENT OF NATIONAL INCOME

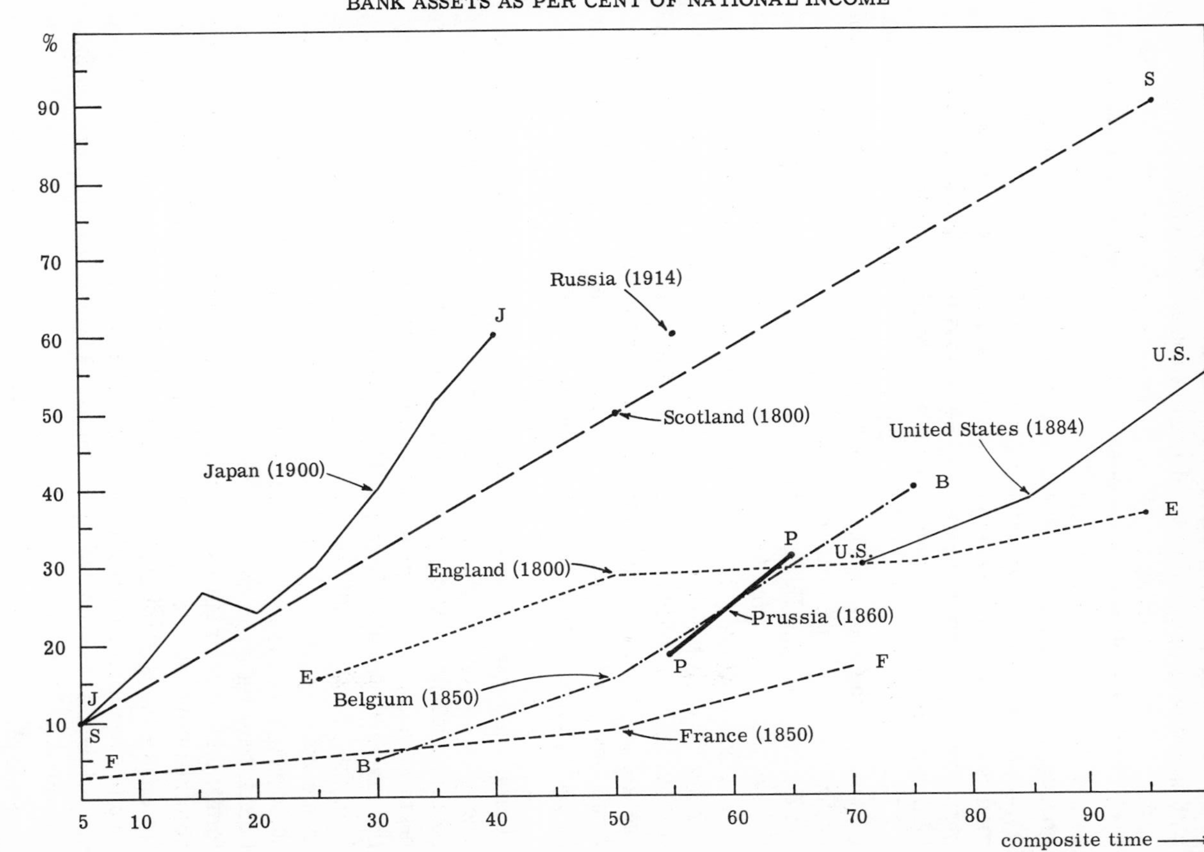

essentially quantitative question is to deal in nonquantitative generalities, with a few percentages thrown in where they are available.

At one time or another all of these countries had one or more very large banks with special privileges—most of which eventually became central banks—and numerous very small banks. The relative importance of the privileged banks tended to diminish over time, but it always remained great. Typically their assets constituted between one-fourth and one-third of the total assets of the banking system; proportions as high as one-half and even higher are not unknown. Usually but not always the large size of the largest bank was related to a monopoly or near-monopoly of note issue. In 1865 the Bank of Prussia controlled 43.6 per cent of the assets of all joint-stock banks in North Germany. The Russian State Bank owned about 30 per cent of the resources of the commercial credit system of Russia until the 1890's. Until after 1905 the Bank of Japan owned between one-fourth and one-third of the assets of the total financial system, and by itself was one-third to one-half the size of the whole commercial banking system.

Nonprivileged banks usually went through two distinct phases with respect to size and concentration. The first phase was that of increasing average size but decreasing concentration. At first the number of private banks (including privately owned joint-stock banks, if any) would be small. The formation of new banks of course reduced the degree of concentration, but average size generally increased as existing banks grew by the reinvestment of profits and new banks entered with larger capitals than earlier banks had. The second phase saw continued growth in average size along with increasing concentration. In most cases the increase in concentration set in at or very near the end of the periods treated in this volume, sometimes (in Germany, for example) shortly afterward. One might almost date the end of the "early stages of industrialization" by reference to increasing concentration in the banking sector. Usually the movement toward concentration was associated with the growth of joint-stock banks and the establishment of branch banking. Joint-stock banks were sometimes created by the transformation or merger of existing private banks. In other cases they frequently absorbed older private banks into their growing chains. The tendency was for private banks to disappear altogether, but a few hardy sports still survive in every country except Scotland and Soviet Russia. After devouring most of the private banks the giant joint-stock banks turned on one another: the ultimate development in each country saw a relatively small number of huge banks, serving the entire nation, engaged in oligopolistic competition. But that development occurred long after the passing of the early stages of industrialization.

Branch Banking vs. Unit Banking

Both the branch banking system and the unit banking system have advantages and disadvantages. At first glance the advantages of branch banking seem greater, as do the disadvantages of unit banking.

Other things being equal, branch chains have larger resources, which enable them to withstand sudden emergencies more easily. They can also diversify their risks to a greater extent, and thus they are less susceptible to emergencies. Branch banks can also shift resources geographically with greater ease and less cost; normally this should result in a smoother functioning national capital market, with a greater tendency toward equalization of rates of return on capital in different regions and industries. Great chain banks can also benefit from economies of scale by employing specialists in various branches of finance such as the call money market, the bond market, etc. Under certain circumstances, depending on governing legislation, they can also work with smaller cash reserves in proportion to total assets.

Offsetting these advantages, large chain banks can suffer from the diseconomies of scale involved in the multiplication of supervisory officers and other staff positions characteristic of large-scale bureaucratic organizations. How important these diseconomies will be depends in part on the geographic spread of the branch network and the technology of communications. The general tendency of the progress of communications has been to reduce their significance. Prior to the advent of the railway and electric telegraph only Scotland had developed branch banking to any significant extent. More serious is the loss of intimate personal contact and detailed knowledge, both within the bank organization and between the bank and the public. The Scottish pioneers of branch banking solved this problem by selecting their "agents" (not branch managers) from the outstanding businessmen of the communities in which they located branches, giving them a large measure of decentralized decision-making authority, and at the same time involving them in the financial responsibility for their operations. Subsequently both the Scottish banks and other chain banks adopted more bureaucratic forms of organization.

Another potential danger of branch banking is the reduction of competition that may result if the banking system falls into the hands of a few oligopolistic chains through the elimination of independent local banks. A related danger, one that showed itself in France after 1870 in particular, is that the large banks may use their network of branches merely as a means of draining the hinterland of surplus funds, and then use those funds in low risk but relatively unproductive employments in the metropolis or abroad, without seeking to develop local resources. How serious a problem this was in other nations is difficult to ascertain with the evidence available. No doubt it tends to be more serious in nations such as France where there is a high degree of concentration of both political and financial power in a single city.

The disadvantages of unit banking are virtually the mirror image of the advantages of chain banking: relatively limited resources (this does not rule out the possibility of a few large unit banks in major cities, or of joint-stock banks of the *mobilier* type that operate on a national scale from a single location); difficulties in the way of diversification of risks and of forming a unified, efficient nationl market; and inability to benefit from economies of scale. The major compensating advantage of independent local banks is that they are more likely to be attuned to the needs and potentialities of local communities and interested in developing local resources. The contrast between the English country banks and the local Scottish banks, on the one hand, and the French and Russian joint-stock banks of the late nineteenth century, on the other, is striking both in methods of operations and results. For that matter, though the English and Scottish systems after mid-century lie outside the scope of this study, it would be interesting to compare the performance of the country banks with that of their latter-day successors, the branches of the English "Big Five." It was one of the last surviving private banks that, in 1910, enabled the founder of Morris Motors to get his start (see above, p. 57). One wonders if he would have been so fortunate in dealing with a branch manager of one of the Big Five.

In considering the relative utility of branch and unit banking, one must take into account the historical trend, which seemingly favored the former. The earliest banks in all countries engaged initially in unit banking. Widespread branch banking had to await the adoption of the joint-stock form of organization for banking; after that branch banking grew rapidly at the expense of unit banks, except for special purpose banks or where branch banking was restrained by special legislation, as in the United States. This record would seem to indicate the overwhelming superiority of branch banking, at least from the viewpoint of stockholders. Yet one wonders if there may not have been a divergence between private and social benefits in that case.

No account has been taken in this discussion of branch systems of central banks or banks with monopoly privileges in the matter of note issue. The historical record is mostly negative on this point. Neither the Bank of England nor the Bank of France, the two leading examples, established branches until forced to by competition or governmental pressure. The Prussian Bank, the Banque Nationale de Belgique, and the Bank of Japan were all latecomers to their respective scenes, and were all creatures of the government, as was the State Bank of Russia. The evidence, such as it is, seems to indicate that insofar as such banks act as lenders of last resort and monopolistic note issuers—if there is to be monopoly—they should be endowed with a network of branches.

Competition in Banking

The question of competition in banking is intimately related to the legal status of banking, bank density, size and concentration, and the relative merits of unit and branch banking. What follows, therefore, is in the nature of a summary of summaries.

Majority opinion, even among groups otherwise favorable to competition in economic life, seems to have regarded the banking system as an area to be preserved from competition or, at least, protected from "excessive" competition. Virtually every country at one time or another has imposed restrictions on banking, with the effect—intentional or not—of limiting competition among banks. In view of this well-nigh universal current of opinion it should be stated in the most unequivocal terms that there is no historical justification whatever for believing that competition in banking is, in general, detrimental to the interests of society as a whole. On the contrary, insofar as the criterion for judging bank performance is the contribution of banks to growth, the best results have been achieved when competition was freest and most unfettered. Once again the examples of Scotland and Japan (and of some American states during the period of free banking) spring to mind. Even Germany in the era of the "great banks," when competition was free if not perfect, was no exception. This suggests that the theoretically optimal growth path of the ratio of bank assets to national income is also the "natural" growth path that would result from free competition. Competition in banking is also, in general, favorable to financial innovation, although in certain circumstances the artificial restrictions placed on banking may likewise serve as a spur to financial innovation if the demand for financial services is strong.

Competition in banking is related to the question of competition in industry. In general the two flourish—and decline—together. Whether this phenomenon is a joint by-product of other circumstances, or whether it results from the decline or restriction of competition among banks, is a matter worthy of further research. It is a striking coincidence, in any case, that industrial structure—competitive, oligopolistic, or monopolistic—tends to mirror financial structure.

FINANCIAL INNOVATION

A financial innovation is any new financial technique or institution intended to facilitate the exchange of goods and services, the settlement of debts, or the provision of producers of goods and services with the resources they require. In the broad sense, banks and even money itself were at one time financial innovations, although far antedating the period of concern in this volume. Just as industry and agriculture progress by means of new techniques—innovation—so the introduction of new financial techniques is the mark of progress in the financial sector. Not uncommonly financial innovation has been the prerequisite of successful technical innovation.

Theoretically the success of an innovation can be measured by reduction in cost or the increased productivity of labor and other resources it permits. The same is true in principle of financial innovations, but measurement of the productivity of new techniques of finance may be extremely difficult because the benefits may be external to the firm introducing the innovation. Some financial innovations, such as the introduction of clearing houses or the use of business machines for record keeping, are not substantively different from technical innovation in industry, and the measurement of their productivity can be easily handled by conventional methods. Other, more important types of financial innovation, such as the introduction of banknotes and the practice of making payments by check in place of currency, are essentially social innovations. Benefits to the firms introducing them accrue not in the form of cost reductions for services performed, but in the long-run expansion of their business. The reduction in cost is widely dispersed throughout society as a form of social saving.

Financial innovations by banks may be classified under three headings: (1) those relating to a bank's ability to attract resources (i.e. those affecting its liabilities); (2) those relating to its use of resources (i.e. its assets); and (3) innovations in the form of financial institutions. The first is of special interest, in that certain bank liabilities performed the functions of money. The eighteenth and nineteenth centuries were prolific in financial as in technical innovations. It is therefore a matter of some interest to know who made the innovations, when, why, under what conditions, and what effects they had.

In the middle of the eighteenth century the dominant form of money was commodity money, principally gold, silver, and baser metals. Banknotes existed, but they were of limited use in a few localities only. Payment by assignment in bank (checks, *giro*) had been practiced for several centuries, but also on a very restricted basis. Bills of exchange may also have been used as a means of current payment, although their characteristic use was for distant payments at deferred dates.

The outstanding feature of the monetary history of the last two centuries, the nineteenth in particular, has been the substitution of various forms of bank-created money for commodity money.[14] The first modern banknotes were issued by the Bank of Stockholm, forerunner of the Swedish Riksbank, in 1656. The experiment was not successful and they were soon withdrawn. Soon afterward goldsmith bankers in London began to issue deposit receipts payable on demand, which, in effect, were banknotes. The Bank of England issued banknotes from the beginning of its operations, and John Law's Banque Générale in France issued them in superabundance. But it was the Scottish banks, soon followed by English country banks, that generalized banknotes in practice. Their major refinement was the introduction of notes of relatively small denominations, £1 and even less. The motivation in both cases seems to have been the scarcity of specie, especially coins of small denomination. This was brought about in England by the inefficiency of the Mint, but it was aggravated in the case of Scotland by its unfavorable balance of payments with England. From Britain the use of banknotes spread to the Continent, though haltingly at first. Eventually banknotes became the most important component in the money supply of several countries. Unlike Britain, most Continental countries did not tolerate the private issue of money claims, or did so only under strict government control. The result was that the issue of paper money came to be centralized in the hands of specially chartered and regulated institutions, as indeed it did in England after 1844.

Bank deposits first existed in medieval Italy in the form of *giro* accounts, which required that both payor and payee have accounts with the same bank. They were not widely used in the sixteenth and seventeenth centuries except in Amsterdam and two or three other major commercial cities. The goldsmith bankers of London also accepted deposits payable on demand, but such payments were usually made directly over the counter to the drawee or his agent rather than being settled by transfers on the bankers' books. The London Clearing House, dating from 1773, indicates that checks were becoming increasingly common, at least among the more important merchants and bankers of the metropolis. Probably not until the 1820's or 1830's, however, with the growth of non-note-issuing joint-stock banks, did deposits subject to check come to occupy an important place in the stock of money or current means of payment in England. By that time they were also widely used in Scotland. Scottish banks originally operated almost entirely on the basis of note issues, but with the strong demand for capital

[14] Cf. Triffin, *International Monetary Standard.*

that arose in the 1780's they made vigorous efforts to attract deposits by means of interest differentials for demand, or current account, deposits and time deposits. The Scottish banks also democratized deposit banking, as they had note issues, by accepting deposits for as little as £10.

The use of checks in Britain was facilitated by legislation and judicial decisions dating from the seventeenth century which provided for summary diligence against drawers of bad checks. Curiously, no similar legal provisions appear to have existed on the Continent. German bankers made fairly extensive use of *giro* credit and current account overdrafts, but demand deposits subject to check made very slow headway on the Continent in spite of the British example. This was no doubt partly due to the lack of legal definition until the 1860's, but since checking remained of secondary importance even afterward it may have reflected the preference of bankers for liabilities over which they had greater control, such as acceptance credits and time deposits. Russian banks followed Continental practice, whereas Japan adopted and adapted the British and American systems.

One other attempted innovation affecting bank liabilities failed, apparently due to official hostility, although lack of market demand may also have been a factor. The Société Général de Belgique raised additional funds in the 1830's by issuing its own debentures. In later years some German, Russian, and Japanese banks, especially special purpose banks, did likewise Jacques Laffitte in the 1830's and the founders of the Crédit Mobilier in the 1850's attempted to carry the idea one step further by issuing short-term interest-bearing bonds as a means of circumventing the Bank of France's monopoly of note issue. Laffitte had moderate success, but the crisis of 1848 put an end to his bank. The Crédit Mobilier made only one issue, then bowed to official pressure against them and made no others. Interestingly, the idea has been picked up again in modified form by large New York and London banks in the twentieth century.

The gradual assumption by bankers of the function of money supply not only made the stock of money more elastic and expansive, but also facilitated economic growth by economizing on the use of specie, a form of money with much higher real cost. It is significant that France, the country that made a fetish of the use of specie, also suffered the lowest rate of growth. The most decisive advantage of the use of bank money, however, was that it gave to bankers, the specialists and presumed experts in the business of lending to deficit units, a large leverage over real resources which they could transfer directly to enterprising entrepreneurs.

Innovations with respect to the use of bank assets mostly took the form of novel ways of granting credit. Loans on mortgages and promissory notes were already standard in the eighteenth century, but the former had the disadvantage of tying up bank assets for long periods of time, whereas the latter frequently lacked the guarantees looked for by cautious bankers. Moreover, until after the French Revolution usury laws effectively hindered the use of promissory notes on the Continent. As a result self-liquidating bills of exchange became the favored instrument of credit in orthodox circles. Bills of exchange had the additional advantage that they could be used as means of current payment. In areas where banknotes were not permitted, or where, as a result of sad experience, the public preferred not to use them, businessmen resorted to the use of bills of exchange as means of payment on a large scale. The effective use of bills in this manner required the existence of banks as ultimate sources of credit by means of discount.

Not all areas nor all entrepreneurs could offer the kinds of security required for bills of exchange. Frequently the need for fixed capital in modest amounts, or even working capital with a turnover period longer than the customary 90 days, took precedence over the need for short-term credit for the movement of goods. In such cases entrepreneurs and their bankers had to devise new methods of finance. Where banks depended upon note issues for their profits—principally in Scotland and England (and also in Japan under its national banking system)—current account advances or "cash credits" sufficed. Elsewhere—in Germany, for example—more subtle and elaborate devices were needed, and banks came to use current account overdrafts and eventually bankers' acceptances. Out of these practices developed a highly elaborate system of *giro* accounts with bankers performing the function of a clearing house for payments between its client firms.

Institutional innovation took the form of the creation of new institutions to perform new functions, and of adaptation of existing types of institutions to suit special circumstances. Among the former were savings banks, mortgage banks, and mutual credit societies. The most important from the standpoint of industrial finance was the joint-stock investment-promotional bank, of which the outstanding examples were the Société Général de Belgique and the Crédit Mobilier of France. Outstanding examples of institutional adaptation were the amalgam of banks of the *mobilier* type with the practices of the German private bankers in the great German Kreditbanken, which performed "mixed" banking functions, and the adaptation by the Japanese of American, British, and Continental models to suit the peculiar needs and circumstances of the Japanese economy.

The significance of this record for contemporary underdeveloped economies is that they should not depend upon slavish imitation of the financial techniques and institutions borrowed from their wealthier neighbors, but should not hesitate to adapt them to their own particular circumstances and, where possible or necessary, to invent new devices to solve their own special problems.

PAST AND PRESENT

One of the clearest lessons to be derived from this study of history is that no single model of a banking system is appropriate for all economies. It is not to be expected, therefore, that the historical experience of the industrialized nations of Europe or elsewhere will be directly applicable in countries that differ widely in culture, resources, historical traditions, and many other respects. In any case it would be the height of folly to attempt to prescribe banking or monetary policy or reforms for a given country on the basis of either history or theory without a detailed and intimate knowledge of that country's economy and society. We make no such prescription. It does not follow, however, as we have already argued, that nothing at all can be learned from history.

In order to ascertain whether and to what extent the experience of the past is valid in the world of the present it is necessary to specify the major similarities and differences in the respective circumstances relevant to our problem. Apart from the obvious differences in culture, tradition, level of technology and the like, there are a number of fundamental differences relating specifically to financial, monetary, and banking matters. Unlike the people of Europe at the beginning of the nineteenth century, today there is virtually no sizable social group that is not familiar with banknotes or other forms of paper money, and that does not have at least a rudimentary consciousness of the existence of banks and their functions. Although many underdeveloped economies are as yet incompletely monetized (that is one of the measures of their backwardness), the scope for industrial capital formation by means of rapid monetization through the banking system is greatly reduced.

With respect to monetization, today's underdeveloped countries are considerably more "advanced" than were their counterparts of 150 or 200 years ago. In other respects, however—proportion of labor force in agriculture, standards of literacy and education, industrial and commercial traditions, etc—many of them are considerably more backward. This indicates that not only will extensive—and expensive—programs of agrarian reform, educational development, and such be required to increase productivity and habituate the populace to modern techniques and procedures, but also that novel financial institutions and practices may be necessary to activate the latent entrepreneurial talents and productive energies of hitherto tradition-minded peoples. In that connection it should be pointed out that, in most contemporary underdeveloped economies, banking practice and policy, although not exactly "orthodox" (central banks in particular), follow far too slavishly the canons of their more advanced neighbors, where conditions and traditions are quite different.

In one important respect contemporary underdeveloped countries have liberated themselves from bondage to an outmoded and expensive fetish. No longer do gold and silver figure prominently—or at all—in the monetary circulation of any nation. As everywhere, however, liberty has its price. Perhaps the outstanding merit of a metallic monetary standard for nations that were committed to one was that it kept governments as well as bankers and businessmen within reasonable bounds when computing expected income and expenditure. Today's underdeveloped nations no longer have to bear the burden of a large stock of unproductive capital in their monetary systems, but all too often they must pay an even higher price in the form of an improvident, unproductive, and corrupt government bureaucracy and a derangement of the monetary system.

Central banks under state control with legal monopolies of note issue are probably here to stay. This seems to be an unavoidable but not necessarily felicitous conclusion. Historically local banks of issue have played an important role not only in habituating the populace to the use of financial instruments and institutions, but also in the development of small-scale local industry and agriculture. Conceivably this can be done by means of deposit money, but in relatively primitive conditions of production and marketing, where laborers and entrepreneurs alike have but little sophistication in the use of modern financial instruments, there is much to be said for local banks of issue, using, perhaps, a standard form of banknote such as the national banknotes of the United States and Japan. It would, in any case, be highly instructive if such experiments could be carried out in countries like Brazil and Nigeria, where there are still some traditions of regional autonomy.

It is frequently argued that the shortage of capital and of entrepreneurs in contemporary underdeveloped economies are reasons why the state must play a larger direct role in economic development than was characteristic of the now-industrialized nations in their respective early stages of industrialization. Such arguments are unsound historically. It is by now abundantly clear that the rate of savings and capital formation among the industrializing nations of the eighteenth and early nineteenth centuries was much less than had previously been supposed. Many if not most of today's developing nations have higher rates of capital formation. If the results are not wholly satisfactory, it may be due to the efficiency—or inefficiency—with which the capital is used.

As for the shortage of entrepreneurs, that argument can only be tested after the fact. There was no reason to believe in 1750 that the Scots would soon people the world—the English-speaking world at least—with a race of hardy entrepreneurs (witness the fate of the inglorious Darien expedition at the end of the seventeenth century), or to believe in 1870 that Japan would soon produce some of the world's foremost industrial and financial entrepreneurs. (As late as 1930 most Westerners still regarded the Japanese as "quaint.")

Arguments for a larger direct entrepreneurial role for the state also overlook the fact that decisions and actions must still be made by men. The kinds of men to be found in the service of the state—and, more importantly, the kinds of incentives that impel them—are not necessarily those most conducive to innovation and economic growth. There is, in fact, a considerable danger—and much contemporary evidence—that such efforts will duplicate the mistakes of Colbert and the cameralists: a sobering example of Santayana's warning. There is little doubt that government officials today are much more "growth-minded" than their counterparts in the past, but this is not necessarily a valid reason for substituting their energies and decisions for those of private entrepreneurs. While there will obviously be exceptional cases, in general the state would do better to devote its own limited resources to creating the conditions in which private entrepreneurs and private capital can flourish. This hortatory suggestion is intended specifically to include private entrepreneurs in banking. It should be evident from the historical record that the banking system is a strategic location with a large leverage for economic development. Therefore, insofar as there is an actual shortage of capable entrepreneurs, the argument for attracting them into the banking system gains force.

Another advantage in allowing greater latitude for the private banking system is that it decentralizes decision-making and encourages initiative on a broad front. It is a common observation that state-sponsored development projects tend toward the grandiose and monumental, and are frequently of doubtful economic value, while small-scale industry and agriculture are often neglected. The most successful historical cases of industrialization, however, show the prominence if not the predominance of small-scale enterprise in the earliest stages of industrialization. If small enterprises are successful, it is because they have met the test of the market, and they will inevitably grow larger. On the other hand, if they fail the losses to society are much less than in the case of the failure of a large government-sponsored enterprise, which for political reasons may not be allowed to appear to have failed. Of the countries in our sample, Russia is the one in which the government played the largest role, both directly and indirectly; and although it had some credits to its record, over-all its achievements were more spectacular than solid. The comparison of the precise role of government in Russia and Japan, two countries with much in common as far as their conditions of backwardness were concerned, is extremely instructive.

In the final analysis, today's developing nations must work out their own problems with such assistance as they can obtain from their wealthier and technically more advanced neighbors. Conditions are different now from what they were in the past, and they will be different in the future from what they are in the present. But present and future grow gradually and ineluctably from the past. A knowledge of history on the part of the leaders of today is the best guarantee that the world will benefit from the mistakes of the past as well as from its triumphs.

BIBLIOGRAPHY

A Note on Sources

Although we have not, as noted in the Preface, made a fetish of exhuming previously unutilized primary sources, we have all made use of unpublished documents and other sources of information not easily available to the casual student. Dr. Crisp has drawn on her long familiarity with archival sources in France pertaining to Russian economic and financial affairs, in particular the Archives Nationales and the Archives de la Ministère des Affaires Étrangères. I have also consulted documents in these same depositories on the financial history of France and Belgium, as well as others indicated in my study of *France and the Economic Development of Europe, 1800–1914* (Princeton, 1961); interested readers are referred to it for a more detailed discussion of the nature and uses of these sources. Professor Tilly has drawn heavily on both public and private archives in the German Federal Republic; fuller descriptions of these sources may be found in his book, *Financial Institutions and Industrialization in the Rhineland, 1815–1870* (Madison, Wis., 1966). Professor Patrick's chapter on Japan has benefited from his intimate personal knowledge of Japanese banks and bankers as well as his mastery of the Japanese literature on finance, banking, and economic history.

I should like to acknowledge here the kindness of Dr. R. M. Hartwell, librarian of Nuffield College, Oxford, for allowing me to consult at length some unpublished manuscripts and research notes by the late H. A. Shannon on English country banks. My debt to the Scottish banks for permission to consult their records has been acknowledged in the footnotes to Chapter III.

The most important manuscript collections, apart from those just mentioned, are indicated in Section A below. Bibliographical information on the published sources actually cited in the footnotes follows in the remaining sections.

A. MANUSCRIPT COLLECTIONS

Archives des Affaires Étrangères, Paris (AE). Contains the *correspondance politique* (CP) and the *correspondance consulaire* (CC) of the French foreign ministry with its diplomatic and consular representatives abroad. Especially valuable for the history of Russian finance.

Archives Générales du Royaume, Brussels (AGR). Its most important collection for the subject of this book is the surviving records of the early history of the Société Générale de Belgique (SG).

Archives Nationales, Paris (AN). The most important *sous-série* is F30, emanating from the Ministry of Finance, which contains documents of great value for the financial history of foreign countries as well as that of France.

Banque de France (BF). The massive archieves of this institution, of primordial importance for the financial history of modern France, are gradually being opened to qualified scholars on a selective basis.

Historisches Archiv der Stadt Köln, Cologne (HASK). Contains a number of private collections, among them those of the Rheinische Eisenbahn Gesellschaft and the important entrepreneur Gustav Mevissen.

Oppenheim Hausarchiv, Cologne (OHA). The magnificent private archives of Sal. Oppenheim Jr. & Cie, one of the most important private banking firms in Germany.

Rheinisch-Westfälische Wirtschafts-Archiv, Cologne. A privately supported archive for business documents, containing records from a number of important banking and industrial enterprises as well as the records of the Cologne Chamber of Commerce and Industry.

Stadt Archiv Barmen. Municipal archives of an important textile center.

Staatsarchiv Düsseldorf. Official records of the most important regional administrative headquarters in the Rhine-Ruhr district.

B. OFFICIAL PUBLICATIONS

United Kingdom

Parliamentary Papers (PP) or *British State Papers* (BSP).

Committee on Resumption of Cash Payments, 1819.

Report from the Commission of Secrecy on the Bank of England Charter, 1832.

Select Committee on Banks of Issue, 1836.

Select Committee on Banks of Issue, 1840.

France

Annuaire statistique de la France.

Conseil supérieur de l'agriculture, du commerce et de l'industrie, *Enquête sur les principes et les faits généraux qui régissent la circulation monétaire et fiduciare,* 6 vols., Paris, 1865–67.

Belgium

Annuaire statistique de la Belgique.

Russia

Ministerstvo finansov, 1802–1902, Ekspeditsiya zagatovleniya gosudarstvennykh bumag, St. Petersburg, 1902.

Ocherk razvitiya deyatel'nosti gosudarstvennykh sberegatel'nykh kass (*Outline of the development of the activities of state savings banks*), St. Petersburg, 1912.

Otchety gosudarstvennykh sberegatel'nykh kass (*Reports of state savings banks*).

Ustav Gosudarstvennogo banka po ofitsyal'nom izdaniyu 1895 g. (*Statutes of the State Bank according to official publication, 1895*), St. Petersburg, 1905 (unofficial edition, with supplements).

"Yezhegodnik Ministerstva Finansov" ("Annual Journal of the Ministry of Finance"), St. Petersburg.

Japan

Bank of Japan, Statistics Dept.: *Historical Statistics of Japanese Economy,* 1962.

Matsukata, Masayoshi, *Report on the Adoption of the Gold Standard in Japan,* Tokyo: Government Press, 1899.

Ministry of Education: *Japan's Growth and Education,* July 1963.

Ministry of Finance: *Dainihon Gaikokuboekinempyo* (*Annual Statistics of Foreign Trade in Japan*); *Financial and Economic Annual of Japan.*

C. NEWSPAPERS, PERIODICALS, COLLECTIVE WORKS

Bulletin de statistique et législation financière (Paris).

The Economist (London).

Économiste français (Paris).

Fiji Bank Bulletin, "Banking in Modern Japan," XI (December 1961), 4 (special issue).

Der Frankfurter Aktionär (Frankfurt).

Istoriya Moskovy, Akademiya Nauk SSSR, Institut istorii, 6 vols., Moscow, 1952–59.

Ocherki Istorii Leningrada, M. P. Vyatkin (gen. ed.), Akademiya Nauk SSSR, Institut istorii, Leningradskoye otdelenie, 4 vols., Leningrad and Moscow, 1955–64.

Scots Magazine (Edinburgh).

Vestnik finansov (*Financial Herald*), No. 6, 1928, publ. by Narodnyy komissariat finansov (People's Commissariat of Finances), 1923–current.

D. OTHER WORKS CITED

Abramovitz, Moses (ed.), *Capital Formation and Economic Growth,* Princeton, 1955.

Adams, T. F. M., *A Financial History of Modern Japan,* Tokyo, 1964.

Agahd, E., *Grossbanken und Weltmarkt,* Berlin, 1914.

Akashi, Teruo, and Norihasa Suzuki, *Nihon Kinyushi* (*Financial History of Japan*), vol. I, *Meiji Hen* (*Meiji Period*), Tokyo: Toyo Keizai Shimposha, 1957.

Anan'ich, B. V., "Uchetno-Ssudnyy bank Persii v 1894–1907 g.," in *Monopolii i inostrannyy kapital v Rossii,* M. P. Vyatkin (gen. ed.), Akademiya Nauk SSSR, Institut istorii, Leningradskoye otdelenie, Leningrad–Moscow, 1962.

Arai, Masao, *Development of Local Banking in Japan,* Tokyo: Science Council of Japan Economic Series No. 19, September 1958.

Asakura, Kokishi, *Meiji Zenki Nihon Kinyu Kozoshi* (*A History of the Japanese Financial Structure in the Meiji Era*), Tokyo, 1963.

Ashton, T. S., "The Bill of Exchange and Private Banks in Lancashire, 1790–1830," *Economic History Review,* XV (1945); reprinted in T. S. Ashton R. S. Sayers (eds.), *Papers in English Monetary History,* Oxford, 1953.

———, *An Eighteenth-Century Industrialist: Peter Stubs of Warrington,* 1765–1806, Manchester, 1961.

———, *Iron and Steel in the Industrial Revolution,* 2nd ed., Manchester, 1951.

Atlas, M.S., *Natsyonalizatsiya bankov v SSSR,* Moscow, 1948.

Balston, Thomas, *William Balston—Paper Maker, 1759–1849,* London, 1954.

Banck, Rudolph, *Geschichte der sächsischen Banken mit Berücksichtigung der Wirtschaftsverhältnisse,* Dissertation, Friedrich Wilhelms-Universität, Berlin, 1896.

Barker, T. C., and J. R. Harris, *A Merseyside Town in the Industrial Revolution: St. Helens 1750–1850,* Liverpool, 1954.

Baxter, Robert, "On the Principles which Regulate the Rate of Interest and on the Currency Laws," *Journal of the Royal Statistical Society,* XXXIX (June 1876).

Bellamy, J. M., "Cotton Manufacture in Kingston upon Hull," *Business History,* IV (1962), 91–108.

Benaerts, Pierre, *Les Origines de la grande industrie allemande,* Paris, 1933.

Berdrow, Wilhelm, *Alfred Krupps Briefe, 1826–1887,* Berlin, 1928.

———, *Friedrich Krupp, der Gründer der Gusstahlfabrik in Briefen und Urkunden,* Essen, 1915.

Bergengrün, Alexander, *David Hansemann,* Berlin 1901.

Bergius, C. J., "Eine Deutsch oder Preussische Münzreform?," *Zeitschrift für die gesammte Staatswissenschaft,* X (1854), 419–96.

———, Geschichte des Preussischen Papiergeldes," *Zeitschrift für die gesammte Staatswissenschaft,* XXVI (1870), 225–60.

———, *Preussische Zustände,* Münster, 1844.

Bigo, Robert, *Les Banques françaises au cours du XIXe siecle,* Paris, 1947.

Blumburg, Horst, "Die Finanzierung der Neugründungen und Erweiterungen von Industriebetrieben in Form der Aktiengesellschaften während der fünfziger Jahre des 19. Jahrhunderts in Deutschland, am Beispiel der preussischen Verhältnisse erläutert," in Hans Mottek (ed.), *Studien zur Geschichte der Industriellen Revolution in Deutschland,* Berlin, 1960.

Boase, C. W., *A Century of Banking in Dundee,* Dundee, 1864.

Borchardt, Knut, "Zur Frage des Kapitalmangels in der ersten Hälfte des 19. Jahrhunderts," *Jahrbücher für Nationalökonomie und Statistik,* 173 (1963).

Borovoy, S. Y., *Kredit i banki v Rossii, 1650–1861,* Moscow, 1958.

Bouvier, J., *Le Crédit Lyonnais de 1863 à 1882,* 2 vols., Paris, 1961.

Bräutigam, H., *Das Bankiergewerbe des Regierungs-Bezirks Aachen von Beginn des 19. Jahrhunderts bis zum Jahre 1933,* Doctoral dissertation, Cologne University, 1949.

Briavoinne, N., *De l'Industrie en Belgique,* 2 vols., Brussels, 1839.

Brockhage, B., "Zur Entwicklung des preussisch-deutschen Kapital-exports," *Schmollers Forschungen,* Leipzig, 1910.

Bukovetsky, A. I., "Svobodnaya nalichnost' i zolotoy zapas," in *Monopolii i inostranny kapital v Rossii,* M. P. Vyatkin (gen. ed.), Akademiya Nauk SSSR, Institut istorii, Leningradskoye otdelenie, Leningrad–Moscow, 1962.

Cameron, R. E., "The Banker as Entrepreneur," *Explorations in Entrepreneurial History,* 2nd series, vol. 1, no. 1, pp. 50–55.

———, "Founding the Bank of Darmstadt," *Explorations in Entrepreneurial History,* VIII (1956).

———, *France and the Economic Development of Europe, 1800–1914,* Princeton, 1961.

Campbell, R. H., "The Anglo-Scottish Union of 1707—II—The Economic Consequences," *Economic History Review,* 2nd series, XVI, 3 (1964), 468–77.

———, "An Economic History of Scotland in the Eighteenth Century," *Scottish Journal of Political Economy,* XI, 1 (February 1964), 17–24.

———, *Scotland since 1707, The Rise of an Industrial Society,* Oxford, 1965.

Chlepner, B. S., *La Banque en Belgique,* Brussels, 1926.

———, *Le Marché financier belge depuis cent ans,* Brussels, 1930.

Choi, K. I., "Shibusawa Eiichi and his Contemporaries," unpublished dissertation, Harvard University, 1958.

Church, R. A., "An Aspect of Family Enterprise in the Industrial Revolution," *Business History,* IV (1962), 120–25.

Clapham, Sir John, *The Bank of England,* 2 vols., Cambridge, England, 1948.

Clark, W. A. G., *Cotton Goods in Japan,* Washington, D.C.: U.S. Department of Commerce, Special Agent Series No. 86, 1914.

Cockburn, Henry A., *Memorials of His Own Times,* Edinburgh, 1856.

Cooke, C. A., *Corporation, Trust, and Company,* Cambridge, England, 1951.

Courtois *fils,* Alph., *Histoire des banques en France,* Paris, 1881.

Cowan, D. C. (ed.), *The Economic Development of China and Japan,* London, 1964.

Craig, J. H. M., *The Mint—A History of the London Mint from A.C. 287 to 1948,* Cambridge, England, 1953.

Crawcour, Sydney, "The Development of a Credit System in Seventeenth Century Japan," *Journal of Economic History,* XXI, 3 (September 1961).

Crick, W. F., and J. E. Wadsworth, *A Hundred Years of Joint Stock Banking,* London, 1936.

Crisp, Olga, "The Financial Aspect of the Franco-Russian Alliance," unpublished Ph.D. Thesis, University of London, 1954.

———, "French Investment in Russian Joint Stock Companies," *Business History,* II (1958).

———, "Russian Financial Policy and the Gold Standard at the End of the Nineteenth Century," *Economic History Review,* 2nd series, VI (1954).

———, "Some Problems of French Investment in Russian Joint Stock Companies, 1894–1914," *Slavonic and East European Review,* 1955.

Crouzet, Francois, "La Formation du capital en Grande-Bretagne pendant la révolution industrielle," Second International Conference of Economic History (Aix-en-Provence, 1962), Paris, 1965.

Crump, W. B. (ed.), *The Leeds Woolen Industry, 1780–1820,* Leeds, 1931.

Däbritz, Walther, *Bochumer Verein für Bergbau und Gusstahfabrikation,* Düsseldorf, 1934.

———, *Denkschrift zum fünfzigjährigen Bestehen der Essener Credit-Anstalt,* Essen, 1922.

———, *David Hansemann und Adolph von Hansemann,* Krefeld, 1954.

———, *Gründung und Anfänge der Disconto-Gesellschaft,* Berlin, 1931.

Daniels, G. W. (with an Introduction by George Unwin), *The Early English Cotton Industry,* Manchester, 1920.

Dean, Phyllis, "Capital Formation in Britain before the Railway Age," *Economic Development and Cultural Change,* IX (April 1961).

———, and W. A. Cole, *British Economic Growth, 1688–1959, Trends and Structure,* Cambridge, England, 1962.

Delbrück, M. F. R. v., *Lebenserinnerungen . . . 1817–1867, mit einem nachtrag aus dem Jahre 1870,* 2 vols., Leipzig, 1905.

Dieterici, C. F. W., *Handbuch der Statistik des Preussischen Staats,* Berlin, 1861.

Dikhtyar, G. A., *Vnutrennyaya torgovlya dorevolyutsyonnoy Rossii,* Moscow, 1960.

Dolléans, Edouard (ed.), *Questions monétaires contemporaines,* Paris, 1905.

Dubois, A. B., *The English Business Company after the Bubble Act,* New York, 1938.

Dun, John, "The Banking Institutions, Bullion Reserves, and Non-Legal Tender Note Circulation of the United Kingdom Statistically Investigated," *Journal of the Royal Statistical Society,* XXXIX (March 1876).

Eckert, C., *J. H. Stein; Werden und Wachsen eines Kölner Bankhauses in 150 Jahren,* Berlin, 1941.

Eichborn, K. v., *Das Soll und Haben von Eichborn & Co. in 200 Jahren,* Munich and Leipzig, 1928.

Eichholtz, Dietrich, *Junker und Bourgeoisie in der Preussischen Eisenbahngeschichte,* Berlin, 1962.

Elster, Julius, "Die Banken Norddeutschlands im Jahre 1865 und während des Krieges 1866," *Zeitschrift des Königlich Preussischen Statistischen Bureaus,* VII (1867).

Emi, Koichi, "An Approach to the Measurement of National Saving in Japan, 1878–1940," *Hitotsubashi Journal of Economics,* 6, 1 (June 1965).

———, *Government Fiscal Activity and Economic Growth in Japan, 1868–1960,* Tokyo, 1963.

Epstein, E., *Les Banques de commerce russes,* Paris, 1925.

Feaveryear, Albert, *The Pound Sterling—A History of English Money,* Oxford, 1963.

Fischer, Wolfram, *Der Staat und die Anfänge der Industrialisierung in Baden, 1800–1850,* Berlin 1962.

Fishlow, Albert, "The Trustee Savings Banks, 1817–1861," *Journal of Economic History,* XXI (March 1961), 26–39.

Flinn, F. W., *Men of Iron, The Crowleys in the Early Iron Industry,* Edinburgh, 1962.

Frère, Louis, *Étude historique des sociétés anonymes belges,* 2 vols., Brussels, 1951.

Friedman, Milton, and A. J. Schwartz, *A Monetary History of the United States, 1867–1960,* Princeton, 1963.

Fujino, Shozaburo, *Nihon no Keiki Junkan* (*Business Cycles in Japan*), Tokyo, 1965.

Gayer, A. D., W. W. Rostow, and A. J. Schwartz, with the assistance of Isaiah Frank, *The Growth and Fluctuation of the British Economy, 1790–1850,* Oxford, 1953.

Gerschenkron, Alexander, *Economic Backwardness in Historical Perspective,* Cambridge, 1962.

———, "The Rate of Growth of Industrial Production in Russia since 1885," *Journal of Economic History,* VII-S (1947).

Gille, Bertrand, *La Banque et le crédit en France de 1815 à 1848,* Paris, 1959.

Gindin, I. F., "Moskovskiye banki v period imperializma (1900–1917)," *Istoricheskiye zapiski,* vol. 58.

———, "Neustavnyye ssudy gosudarstvennogo banka i ekonomicheskaya politika tsarskogo pravilet'stva," *Istoricheskiye zapiski,* vol. 35.

———, *Russkiye Kommercheskiye Banki,* Moscow, 1948.

———, and L. E. Shepelev, "Bankovskiye monopolii v Rossii nakanune Velikoy Oktyabrskoy sotsyalisticheskoy revolyutsii," *Istoricheskiye zapiski,* vol. 66.

Glover, F. J., "Thomas Cook and the American Blanket Trade in the Nineteenth Century," *Business History Review,* XXXV, 2 (1961), 226–46.

Goldsmith, R., *Financial Intermediaries in the American Economy since 1900,* Princeton, 1955.

———, "Financial Structure and Economic Growth in Advanced Countries," in Moses Abramovitz (ed.), *Capital Formation and Economic Growth,* Princeton, 1955.

Gossudarstvennyy Bank, *Kratkiy ocherk deyatel'nosti s 1860 po 1910 g.*, St. Petersburg, 1910.

Gulich, G. v., *Geschichtliche Darstellung des Handels, der Gewerbe und des Ackerbaus,* 4 vols., Jena, 1830–45.

Gurley, J. G., and E. S. Shaw, "Financial Aspects of Economic Development," *American Economic Review,* XLV (1955), 515–38.

———, "Financial Intermediaries and the Saving-Investment Process," *Journal of Finance,* II, 2 (May 1956), 257–76.

———, "The Growth of Debt and Money in the United States, 1800–1950," *Review of Economics and Statistics,* XXXIX (1957), 250–62.

———, *Money in a Theory of Finance,* Washington, D.C., 1960.

Hamilton, Henry, *An Economic History of Scotland in the Eighteenth Century,* Oxford, 1963.

———, *The Industrial Revolution in Scotland,* Oxford, 1932.

Harkort, Fritz, "Plan einer Gesellschaft für die Eisenbahn," in Hermann, *Zeitschrift für das Lande zwischen der Weser und Maas,* 9 February 1833 (in *Stadt Archiv Barmen*).

Heaton, Herbert, *The Yorkshire Woollen and Worsted Industries,* Oxford, 1920.

Helfferich, Karl, *Beiträge zur Geschichte der deutschen Geldreform,* Leipzig, 1898.

Henderson, W. O., *The State and the Industrial Revolution in Prussia, 1740–1870,* Liverpool, 1958.

Hueschling, Xavier, *Résumé de la statistique générale de la Belgique,* Brussels, 1852.

Hicks, J. R., *Capital and Growth,* Oxford, 1965.

Hilton, G. W., *The Truck System,* Cambridge, England, 1960.

Hirschman, A. O., *The Strategy of Economic Development,* New Haven, Conn., 1958.

Hirschmeier, Johannes, *The Origins of Entrepreneurship in Meiji Japan,* Cambridge, Mass., 1964.

———, "Shibusawa Eiichi and Modern Business Enterprise," in W.W. Lockwood (ed.), *The State and Economic Enterprise in Modern Japan,* Princeton, 1965.

Hobson, O. R., *A Hundred Years of the Halifax—The History of the Halifax Building Society, 1853–1953,* London, 1953.

Hodges, T. B., "The Iron King of Liege: John Cockerill," unpublished Ph.D. Thesis, Columbia University, 1957.

Hoekendorf, W. C., "The Secular Trend of Income Velocity in Japan, 1879–1940," unpublished Ph.D. Thesis, University of Washington, 1961.

Hoffmann, J. G., *Die Lehre vom Geld,* Berlin, 1938.

Hoffmann, Walther, *British Industry, 1700–1950,* trans, by W. O. Henderson and W. H. Chaloner, Oxford, 1955.

———, *Das Deutsche Volkseinkommen, 1851–1957,* Tübingen, 1959.

———, "The Take-Off in Germany," in W. W. Rostow (ed.), *The Economics of the Take-Off into Sustained Growth,* New York, 1963.

Hollingsbery, R. H., *A Handbook on Gold and Silver,* London, 1878.

Horne, H. O., *A History of Savings Banks,* Oxford, 1947.

Horsefield, J. K., "British Banking Practices, 1750–1850: Some Legal Sidelights," *Economica,* 2nd series, XIX (August 1952), 308–21.

———, *British Monetary Experiments, 1650–1710,* Cambridge, Mass., 1960.

———, "The Duties of a Banker," I, *Economica,* February 1941; II, *Economica,* May 1944; reprinted in T. S. Ashton and R. S. Sayers (eds.), *Papers in English Monetary History,* Oxford, 1953.

Hughes, J. R. T., *Fluctuations in Trade, Industry and Finance—A Study of British Economic Development, 1850–1860,* Oxford, 1960.

Hunt, B. C., *The Development of the Business Corporation in England,* Cambridge, Mass., 1936.

Hypothec Bank, *Nippon Kangyo Ginko Shi* (*History of the Hypothec Bank of Japan*), Tokyo, 1953.

Imlah, Albert Henry, *Economic Elements in the Pax Britannica: Studies in British Foreign Trade in the Nineteenth Century,* Cambridge, Mass., 1958.

Industrial Bank, *Nippon Kogyo Ginko Gojunen Shi* (*Fifty-year History of the Industrial Bank of Japan*), Tokyo, 1957.

James, F. G., "Charity Endowments as Sources of Local Credit in Seventeenth and Eighteenth Century England," *Journal of Economic History,* VIII (1948), 153–70.

John, A. H., *The Industrial Development of South Wales, 1750–1850,* Cardiff, 1949.

Joslin, D. M., "London Private Bankers, 1720–1785," *Economic History Review,* 2nd series, VIII (1956); reprinted in E. M. Carus-Wilson (ed.), *Essays in Economic History,* vol. II, Economic History Society, London, 1963.

Käding, Emil, *Beiträge zur Preussischen Finanzpolitik in den Rheinlanden, 1815–1840,* Bonn, 1913.

Kato, Toshihiko, "Development of the Monetary System," in *Keizo Shibusawa* (ed.), *Japanese Society in the Meiji Era,* Tokyo, 1957.

———, *Hompo Ginko Shi Ron* (*A History of Japanese Banks*), Toyko, 1957.

Katzenellenbaum, S. S., *Kommercheskiye banki i ikh torgovo-kommissyonnye operatsii,* Moscow, 1912.

———, *Russian Currency and Banking, 1914–1924,* London, 1925.

Kauch, P., *La Banque Nationale de Belgique,* Brussels, 1950.

Keith, Alexander, *The North of Scotland Bank Limited, 1836–1936,* Aberdeen, 1936.

Kerr, A. W., *History of Banking in Scotland,* Glasgow, 1884.

Khromov, P. A., *Ekonomicheskoye razvitiye Rossii v XIX–XX vekakh,* Moscow–Leningrad, 1950.

———, *Ocherki ekonomiki Possii perioda monopolisticheskogo kapitalisma,* Moscow, 1960.

King, W. T. C., *History of the London Discount Market,* London, 1936.

Klersch, Josef, *Die Sparkasse der Stadt Köln,* Cologne, 1926.

Kluitmann, Leo, *Der gewerbliche Geld- und Kapitalverkehr im Ruhrbiet im 19. Jahrhundert,* Bonn, 1931.

Koenigs, Ernst, *Erinnerungschrift zum fünfzigjähren Besten des A. Schaaffhausen'schen Bankvereins, in Bibliothek der Industrie- und Handelskammer zu Köln,* Cologne, 1898.

Kondrat'ev, N. D. (ed.), *Mirovoye Khozyastvo 1913–1925,* Moscow, 1926.

Krüger, Alfred, *Das Kölner Bankiergewerbe vom Ende des 18. Jahrhunderts bis 1875,* Cologne, 1925.

Kubitschek, Helmut, "Die Börsenverordnung vom 24. Mai 1844 und die Situation im Finanz- und Kreditwesen Preussens in den vierziger Jahren des 19. Jahrhunderts," *Jahrbuch für Wirtschaftgeschichte,* 1962.

Kumpmann, Karl, *Die Entstehung der Rheinischen Eisenbahn Gesellschaft,* Essen, 1910.

Kurzrock, Hans, *200 Jahre von der Heydt-Kersten & Söhne,* Elberfeld, 1954.

Kuznets, Simon, *Capital in the American Economy: Its Formation and Financing,* Princeton, 1962.

———, (ed.), *Income and Wealth,* Series V, London, 1955.

Leatham, William, *Letters on the Currency, addressed to Charles Wood,* 2nd ed., London, 1840.

Lenz, F., and O. Unholz, *Geschichte des Bankhauses Gebrüder Schickler,* Berlin, 1912.

Leslie, J. O., *The Note Exchange and Clearing House System,* Edinburgh, 1950.

Lévy-Leboyer, Maurice, *Les Banques européennes et l'industrialisation internationale dans la première moitié du XIXe siècle,* Paris, 1964.

Lewis, W. A., *The Theory of Economic Growth,* Homewood, Illinois, 1955.

Lockwood, W. W., *The Economic Development of Japan,* Princeton, 1954.

———, (ed.), *The State and Economic Enterprise in Modern Japan,* Princeton, 1965.

Lüke, R., *Die Berliner Handelsgesellschaft in einem Jahrhundert deutschen Wirtschaft,* Berlin, 1956.

Lyashchenko, P. I., *Istoriya narodnogo khozyastva SSSR,* 2 vols., Moscow–Leningrad, 1952.

Malcolm, C.A., *The Bank of Scoland, 1695–1945,* Edinburgh, n.d.

———, *History of the British Linen Bank,* Edinburgh, 1950.

Malou, J., *Notice historique sur la Société Générale,* Brussels, 1863.

Marczewski, Jean, *Introduction à l'histoire quantitative,* Geneva, 1965.

Marshall, Alfred, *Industry and Trade,* London, 1919.

Mathews, R. C. O., *A Study in Trade-cycle History, Economic Fluctuations in Great Britain, 1833–42,* Cambridge, England, 1954.

Mathias, Peter, *The Brewing Industry in England, 1700–1830,* Cambridge, England, 1959.

Mauer, H., *Das Landschaftlichen Kreditwesen Preussens,* Strassburg, 1907.

Mayer, A. v., *Geschichte und Geographie der Deutschen Eisenbahnen von ihrer Entstehung bis auf die Gegenwart,* Berlin, 1891.

Migulin, P., *Nasha bankovaya politika,* Kharkov, 1904.

"Mirovyye ekonomicheskiye krizisy 1848–1935 gg," Moscow–Leningrad, 1937.

Mitchell, B. R., with the collaboration of Phyllis Deane, *Abstract of British Historical Statistics,* Cambridge, England, 1962.

Mottek, Hans (ed.), *Studien zur Geschichte der Industriellen Revolution in Deutschland,* Berlin, 1960.

Muloseyev, V. A., "Money and Credit," in A. Raffalovich (ed.), *Russia: Its Trade and Commerce,* London, 1918.

Munro, Neil, *The History of the Royal Bank of Scotland, 1727–1927,* Edinburgh, 1928.

Nakamura, James I., "Agricultural Production in Japan, 1878–1922," in W. W. Lockwood (ed.), *The State and Economic Enterprise in Modern Japan,* Princeton, 1965.

"Narodnoye Khozyastvo," St. Petersburg, 1914.

Nasse, Edwin, "Zur Banknoten- und Papiergeldfrage mit spezieller Beziehung auf den Preussischen Staat," *Zeitschrift für die gesammte Staatswissenschaften,* XII (1856).

Nevin, E., *Capital Funds in Underdeveloped Countries: The Role of Financial Institutions,* London, 1961.

Newmarch, William, "An Attempt to Ascertain the Magnitude and Fluctuations of the Amount of Bills of Exchange in Circulation at One Time in Great Britain," *Journal of the Royal Statistical Society,* XIV (1851), 166–75.

Niebuhr, Markus, *Geschichte der Königlichen Bank zu Berlin,* Berlin, 1854.

Ohkawa, Kazushi, et al., *The Growth Rate of the Japanese Economy since 1878,* Tokyo, 1957.

Ol', P. V. *Inostrannye kapitaly v Rossii,* Petrograd, 1922.

Oshima, Harry T., "Government Revenues and Expenditures in Meiji Economic Growth," in W. W. Lockwood (ed.), *The State and Economic Enterprise in Modern Japan,* Princeton, 1965.

Ott, David J., "The Financial Development of Japan, 1878–1958," *Journal of Political Economy,* LXIX, 2 (April 1961).

Ouchi, Tsutomu, and Toshihiko Kato, *Kokuritsu Ginko no Kenkyu* (*Studies on National Banks*), Tokyo, 1963.

Owen, Robert, *The Life of Robert Owen Written by Himself,* London, 1857.

Palmade, G. P., *Capitalistes et capitalisme français au XIXe siècle,* Paris, 1961.

Paasche, H., "Die neueste Entwicklung der Banknoten- und Papiergeld- Zirkulation in den hauptsächlichsten Kulturländern der Gegenwart," *Jahrbücher für Nationalökonomie und Statistik,* XXX (1878), 331–64.

Patrick, H. T., "External Equilibrium and Internal Convertibility: Financial Policy in Meiji Japan," *Journal of Economic History,* XXV, 2 (June 1965).

———, "Financial Development and Economic Growth in Underdeveloped Countries," *Economic Development and Cultural Change,* XIV, 2 (January 1966).

Péreire, I. and E., *Œuvres de Émile et Isaac Péreire, rassemblées et commentées par Pierre-Charles Laurent de Villeduil . . .*, 28 vols. in 10 series, Paris, 1912.

Perroux, François, "Prise de vues sur la croissance de l'économie française, 1780–1950," in Simon Kuznets (ed.), *Income and Wealth,* Series V, London, 1955.

Pokrovsky, V. I. (ed.), *Sbornik svedeniy po istorii i statistike vneshney torgovli,* vol. 1, St. Petersburg.

Pogrebenskiy, A. P., *Ocherki finansov dorevolyutsyonnoy Rossii,* Moscow, 1954.

Pollard, Sydney, "Fixed Capital in the Industrial Revolution," *Journal of Economic History,* XXIV (September 1964), 299–314.

Poppelreuter, R., and G. Witzel, *Barmer Bank-Verein: Hinsberg, Fischer & Co., 1867–1917,* Essen, 1918.

Porter, G. R., "On the Accumulation of Capital by the Different Classes of Society," *Journal of the Royal Statistical Society,* XIV (September 1851).

Poschinger, H. v., *Bankwesen und Bankpolitik in Preussen,* 3 vols., Berlin, 1878–79.

Pressnell, L. S., *Country Banking in the Industrial Revolution,* Oxford, 1956.

Prokopovich, S. N., "Ueber die Bedingungen der industriellen Entwicklung Russlands," *Archiv für Soziale Gesetzgebung und Statistik, Ergänzungsheft,* No. 10, 1913.

Radcliffe, William, *Origin of the New System of Manufacture commonly called "Power-Loom Weaving,"* Stockport, 1840.

Raffalovich, A. (ed.), *Russia: Its Trade and Commerce,* London, 1918.

Raistrick, Arthur, *Dynasty of Ironfounders, The Darbys and Coalbrookdale,* London, 1953.

Rait, Sir Robert S., *The History of the Union Bank of Scotland,* Glasgow, 1930.

Ramon, Gabriel, *Histoire de la Banque de France,* Paris, 1929.

Reid, J. M., *The History of the Clydesdale Bank, 1838–1938,* Glasgow, 1938.

Redlich, Fritz, "The Leaders of the German Steam Engine Industry during the First Hundred Years," *Journal of Economic History,* IV (1944), 121–48.

Riesser, Jakob, *The Great German Banks and Their Concentration in connection with the Economic Development of Germany,* Washington, 1911.

Rimmer, W. G., *Marshalls of Leeds, Flax-Spinners, 1788–1886,* Cambridge, England, 1960.

Ronin, S., *Inostrannyy kapital i russkiye banki,* Moscow, 1926.

Rosovsky, Henry, *Capital Formation in Japan,* New York, 1961.

———, "The Take-Off into Sustained Controversy," *Journal of Economic History,* XXV (June 1965), 271–5.

Rostow, W. W. (ed.), *The Economics of the Take-Off into Sustained Growth,* New York, 1963.

Rozkova, M. K., "Ekonomicheskaya politika pravitel'stva," Akademiya Nauk SSR (ed.), *Ocherki ekonomicheskoy istorii Rossii pervoy poloviny XIX veka,* Moscow, 1959.

Sakurai, Kinichiro, *Financial Aspects of the Economic Development of Japan,*

Tokyo: Science Council of Japan, Economic Series No. 34, February 1964.

Sarasas, Phra, *Money and Banking in Japan,* London, 1936.

Sayers, R. S., *Lloyds Bank in the History of English Banking,* Oxford, 1957.

Schauer, Curt, *Die Preussische Bank,* Halle, 1912.

Schnee, Heinrich, *Die Hoffinanz und der Moderne Staat,* 3 vols., Berlin, 1953.

Schoubroeck, A. v., *L'Évolution des banques belges en fonction de la conjoncture de 1850 à 1872,* Brussels, 1951.

Schulte, Franz, *Das Bedürfniss von Aktienbanken in volkswirtschaftlicher Beziehung mit besonderen Rücksicht auf die Preussische Rheinprovinz,* Cologne, 1845.

Schumpeter, J. A., *Business Cycles: A Theoretical and Statistical Analysis of the Capitalist Process,* 2 vols., New York and London, 1939.

———, *The Theory of Economic Development,* Cambridge, Mass., 1933.

Schwann, Matthieu, *Ludolph Camphausen als Wirtschaftspolitiker,* 3 vols., Essen, 1915.

Schwarz, Paul, *Die Entwicklungstendenzen im deutschen Privatbankiergewerbe,* Doctoral dissertation, Strasbourg University, 1915.

Scott, W. R., *The Constitution and Finance of English Scottish, and Irish Joint-Stock Companies to 1720,* 3 vols., Cambridge, England, 1910–12.

Seki, Keizo, *The Cotton Industry of Japan,* Tokyo, 1956.

Shatsillo, K. F., "Formirovaniye finansovogo kapitala v sudostroitel'noy promyshlennosti Yuga Rossi," in *Iz istorii imperializma,* M. P. Vyatkin (gen. ed.), Akademiya Nauk SSSR, Institut istorii, Leningradskoye otdelenie, Moscow–Leningrad, 1959.

Shepelev, L. E., "AKtsyonernoye uchreditel'stvo v Rossii," in *Iz istorii imperializma,* M. P. Vyatkin (gen. ed.), Akademiya Nauk SSSR, Institut istorii, Leningradskoe otdelenie, Moscow–Leningrad, 1959.

———, "Arkhivnyye fondy aktsyonernykh bankov," in *Problemy istochnikovedeniya,* vol. 7, 1959.

Shibusawa, Keizo (ed.), *Japanese Society in the Meiji Era,* Tokyo, 1958.

Shinohara, Miyohei, "Economic Development and Foreign Trade in Pre-War Japan," in D. C. Cowan (ed.), *The Economic Development of China and Japan,* London, 1964.

Shionoya, Yuichi, "Waga Kuni Kogyokan no Nibumon Pattern" ("The Two-Sector Pattern of Japan's Industrialization"), *Ikkyo Ronso,* 52, 5 (November 1964).

Sidorov, A. L., "O strukture promyshlennosti Rossii v kontse XIX v.," *Istoricheskiye zapiski,* vol. 69.

Sigsworth, E. M., *Black Dyke Mills,* Liverpool, 1958.

Smith, Adam, *An Inquiry into the Nature and Causes of the Wealth of Nations,* Edwin Cannan (ed.), New York: Modern Library, 1937.

Smout, T. C., "The Anglo-Scottish Union of 1707—The Economic Background," *Economic History Review,* 2nd series, XVI, 3 (1946), 455–67.

Solov'voya, A. M., "K voporsu o roli finansovogo kapitala v zheleznodorozhnom stroitel'stve Rossii Nakanune pervoy miróvoy voyny," *Istoricheskiye zapiski,* vol. 69.

Soyeda, J., "A History of Banking in Japan," in *A History of Banking in All the Leading Nations, published by Journal of Commerce and Commercial Bulletin,* New York, 1896.

Spangenthal, S., *Die Geschichte der Berliner Börse,* Berlin, 1903.

Spiethoff, Arthur, *Die Wirtschaftlichen Wechsellagen,* 2 vols., Tübingen and Zurich, 1955.

Strumilin, S. G., *Ocherki sovetskoy ekonomiki,* Moscow–Leningrad, 1926.

Takatera, S., "Early Experiment of Depreciation Accounting in National Banks, 1875–1878," *Kyoto University Economic Review,* XXXII, 1 (April 1962).

Taylor, A. M., *Gilletts, Bankers at Banbury and Oxford,* Oxford, 1964.

Thomas, S. G., *The Rise and Growth of Joint Stock Banking,* London, 1934.

Thorwärt, F., "Die Entwicklung des Banknotenumlaufs in Deutschland, 1851–1880," *Jahrbücher für Nationalökonomie und Statistik,* XLI (1883), 202–3.

Tilly, Richard, *Financial Institutions and Industrialization in the German Rhineland, 1815–1870,* Madison, Wis., 1966.

Tooke, Thomas, and William Newmarch, *A History of Prices and of the State of the Circulation from 1792 to 1856,* 6 vols., London, 1857.

Toyo Keizai Shimposha (ed.), *Meiji Taisho Kakusei Soron* (*Survey of the State of the Nation in the Meiji-Taisho Periods*), Tokyo, 1927.

Triffin, Robert, *The Evolution of the International Monetary Standard,* Princeton, 1964.

Tugan-Baranovsky, M., *Russkaya fabrika. v proshlom i nastoyashchem,* Moscow, 1934.

Unwin, George (with chapters by Arthur Hulme and George Taylor), *Samuel Oldknow and the Arkwrights,* Manchester, 1924.

Veblen, Thorstein, *Imperial Germany and the Industrial Revolution,* New York, 1915.

Vigne, Marcel, *La Banque à Lyon du 15ᵉ au 18ᵉ siecle,* Lyon, 1903.

Viner, Jacob, *Studies in the Theory of International Trade,* London, 1934.

Von Laue, Theodore, *Sergei Witte and the Industrialization of Russia,* New York, 1963.

Voye, E., *Ueber die Höhe der verschiedenen Zinssätze und ihre wechselseitige Abbängigkeit,* Berlin, 1902.

Wadsworth, A. P., and J. L. Mann, *The Cotton Trade and Industrial Lancashire,* Manchester, 1931.

Wagner, Adolph, *Beiträge zur Lehre von den Banken,* Leipzig, 1857.

Wallich, H. C., "Comparison of Monetary Systems," paper prepared for VII Reunião de téchnicos dos bancos centrais do continente americano, Rio de Janeiro, October, 1963.

Westebbe, R. M., "State Entrepreneurship: King Willem I, John Cockerill, and the Seraing Engineering Works, 1815–1840," *Explorations in Entrepreneurial History,* VIII, 4 (April 1956), 205–32.

Wichelhaus, R., *Bankhaus Johann Wichelhaus Peters Sohn,* Elberfeld, 1930.

Woltmann, Arnold, and Fr. Frölich, *Die Gutenhoffnungshütte, Oberhausen 1810–1910,* Oberhausen, 1910.

Yoshino, T., *Waga Kuni Kinyu Seido to Kinyu Seisaku* (*Japan's Financial System and Monetary Policy*), Tokyo, 1954.

———, "Waga Kuni Shichu Ginko no Obaaron ni Tuite" ("Overloan of Commercial Banks in Japan"), Bank of Japan *Chosa Geppo,* (February 1954), 1–39.

INDEX

N.B. References to specific countries which appear in the chapters devoted to those countries have not been indexed.